Mathematics 10

Exercise and Homework Book

AUTHORS

Len Bonifacio
B.Ed.
Edmonton Catholic Separate School
 District No. 7
Alberta

Scott Carlson
B.Ed., B.Sc.
Golden Hills School Division No. 75
Alberta

Darlene Couwenberghs
B.Ed., M.Ed.
School District 37 (Delta)
British Columbia

David DeGrave
B.P.E., B.Ed.
Winnipeg School Division
Manitoba

Victor Epp
Hon. B.A., M.Ed.
Mathematics Consultant
Vancouver, British Columbia

Reg Fogarty
B.Ed., M.A.
School District 83 (North
 Okanagan/Shuswap)
British Columbia

Emily Kalwarowsky
B.Sc., B.Ed.
Mathematics Consultant
Edmonton, Alberta

Thomas Kelly
B.Sc., B.Ed.
School District of Mystery Lake
Manitoba

Gerald Krabbe
B.Ed.
Calgary Board of Education
Alberta

Stephanie MacKay
B.Ed.
Edmonton Catholic Separate School
 District No. 7
Alberta

Robert Wong
B.Sc., B.Ed.
Edmonton Public Schools
Alberta

Rick Wunderlich
B.Ed.
School District 83 (North
 Okanagan/Shuswap)
British Columbia

Chris Zarski
B.Ed., M.Ed.
Wetaskiwin Regional Division No. 11
Alberta

REVIEWERS

Shannon Dougall
Calgary Roman Catholic Separate
 School District No. 1
Alberta

Ken Gordon
The Winnipeg School Division
Manitoba

Sandra Harazny
Regina Roman Catholic Separate
 School Division No. 81
Saskatchewan

Heather Lait
School District 62 (Sooke)
British Columbia

NELSON

NELSON

For more information contact
Nelson Education Ltd.,
1120 Birchmount Road, Toronto,
Ontario M1K 5G4.
Or you can visit our website
at nelson.com.

Mathematics 10

ISBN-13: 978-0-07-012733-3
ISBN-10: 0-07-012733-6

8 9 10 24 23 22

Printed and bound in Canada

ASSOCIATE PUBLISHER: Kristi Clark
PROJECT MANAGER: Helen Mason
DEVELOPMENTAL EDITORS: Kelly Cochrane, Paul McNulty, Rita Vanden Heuvel
MANAGER, EDITORIAL SERVICES: Crystal Shortt
SUPERVISING EDITOR: Jeanette McCurdy
COPY EDITOR: Laurel Sparrow
ANSWER CHECKER: Daniela Spiroska
EDITORIAL ASSISTANT: Erin Hartley
MANAGER, PRODUCTION SERVICES: Yolanda Pigden
TEAM LEAD, PRODUCTION: Paula Brown
PRODUCTION COORDINATOR: Sheryl MacAdam
COVER DESIGN: Michelle Losier
ELECTRONIC PAGE MAKE-UP: APTARA
ART DIRECTION: Tom Dart, First Folio Resource Group, Inc.
COVER IMAGE: Courtesy of Getty Images; Don Bishop, Photographer

Contents

Unit 4 Systems of Equations

Chapter 8 Solving Systems of Linear Equations Graphically

Chapter 9 Solving Systems of Linear Equations Algebraically

Overview

Mathematics plays an important role in many exciting activities, from art and music to industrial design and engineering, from sports management and astronomy to forensic sciences and archeology, and from air and water conservation to flying and space technology. The skills needed for many of these activities are provided in *McGraw-Hill Ryerson Mathematics 10* student book. This *McGraw-Hill Ryerson Mathematics 10 Exercise and Homework Book* is designed to complement the student book.

Exercise and Homework Book Organization
Like the student book, the exercise and homework book is divided into four units, each with a number of chapters.

Unit 1—Unit 1 investigates linear measurement, surface area, and volume using the SI and imperial measurement systems.

In Chapter 1, you use referents for linear measurements and make measurements in both imperial and SI units. You review similarities and differences between the SI system and the imperial system and estimate linear measurements in both imperial and SI units. You use a variety of techniques to convert linear measurements within and between imperial and SI systems.

Chapter 2 extends your knowledge of SI and imperial measurements to work with surface area and volume of 3-D objects. You determine the surface area and volume of right cones, right pyramids, spheres, right cylinders, right prisms, and composite objects. As part of these calculations, you may need to determine square roots and cube roots of numbers.

Chapter 3 deals with the relationships among sides and angles of a right triangle. You use primary trigonometric ratios (sine, cosine, and tangent) to determine missing sides or missing angles. You may also use the Pythagorean relationship to determine the missing side of a right triangle given two other sides.

Unit 2—Unit 2 extends your knowledge of powers and exponents. You solve problems involving square roots and cube roots and apply the exponent laws to expressions involving powers with integral and rational exponents. You represent, identify, and order irrational numbers. You also develop and use algebraic skills for multiplying and factoring polynomials.

In Chapter 4, you determine square roots and cube roots and solve problems involving square roots and cube roots. You apply the exponent laws to expressions involving rational numbers or variables as bases and integers and rational numbers as exponents. You also convert between powers with rational exponents and radicals, and mixed radicals and entire radicals, and solve problems involving radicals.

In Chapter 5, you multiply and factor polynomial expressions. You use algebra tiles to examine patterns that occur when multiplying polynomials. You also work with special products and factor the difference of squares and perfect square trinomials.

Unit 3 —Unit 3 deals with graphing functions and relations in a variety of ways, including with technology. This unit also deals with three different forms of writing linear equations: slope-intercept form, general form, and slope-point form. You determine the y-intercept, slope, and x-intercept and use this information to graph linear equations.

In Chapter 6, you graph functions and relations in a variety of ways. You distinguish between a function and a relation and determine the domain and range of a function or relation. You also express the domain and range in different formats, including interval notation. You use function notation to express and work with functions. Finally, you explore the slope of a line, including lines that are horizontal or vertical.

Chapter 7 introduces three different forms of writing linear equations:
- slope-intercept form ($y = mx + b$),
- general form ($Ax + By + C = 0$), and
- slope-point form [$y - y_1 = m(x - x_1)$].

You use the information that can easily be obtained from each form to graph linear equations. You also convert linear equations among the three forms presented and write the equation of a line given a graph.

Unit 4—Unit 4 extends your knowledge of linear relations. You identify the solution to a system of linear equations shown on a graph and use algebraic manipulation to solve a linear system. You analyse various types of linear systems where the system of equations may have no solution, one solution, or an infinite number of solutions.

In Chapter 8, you graph and solve systems of linear equations with two variables. You work with systems expressed algebraically, as well as in words, and solve the systems graphically. You examine various systems of equations and identify the possible number of solutions.

Chapter 9 continues the work with linear systems. You construct a system of linear equations from a problem and then solve the linear system algebraically. You compare algebraic methods of substitution and elimination with the graphical methods used in Chapter 8. You decide on and use strategies to determine which method is most appropriate and efficient for a particular problem.

Study Guide Features
- Each section begins with Key Concepts that summarize the concepts needed to complete the exercises.
- The sections continue with a worked example that guides you through the skills needed to complete the exercises.
- Exercises are organized into four sections: A Practise, B Apply, C Extend, and D Create Connections.
- A review of all sections is included at the end of each chapter.
- Each chapter includes Extend It Further questions that cover the concepts in the chapter, as well as extending your thinking and combining concepts from previous chapters.
- A cumulative review of the skills and concepts handled so far in the exercise and homework book is included at the end of each chapter.
- Selected questions in each section are marked by a star indicating that complete solutions are provided at the back of the book.
- The final two pages of each chapter provide a Study Check that assists you in summarizing the important information in that chapter and identifying what skills and concepts you need to reinforce.
- The end of each unit includes unit review questions.
- A practice exam at the end of the study guide gives you the opportunity to determine if you are ready for the final examination.
- Answers to all questions—and solutions to questions marked with a star—are provided at the back of the book.

Symbols

SYMBOLS

Symbol	Meaning
$\in$	belongs to
$\approx$	is approximately
R	real numbers
N	natural numbers
∞	infinity

GREEK LETTERS

Symbol	Meaning
α	alpha (a)
β	beta (b)
θ	theta (th)
π	pi (p)

Unit Conversions

COMMON ABBREVIATIONS

SI	Imperial
mm = millimetre cm = centimetre m = metre km = kilometre	″ or in. = inch ′ or ft = foot yd = yard mi = mile

INTERNAL CONVERSIONS

SI	Imperial
10 mm = 1 cm 100 cm = 1 m 1000 m = 1 km	12 in. = 1 ft 36 in. = 3 ft 3 ft = 1 yd 1760 yd = 1 mi 5280 ft = 1 mi

CONVERSIONS BETWEEN SYSTEMS

SI to Imperial	Imperial to SI
1 mm ≈ 0.0394 in. 1 cm ≈ 0.3937 in. 1 m ≈ 1.094 yd 1 m ≈ 3.281 ft 1 km ≈ 0.6214 mi	1 in. = 0.0254 m 1 in. = 2.54 cm 12 in. = 30.48 cm 1 ft = 30.48 cm 12 in. = 0.3048 m 1 ft = 0.3048 m 36 in. = 0.9144 m 1 yd = 0.9144 m 1 mi ≈ 1.609 km

Formulas

ALGEBRA

Square Roots	*Perfect Squares* $5^2 = (5)(5)$ $\quad = 25$ $\sqrt{25} = \sqrt{(5)(5)}$ $\quad\quad = 5$	*Imperfect Squares* $\sqrt{5} = 2.236\ldots$
Cube Roots	*Perfect Cubes* $3^3 = (3)(3)(3)$ $\quad = 27$ $\sqrt[3]{27} = \sqrt{(3)(3)(3)}$ $\quad\quad = 3$	*Imperfect Cubes* $\sqrt[3]{5} = 1.709\ldots$
Multiplying Polynomials	*Use the distributive property* $(3x - 2)(4x + 5) = (3x)(4x + 5) - 2(4x + 5)$ $\quad\quad\quad\quad\quad\quad\quad = 12x^2 + 15x - 8x - 10$ $\quad\quad\quad\quad\quad\quad\quad = 12x^2 + 7x - 10$ *Use algebra tiles* $(x - 3)(2x + 1) = 2x^2 - 5x - 3$	
Factoring Polynomials	*Identify the GCF of the numerical coefficients* *In $5a^2b - 30ab + 15ab^2$, the GCF is $5ab$.* $5a^2b - 30ab + 15ab^2 = 5ab(a - 6 + 3b)$ *If the GCF is a binomial expression* $7(a - 2) + 2a(a - 2) = (a - 2)(7 + 2a)$	
Factoring Special Trinomials	*Difference of Squares* $(x - y)(x + y) = x^2 - y^2$ *Perfect Square Trinomial* $(x \pm y)^2 = x^2 \pm 2xy + y^2$	

EXPONENT LAWS

Note that a and b are rational or variable bases and m and n are rational exponents.	
Product of Powers	$(a^m)(a^n) = a^{m+n}$
Quotient of Powers	$\dfrac{a^m}{a^n} = a^{m-n}, a \neq 0$
Power of a Power	$(a^m)^n = a^{mn}$

Power of a Product	$(ab)^m = a^m b^m$
Power of a Quotient	$\left(\dfrac{a}{b}\right)^n = \dfrac{a^n}{b^n}, b \neq 0$
Zero Exponent	$a^0 = 1, a \neq 0$
Negative Exponent	$a^{-n} = \dfrac{1}{a^n}, a \neq 0$ $\dfrac{1}{a^{-n}} = a^n, a \neq 0$ $\left(\dfrac{a}{b}\right)^{-n} = \dfrac{1}{\left(\dfrac{a}{b}\right)^n}$ $\quad = \left(\dfrac{b}{a}\right)^n$
Power With Rational Exponent	$x^{\frac{3}{5}} = x^{0.6}$
Radicals and Fractional Exponents	$\sqrt[n]{x^m} = x^{\frac{m}{n}}$

LINEAR RELATIONS AND FUNCTIONS

Slope	$m = \dfrac{\text{rise}}{\text{run}}$ or $m = \dfrac{y_2 - y_1}{x_2 - x_1}$
	Slope-intercept form $y = mx + b$, where b is the y-intercept *General form* $Ax + By + C = 0$, A, B, and C are real numbers and $B \neq 0$ *Slope-point form* $y - y_1 = m(x - x_1)$ 0 slope $m = \dfrac{\text{rise}}{\text{run}}$ $m = \dfrac{0}{5}$ $m = 0$ *Undefined slope* $m = \dfrac{\text{rise}}{\text{run}}$ $m = \dfrac{5}{0}$ $m = \text{undefined}$

Vertical Lines 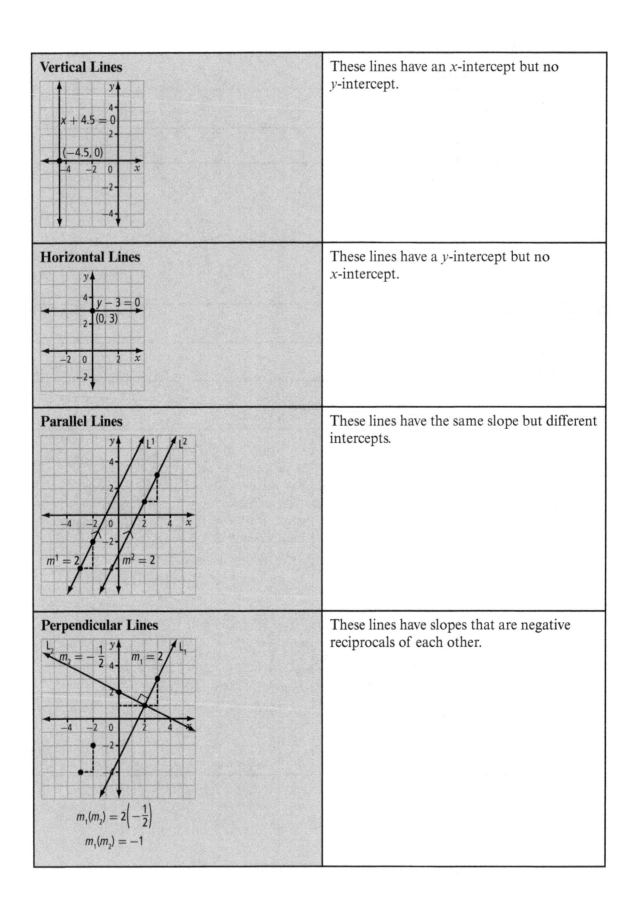	These lines have an x-intercept but no y-intercept.
Horizontal Lines	These lines have a y-intercept but no x-intercept.
Parallel Lines	These lines have the same slope but different intercepts.
Perpendicular Lines	These lines have slopes that are negative reciprocals of each other.

MEASUREMENT

In the following, P represents the perimeter, C the circumference, A the area, V the volume, and SA the surface area.

2-D Shape	
Circle	$C = 2\pi r \text{ or } C = \pi d$ $A = \pi r^2$
Square	$P = 4s$ $A = s^2$
Rectangle	$P = 2l + 2w$ $A = lw$
Triangle	$P = s_1 + s_2 + s_3$ $A = \frac{1}{2}bh$

3-D Object	
Cube	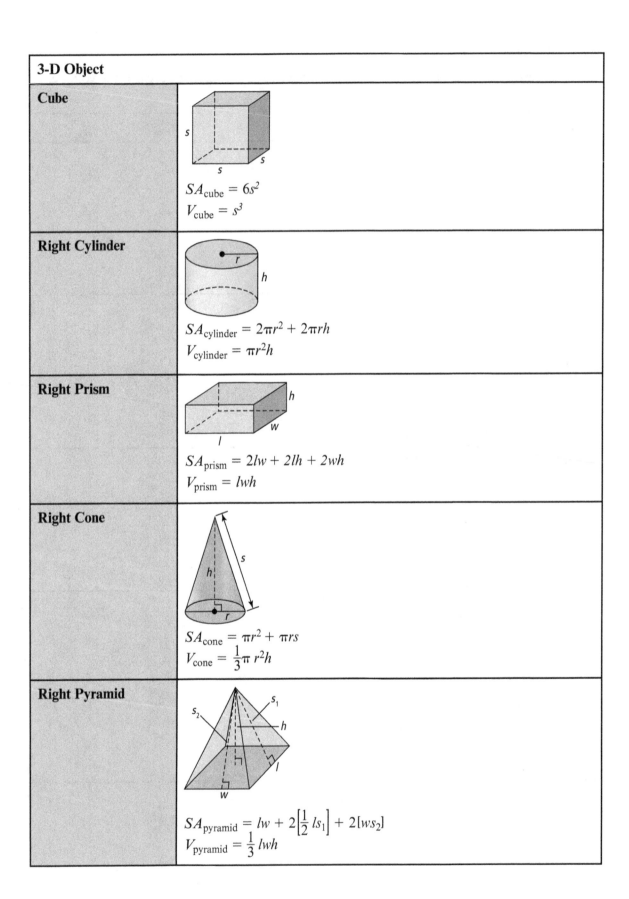 $SA_{\text{cube}} = 6s^2$ $V_{\text{cube}} = s^3$
Right Cylinder	$SA_{\text{cylinder}} = 2\pi r^2 + 2\pi rh$ $V_{\text{cylinder}} = \pi r^2 h$
Right Prism	$SA_{\text{prism}} = 2lw + 2lh + 2wh$ $V_{\text{prism}} = lwh$
Right Cone	$SA_{\text{cone}} = \pi r^2 + \pi rs$ $V_{\text{cone}} = \frac{1}{3}\pi r^2 h$
Right Pyramid	$SA_{\text{pyramid}} = lw + 2\left[\frac{1}{2} ls_1\right] + 2[ws_2]$ $V_{\text{pyramid}} = \frac{1}{3} lwh$

Sphere	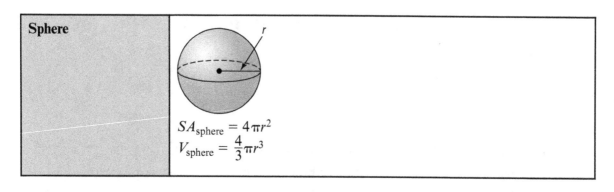 $SA_{\text{sphere}} = 4\pi r^2$ $V_{\text{sphere}} = \dfrac{4}{3}\pi r^3$	

TRIGONOMETRY

Primary Trigonometric Ratios A adjacent hypotenuse B opposite C	$\sin \theta = \dfrac{\text{opposite}}{\text{hypotenuse}}$	$\cos \theta = \dfrac{\text{adjacent}}{\text{hypotenuse}}$	$\tan \theta = \dfrac{\text{opposite}}{\text{adjacent}}$
Pythagorean Theorem AB^2 B BC^2 A C AC^2	$AC^2 + BC^2 = AB^2$	$BC^2 = AB^2 - AC^2$	$AC^2 = AB^2 - BC^2$

Tips for Success in MATH

IN CLASS
✓ Listen carefully to your teacher.
✓ Focus and pay attention to examples and their solutions.
✓ Think about the solutions.
✓ Ask questions when you don't understand.
✓ Use class time efficiently. Begin homework when time is given in class.
✓ Use proper form when solving questions. Show your thinking. Don't skip key steps.
✓ Ask about homework questions you had difficulty with. Make sure you understand how to do them.
✓ Create a Math Vocabulary/Formula List section in your notebook to record all important words, definitions, and formulas.
✓ Read the instructions to a question so that you are familiar with the wording.
✓ Make sure that you answer the question that has been asked.

AT HOME
✓ Complete your math homework after every class. Try each question assigned. Refer to the text and sample solutions to help you.
✓ Review examples and notes. Use them to help you with your homework.
✓ Memorize all formulas, definitions, vocabulary, and steps/procedures for solving longer questions.
✓ Check your answers with those at the back of the book. Highlight homework questions that you had difficulty with or could not do.
✓ For each lesson and chapter, prepare a summary sheet that contains important formulas, definitions, vocabulary, procedures for solutions, and solutions to questions from the homework that you found to be difficult.
✓ Update your study sheet after each lesson. This will save time when studying for tests and the exam.

PREPARING FOR A TEST
Studying for a math test should be easy if you have been keeping up throughout the chapter.
✓ DO NOT CRAM! Begin studying and reviewing at least three days prior to a test. Don't wait until the night before.
✓ Review the summary sheets that you have prepared.
✓ Review each section in the chapter to be tested. Redo homework questions that you found difficult.
✓ Do all review questions. Try extra questions.
✓ Memorize formulas, definitions, vocabulary, and steps for longer solutions.
✓ Study the wording of questions so that you will understand the instructions on a test.
✓ Try to categorize the types and variety of questions done over the entire chapter. Make sure that you understand how to solve each type of question.

Chapter 1 Measurement Systems

1.1 SI Measurement

<< **KEY IDEAS** >>

- SI (Système International d'Unités) is Canada's official measurement system.

- All SI units are based on multiples of 10.

- The *metre* is the basic unit of length.

- Lengths can be measured with SI rulers, metre sticks, or calipers.

- A *referent* is an item that an individual uses as a measurement unit for estimating.

- When measuring, use an appropriate SI unit. Kilometres are appropriate for measuring large distances, such as the distance between cities. Millimetres are appropriate for measuring small units of length, such as a plant's growth in one week.

- To convert from one SI unit to another unit, use *unit analysis* or *proportional reasoning*.

- Some SI units for measuring length are shown in the table. Also shown are each unit's abbreviation, its multiplying factor, and a possible referent.

Unit	Abbreviation	Multiplying Factor	Possible Referent
kilometre	km	1000	length of 12 city blocks
hectometre	hm	100	length of a football field
decametre	dam	10	length of a classroom
metre	m	1	height of a doorknob above the floor
decimetre	dm	0.1	width of a fisted hand
centimetre	cm	0.01	width of a fingernail
millimetre	mm	0.001	thickness of a dime

- Use *unit analysis* to convert one SI unit into another SI unit.
  Convert 109 000 mm to metres.
  1 m = 1000 mm

  So, $109\,000 \text{ mm} \left(\dfrac{1 \text{ m}}{1000 \text{ mm}} \right) = 109 \text{ m}$

- Use *proportional reasoning* to convert one SI unit into another SI unit.

Convert 0.0098 km to metres.
Let x represent the number of metres.

$$1000 \text{ m} = 1 \text{ km}$$
$$\frac{1000 \text{ m}}{1 \text{ km}} = \frac{x \text{ m}}{0.0098 \text{ km}}$$
$$1000(0.0098) = x$$
$$9.8 = x$$

Therefore, 0.0098 km is equivalent to 9.8 m.

- Follow these steps to read a caliper.
   1. Read the value on the fixed scale that is located exactly at or just to the left of the zero on the moving scale.
   2. Identify the next line on the moving scale that aligns with a line on the fixed scale. Read the value on the moving scale.

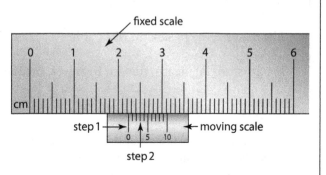

The reading for the caliper shown is 2.23 cm. $(2.2 + 0.03 = 2.23)$

Example

Two students in a Biology class measure the length of an insect specimen. Kelly determines the length to be 8 mm. Caleb states that the length is 0.008 m.
  a) What referent could be used to estimate the length of the specimen?
  b) What unit of measurement of all possible units is the most appropriate for measuring the length? Explain.
  c) How do Kelly's and Caleb's measurements compare? Show your reasoning.

Solution

  a) The width of a fingernail, which is a referent for a centimetre, could be convenient to use to estimate the length.
  b) Since the insect specimen is very small, the most appropriate unit for measuring it is the millimetre (or centimetre).
  c) To compare the two measurements, either convert 8 mm to metres or convert 0.008 m to millimetres.

Use unit analysis to convert 8 mm to metres.

$$1 \text{ m} = 1000 \text{ mm}$$
$$(8 \text{ mm})\left(\frac{1 \text{ m}}{1000 \text{ mm}}\right) = 0.008 \text{ m}$$

Therefore, 8 mm is equivalent to 0.008 m.

or

Use proportional reasoning to convert 0.008 m to millimetres.
Let x represent the number of millimetres.

$$1 \text{ m} = 1000 \text{ mm}$$
$$\frac{1 \text{ m}}{1000 \text{ mm}} = \frac{0.008 \text{ m}}{x \text{ mm}}$$
$$1000(0.008) = x$$
$$8 = x$$

Therefore, 0.008 m is equivalent to 8 mm.

The measurements are equivalent.

A Practise

1. Estimate and measure.

   a) Estimate the perimeter or circumference of each figure.

   i)

   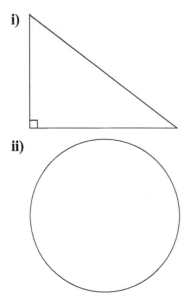

   ii)

   b) Measure and calculate the perimeter or circumference of each figure. Give each answer in both millimetres and centimetres.

   c) What referent could you use to estimate the perimeter of figure i)?

2. What reading is shown on each measuring instrument? Give each reading in both millimetres and centimetres.

   a) SI ruler

   b) SI caliper

   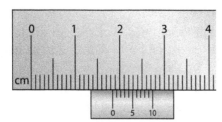

3. Consider each measurement. State whether it is reported in the most appropriate unit. If it is not, explain why and convert to a more appropriate unit.

   a) The length of the Iditarod Trail sled dog race is 1 850 750 m.

   b) The wingspan of a sycamore moth is approximately 0.042 m.

   c) The circumference of the tire of a mountain bike is 207 cm.

B Apply

4. **a)** The front wheel of a motorcycle has a radius of 20.32 cm. On a trip, the wheel rotated 25 000 times. What was the distance of the trip in kilometres?

   b) What referent could you use to estimate a kilometre distance?

★**5.** A running oval with each end in the shape of a semi-circle has the dimensions shown. Stefan runs on the inner track and Vashaal runs on the outer track. The distance between the tracks is 10 dm. Express the difference, in metres, in the distances that the boys run for one lap. Show your reasoning.

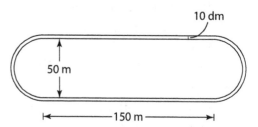

6. **a)** A grass flea can leap a distance 350 times its length in a single jump. What is the length of a grass flea that covered a distance of 70 m in 500 jumps? Express your answer in an appropriate unit.

   b) Justify your choice of unit in part a).

★**7.** A map of Prince Albert National Park is shown.

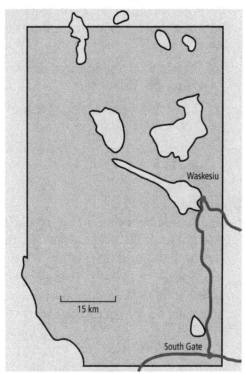

Waskesiu

15 km

South Gate

a) Express the scale of the map as a ratio in lowest terms.

b) Estimate the length and width of the park.

c) Determine the length and width of the park using the scale.

d) Determine the distance from Waskesiu to the South Gate. Express your answer in metres and kilometres.

C Extend

★**8.** The ratio of length to width of an *Edmonton Journal* newspaper page is 15 to 7. A diagonal drawn on the page has a length of 0.0662 dam. What are the dimensions of the page in centimetres?

9. A rancher has 1600 m of fencing to construct two adjoining fields with the greatest area possible. The minimum area a field can have is 10 000 m², or 1 hectare (ha).

a) What are the dimensions of the fields? Explain your thinking.

b) What is the total area of both fields?

10. The oblate spheroid is the approximate shape of many planets. An everyday example of an oblate spheroid is an M&M'S® candy. The oblateness of a spheroid (three-dimensional) or an ellipse (two-dimensional) is the ratio of the polar radius, *b*, to the equatorial radius, *a*, subtracted from 1.

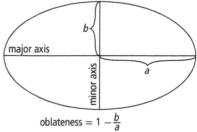

$$\text{oblateness} = 1 - \frac{b}{a}$$

a) Determine the oblateness of the ellipse shown.

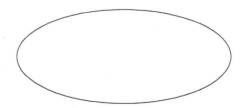

b) What is the oblateness of Earth, if Earth's equatorial diameter is 12 756.274 km and its polar diameter is 12 713.504 km?

c) Determine the oblateness of a sphere. How does it compare to the oblateness of Earth?

D Create Connections

11. Tukani wants to determine the height of his school without actually climbing the school wall with a measuring tape. Instead, he places a metre stick vertically against the wall and takes a photograph showing the ground to the top of the wall and including the metre stick.

a) Explain how Tukani can use the photograph to determine the height of the school.

b) With a partner, try to determine the height of your school.

c) What personal referent could Tukani use instead of the metre stick?

1.2 Imperial Measurement

KEY IDEAS

- The imperial system is based on old English units of measurement derived from nature and everyday activities.

- Canada began a transition from the imperial system to SI in 1970.

- Imperial measurements are used in the United States.

- The imperial system is still used in some instances in Canada.

- From shortest to longest, the basic imperial units for measuring distances are the inch, foot, yard, and mile.

Unit	Abbreviation/ Symbol	Conversion	Possible Referent
mile	mi	1 mi = 1760 yd or 5280 ft or 63 360 in.	length of 15 to 17 city blocks
yard	yd	1 yd = 3 ft or 36 in.	length of a large walking stride
foot	ft or '	1 ft = 12 in.	length from elbow to wrist
inch	in. or "		length from end of thumb to first knuckle

- An imperial ruler or measuring tape can measure distances to the nearest $\frac{1}{16}$ in. A caliper can measure distances to the nearest $\frac{1}{1000}$ in.

- Use *unit analysis* to convert one imperial unit into another one.
  Convert $5\frac{3}{4}$ yd into inches.
  $$1 \text{ yd} = 36 \text{ in.}$$
  $$\left(\frac{36 \text{ in}}{1 \text{ yd}}\right)\left(5\frac{3}{4} \text{ yd}\right) = 207 \text{ in.}$$
  Therefore, $5\frac{3}{4}$ yd is equivalent to 207 in.

- Use *proportional reasoning* to convert one imperial unit into another one.
  Convert 20 240 yd into miles.
  $$1 \text{ mi} = 1760 \text{ yd}$$
  Let x = number of miles
  $$\frac{1 \text{ mi}}{1760 \text{ yd}} = \frac{x \text{ mi}}{20\,240 \text{ yd}}$$
  $$x = 1\left(\frac{20\,240}{1760}\right)$$
  $$x = 11.5$$
  Therefore, 20 240 yd is equivalent to 11.5 mi.

Example

Mary and Ling need to determine the area of a room they wish to paint. The room is rectangular with one window and one door. Mary measures the perimeter of the room to be 52 ft and the window to be $1\frac{1}{2}$ yd by 2 yd. Ling measures the height of the room to be 96 in. and the door to be 78 in. by 42 in. If only the walls are to be painted, what is the area to be painted measured in square feet?

Solution

Convert all measurements to feet. Use unit analysis.

Dimensions of the window:
$$1 \text{ yd} = 3 \text{ ft}$$
$$1\frac{1}{2} \text{ yd} = 1\frac{1}{2} \text{ yd} \left(\frac{3 \text{ ft}}{1 \text{ yd}}\right)$$
$$1\frac{1}{2} \text{ yd} = 4.5 \text{ ft}$$

$$2 \text{ yd} = 2 \text{ yd} \left(\frac{3 \text{ ft}}{1 \text{ yd}}\right)$$
$$2 \text{ yd} = 6 \text{ ft}$$

Dimensions of the door:
$$78 \text{ in.} = 78 \text{ in.} \left(\frac{1 \text{ ft}}{12 \text{ in.}}\right)$$
$$78 \text{ in.} = 6.5 \text{ ft}$$

$$42 \text{ in.} = 42 \text{ in.} \left(\frac{1 \text{ ft}}{12 \text{ in.}}\right)$$
$$42 \text{ in.} = 3.5 \text{ ft}$$

Height of the room:
$$1 \text{ ft} = 12 \text{ in}$$
$$96 \text{ in.} = 96 \text{ in.} \left(\frac{1 \text{ ft}}{12 \text{ in.}}\right)$$
$$96 \text{ in.} = 8 \text{ ft}$$

Calculate the area of the four walls and subtract the area of the window and door.

Area of four walls = (52 ft) (8 ft)
= 416 sq ft

Area of window = (4.5 ft) (6 ft)
= 27 sq ft

Area of door = (6.5 ft) (3.5 ft)
= 22.75 sq ft

Area to be painted = 416 − (27 + 22.75)
= 366.25
The area to be painted is 366.25 sq ft.

A Practise

1. **a)** Use a personal referent to estimate the length and width of the rectangle in an appropriate unit.

   b) Measure the length and width in inches to the nearest $\frac{1}{16}$ in.

   c) What referent did you use in part a)? Justify your choice.

2. Convert each measurement to the unit indicated.

   a) The circumference of a pipe is 1 ft 3 in. (nearest inch)

   b) The Burj Khalifa in the United Arab Emirates is the world's tallest skyscraper, with a height of $905\frac{1}{3}$ yd. (nearest foot)

   c) The elevation of Mount Robson is 12 972 ft. (nearest tenth of a mile)

3. What reading is shown on each measuring scale? For each measurement, name one item that might have this length.

   a)

   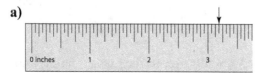

   b)

   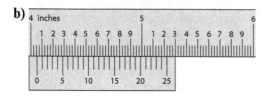

4. Measure each item to the nearest sixteenth of an inch. What device did you use to measure? Explain your choice of measuring device.

   a) length of your calculator

   b) width of your calculator

   c) depth of a key on your calculator

B Apply

⭐5. A snow gauge is a funnel-shaped device to measure snowfall. The device collects falling snow, which is melted and measured. The amount of snowfall in inches is determined by measuring the depth of the water in inches and multiplying that value by 10.

   a) A snow gauge gathered snow over a period of 12 h. The melted snow measured $1\frac{1}{2}$ in. What was the average snowfall per hour?

   b) In an average ski season, a snow gauge in the Sunshine Village area in Banff National Park will measure 36 in. of water. What is the area's average annual snowfall? If the season lasts approximately six months, what is the average snowfall in inches per week?

6. A draftsperson wishes to produce a scale drawing of a house's floor plan. The actual dimensions of the house are to be 60 ft by 32 ft. The scale rate for the drawing is 1 in. represents 1.25 ft.

   a) What is the scale ratio?

   b) What are the dimensions of the scale drawing in inches?

⭐7. Two snowmobilers leave the same place at the same time heading for the same destination, but take different routes. Josephine follows the trail indicated by dashed lines at a speed of 60 mph. Marcus follows the trail indicated by a solid line at a speed of 45 mph.

   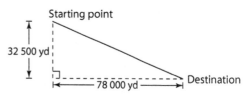

   a) Who arrives first? Show calculations to justify your answer.

   b) How much sooner, to the nearest minute, does the first rider reach the destination?

8. An inchworm is actually a caterpillar of the *Geometridae* moth family. Because an inchworm lacks appendages in the middle of its body, it moves in a looping gait. The inchworm's name describes the length of its smooth, hairless body. If an inchworm can travel the length of its body in 1 s, estimate and then calculate how long it would take to travel one mile. State your answer in seconds, minutes, and hours.

C Extend

9. Line segments MN and PQ are given below.

M_____N

P_____Q

a) PQ is longer than MN by ____ mm.

b) You have an unlimited supply of copies of MN and PQ, and are asked to build two lines the same length by placing your line segments end to end, using only one type in each line. What is the smallest number of MN and PQ pieces that you will need?

★10. A new deck is to be 60 ft long by 10 ft wide. Boards of length 12 ft and width 8 in. are to form the surface of the deck with a space of one quarter of an inch between pairs of boards.

a) How many boards are needed? Explain your reasoning.

b) Will there be any wastage? If so, how much will there be?

11. Tabular icebergs have a flat table-top surface. Suppose a large tabular iceberg floating in the Antarctic Ocean has a length of 8480 yd. The iceberg's length to height ratio is 5 to 1 and 11% of its height extends above the water.

a) Calculate the height of the iceberg above sea level. State your answer in yards and in metres.

b) How far below sea level does the iceberg extend? Express your answer in yards and in metres.

D Create Connections

12. Concrete is measured and sold by the cubic yard.

a) To the nearest whole cubic yard, how much concrete is needed for the foundation of a rectangular building 40 ft by 85 ft if the foundation walls are 8 in. thick and 7 ft 6 in. high?

b) A contractor charges $1.25 per cubic foot to frame the foundation and pour the concrete. If the cost of the concrete is $200 per cubic yard, what is the total cost of the foundation?

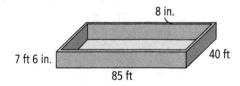

13. In addition to the measurement units described in this section, the imperial system includes other units that came into common usage in the 16th century. These units include the hand, the rod, the chain, and the furlong. Using the stated conversion values, convert each measurement to the unit indicated.

1 hand = 4 in.
1 chain = 22 yd
1 rod = 5.5 yd
1 furlong = 10 chains
1 mi = 8 furlongs

a) 300 furlongs = _____mi

b) 20 hands = _____yd

c) 75 chains = _____mi

d) 15 rods = _____chains

e) 3 furlongs = _____ft

1.3 Converting Between SI and Imperial Systems

KEY IDEAS

- When solving problems involving measurement, it is necessary to work with the same units.

- You may need to convert units from one measurement system to another.

- Conversion Chart

Imperial	Metric
1 in.	2.54 cm (0.0254 m)
1 ft	0.3048 m (30.48 cm)
1 yd	0.9144 m (defined as an exact conversion)
1 mi	1.609 km

Metric	Imperial
1 mm	0.0394 in.
1 cm	0.3937 in.
1 m	3.281 ft (39.37 in. or 1.094 yd)
1 km	0.6214 mi (3 280.84 ft)

- Conversions can be made using unit analysis or proportional reasoning.

  Determine the perimeter of the rectangle.

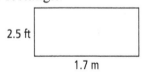

2.5 ft

1.7 m

Use unit analysis to convert 1.7 m to feet.
$$1 \text{ m} = 3.281 \text{ ft}$$

$$(1.7 \text{ m})\left(\frac{3.281 \text{ ft}}{1 \text{ m}}\right) = 5.5777 \text{ ft}$$

Therefore, 1.7 m is approximately 5.58 ft.
The perimeter is:
$P = 2(2.5) + 2(5.58)$
$P = 16.16$
The perimeter of the rectangle is approximately 16.16 ft.

or Use proportional reasoning to convert 2.5 ft to metres.
Let x represent the number of metres in 2.5 ft.
$$1 \text{ ft} = 0.3048 \text{ m}$$

$$\frac{1 \text{ ft}}{0.3048 \text{ m}} = \frac{2.5 \text{ ft}}{x}$$

$$x = 0.762$$

Therefore, 2.5 ft is approximately 0.76 m.
The perimeter is:
$P = 2(1.7) + 2(0.76)$
$P = 4.92$
The perimeter of the rectangle is approximately 4.92 m.

Example

The land speed record is the fastest speed achieved on land by any wheeled vehicle. A turbofan-powered car holds the current record. The car reached a speed of 766.609 mph for one mile, breaking the sound barrier.

   a) Express the statement about the car's speed in kilometres per hour.

   b) At 15°C, the speed of sound is 1116 ft/s. This speed is given a measurement called Mach 1. How many miles per hour above Mach 1 was the car's top speed? How many kilometres per hour above Mach 1 was that speed?

Solution

   a) Convert 766.609 miles to kilometres using proportional reasoning.

   1 mi = 1.609 km

   Let x = the number of kilometres

   $$\frac{1 \text{ mi}}{1.609 \text{ km}} = \frac{766.609 \text{ mi}}{x \text{ km}}$$

   $$x \approx 1233.47 \text{ km}$$

   Converting the measures to SI units, the statement would read: "The car reached a speed of 1233.47 km/h for 1.609 km, breaking the sound barrier."

   b) Convert 1116 ft/s to miles per hour using proportional reasoning.

   1 mi = 5280 ft and 1 h = 3600 s.

   Let x = the number of feet in one hour or 3600 s.

   $$\frac{1116 \text{ ft}}{1 \text{ s}} = \frac{x \text{ ft}}{3600 \text{ s}}$$

   $$x = 4\,017\,600 \text{ ft}$$

   Convert 4 017 600 ft to miles using unit analysis.

   1 mi = 5280 ft

   $$4\,017\,600 \text{ ft}\left(\frac{1 \text{ mi}}{5280 \text{ ft}}\right) = 760.91 \text{ mi}$$

   Mach 1 is approximately 760.91 mph.

   Therefore, the car exceeded Mach 1 by (766.609 mph − 760.91 mph) or 5.699 mph.

   Convert 5.699 mi to kilometres using unit analysis.

   1 mi = 1.609 km

   $$5.699 \text{ mi}\left(\frac{1.609 \text{ km}}{1 \text{ mi}}\right) = 9.170 \text{ km}$$

   The top speed of the car exceeded Mach 1 by 9.170 km/h.

A Practise

1. Use your referent for an inch to estimate the total length of each line.

    a) _____

    b) _____

2. Measure each of the lines in question 1. Express answers to the nearest eighth of an inch.

3. Use the following segment to complete parts a), b), and c).

X _____ Y

a) Measure segment XY to the nearest millimetre.

b) Measure segment XY to the nearest $\frac{1}{16}$ in.

c) Convert the answer in part a) to inches. Compare the conversion to your answer in part b). Are the answers the same? If not, explain a reason for the difference.

4. Convert each unit to the unit specified.

a) The average growth rate for a teenage boy can be as high as $4\frac{1}{4}$ in. per year. (millimetre)

b) The official distance of a marathon is 26 mi 385 yd. (hundredth of a kilometre)

c) The length of a basketball court is 28.65 m. (tenth of a foot)

d) The height of the model Easter egg in Vegreville, Alberta, is 163.2 in. (tenth of a centimetre)

5. The table lists tourist attractions in Saskatchewan. Complete the missing size for each item. Choose an appropriate unit for the conversion.

	Attraction	Size in SI	Size in Imperial
a)	Surveyor	height: 3.7 m	
b)	Tomahawk and Teepee		height: 39.4'
c)	Whooping Crane	wingspan: 2100 cm	
d)	Mac the Moose		height: 384"
e)	Wheat	height: 13.1 m	

B Apply

★**6.** In a triathlon, competitors swim for 1.5 km, run a distance that is $6\frac{2}{3}$ times the length of the swim, and ride a bike for a distance that is 4 times the length of the run.

a) Compute the length of each part of the triathlon to the nearest tenth of a kilometre.

b) Compute the length of each part of the triathlon to the nearest tenth of a mile.

c) What is the total distance of the competition in kilometres? in miles?

7. Use the list of rivers below that flow into the Arctic Ocean to answer the questions.

River	Length
Liard	1 019 556 yd
Smoky	492 000 m
Athabasca	1231 km
Peace	1195 mi

a) Which river is longest?

b) What is the total length, in kilometres, of the four rivers?

c) How many times longer is the longest river than the shortest river?

★**8.** Molly purchased a pattern to make a coat. The pattern gives the measurements for the amount of material needed in imperial units for two widths of fabric. The coat requires 2 yd of fabric 45″ wide, or $1\frac{3}{4}$ yd of fabric 60″ wide.

a) Convert the measurements to SI units.

b) If Molly chooses the first width, how many square metres of fabric will she buy? What is the area of the wider material? How do the two areas compare? Which width would you choose to end up with a lesser amount of fabric left over?

9. The relay that crisscrossed Canada to bring the torch to Vancouver for the 2010 Olympic Winter Games covered a total distance of approximately 28 000 mi. Torch bearers carried the flame for about 2240 of those miles.

   a) If each person in the relay carried the torch for 300 m, approximately how many people took part?

   b) The relay started in Victoria on October 30, 2009, and ended in Vancouver on February 12, 2010. Approximately how far, to the nearest kilometre, was the torch carried each day? What assumptions are you making?

C Extend

☆10. Savario is driving to Brandon, Manitoba, at a fairly constant speed. At 4:30 p.m., he is 240 km from his destination. At 7:00 p.m., he passes an old highway sign that gives the distance to Brandon as 25 mi. If Savario continues at the same rate of speed, will he arrive by 7:30 p.m.? If not, when will he arrive? What assumptions must you make?

11. a) Your cousins from the United States are driving to visit you in St. Walburg, Saskatchewan. The speedometer in their vehicle shows that they are travelling at 53 mph along a secondary road. Are they within the speed limit if the posted maximum speed is 80 km/h?

    b) The route your cousins are taking includes a stretch of four-lane highway where the maximum speed limit is 110 km/h. What will their speed be in miles per hour if they drive at the limit?

    c) Your cousins call you when they reach Turtleford. You tell them they are only 34 km from St. Walburg. How long will it take them to drive the remaining distance if they travel at an average speed of 45 mph?

   d) Show how you can use mental mathematics to verify the reasonableness of your response in part a).

12. The screen of a cell phone measures 3.84 cm × 2.88 cm.

   a) What is the area of the screen in square millimetres? in square inches?

   b) If the screen has a resolution of 160 pixels × 120 pixels, what is the size of a pixel in square millimetres? in square inches?

D Create Connections

13. The adult height of a girl can be predicted using the formula:

$$\frac{(\text{father's height} - 5'' + \text{mother's height})}{2},$$

where the height of each parent is given in inches.

A boy's adult height can be predicted using the formula:

$$\frac{(\text{father's height} + 5'' + \text{mother's height})}{2},$$

where the height of each parent is given in inches.

   a) Suppose your father's height is 6 ft and your mother's height is 5 ft 5 in. Use the appropriate formula to predict your height as an adult measured in inches.

   b) Convert the formula you used to work with SI units. Predict your height as an adult in SI units.

14. Using the conversion factor 1 ft = 30.48 cm, show how to convert from a large imperial unit to a smaller SI unit.

Chapter 1 Review

1.1 SI Measurement

1. Use a personal referent to estimate the diameter of a cylindrical can. Mark off a distance of 2 m on the floor.

   a) Predict how many times the can will rotate to roll the distance of 2 m.

   b) Measure the diameter of the can and calculate how many times it will roll.

   c) Try rolling the can and counting the rotations. Compare your count to your answers in parts a) and b). How do they compare?

2. Determine the distance from X to Y on this SI ruler. Express your answer to the nearest tenth of a centimetre.

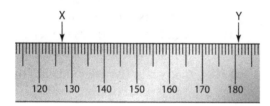

3. Explain how to make a reading using an SI caliper. Draw a diagram to support your explanation.

⋆**4.** Montgomery ran 100 m in 9.78 s. What was the runner's speed in kilometres per hour?

⋆**5.** Radio waves in a vacuum travel a distance equal to seven times the circumference of Earth in 1 s. If the radius of Earth is 6 318 138.7 m, what is the speed of the radio waves in kilometres per hour?

1.2 Imperial Measurement

6. Use your personal referent for an inch to estimate the length and width of your textbook in inches. Measure the length and width using an imperial ruler. Express your answer as a mixed number in simplest form.

7. The greatest rainfall within a 24-hour period occurred in a region of the Indian Ocean. The amount measured was 6′ 1″. Assuming the rain fell at a constant rate, what was the rate in inches per hour?

⋆**8.** A 4″ by 6″ photograph is to be enlarged to fit a 16″ by 20″ frame. Is it possible to make the enlargement without distorting or omitting part of the original image? Show your thinking. If it is not possible, determine a frame size that would hold an enlargement of the photograph without distortion.

9. The height of a microwave tower is 210′. A series of platforms and ladders are installed to allow access to the top. A platform is located every 30′ and rungs on the ladders are 12″ apart.

   a) How many platforms are there? How many ladder rungs are there? What assumptions did you make?

   b) Once a platform is reached, it is necessary to take three steps to reach the next ladder. Including steps on each ladder, how many steps must be taken to reach the top of the tower? What assumptions did you make?

⋆**10.** Drywall is to be used to cover the walls and ceiling of a bedroom. The room is 20′ long by 15′ wide by 10′ high.

   a) Drywall is sold in sheets sized 4′ by 6′, 4′ by 10′, and 4′ by 12′. Which sheet size would be most suitable for the room?

   b) Guidelines for buying drywall recommend that you increase the required amount by 5% to allow for waste, deduct one third of a sheet for each door, and deduct one quarter of a sheet for each window. Using the sheet size from part a), compute how many sheets are needed for the walls and ceiling if the room has two doors and one window.

1.3 Converting Between SI and Imperial Systems

11. Convert each unit to the unit specified.

  a) The men's record for javelin throw is 323′ 1″. (hundredth of metre)

  b) The fastest land mammal is the cheetah, with a speed of 101 km/h. (miles per hour)

  c) A spool contains 274 m of thread. (feet)

12. The fastest time for a 440-yd drag bike race is 7.05 s. Discounting acceleration at the start of the race, what average speed did this bike maintain

  a) in kilometres per hour?

  b) in miles per hour?

13. Bethany and Matt travel with their families to Calgary, AB, for the Calgary Stampede. When the friends arrive, they compare how far they travelled.
  • Bethany lives in Conrad, Montana, and travelled 227 mi.
  • Matt lives in North Battleford, SK, and travelled 439 km.

  a) Bethany is not familiar with SI distances. Explain how to determine the approximate conversion from kilometres to miles.

  b) Who travelled the greater distance?

14. You are hiking in Banff National Park from Lake Louise to the Plain of Six Glaciers. The trail is 5.5 km in length.

  a) How long will it take to reach the plain if you are walking at a speed of 2 mph?

  b) The vertical climb along the trail is 370 m. If Lake Louise is 5675 ft above sea level, what is the elevation at the upper end of the trail? Express your answer in meters and in feet?

☆**15.** If a space shuttle makes one complete orbit of Earth at a rate of 25 500 mph in a time of 1 h, how far above Earth is the ship orbiting in miles? in kilometres? (Use 6318.1387 km as the radius of Earth.)

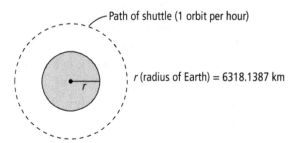

16. The passing lines on a highway consist of dashed yellow-painted segments, alternating with unpainted sections. A 13-m stretch of road that begins and ends with painted sections contains five painted segments. The length of each painted segment is 1.8 times the length of each unpainted segment.

  a) How many painted segments are there in a 1-km stretch of highway?

  b) What is the length of each painted segment in centimetres?

  c) How many painted segments are there in a 1-mi stretch of highway?

  d) What is the length of each painted segment in inches?

  e) Show how you can use mental mathematics to show the reasonableness of your answer to part d).

Chapter 1 Cumulative Review

1. Use a personal referent to estimate the perimeter of each figure in an appropriate SI unit.

   a)

   b)

   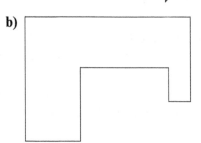

2. Measure the perimeter of each figure in question 1. Convert each measurement into an appropriate imperial unit. Justify your choice of unit.

3. Convert each measurement to the unit specified.

   a) The thickness of a penny is 0.06 in. (hundredth of a millimetre)

   b) The length of a CFL football field is 137.16 m. (feet)

   c) The length of the West Coast Trail in British Columbia is 46 mi 1061 yd. (hundredth of a kilometre)

   d) A computer speaker has a height of $8\frac{3}{4}$ in. (hundredth of a centimetre)

4. Determine the distance from A to B on this SI ruler. Express your answer to the nearest tenth of a centimetre.

   a) What is the reading in SI units?

   b) What is the reading in imperial units?

   c) Name an object that could be this length.

5. **a)** The Calgary Tower is 626 ft $\frac{1}{5}$ in. Suppose the tower's height is stated to be 191 m. Would this be an approximate or an exact measurement? Justify your answer.

   b) If the height of the tower in a photograph is 4.6 cm, by what scale factor has the picture been reduced?

6. **a)** What is the reading on this SI caliper? Name an object that could be this length.

   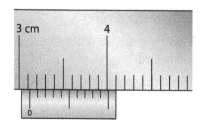

   b) Estimate and then calculate the equivalent measurement in the imperial system.

   c) Use unit analysis to verify your answer to part b).

7. Read the following paragraph about Mount Logan. Convert each SI measurement to an equivalent imperial measurement. Round to the nearest unit.

   Mount Logan is the highest mountain in Canada. Mount Logan is located within Kluane National Park and Reserve in southwestern Yukon. Due to active tectonic uplifting, Mount Logan is still rising in elevation. Before 1992, the exact height of Mount Logan was unknown and measurements ranged from 5959 m to 6050 m. In May 1992, an expedition climbed Mount Logan and fixed the current height of 5959 m. Minimal snow melt leads to a significant ice cap, reaching almost 300 m in certain spots.

8. Use the map of Vancouver Island to help answer the following questions.

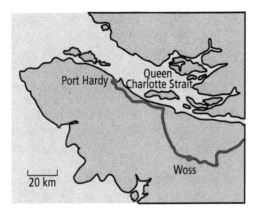

a) Express the scale of the map as a ratio in lowest terms.

b) How many kilometres are represented by 1 cm?

c) Estimate the distance from Woss to Port Hardy.

9. Chelsea wants to enlarge this 4″ by 6″ picture to fit into a 9″ by 12″ frame.

a) Can the photograph be enlarged proportionately to fill the new frame? Explain using measurements and ratios.

b) If not, which frame size would work so that the picture would not need to be cropped? 5″ by 7″, 8″ by 10″, $8\frac{1}{2}$″ by 11″, 11″ by 14″, 10″ by 15″, 14″ by 18″, 16″ by 20″

10. Jason wants to build a trundle wheel. He wants the wheel to go around once for every 50 cm the trundle is pushed. What will be the radius of his trundle wheel? Round your answer to the nearest hundredth of a centimetre.

11. Jeremy wants to lay laminate flooring in his room. The room measures 9 ft by $11\frac{1}{4}$ ft.

a) What is the area that needs to be covered?

b) The laminate Jeremy selects is $4\frac{1}{2}$ ft by 4 in. How many pieces of laminate are needed to cover his bedroom floor?

c) If the laminate costs $4.59 per square foot, how much will it cost to cover the room?

12. a) The Grand Canyon in Arizona is 6000 ft deep at its deepest point. At Hell's Gate, near Boston Bar, British Columbia, the Fraser Canyon's walls rise about 1000 m. Compare the depth of the Grand Canyon with the depth of the Fraser Canyon at Hell's Gate. Which canyon is deeper, and by how much? Give your answer to the nearest tenth of a metre.

b) Use another method to verify your answer to part a).

13. a) Calculate the perimeter of the following figure. Express your answer to the nearest quarter of an inch.

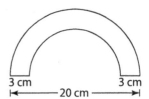

b) Show how you can use mental mathematics to check the reasonableness of your answer to part a).

1. How many metres are there in 0.74 km 36 m 79 cm?

   A 117.9 m   B 189 m

   C 776.79 m   D 783.9 m

2. Which of the following is the smallest measurement?

   A 1 m 56 cm   B 149 cm

   C 0.001 09 km   D 0.0099 km

3. _____ is longer than 16 feet 7 inches by 8 yards 2 feet and 9 inches.

   A 12 yards 2 feet 4 inches

   B 13 yards 4 feet 4 inches

   C 14 yards 1 foot 4 inches

   D 24 yards 2 feet 4 inches

4. Peter ran a distance of 3 km 435 m in 12 min 30 s. What is his speed in metres per second?

   A 4.58 m/s   B 5.12 m/s

   C 5.34 m/s   D 6.14 m/s

5. To commemorate the 1996 Olympic Summer Games in Atlanta, Georgia, a company made a hot dog that was 1996 feet long. About how many regular-sized (15-cm) hot dogs could be made from the large hot dog?

   A 3992   B 4014

   C 4023   D 4055

6. A marathon is a long-distance foot race with an official distance of 42.196 km.

   a) Express the distance in terms of miles and yards.

   b) For a marathon course to be certified, the length must not be less than 42.195 km and the uncertainty in measurement shall not exceed 0.1%. Express the length in metres as well as in feet.

7. A 2″ by 4″ by 8′ piece of lumber is actually 1.5″ by 3.5″ by 8′. Each cut from a table saw will remove $\frac{1''}{8}$ of wood. You need to cut smaller pieces that are 1.5′ long. How many smaller pieces at most can be cut from a single piece of lumber?

8. The incline on the roof of a house is 8 : 12. This means that for every 8 units of vertical change there are 12 units of horizontal change. The width of a house is 32 ft. How many yards of trim are needed on the roof ends, which have an overhang of 2 ft?

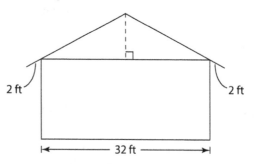

9. George is taller than Mandy by 8 cm. Mandy is shorter than Cindy by 3 in. Who is taller, Cindy or George? by how much? Justify your choice of unit.

10. A decorative block is about 7 in. high. A section of a garden retaining wall is 8 blocks high with 2.5 blocks covered by soil. Measured in feet and inches, how high is the retaining wall above ground?

11. Calculate the total cost of material for the three suits including any retail sales tax in your province or territory.

    Suit 1: fabric – 3 yd at $4.50/yd with 40% off

    Suit 2: first fabric – 1 yd at $4.50/yd; second fabric – 2 yd at $8.50/yd; lining – 2 yd at $2.00/yd

    Suit 3: fabric – 3 yd at $8.00/yd with 25% off

Chapter 1 Study Check

Use the chart below to help you assess the skills and processes you have developed during Chapter 1. The references in italics direct you to pages in *Mathematics 10 Exercise and Homework Book* where you could review the skill. How can you show that you have gained each skill? What can you do to improve?

Big Idea	Skills	This Shows I Know	This Is How I Can Improve
Solve linear measurement problems involving SI and imperial units of measure, estimation, and measurement *pages 1–8, 11, 13, 15–16*	✓ Provide referents for linear measurements *pages 3–4, 6–7, 13, 15*	Example: page 3, #1	Example: I need to review personal referents for imperial units
	✓ Use a referent to estimate a linear measurement and justify the choice of units *pages 3–4, 6–7, 13, 15*		
	✓ Choose and use instruments such as rulers, calipers, or tape measures to complete linear measurements *pages 3–4, 6–8, 11, 13, 15–16*		
	✓ Choose and justify units to use for a linear measurement *pages 3–4, 7–8, 11–13, 15, 17*		
Apply proportional reasoning to convert between SI and imperial units of measure in order to solve problems *pages 9–12, 14–17*	✓ Convert within and between SI and imperial units of measurement *pages 11–12, 14–17*		
	✓ Use mental math to check the reasonableness of conversion results *pages 11–12, 14–16*		
	✓ Use unit analysis to verify conversion results *pages 11–12, 14–16*		

Organizing the Ideas

In the Venn diagram below, show the common linear units of measure in each system. Show how to convert from one unit to another within each system. One example is provided.

How can you use this Venn diagram to help you convert from SI units to imperial? from imperial units to SI?

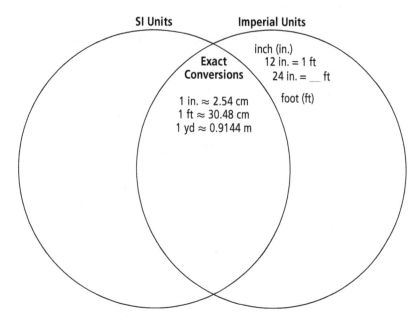

SI Units   Imperial Units

inch (in.)
12 in. = 1 ft
Exact   24 in. = ___ ft
Conversions

foot (ft)
1 in. ≈ 2.54 cm
1 ft ≈ 30.48 cm
1 yd ≈ 0.9144 m

Study Guide

Review the types of problems you handled in Chapter 1. What do you need to remember to help you do similar problems?

```
 Things to Remember

Perimeter Problems                    Speed Problems




Working With Scale
```

Chapter 2 Surface Area and Volume

2.1 Units of Area and Volume

> ### 》 KEY IDEAS 》》
>
> • Area is measured in square units. Volume is measured in cubic units.
>
> Proportional reasoning can be used to
> • solve problems involving area or volume units within SI
>
> • solve problems involving area or volume units within the imperial system
>
> • solve problems requiring the conversion of area or volume within and between the SI and imperial systems using linear dimensions
>
> | | |
> |---|---|
> | Convert 0.62 m² to square centimetres.

$1 \text{ m} = 100 \text{ cm}$
$1 \text{ m}^2 = (100 \text{ cm})(100 \text{ cm})$
$\quad\quad = 10\ 000 \text{ cm}^2$
$0.62 \text{ m}^2 = (0.62)(10\ 000 \text{ cm}^2)$
$\quad\quad = 6200 \text{ cm}^2$
0.62 m² is equal to 6200 cm². | Calculate the volume of a rectangular prism with dimensions 1 ft by 3 ft by 5 ft in cubic metres.

$1 \text{ ft} = 0.3048 \text{ m}$
$3 \text{ ft} = 3(0.3048 \text{ m})$
$\quad\quad = 0.9144 \text{ m}$
$5 \text{ ft} = 5(0.3048 \text{ m})$
$\quad\quad = 1.524 \text{ m}$

$V = (0.3048 \text{ m})(0.9144 \text{ m})(1.524 \text{ m})$
$V = 0.424\ 752\ 698\ 9 \text{ m}^3$
The volume of the prism is approximately 0.42 m³. |

Example

For a friend's birthday, Sam plans to wrap the door of her locker with wrapping paper and fill the locker with balloons. The dimensions of the locker are shown.
  a) How much wrapping paper will he need to cover the door?
  b) How much space is there inside the locker for the balloons?

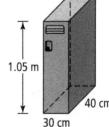

1.05 m
40 cm
30 cm

Solution

  a) The amount of wrapping paper required is equal to the area of the door. Sam decides to work in metres and converts 30 cm to 0.3 m.

  Calculate the area of the door.

  $A = lw$

  $A = (1.05)(0.30)$

  $A = 0.315$

  The area of the door is 0.315 m².

Sam learns that the wrapping paper is available only in square centimetres. Sam decides to convert to square centimetres.

$$\left(\frac{0.315 \text{ m}^2}{1}\right)\left(\frac{10\,000 \text{ cm}^2}{1 \text{ m}^2}\right) = 3150 \text{ cm}^2 \quad \text{Recall that } 10\,000 \text{ cm}^2 = 1 \text{ m}^2.$$

Sam needs 0.315 m² or 3150 cm² of wrapping paper.

b) Sam plans to fill the locker with balloons. She calculates the volume of the locker. Sam decides to work in metres and converts 30 cm to 0.3 m and 40 cm to 0.4 m.

$V = lwh$

$V = (1.05)(0.3)(0.4)$

$V = 0.126$

The volume of the locker is 0.126 m³.

Sam decides to convert to cubic centimetres by solving a proportion.

$$\left(\frac{x}{0.126 \text{ m}^3}\right) = \left(\frac{1\,000\,000 \text{ cm}^3}{1 \text{ m}^3}\right) \quad \text{Recall that } 1\,000\,000 \text{ cm}^3 = 1 \text{ m}^3.$$

$$x = 126\,000 \text{ cm}^3$$

The balloons will occupy 0.126 m³ or 126 000 cm³ of space.

A Practise

Refer to the table of conversion factors to help answer #1 and #2.

Imperial Unit	SI Unit
1 in.	2.54 cm
1 ft	0.3048 m
1 yd	0.9144 m
1 mi	1.609 km

1. Determine the following areas to the indicated unit. Express the answers to the nearest hundredth of a square unit where necessary.

a)
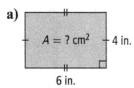
$A = ?$ cm² 4 in.
6 in.

b)
$A = ?$ m² 2 ft
2.5 ft

c)
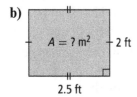
42 cm
$A = ?$ m² 18 cm

d)
$A = ?$ ft² 1.2 m
2.5 m

2. Determine possible dimensions for each area. Then, use the dimensions to calculate the area to the indicated equivalent, to the nearest tenth of a square unit.

a)
$A = 500$ cm²
$A = ?$ mm²

b)
$A = 15$ ft²
$A = ?$ cm²

3. What is each volume in cubic centimetres? Express the answer to the nearest tenth of a cubic centimetre.

a)
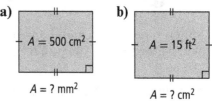
10 in.
10 in.
10 in.

b)
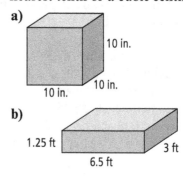
1.25 ft
3 ft
6.5 ft

4. Calculate the volume of each prism to the indicated unit. Express the answer to the nearest hundredth of a cubic unit.

a)

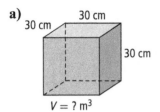

$V = ?\text{ m}^3$

⭐ **b)**

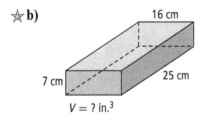

$V = ?\text{ in.}^3$

B Apply

Unless otherwise indicated, express the answers to the nearest tenth of a unit.

5. A utility trailer has the measures shown. What is the volume of the box in cubic metres?

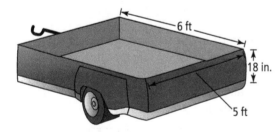

6. Shannon is painting a mural on one wall in her bedroom. The wall measures 10′ 6″ by 8′.

  a) She plans to paint a primer coat. What is the total area to be painted in square metres?

  b) One can of paint is expected to cover 15 m². How many cans of paint will Shannon need to buy?

7. The drama club sells advertising space in their playbill. The cost of an ad depends on the size of the ad. Each square centimetre costs $0.25. If the available space on each page of the playbill is 8″ by 10.5″, what is the cost of a full-page ad?

8. For a graduation ceremony, the floor of a school gymnasium is covered with a tarp to protect its finish. The gym measures 110 ft by 80 ft. What is the area of the tarp in square metres?

9. A recycling business provides customers with containers in which to place recycled materials. The business charges for recycling based on the size of the container. The largest container available measures 20 in. by 21 in. by 1 yd. Determine the volume of the container in cubic feet, to the nearest hundredth of a cubic foot.

⭐**10.** A hotel manager plans to replace the carpet in a meeting room with hardwood. The meeting room measures 6 m by 10 m.

  a) Determine the area of the room in square feet.

  b) The hardwood is available in strips measuring 4 in. by 4 ft. Determine the area of each strip in square feet.

  c) The hotel manager was advised to buy extra hardwood. If she needs to buy 12% more than the area of the floor, how many strips of hardwood should she order?

11. A community is setting up a WiFi network. Each tower can reliably transmit a signal for a circular area of radius 5 mi. What is this area in SI units, to the nearest square unit?

12. For each container, determine the unknown dimension.

  a) A rectangular prism has volume 504 cm³ and base 12 cm by 14 cm. Determine the height of the prism.

  b) A box with a square base has height 3 in. and volume 243 in.³. Determine the dimensions of the base.

13. a) A square table has an area of 16 ft². Determine the side lengths of the table in centimetres, to the nearest centimetre.

b) A window has an area of 1728 in.². If the width of the window is 3 ft, what is its length in feet?

⭐**14.** David installed a rain barrel to store rainwater for use in his garden. The barrel has a height of 34 in. and a diameter of 23.5 in. Determine the volume of rain that the barrel can hold in cubic metres, to the nearest hundredth of a cubic metre.

C Extend

⭐**15.** Amy is organizing a day for volunteers to clean up litter in a park.

a) She estimates that each volunteer will fill one large garbage bag. Each bag measures 19 in. by 11 in. by 34 in. Determine the capacity of each bag in cubic feet.

b) Amy needs to rent a dumpster for the litter. She can choose either a dumpster with a capacity of 10 yd³ or one with a capacity of 15 yd³. If 80 volunteers have signed up, which dumpster should she rent? Justify your answer mathematically.

16. In the late 1800s, in Western Canada, farmers were offered a quarter section of land to grow crops and raise livestock. This is equal to $\frac{1}{4}$ mi².

a) Each quarter section usually formed a square. Determine the length of each side of the section, in miles and in kilometres.

b) What is $\frac{1}{4}$ mi² to the nearest tenth of a square kilometre?

c) Today, the average farm in Saskatchewan is about $2\frac{1}{4}$ mi². Assuming that the land for an average farm forms a square, determine the length of each side, in miles.

d) How many times larger is the area of a farm today than a farm in the 1800s?

e) How many times longer is the length of each side of a farm today than a farm in the 1800s?

17. Wascana Park, which is located in Regina, SK, is one of the largest urban parks in Canada. The area of the park is about 2325 acres.

a) One acre is equal to 43 560 ft². What is the area of Wascana Park in square feet?

b) Determine the area of the park in square metres, to the nearest square metre.

c) The SI unit for large areas is the hectare. One hectare is equal to 10 000 m². What is the area of Wascana Park in hectares, to the nearest hectare?

D Create Connections

18. a) Identify an item you prefer to measure using imperial units.

b) Choose a quantity for the item in part a). Show how to convert the quantity from imperial to SI measure.

c) What is a quick estimate you could use for the conversion in part b)?

19. a) Identify an item you prefer to measure using SI units.

b) Choose a quantity for the item in part a). Show how to convert the quantity from SI to imperial measures.

c) What is a quick estimate you could use for the conversion in part b)?

2.2 Surface Area

- The surface area of a right cylinder and of a right prism can be calculated using the area of the bases (top and bottom) plus the lateral area.

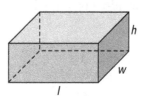 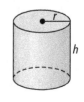

$SA_{prism} = 2lw + 2lh + 2wh$ $SA_{cylinder} = 2(\pi r^2) + 2\pi rh$

- The surface area of a right pyramid and of a right cone can be calculated using the area of the base plus the lateral area.

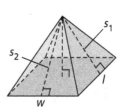 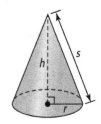

$SA_{pyramid} = lw + 2\left[\frac{1}{2}ls_1\right] + 2\left[\frac{1}{2}ws_2\right]$ $SA_{cone} = \pi r^2 + \pi rs$

- The surface area of a sphere depends on the radius only.

$SA_{sphere} = 4\pi r^2$

Example

Colby is taking a pottery class. He sketches a set of geometric objects as shown.

Before he makes clay models, he adds dimensions to each object.

Given the measurements, determine the surface area of each object. Express the answers to the nearest tenth of a square centimetre.

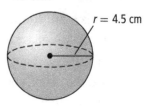

a) The right cone has radius 4.5 cm and slant height 12 cm.

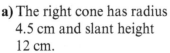
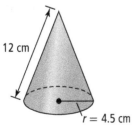

b) The right pyramid has a square base with side length 16 cm and slant height 12 cm.

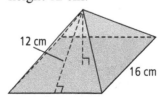

c) The sphere has radius 4.5 cm.

$r = 4.5$ cm

Solution

a) The surface area of a right cone is the sum of the area of the base and the lateral area.

$SA = $ base $+$ lateral area

$SA = \pi r^2 + \pi r s$

$SA = \pi(4.5)^2 + \pi(4.5)(12)$

$SA = 233.2632...$

The surface area of the cone is approximately 233.3 cm^2.

b) The surface area of a right pyramid is the sum of the area of the base and the lateral area.

$SA = $ base $+$ lateral area

$SA = (\text{length})(\text{width}) + 2\left[\frac{1}{2}(\text{length})(\text{slant height}_1)\right] + 2\left[\frac{1}{2}(\text{width})(\text{slant height}_2)\right]$

$SA = (\text{length})(\text{width}) + 4\left[\frac{1}{2}(\text{length})(\text{slant height})\right]$

In this case, why can you multiply by 4?

$SA = (16)(16) + 4\left[\frac{1}{2}(16)(12)\right]$

$SA = 640$

The surface area of the pyramid is 640.0 cm^2.

c) The formula for the surface area of a sphere is $SA = 4\pi r^2$.

$SA = 4\pi(4.5)^2$

$SA = 254.469$

The surface area of the sphere is approximately 254.5 cm^2.

A Practise

Express your answers to the nearest hundredth of a unit where necessary.

1. Determine the surface area of each of the following.

a)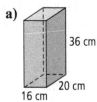
36 cm
20 cm
16 cm

b)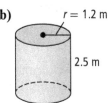
$r = 1.2$ m
2.5 m

c)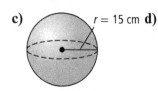
$r = 15$ cm

d)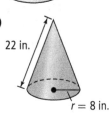
22 in.
$r = 8$ in.

e)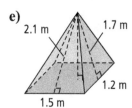
2.1 m
1.7 m
1.2 m
1.5 m

2. What is the surface area of each of the following?

a)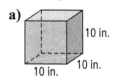
10 in.
10 in.
10 in.

b)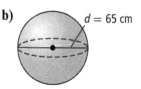
$d = 65$ cm

c)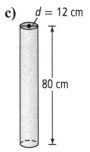
$d = 12$ cm
80 cm

d)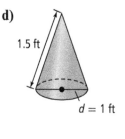
1.5 ft
$d = 1$ ft

3. A jewellery box has a surface area of 148 in.^{2}. The base of the box is 6 in. by 4 in. Sketch a diagram to help determine the height of the box.

4. What is the surface area of the right pyramid?

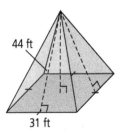

44 ft

31 ft

5. The surface area is given for each object. Determine the unknown dimension.

☆**a)** $SA = 4 \text{ m}^2$

$d = 1.2$ m

h

b) $SA = 84.5 \text{ in.}^2$

r

c) $SA = 5.7 \text{ cm}^2$

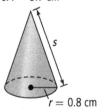
s

$r = 0.8$ cm

d) $SA = 2443.8 \text{ ft}^2$

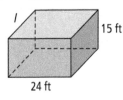
l

15 ft

24 ft

6. Determine the surface area of each composite object.

a) $d = 25$ cm

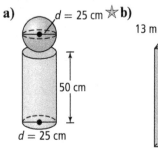

50 cm

$d = 25$ cm

☆**b)** 15 m

13 m

38 m

18 m

10 m

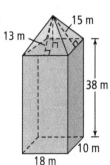

B Apply
Express your answers to the nearest tenth of a unit where necessary.

7. Andrea wants to make a leather case for her new smartphone. The phone measures 55 mm by 12 mm by 114 mm.

a) How much leather is needed for a case that completely encloses the smartphone?

b) How much leather is needed for a case that is open at one end? Hint: Do not include the overlap of the leather pieces when they are sewn together.

8. The diameter of Earth is approximately 12 740 km. Determine the surface area of Earth to the nearest square kilometre.

9. A skylight has the shape of a right pyramid. The square base measures 1.2 m by 1.2 m and the height is 1.6 m.

a) Determine the slant height of each face of the skylight.

b) Determine the surface area of the pyramid that represents the skylight.

c) How much glass is needed for the skylight? Hint: There is no glass in the base of the pyramid.

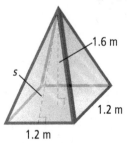

1.6 m

s

1.2 m

1.2 m

10. A manufacturer is designing a new cylindrical paint can with diameter 20 cm. He plans to use 2200 cm^2 of material to make the can. What is the height of a can that uses all available material?

11. Obelisks are sometimes used to mark the border between Canada and the United States. One stone obelisk is a right prism topped by a right pyramid. The obelisk has a base 15 cm by 15 cm by 95 cm and a top in the shape of a pyramid with height 10 cm. Determine the surface area of the obelisk.

12. Daniel needs to paint four cylindrical columns that support the ceiling in the hall of his home. The columns have height 10 ft and diameter 10 in. Determine the total surface area, in square feet, requiring paint.

13. The surface area of a cone is 3520 cm^2. If the radius of the cone is 20 cm, determine the slant height, to the nearest centimetre.

☆14. Breanne makes and sells bracelets. She uses a bracelet mandrel to shape, stretch, and size the bracelets. The mandrel is a cone with the circumference marked at different locations on the lateral face of the cone. The mandrel is 6 in. tall and has a base circumference of 12 in. Determine the surface area of the mandrel.
Hint: $C = 2\pi r$.

15. a) Determine the edge length of a cube with surface area 62 m^2.

   b) Write a formula for determining the edge length of a cube, when the surface area is known.

C Extend

16. A sheet of aluminum measures 4 ft by 8 ft.

   a) If David uses all of the aluminum, what is the diameter of the largest sphere that he can make?

   b) If he uses all of the aluminum, what are the dimensions of the largest cube that he can make?

   c) Is it realistic for David to expect that all of the aluminum will be used? Explain why or why not.

17. A farmer is filling a bin with grain. The grain forms a cone near the top of the bin.

   a) The grain cone has height 5.2 m and circumference 32 m. Determine the slant height of the grain, to the nearest tenth of a metre.

   b) The farmer plans to treat the outside surface of the grain pile to reduce rot. Determine the area to be treated, to the nearest square metre.

D Create Connections

18. A formula for the surface area of a cylinder is $SA = 2\pi r^2 + 2\pi rh$.

   a) Write a formula that you can use to determine the surface area of a cylinder using the diameter instead of the radius.

   b) Write a formula that you can use to determine the surface area of a cylinder using the circumference instead of the radius.

   c) For parts a) and b), identify a situation in which each form of the formula would be more useful.

<< **KEY IDEAS** >>

- The volume of a right cone is found by calculating one third of the volume of its related right cylinder.

$$V_{\text{cone}} = \tfrac{1}{3}\pi r^2 h$$

- The volume of a right pyramid is found by calculating one third of the volume of its related right prism.

$$V_{\text{pyramid}} = \tfrac{1}{3} lwh$$

- The volume of a sphere is found by using the formula

$$V_{\text{sphere}} = \tfrac{4}{3}\pi r^3$$

- If you know the volume of an object, you can calculate an unknown dimension.

- The volume of the right pyramid with square base w is 384 ft³. Find the dimensions of the base.

$$V = \tfrac{1}{3} Bh$$
$$384 = \tfrac{1}{3}w^2(8)$$
$$3(384) = 3[\tfrac{1}{3}w^2(8)]$$
$$1152 = w^2(8)$$
$$\tfrac{1152}{8} = w^2$$
$$144 = w^2$$
$$12 = w$$

The dimensions of the base are 12 ft × 12 ft.

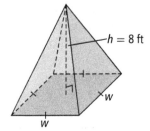

$h = 8$ ft

w

w

Example

Julie makes glass beads and is experimenting with two new designs: a conical bead and a spherical bead. Determine how much glass is needed to make each bead. Express the answers to the nearest tenth.

a)

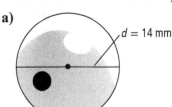

$d = 14$ mm

b)

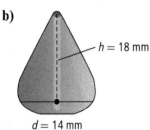

$h = 18$ mm

$d = 14$ mm

Solution

a) For the sphere,

$r = 14 \div 2$

$\quad = 7$

Substitute into the formula $V = \frac{4}{3}\pi r^3$.

$V = \frac{4}{3}\pi r^3$

$V = \frac{4}{3}\pi(7)^3$

$V \approx 1436.755\,04...$

The volume of glass needed per spherical bead is approximately 1436.8 mm³.

b) For the cone,

$V = \frac{1}{3}\pi r^2 h$

$V = \frac{1}{3}\pi(7)^2(18)$

$V \approx 923.628\,24...$

The volume of glass needed per conical bead is approximately 923.6 mm³.

A Practise

Express your answers to the nearest hundredth of a unit where necessary.

1. Determine the volume of each solid.

a)

26.8 in.

17 in.

10.2 in.

b)

$r = 2\,\text{m}$

3.3 m

c)

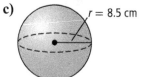

$r = 8.5$ cm

d)

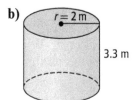

$h = 5$ ft

$r = 12$ ft

e)

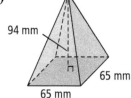

94 mm

65 mm

65 mm

2. Calculate the volume of each solid.

a)

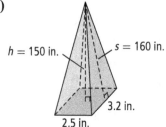

$h = 150$ in.

$s = 160$ in.

3.2 in.

2.5 in.

b)

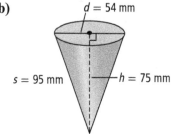

$d = 54$ mm

$s = 95$ mm

$h = 75$ mm

3. Determine the unknown dimension of each solid.

a) $V = 150$ in.³

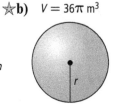

h

4.1 in.

4.3 in.

⭐**b)** $V = 36\pi$ m³

r

c) $V = 7$ m³

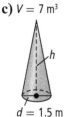

h

$d = 1.5$ m

d) $V = 2.2$ ft³

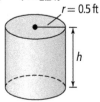

$r = 0.5$ ft

h

4. What is the volume of each solid, in cubic centimetres?

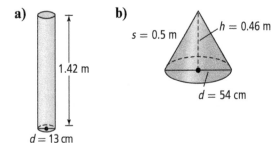

a) $d = 13$ cm, 1.42 m

b) $s = 0.5$ m, $h = 0.46$ m, $d = 54$ cm

5. Determine the volume of each composite object, in cubic centimetres.

a)

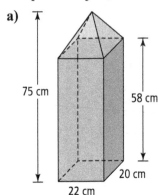

75 cm, 58 cm, 20 cm, 22 cm

b)

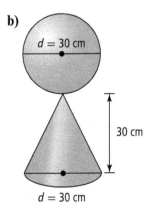

$d = 30$ cm, 30 cm, $d = 30$ cm

B Apply
Express your answers to the nearest tenth of a unit where necessary.

6. Earth has a diameter of approximately 12 740 km. What is Earth's volume?

7. Kyle plans to operate a snow cone stand. He determines that his right conical cups need a capacity between 75 cm³ and 100 cm³. Will either of the following cups meet this standard? Justify your answer mathematically.

a) a conical cup with height 10 cm and diameter 6 cm

b) a conical cup with height 6 cm and diameter 10 cm

8. Sketch the object and determine the volume.

a) a right cone with height 44 in. and radius $\frac{1}{4}$ of the height

b) a right pyramid with base 12.3 cm by 12.3 cm and height 18.8 cm

c) a right pyramid with base 68 cm by 85 cm and height 1 m

d) a sphere with diameter 1.1 m

9. A can of juice has height 11.5 cm and diameter 5 cm.

a) What is the volume of the can?

b) The can is labelled 225 mL. What is the relationship between millilitres and cubic centimetres?

★**10.** The right pyramid shown has height 24 cm and slant height 25 cm. What is its volume?

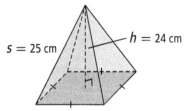

$s = 25$ cm, $h = 24$ cm

11. A cylindrical water bottle must hold 1000 cm³ and can be no more than 25 cm high. Determine the required radius. Is this the minimum radius or the maximum radius? Justify your answer.

12. The volume of each solid is given. Sketch the object and determine the unknown dimension.

a) A cylinder has a volume of 700 m^3 and a height of 16 m. Calculate its radius.

b) A cone has a capacity of 250 cm^3 and a diameter of 15 cm. Determine its height.

c) A square-based pyramid has a volume of 0.015 m^3. The height of the pyramid is 50 cm. Determine the dimensions of the base.

13. The roof of a house is shaped like a right pyramid with a square base. The base of the pyramid measures 32 ft by 32 ft. The roof must enclose a volume of at least 7300 ft^3 of air. What is the minimum height for the apex of the roof?

14. Lori designed a cylindrical can that must have a capacity of 250 cm^3. Her can has a diameter of 5 cm and a height of 10 cm.

a) Calculate the capacity of the can.

b) Does it meet the design requirements? Explain.

☆c) Modify the height of Lori's can so that it will have the correct capacity. Justify your answer mathematically.

15. Bree has 1000 cm^3 of melted wax to make a candle.

a) Sketch a cylindrical candle with height 20 cm. Determine the radius.

b) Sketch a cylindrical candle with height 15 cm. Determine the radius.

c) Suppose Bree makes a right conical candle with height 25 cm. Sketch the candle and determine the radius of its base.

d) Suppose Bree makes a candle shaped like a pyramid with a square base and a height of 20 cm. What is the area of the base of the pyramid?

16. The Luxor Hotel in Las Vegas, Nevada, is a square-based pyramid with a height of about 350 ft and a slant height of about 447 ft. Determine the volume of the hotel.

☆17. A ceramic bead is half a sphere with a diameter of 1.85 cm. Determine the volume of the bead.

C Extend

18. Stan's company is designing a container that must have a volume of 750 cm^3.

a) What is the height of a cylindrical container with a diameter of 10 cm?

b) What is the height of a right prism with a square base measuring 10 cm by 10 cm?

c) Determine the surface area of the container in parts a) and b).

d) Which container do you recommend that Stan's company produce? Explain why.

19. Determine the volume of the building block.

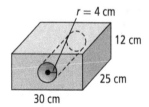
r = 4 cm
12 cm
25 cm
30 cm

20. a) What are the dimensions of a cube with a surface area numerically equal to its volume?

b) Determine the radius of a sphere with a surface area numerically equal to its volume.

D Create Connections

21. Suppose that each dimension of a solid is doubled. Which will change more—the surface area or the volume of the object? Explain your reasoning using an example.

Chapter 2 Review

2.1 Units of Area and Volume
Express your answers to the nearest hundredth of a unit where necessary. You may need to refer to the table of conversion factors on page 21.

1. Calculate each area using the indicated unit.

    a)
    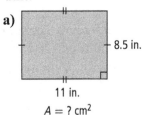
    8.5 in.

    11 in.
    $A = ?$ cm^2

    b)
    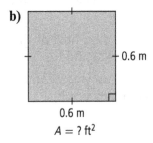
    0.6 m

    0.6 m
    $A = ?$ ft^2

2. Calculate each volume using the indicated unit.

    a) **b)**
    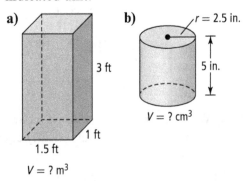
    3 ft

    1 ft
    1.5 ft
    $V = ?$ m^3

    $r = 2.5$ in.
    5 in.
    $V = ?$ cm^3

3. Cassidy wants to replace her kitchen countertop. The dimensions are 65 cm by 1.5 m. The building supply store sells countertop material by the square foot. Determine the area of her countertop, in square feet.

★4. Ken is researching the cost of topsoil for his lawn. One supplier quotes a price of $50 per cubic yard, and another quotes a price of $62 per cubic metre. Which supplier offers a better price? Justify your answer mathematically.

2.2 Surface Area
Express your answers to the nearest hundredth of a unit where necessary.

5. Sketch each solid and determine its surface area.

    a) A right cone has radius 3.5 m and slant height 12 m.

    b) A right cone has diameter 12 cm and slant height 10 cm.

    c) A sphere has diameter 8.5 in.

    d) A pyramid has a square base with sides 4 ft and slant height 5.5 ft.

6. Calculate the unknown dimension in each of the following.

    a) A sphere has surface area 450 in.^{2}.

    b) The base of a right pyramid has sides 12 cm by 10 cm. The slant height of the face with base 10 cm is 10 cm. The surface area is 333.2 cm^2.

    c) A right cone has surface area 20 ft^2 and radius 2 ft.

    d) A right cone has surface area 500 m^2 and the base of the cone has area 314 m^2.

★7. The floor of a storage shed has sides 8 ft by 10 ft. The height of the walls is 7 ft. The roof is shaped like a pyramid. The slant height of the face with the shorter side of the shed is 5.4 ft. The slant height of the face with the longer side is 4.5 ft. Sketch the shed and determine the total surface area of the shed.

8. A concrete pillar has a diameter of 12 in. If the pillar is 10 ft tall, what is its surface area?

9. The surface of a sphere with diameter 50 cm is composed of small mirrors. The construction company purchased 5% extra material to cover the sphere. If the mirrors cost $10 per square foot, how much did it cost to cover the sphere?

10. A conical sculpture has diameter 10 ft and height 12 ft.

    a) Sketch and label a cross-section of the cone.

    b) Determine the radius and slant height of the cone.

    c) Determine the surface area of the cone.

2.3 Volume

Express your answers to the nearest hundredth of a unit where necessary.

11. Calculate the volume of each solid.

    a) A right cylinder has radius 9 in. and height 4 ft.

    b) A right pyramid has a base with sides 2 m by 2.5 m and a height of 3.2 m.

    c) A sphere has diameter 1 m.

    d) A right cone has height 18 cm and radius 6.5 cm.

12. What is the unknown dimension of each solid?

    a) A square-based prism has volume 33 750 m³ and height 50 m.

    b) A right cone has height 12.5 cm and volume 325 cm³.

    c) A sphere has volume 905 in.³.

    d) A right pyramid has a base with sides 1 ft by 1.5 ft and a volume of 3 ft³.

13. Mike is building a patio with an area of 700 ft². The concrete pad will have a thickness of 4 in.

    a) Determine the volume of concrete required for the patio, in cubic feet.

    b) Mike estimates that for every 35 ft³, he will need 1 m³ of concrete. How many cubic metres of concrete will he need? Convert from cubic feet to cubic metres and check the accuracy of his estimate.

✮14. Astrid has a cylindrical compost bin with a height of 1.1 m and a diameter of 1.25 m.

    a) Determine the volume of compost in a full bin.

    b) Astrid's garden is rectangular and measures 12 ft by 20 ft. If she spreads the compost uniformly on her garden, how deep will the compost be, in inches?

15. Liam made a ceramic mug with a diameter of 8 cm and a height of 10 cm. Determine the capacity of the mug.

16. Suppose Liam makes a cylindrical mug with twice the capacity of the mug in #15.

    a) If the diameter stays the same, predict the height of a mug with the desired capacity. Check your prediction.

    b) If the height stays the same, predict the diameter of a mug with the desired capacity. Check your prediction.

17. A pile of gravel is shaped like a cone. It has a diameter of 12 ft and a height of 4.5 ft.

    a) What is the volume of gravel in the pile?

    b) Gravel is often sold in cubic yards. If one cubic yard sells for $15, determine the value of the gravel pile. Hint: 1 yd³ = 27 ft³.

Chapter 1–2 Cumulative Review

Unless otherwise indicated, express the answers to the nearest hundredth of a unit. You may need to refer to the table of conversion factors on page 21.

1. Calculate each area using the indicated unit.

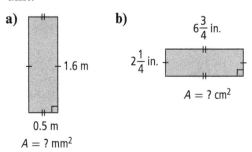

a)

1.6 m

0.5 m

$A = ?\ mm^2$

b)

$6\frac{3}{4}$ in.

$2\frac{1}{4}$ in.

$A = ?\ cm^2$

2. On a plain piece of paper, draw a letter O whose curve length you estimate to be each distance.

   a) 35 mm   b) 15 cm

3. a) Explain how you could measure the distance of each curved letter you drew for #2.

   b) Measure each O and compare your measurements with the required distances. If you are out by more than 5 mm for part a) or 2 cm for part b), try drawing the letter again.

4. Determine each volume using the indicated unit.

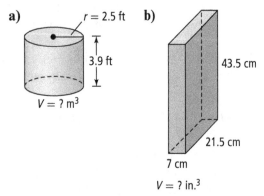

a) $r = 2.5$ ft

3.9 ft

$V = ?\ m^3$

b)

43.5 cm

21.5 cm

7 cm

$V = ?\ in.^3$

5. Work with a partner and create a list of unit conversions you have used in Chapters 1 and 2.

6. What reading is shown on each measuring device? Give each reading in both millimetres and centimetres.

   a) SI ruler

   b) SI caliper

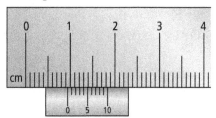

7. Chloe plans to build a chest with the dimensions shown. The store sells wood by the square foot. Determine the total amount of wood she needs to build the chest, including the base of the chest and the lid. Assume that there is no overlap and no waste. Express the answer to the nearest quarter of a square foot.

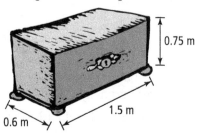

0.75 m

1.5 m

0.6 m

8. Suppose the actual height of the flag pole is 7.6 m. What are the dimensions of the flag? Hint: Measure the dimensions of the flag in the picture.

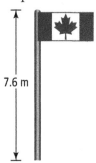

7.6 m

9. Describe how you would determine each volume in the indicated units. Calculate the volume to the nearest tenth of a cubic unit.

   a) a sphere with radius 6.2 cm

   b) a right pyramid with base 1.5 m by 0.7 m and height 2 m

   c) a right cone with radius 4 mm and height 7 mm

10. What reading is shown on this imperial ruler? Name one item that might be this length.

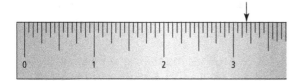

11. Sketch each solid and calculate the surface area, to the nearest tenth of a square unit.

   a) A right cone has slant height 17 in. and diameter 12 in.

   b) A pyramid has a square base with sides 14 cm and slant height 21 cm.

   c) A sphere has diameter 5 ft.

12. Convert each measurement to the unit indicated.

   a) The world's tallest man is 8′ 11″. (yard)

   b) Mount Everest is 29 029 ft. (tenth of a mile)

   c) The world's tallest tree is 126.4 yd. (inch)

13. Determine the missing dimension.

   a) A right cone has surface area 16 ft² and radius 1.6 ft.

   b) The square base of a pyramid has area 20 cm² and surface area 948 cm².

   c) A sphere has surface area 56.4 m².

14. Tim needs to shingle the roof of his gazebo. The roof is a pyramid with a square base 4.1 m by 4.1 m and a slant height of 2.1 m.

   a) How much roofing material is needed for the roof? Express the answer to the nearest square metre.

   b) If the roofing tiles measure 265 mm by 165 mm, how many tiles will he need? Assume that there is no overlap.

15. What is the height of the cone funnel?

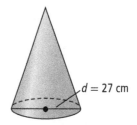

$d = 27$ cm

$V = 4019.2$ cm³

16. Jon is driving home from Seattle, Washington, to Vancouver, British Columbia. A highway sign just outside Seattle indicates that the Canada–U.S. border is 138 mi. away. As Jon passes the border, he sees another sign indicating that Vancouver is 49 km away. What is the total driving distance between Seattle and Vancouver in SI units?

17. Charlotte wants to buy a bracelet made of rhodonite. The cost of the bracelet depends on the amount of rhodonite in the bracelet. If there are 30 beads and each bead is 6 mm in diameter, what is the amount of rhodonite in the bracelet, in cubic centimetres?

1. In 2009, the most expensive home in Canada was listed at $14 million CDN for 789 m². The world's most expensive home was listed at $2 billion US for 400 000 ft². Assume the exchange rate is $1 CDN = $0.9372 US. In terms of Canadian dollars per square foot, by how many times is the world's record home more expensive than Canada's record home?

   A between 2 and 3 times

   B between 3 and 4 times

   C between 4 and 5 times

   D between 5 and 6 times

★2. A cylindrical glass has an inner diameter of 6 cm and contains juice with a height of 10 cm. Two spherical scoops of ice cream are added to the glass. Each scoop has a radius of 2 cm. What is the new height of the juice?

   A 1.7 cm   B 2.4 cm

   C 11.7 cm   D 12.4 cm

3. The inner core of a toilet paper roll is shown. Point D is directly below point A. The paper core has diameter 4 cm and height 10 cm. Delia draws a curve along the surface of the roll starting at point D and wrapping around the roll twice before reaching point A. What is the length of the curve she draws?

   A 27 cm   B 30 cm

   C 31 cm   D 34 cm

4. A cylinder that is 40 cm tall is inscribed in a cone that is 50 cm tall. The radius of the base of the cone is 30 cm. What is the lateral surface area of the cylinder?

   A 360π cm²   B 480π cm²

   C 500π cm²   D 520π cm²

★5. A test tube is made of a cylindrical tube joined to a hemispherical bowl of the same radius. The capacity of the hemispherical part is $\frac{1}{6}$ that of the whole test tube. What is the ratio of the radius to the height?

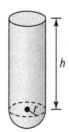

★6. The pencil is composed of a cone, a cylinder, and a hemisphere, all of the same radius. If the volumes of the three components are equal, what is the ratio $x:y:z$?

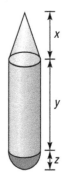

Chapter 2 Study Check

Use the chart below to help you assess the skills and processes you have developed during Chapter 2. The references in italics direct you to pages in *Mathematics 10 Exercise and Homework Book* where you could review the skill. How can you show that you have gained each skill? What can you do to improve?

Big Idea	Skills	This Shows I Know	This Is How I Can Improve
Solve surface area and volume problems that involve right cones, right cylinders, right prisms, right pyramids, and spheres, using SI and imperial units *pages 20–36*	✓ Determine surface area of 3-D objects *pages 20–27, 32–36*		
	✓ Determine volume of 3-D objects *pages 20–23, 28–36*		
	✓ Determine the volume or surface area of a composite 3-D object *pages 26–27, 30–32, 36*		
	✓ Given surface area and other dimensions, determine the unknown dimension of a 3-D object *pages 23, 25–27, 32, 35*		
	✓ Given volume and other dimensions, determine the unknown dimension of a 3-D object *pages 22, 29–31, 33, 35*		
	✓ Create diagrams to represent and solve problems involving 3-D objects *pages 22–23, 25–27, 30–36*		
	✓ Convert within and between SI and imperial units of area or volume *pages 20–23, 30–36*		
	✓ Use mental math to judge the reasonableness of answers *pages 21–23, 25–27, 29–36*		

Organizing the Ideas

Use the table below to make comparisons among the solids you have studied in Chapter 2.
Compare the solids and how to calculate their surface area and volume.

Surface Area and Volume of 3-D Objects				
Characteristics	Right Cones	Spheres	Right Pyramids	
Surface Area				Similarities
				Differences
Volume				Similarities
				Differences

Study Guide

Review the types of surface area and volume problems you handled in Chapter 2. What do you
need to remember to help you do similar problems? Develop a series of cards or file folders for
each type of 3-D object you studied in Chapter 2.

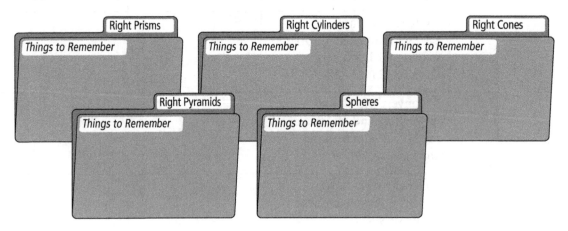

Chapter 3 Right Triangle Trigonometry

3.1 The Tangent Ratio

- In similar triangles, corresponding angles are equal, and corresponding sides are in proportion. Therefore, the ratios of the lengths of corresponding sides are equal.

- The sides of a right triangle are labelled according to a reference angle.

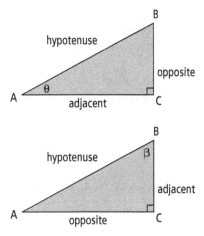

- The tangent ratio compares the length of the side opposite the reference angle to the length of the side adjacent to the angle in a right triangle. For the reference angle θ in the upper triangle,

$$\tan \theta = \frac{\text{length of side opposite } \theta}{\text{length of side adjacent to } \theta}$$

For the reference angle β in the lower triangle,

$$\tan \beta = \frac{\text{length of side opposite } \beta}{\text{length of side adjacent to } \beta}$$

- You can use the tangent ratio to
  - determine the measure of one of the acute angles when the lengths of both legs in a right triangle are known
  - determine a side length if the measure of one acute angle and the length of one leg of a right triangle are known

Example

A housing contractor is required to build a roof on a house with a 38° slope from the horizontal. Additionally, the peak of the roof is to align with the centre of the end walls. The house is 16 m wide and has that are 4 m high. To the nearest tenth of a metre, how high will the peak be above the ground once the house is completed?

Solution

Organize the information and sketch a diagram to illustrate the problem.

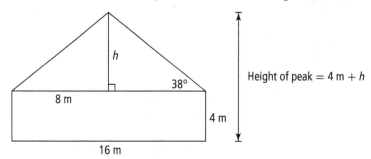

Since the peak must be in the centre of a wall that is 16 m wide, it means that any point directly below the peak is 8 m from either side. Create a right triangle (two right triangles, actually) using the top of the wall, the height of the roof, and the roofline.

Let h represent the height, in metres, of the roof above the top of the wall.
Identify the sides in terms of the given angle of 38°: opposite $= h$ and adjacent $= 8$ m.
Apply the tangent ratio using $\theta = 38°$:

$$\tan \theta = \frac{\text{opposite}}{\text{adjacent}}$$

$\tan 38° = \frac{h}{8}$

Isolate the value h and solve. (Remember to set your calculator to degrees.)

$8(\tan 38°) = h$
$8(0.7812) = h$
$6.2496 = h$

The height, h, of the roof above the wall is 6.25 m, to the nearest tenth of a metre. Therefore, the height of the peak above the ground once the house is completed is 6.25 m + 4 m (height of wall) = 10.25 m.

A Practise

1. For $\angle B$ in right $\triangle ABC$, identify

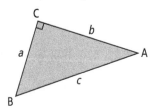

   a) the hypotenuse
   b) the adjacent side
   c) the opposite side

2. Refer to right $\triangle ABC$ in question 1.

   a) State the tangent ratio of $\angle A$.
   b) State the tangent ratio of $\angle B$.

3. Refer to right $\triangle ABC$ in question 1.

   a) If $a = 10$ cm and $b = 12$ cm, what is the value of tan A?
   b) If $a = 1.9$ m and $b = 2.4$ m, what is the value of tan B?
   c) If $\tan A = \frac{5}{6}$ and $a = 15$, what is the value of b?

4. In right △RST, determine the length of side *t* if ∠R = 39° and *r* = 4.3 m.

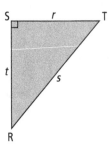

☆**5.** Use the tangent ratios and a calculator to determine the measure of each angle, to the nearest tenth of a degree.

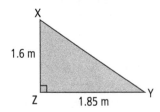

a) ∠X

b) ∠Y

B Apply

6. Calculate ∠A and ∠B in right △ABC where ∠C = 90°, side *a* measures 3.2 m, and side *b* measures 2.5 m. What is the measure of side *c*? Explain how you determined the length of this side.

7. Ms. Singh's design class is required to build model cars. The models are tested for efficiency by releasing them at the top of a ramp and comparing the distances they travel. The ramp extends over a horizontal distance of 375 cm and forms an angle of 38° with the floor. Calculate the height of the ramp to the nearest centimetre.

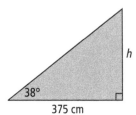

8. Determine the value of each variable. Express your answer to the nearest tenth of a unit.

a)

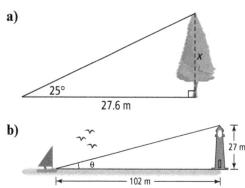

b)

9. The length of a shadow cast by an elm tree is 6.2 m. At the same time, a woman who is 165 cm tall casts a shadow that is 285 cm in length. What is the height of the tree?

10. A wheelchair ramp on a bus forms an angle of 18° with the ground. If the floor of the bus is 65 cm above the ground, how much width does the ramp require beside the bus?

☆**11.** The minute hand of a clock has a length of 14 cm. The length of the hour hand is 11 cm.

a) If a line is drawn between the ends of the two hands at the 9 o'clock position, what angle is formed between the line and the minute hand?

b) What is the angle between the line in part a) and the hour hand?

C Extend

12. An access road runs 75 m from and parallel to a high voltage power line. Two maintenance crews working along the road at different positions can see the same transmission tower. Looking from the north, crew #1 sees the tower 28° to the west of the road. From the south crew #2 sights the tower 19° to the west of the road. How far apart are the crews?

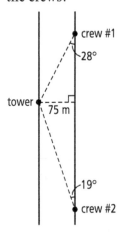

13. A plane flying at an altitude of 1200 m is directly over a small island. After a few minutes, the island is sighted at an angle 5.2° below and behind the plane. Determine the distance the plane travelled, to the nearest metre.

14. Different types of gravel will form different slopes when piled up. Coarse gravel can sustain an angle of 29° with the horizontal, whereas fine gravel can sustain an angle of 24°. Maria and Nathan are landscapers who need to create a circular mound 1.7 m high. To the nearest tenth of a metre, what is the minimum diameter of mound they can create using

a) coarse gravel?

b) fine gravel?

D Create Connections

15. Jasmine and Ivan are monitoring a pair of falcons nesting on a building ledge that is 112 m above the street. They position their telescope (on a 1.4-m tripod) at street level at a distance of 245 m from the building. At what angle does the telescope need to be set? Calculate your answer to the nearest tenth of a degree.

☆**16.** Guy wires are lengths of cord or cable used to support towers or poles. For greatest support, four guy wires should be used. They should be spaced evenly around a tower or pole and attached at least two thirds of the way up the structure. They should form an angle with the ground of 60° or less. Ramon wishes to erect a radio tower 6.5 m tall on a piece of property measuring 10 m by 4.2 m.

a) Does Ramon have enough space for proper guy wires?

b) How high a tower, to the nearest tenth of a metre, could Ramon build and support safely in the space?

17. △ABC is a right triangle with the right angle at vertex C.

a) If the triangle has a tangent ratio of 2, state two possible values for each of side a and side b.

b) If the triangle has a tangent ratio of $\frac{1}{2}$, state two possible values for each of side a and side b.

c) What do you notice about the values in parts a) and b)? Why is this?

3.2 The Sine and Cosine Ratios

• The sine ratio and cosine ratio compare the lengths of the legs of a right triangle to the length of the hypotenuse.

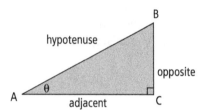

• The sine ratio compares the length of the side opposite an acute angle to the length of the hypotenuse.

$$\sin \theta = \frac{\text{length of side opposite } \theta}{\text{length of hypotenuse}}$$

• The cosine ratio compares the length of the side adjacent to an acute angle to the length of the hypotenuse.

$$\cos \theta = \frac{\text{length of side adjacent to } \theta}{\text{length of hypotenuse}}$$

• The sine and cosine ratios can be used to calculate side lengths and angle measures of right triangles.

• Visualizing the information that you are given and that you need to find is important. It helps you determine which trigonometric ratio to use and whether to use the inverse trigonometric ratio.

• Determine the value of θ, to the nearest degree.

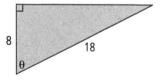

$$\cos \theta = \frac{\text{length of side adjacent } \theta}{\text{length of hypotenuse}}$$

$$\cos \theta = \frac{8}{18}$$

$$\theta = \cos^{-1}\left(\frac{8}{18}\right)$$

$$\theta = 63.6122...°$$

Angle θ is approximately 64°.

Example

Traditionally, ships were constructed in docks on land and then launched by sliding them down a ramp into the water. If the ramp was too steep, there was a risk of capsizing the ship; if it was not steep enough, the ship could get stuck. Engineers determined that a ramp angle of 32° was ideal. At a shipyard, the vertical distance from the construction dock to the water is 6.8 m. Calculate to the nearest tenth of a metre the length of ramp needed to launch a ship safely.

Solution

Organize the information by sketching a diagram to illustrate the problem.

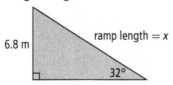

Choose the appropriate trigonometric ratio.
In relation to the 32° angle, the side that measures 6.8 m is the opposite side. The side of unknown length, x, is the hypotenuse. Therefore, use the sine ratio.

$$\sin \theta = \frac{\text{opposite}}{\text{hypotenuse}}$$

$$\sin 32° = \frac{6.8 \text{ m}}{x}$$

Isolate the value of x and solve.

$$\sin 32°(x) = 6.8 \text{ m}$$

$$x = \frac{6.8 \text{ m}}{\sin 32°}$$

$$x = \frac{6.8 \text{ m}}{0.5299}$$

$$x = 12.83 \text{ m}$$

The length of the ramp must be 12.8 m, to the nearest tenth of a metre.

A Practise

1. Express each trigonometric ratio in relation to right △ABC.

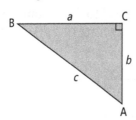

   a) sin A

   b) cos A

   c) sin B

   d) cos B

2. Using right △ABC in question 1 and the stated values, determine each unknown value.

   a) If $b = 12$ cm and $c = 17$ cm, what is the value of cos A?

   b) If $a = 10$ cm and $c = 15$ cm, what is the value of sin A?

   c) If $b = 1.9$ m and $c = 2.4$ m, what is the value of sin B?

   d) If $a = 2.6$ mm and $c = 3.9$ mm, what is the value of cos B?

   e) If $\sin A = \frac{5}{6}$ and $c = 15$, what is the value of a?

   f) If $\cos B = \frac{9}{45}$ and $c = 15$, what is the value of a?

3. Use the sine and cosine ratios and a calculator to determine the measure of each angle, to the nearest tenth of a degree.

   a) ∠R

   b) ∠S

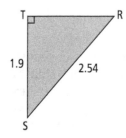

4. Use a calculator to determine the measure of each angle, to the nearest tenth of a degree.

a) $\cos A = 0.5835$

b) $\sin B = 0.8358$

c) $\sin \theta = 0.2181$

d) $\cos \theta = 0.0488$

5. For right $\triangle XYZ$, determine the length of side x to two decimal places if

a) $\angle Y = 38°$ and $z = 2.35$ cm

b) $\angle X = 59°$ and $z = 5.12$ m

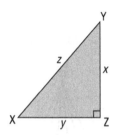

6. For right $\triangle XYZ$ in question 5, calculate the length of side z to two decimal places if

a) $\angle Y = 41°$ and $x = 54.7$ mm

b) $\angle X = 52°$ and $x = 7.64$ m

B Apply

7. Some students in Mr. Pang's wood shop class are building a shelf. The shelf is 28 cm deep and is supported by a 32-cm diagonal brace on each side. Calculate the angle that the brace forms with the backing piece, to the nearest degree. Calculate the required height of the backing piece, to the nearest millimetre.

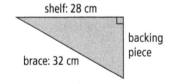

8. A 14-ft ladder is leaning against a wall 9 ft high in such a way that the top 3 ft of the ladder extend above the top of the wall.

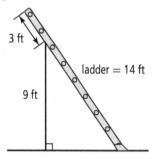

a) What is the horizontal distance from the bottom of the ladder to the wall? Round your answer to the nearest tenth of a foot.

b) What angle does the ladder form with the ground, to the nearest tenth of a degree?

9. A zip line is to be set up from a tree to the ground in the Cortez family's backyard. To prevent people from zipping down too quickly, the line should form an angle of 35° with the ground. To the nearest metre, how long can the zip line be if it is anchored 28 m from the base of the tree?

★**10.** In areas with extreme winds, houses are constructed with steel rods that run diagonally inside walls to help keep walls square. Rods are sold in standard lengths of 4 m and 5 m.

If standard walls are 2.5 m high, what angle does the 5-m rod make with the floor? What angle with the floor does the 4-m rod make? State your answers to the nearest degree.

C Extend

11. A boat ramp with a cable winch is to be constructed to allow the McKenzie family to pull their boat from the water for the winter. If the shore has a slope of 39° and the front of the boat must be lifted 3 m above the water, what length does the ramp have to be?

☆12. A 2″ by 4″ length of lumber actually measures 1.5″ by 3.5″. To make a top rail for a deck, a carpenter stacks two pieces of lumber together to create a rail that is 3″ thick. However, the carpenter has only 3.5″ wood screws available. At what angle must he drive the screws in from underneath so that none of the points sticks through the top rail? Round your answer to the nearest degree.

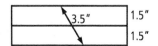

13. A water gun at Splasher's water park is positioned at the centre of the long side of a 10-m by 6-m rectangular pool. The gun can spray to a maximum distance of 7 m.

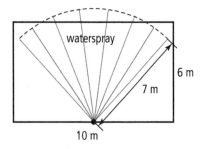

a) How much of the opposite side of the pool can be sprayed?

b) How much of the opposite side cannot be sprayed?

c) What spray distance would the gun need for the spray to reach the entire opposite side? Round each answer to the nearest tenth of a metre.

D Create Connections

14. Determine the length of CD, to the nearest tenth of a centimetre.

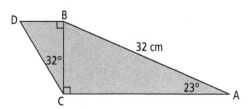

☆15. A traditional teepee uses 13 poles to form its conical shape. The poles are inclined at an angle of 65° to the ground and tied together 4.8 m up their length. Calculate the diameter of this structure, to the nearest tenth of a metre.

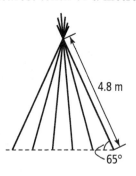

16. a) Copy the table and determine the trigonometric values for each stated value of θ, to four decimal places.

θ	tan θ	sin θ	cos θ
15°			
30°			
45°			
60°			
75°			

b) Describe any pattern you see in each column.

c) Do you see any relationship between the sine and cosine values? Explain.

3.3 Solving Right Triangles

- An angle of elevation is the angle between the line of sight and the horizontal when an observer looks upward.

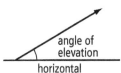

- An angle of depression is the angle between the line of sight and the horizontal when the observer looks downward.

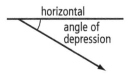

- To solve a triangle means to calculate all unknown angle measures and side lengths.

Example

Two adjoining properties are bordered by three roads, as shown in the diagram. The property owners agree to put a fence around and between both lots. What total length of fencing is required, to the nearest metre? Explain why you should round up or down.

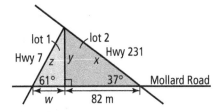

Solution

First, determine the length of fence around the first lot.
Let x represent the length, in metres, of fence required along Hwy 231. Let y represent the length, in metres, of fence required along the property line.
Use the given information and choose the appropriate trigonometric ratio to solve for each value.

For x:
$$\cos 37° = \frac{82 \text{ m}}{x}$$
$$\cos 37°(x) = 82 \text{ m}$$
$$x = \frac{82 \text{ m}}{\cos 37°}$$
$$x = \frac{82 \text{ m}}{0.7986}$$
$$x = 102.68 \text{ m}$$

For y:
$$\tan 37° = \frac{y}{82 \text{ m}}$$
$$(82 \text{ m})(\tan 37°) = y$$
$$(82 \text{ m})(0.7536) = y$$
$$y = 61.79 \text{ m}$$

Next, calculate the length of fence needed to complete the fence around the second lot.

Let w represent the length, in metres, of fence required along Mollard Road. Let z represent the length, in metres, of fence required along Hwy 7.

Use the given information and choose the appropriate trigonometric ratio to solve for each value.

For w:

$$\tan 61° = \frac{61.79 \text{ m}}{w}$$

$$w = \frac{61.79 \text{ m}}{\tan 61°}$$

$$w = \frac{61.79 \text{ m}}{1.804}$$

$$w = 34.25 \text{ m}$$

For z:

$$\sin 61° = \frac{61.79 \text{ m}}{z}$$

$$z = \frac{61.79 \text{ m}}{\sin 61°}$$

$$z = \frac{61.79 \text{ m}}{0.8746}$$

$$z = 70.65 \text{ m}$$

Total length of fence needed $= 82 \text{ m} + 102.68 \text{ m} + 61.79 \text{ m} + 34.25 \text{ m} + 70.65 \text{ m}$
$= 351.37 \text{ m}$

The two properties require a total of approximately 352 m of fencing. Round up to make sure that there is enough fencing.

A Practise

1. Solve each triangle. State each answer to the nearest tenth of a unit.

   a)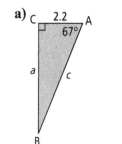

   b)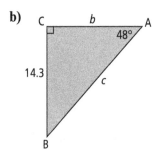

   c)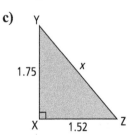

   d) Use a second strategy to solve part c).

2. Using the diagram, name

   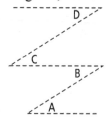

   a) two angles of elevation

   b) two angles of depression

   c) two pairs of equal angles

3. Paolo and Chandra are on two balconies facing each other across a courtyard. Chandra sends a text message to Paolo to tell him that she sees him at an angle of depression of 23°. Paolo replies that Chandra is wrong and that Chandra is actually at an angle of elevation of 23°.

   a) Who is right? Explain.

   b) What is the relationship between angles of elevation and angles of depression?

4. For each figure, solve all variables. For side lengths, state your answers to the nearest tenth of a unit. For angle measures, give your answers to the nearest degree.

a)

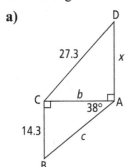

b)

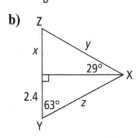

5. Determine the value of each variable. Express your answer to the nearest tenth of a unit.

a)

b)

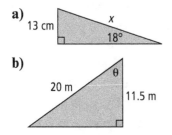

B Apply

⭐**6.** A car is parked on a street 4.8 m from the bottom of Ruthie's apartment building. From her window above the street, Ruthie views the car at an angle of depression of 73°. Kenneth lives directly across the street from Ruthie. From his window at exactly the same height as Ruthie's, Kenneth sees the car at an angle of depression of 59°. Determine the distance between Ruthie's and Kenneth's windows, to the nearest tenth of a metre.

7. There are two sails on the mast of a sailboat. The mast measures 8.5 m from the booms at the bottom of the sails to the top. The main sail meets the mast at an angle of 32° and the secondary sail meets the mast at an angle of 21°. Determine the combined length of the two booms, to the nearest tenth of a metre.

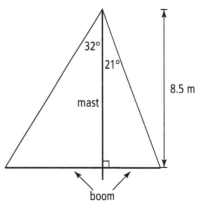

8. Pit mines are cone-shaped excavations often used in diamond mining. The side of one pit mine has an angle of depression of 35° so that it will not collapse.

a) If the mine has a diameter of 576 m, how deep is it?

b) If the mine is required to extend down 250 m, then how wide should it be at the top?

c) If the bottom of the mine is 250 m below the surface, what length does a conveyor belt to the top need to be if it follows the slope of the excavation?

In each case, round your answer to the nearest metre.

C Extend

9. A footbridge across a river is 12 m above the water. On one side, a ramp slopes to the bridge at an angle of 7°. On the other side, there is a set of stairs. The bottom of the stairs is 10 m from the bridge.

a) What is the distance from the bottom end of the ramp to the bridge?

b) At what angle do the stairs climb to the bridge?

10. A box measures 55 cm deep, 28 cm high, and 105 cm long.

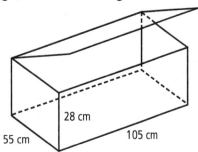

28 cm

55 cm

105 cm

José wishes to use this box to hold his great-grandfather's cane, a family heirloom. The cane has a length of 120 cm.

a) Can the cane fit flat in the box?

b) Can José put the cane completely in the box without interfering with the lid? Explain.

☆**11.** A section of dike is to be constructed to hold water in a reservoir for a hydro-electric power dam. The dike needs to be built to a height of 36.5 m, with a slope of 55° on the reservoir side and a slope of 42° on the outside.

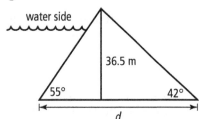

water side

36.5 m

55°   42°

d

a) How wide is the dike at its base?

b) A wire mesh is to be attached to the outside slope of the dike to prevent rock slides.

Determine the length required for the wire mesh.

c) A different section of dike requires a height of 39 m. What is the width of its base?

d) A student engineer believes that for a 31-m-high section, the base needs to be 54.8 m wide. Is she correct? Explain.

Express each answer to the nearest tenth of a metre.

D Create Connections

☆**12.** In order to accurately measure the height of a mountain that cannot be climbed, two right triangles can be used. One lies horizontally along the ground and the other stands vertically with a vertex at the mountain's peak.

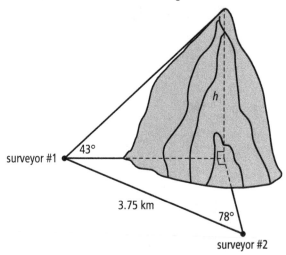

surveyor #1   43°

3.75 km

78°

surveyor #2

Two surveyors are 3.75 km apart. Surveyor #1 is directly west of the peak and surveyor #2 is directly south. From the position of the second surveyor, the first is at an angle of 78° west of north. Surveyor #1 can see the peak at an angle of elevation of 43°.

a) Determine the height of the mountain, to the nearest metre.

b) How long would a cable need to be, to the nearest metre, in order to connect the peak with the position of surveyor #1?

c) Solve this problem using a second set of strategies.

3.1 The Tangent Ratio

1. For ∠Y in right △XYZ, identify

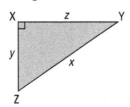

   a) the hypotenuse

   b) the adjacent side

   c) the opposite side

2. Refer to right △XYZ in question 1.

   a) State the tangent ratio of ∠Y.

   b) State the tangent ratio of ∠Z.

3. For right △LMN, determine the length n if ∠N = 68° and l = 12.4 cm.

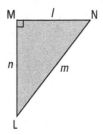

4. Calculate the smallest angle in right △ABC where ∠C = 90°, side a measures 32.7 m, and side b measures 27.2 m.

5. A ramp on a moving truck forms an angle of 30° with the ground, allowing movers to load heavy items easily. If the truck bed is 1.35 m above the ground, how far will the ramp extend behind the truck?

6. The length of a shadow cast by a building is 25 m. Nearby, a 1.8-m shadow is cast by a man who is 2.2 m tall. Calculate the height of the building.

3.2 The Sine and Cosine Ratios

7. For right △ABC, state each of the following ratios.

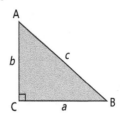

   a) sin A

   b) cos A

   c) sin B

   d) cos B

8. Calculate the value of b in △ABC in question 7 if

   a) ∠B = 23° and c = 12

   b) ∠A = 67° and c = 9.2

9. A ladder 7 m in length is leaning against a wall. The top of the ladder forms an angle of 20° with the wall. Determine the distance from the bottom of the wall to the bottom of the ladder.

10. Inflatable slides are used to evacuate people from airplanes. If a slide must form an angle of 35° with the ground and its bottom will be 4.5 m from the plane, what length does the slide need to be?

11. The length of a ramp from the ground level of a parking garage to the upper level is 54 ft.

    a) If the height of the upper level is 8 ft, what angle does the ramp make with the ground?

    b) Over what horizontal distance does the ramp extend?

    Round your answers to the nearest tenth of a unit.

3.3 Solving Right Triangles

12. Solve each triangle, to the nearest tenth of a unit.

a)

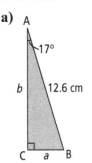

b)

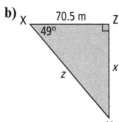

c)

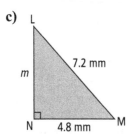

d)

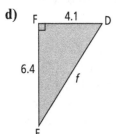

e)

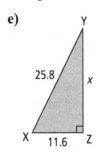

f) Use a second strategy to solve part c).

13. Consider adjacent right triangles KLM and KMN shown in the figure.

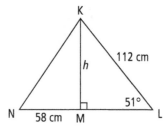

a) What is the height of side *h*, to the nearest centimetre?

b) What is the measure of ∠MKN, to the nearest degree?

14. A surveyor is trying to determine the height of a cliff. From her location, 1375 m from the base of the cliff, the angle of elevation to the top of the cliff is 27°. What is the height of the cliff, to the nearest metre?

15. A hot-air balloon is floating 105 metres above a soccer field 100 m long. A photographer in the balloon's basket can see the two goalkeepers standing on their goal lines. One is at an angle of depression of 53.39°. The other is at an angle of depression of 78.17°. If the balloon is directly between the goalies, how far, to the nearest metre, is each goalie from a point on the ground directly under the balloon?

16. The top of a skyscraper is 200 m above the ground. You are standing 100 m from the base of the building. Your friend is 20 m behind you. Each of you has a clear view of the top of the building.

a) What is the distance between the top of the building and your friend?

b) What is the distance between the top of the skyscraper and you?

c) From your position, at what angle of elevation does the top of the building appear to be?

Round your answers to the nearest tenth of a unit.

Chapters 1–3 Cumulative Review

1. **a)** Estimate the perimeter of the figure in an appropriate SI unit.

   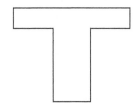

   b) Measure the perimeter of the figure.

   c) Calculate the area of the figure, to the nearest hundredth of a unit.

2. Sketch a diagram to illustrate a right pyramid with a square base measuring 14 ft by 14 ft and a slant height of 9 ft. What is the surface area of the pyramid?

3. Draw right $\triangle FGH$ in which $\angle G$ is the right angle.

   a) Label the leg opposite $\angle H$, the leg adjacent to $\angle H$, and the hypotenuse.

   b) State the tangent, sine, and cosine ratios of $\angle H$.

4. Calculate the missing dimension in each of the following. Round each answer to the nearest hundredth of a unit.

   a) A right cone has a surface area of 15 m² and a radius of 1.7 m.

   b) The square base of a right pyramid has an area of 1521 cm². The pyramid has a total surface area of 4407 cm².

   c) A sphere has a surface area of 475 mm².

5. Calculate the measure of each angle, to the nearest degree.

   a) $\cos A = 0.2345$

   b) $\sin C = 0.8860$

   c) $\tan \theta = \frac{4}{3}$

6. What is the reading on each measuring device? Estimate and then calculate each equivalent measurement in the other system (SI or imperial), to the nearest hundredth of a unit.

   a)

   b)

7. Calculate the surface area of this object composed of a rectangular prism and a cylinder.

   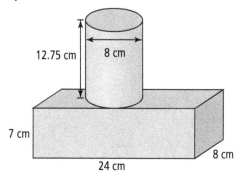

8. Calculate the volume of each of the following. Where necessary, express your answers to the nearest hundredth of a unit.

   a) A cylinder has a radius of 16 ft and a height of 12 ft.

   b) A cone has a height of 19 cm and a diameter of 7.5 cm.

   c) A rectangular pyramid has a base measuring 6 ft by 8 ft and a height of 12 ft.

   d) A sphere has a radius of 6.2 cm.

   e) A cylinder has a height of 6 in. and a radius of 3 in.

   f) A rectangular prism has a height of 3 m, a width of 4 m, and a length of 5 m.

9. Calculate the missing dimension in each of the following, to the nearest hundredth of a unit.

a) A cylinder has a volume of 3 m^3 and a height of 1.2 m.

b) A cone has a radius of 35 cm and a volume of 9500 cm^3.

c) A square-based pyramid has a height of 85 cm and a volume of 4.6 m^3.

d) A sphere has a volume of 3467 cm^3.

e) A cylinder has a volume of 6 in.^{3} and a height of 5 in.

f) A rectangular prism has a volume of 252 ft^3, with a length of 12 ft, and a width of 7 ft.

10. Solve each triangle to the nearest tenth of a unit.

a)

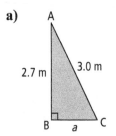

b)

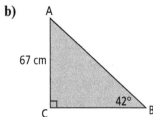

11. Two forest fires are spotted on opposite sides of an observation tower. From the top of the tower, the angle of depression to one fire is 3°. The angle of depression to the other fire is 7°.

a) If the observation tower is 75 m high, how far apart are the fires?

b) Suppose the two fires were on the same side of the tower on the same compass heading. How far apart would they be then?

12. A standard shipping container is in the form of a rectangular prism with a length of 12.01 m, a width of 2.33 m, and a height of 2.38 m. Suppose a fully loaded ship arriving in the Port of Vancouver is carrying 5000 such containers.

a) What is the storage capacity of each container? of the ship?

b) If the trailer of a transport truck measures 2.74 m by 2.54 m by 16.15 m, how many truckloads of cargo can one container hold? How many truckloads would it take to fill all the containers on the ship?

c) What is the total surface area of the 5000 containers?

Where appropriate, round your answers to the nearest hundredth of a unit.

13.

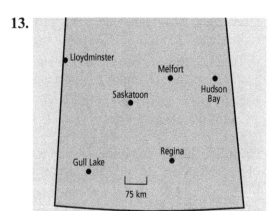

a) Express the scale of the map as a ratio in lowest terms.

b) How many kilometres are represented by one inch?

c) Estimate the distance from Gull Lake to Regina. Give your answer in miles.

d) The distance from Saskatoon to Melfort is shorter than the distance from Saskatoon to Lloydminster. How many miles shorter is it?

Chapter 3 Extend It Further

For 1 to 3, choose the best answer.

1. What is the length of the base n?

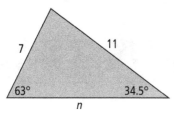

   A 12.3   **B** 16.1

   C 17.2   **D** 19.2

★2. A child swings back and forth, reaching a maximum angle of 32° with the vertical. The swing is 3.4 m long and 0.75 m from the ground when at rest. What maximum height above the ground does the child reach?

   A 2.64 m   **B** 2.18 m

   C 1.27 m   **D** 0.98 m

3. Dad used to walk uphill to school every day. He travelled a distance of 2 km at a slope of 12°, then another 3 km horizontally. Finally, he walked a further distance of 1.5 km at a slope of 15° before reaching school. How far vertically was the school from the starting point?

   A 0.7 km   **B** 0.8 km

   C 0.9 km   **D** 1.0 km

4. Romeo has a ladder 4 m long. He leans the ladder against a vertical wall, making an angle of 26°. As Romeo reaches Juliet's window, the ladder slips, then stops when it is making an angle of 34° with the wall.

   a) How far vertically has the ladder slipped?

   b) How far horizontally has the ladder slipped?

   c) Compare the two distances. What do you notice? Explain.

5. ABCD is a rhombus of side 10 cm and ∠A = 80°. Determine lengths AC and BD, to one decimal place. Hint: AC ⊥ BD.

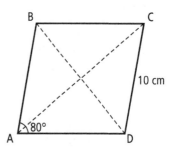

6. ABCDE is a pentagon. Each side is 10 cm long. Determine

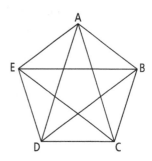

   a) the measure of ∠EDC

   b) the total length of a pentagonal star connecting A to D to B to E to C, and back to A

7. A fuel tank has a length of 1 m and a cross-section that is a quarter of a circle having a radius of 40 cm. The tank is filled with gasoline to a height of 20 cm. What is the volume of the fuel?

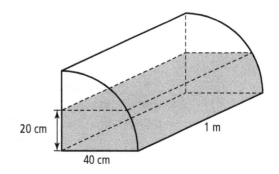

Chapter 3 Study Check

Use the chart below to help you assess the skills and processes you have developed during Chapter 3. The references in italics direct you to pages in *Mathematics 10 Exercise and Homework Book* where you could review the skill. How can you show that you have gained each skill? What can you do to improve?

Big Idea	Skills	This Shows I Know	This Is How I Can Improve
Use Pythagoras and trigonometry to solve problems *pages 39–55*	✓ Apply the Pythagorean theorem to calculate the length(s) of missing side(s) *pages 48–50, 52, 54*		
	✓ Use trigonometric ratios to calculate the value(s) for missing side(s) and angle(s) *pages 39–55*		
	✓ Solve direct measurement problems using Pythagoras and/or trigonometry *pages 39–55*		
	✓ Solve indirect measurement problems using Pythagoras and/or trigonometry *pages 42, 46, 49–50, 52, 54–55*		
Solve right triangles *pages xx*	✓ Apply the Pythagorean theorem to solve for the length(s) of missing side(s) *pages 48–50, 52, 54–55*		
	✓ Use trigonometric ratios to solve for the length(s) of missing side(s) of right triangles *pages 39–55*		
	✓ Use trigonometric ratios to solve for the value(s) of missing angle(s) of right triangles *pages 44–46, 48–55*		

Organizing the Ideas

How can you use this Venn diagram to help you decide which procedure to use in various circumstances? Show how the information provided in a particular problem affects the procedure used to solve it. Show an example of the procedure itself, then identify the information from the problem that must be present to use that procedure.

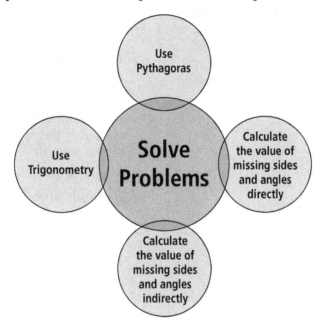

Study Guide

Review the types of problems you handled in Chapter 3. What do you need to remember to help you do similar problems?

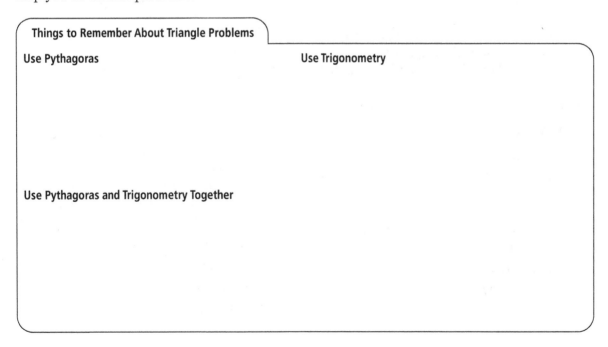

Things to Remember About Triangle Problems

Use Pythagoras

Use Trigonometry

Use Pythagoras and Trigonometry Together

Multiple Choice

For #1 to #16, choose the best answer.

1. Mike wants to measure the length of his bicycle to determine if it will fit in his parents' garden shed for storage during the winter. Which unit of measurement is the most appropriate for Mike to use?

   A millimetres

   B inches

   C feet

   D kilometres

2. Sarah needs to mark the position for a showerhead that is recommended to be installed at a height of 6' 6". Which referent and estimate are best for Sarah to approximate that height?

   A body height 5' 3", just above her head

   B hand span $8\frac{1}{2}$ in., just over 9 hand spans

   C length of foot $9\frac{1}{2}$ in., 6 and one half foot lengths

   D length of forearm 17", six forearm lengths

3. The length of a Canadian flag is always twice its width. If the length of a particular flag is 52 in., what is its width in centimetres?

   A 26 cm

   B 66.04 cm

   C 104 cm

   D 132.08 cm

4. If 1 ft = 0.3048 m, what is the correct conversion to express the number of inches in metres?

   A 1 in. = 0.0254 m

   B 1 m = 39.37 in.

   C 1 m = 100 in.

   D 3.6576 in. = 1 m

5. Which unit would be the most appropriate to measure the volume of concrete used for a driveway?

   A cubic millimetres

   B cubic yards

   C square inches

   D square metres

6. Which of the following could be used to accurately determine the circumference of a basketball?

   A hand span

   B trundle wheel

   C string and ruler

   D arm length

7. What is the surface area of the right pyramid?

   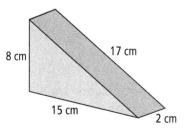

   A 140 cm²

   B 200 cm²

   C 240 cm²

   D 260 cm²

8. A stress ball is squeezed in the hand and manipulated by the fingers to help relieve stress and muscle tension or to exercise the muscles of the hand. If a stress ball has a diameter of 7 cm, what is the surface area of its covering?

   A 4310.3 cm²

   B 1372 cm²

   C 538.8 cm²

   D 153.9 cm²

9. If the volume of a sphere is 905 cm³, the diameter of the sphere is

A 6 cm

B 12 cm

C 216 cm

D 432 cm

10. Which equation regarding triangle ABC is true?

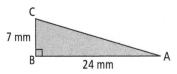

A $\tan C = \frac{25}{7}$

B $\tan C = \frac{7}{24}$

C $\sin A = \frac{7}{25}$

D $A = \cos^{-1}\left(\frac{24}{25}\right)$

11. Determine the measure of angle x, to the nearest tenth of a degree.

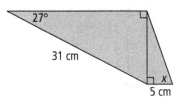

A 79.7°

B 70.4°

C 63°

D 19.6°

12. The surface area of a cone with a diameter of 10 cm is determined to be 65π cm². The slant height of the cone is

A 3.5 cm

B 8 cm

C 25 cm

D 35 cm

13. The standard height of a basketball hoop above the floor is 3.048 m. Colin is 5′ 9″ tall and can reach an additional 21″ when extending his arm above his head. How high must Colin jump to be able to touch the hoop?

A 1.573 m

B 2′ 6″

C 36 cm

D 40 in.

14. If a vehicle travels a distance of 2 km along an incline of 9°, how far does it actually travel along a horizontal distance?

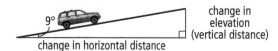

A 0.323 km

B 1.869 km

C 1970 m

D 3168 m

15. Using the measurements given in the diagrams of the similar triangles, which of the primary trigonometric ratios could be used to determine the measure of the indicated angle in the larger triangle?

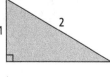

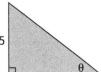

A tangent

B sine

C cosine

D Pythagorean theorem

16. If the tangent ratio of a reference angle in a right triangle is calculated to be 0.6249, then the cosine ratio of the same angle is

A 32.0013

B 1

C 0.8480

D 0.0109

Numerical Response

17. What is the value of the reading, as a mixed fraction, represented by the arrow on the imperial ruler?

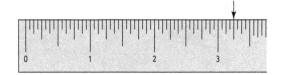

18. In the SI system, 0.0305 metres is the same as how many millimetres?

19. In the imperial system, how many inches are there in $2\frac{1}{2}$ yards?

20. Calculate the surface area of a square-based pyramid with a side length of 8 cm and a height of 5 cm, to the nearest hundredth of a centimetre.

21. The surface area of the triangular-based right prism shown is 1440 m². Determine the missing dimension.

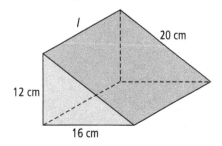

22. Kayla is playing golf and needs to make a putt of 3.7 yd to get the ball into the cup. What is the length of the putt in feet, rounded to the nearest foot?

23. A gravel pile in the shape of a cone has a height of 2 yd and a radius of 3.5 yd. What is the volume of gravel in the pile, to the nearest tenth of a cubic yard?

24. The ice surface in a hockey arena measures 200 ft by 85 ft. A spectator stands along the boards at the centre line. At each end of the rink, the goal line is 11 ft from the boards. From the perspective of the spectator, what is the angle between the two goalies, to the nearest tenth of a degree?

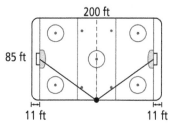

Extended Response

25. A cone-shaped oil filter, open at the base, has a diameter of 10″ and a depth of 12″.

a) What are the measurements of the filter's radius and depth, to the nearest tenth of a centimetre?

b) A paper cone is used to line the filter. What is the surface area of paper, to the nearest tenth of a cubic centimetre?

c) What is the capacity of the filter, to the nearest tenth of a cubic centimetre?

26. Two trees are 70 m apart. From the point on the ground halfway between the trees, the angle of elevation to the top of one tree is 15° and to the top of the other tree is 22°.

a) Sketch and label a diagram to represent the given information.

b) Which trigonometric ratio would you use to determine the heights of the trees? Explain your reasoning.

c) Determine the difference between the heights of the trees, to the nearest tenth of a metre.

27. A boy spots a bird sitting on a power line 3.7 m above the ground. The boy is 1.2 m tall and is standing 5 m from the point on the ground that is directly below the bird.

   a) Sketch and label a diagram to represent the given information.

   b) Determine the angle at which the boy is looking up at the bird, to the nearest tenth of a degree.

28. A bin to store grain has a diameter of 16 ft. The slope of the bottom cone is 40° from the horizontal.

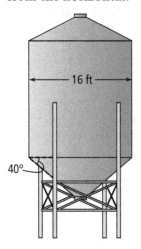

   a) What is the depth of the cone-shaped bottom, to the nearest tenth of a foot?

   b) What volume of grain could be held in the bottom cone, to the nearest cubic foot?

   c) Suppose that the volume of grain that can be stored in the bin, not including the top conical section, is 4042 ft³. What is the length of the cylindrical section, to the nearest tenth of a foot?

29. A regular tetrahedron is an object with four congruent equilateral triangular faces.

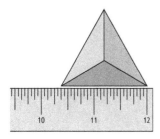

   a) Use the diagram to determine the length of the tetrahedron, to the nearest $\frac{1}{8}$ in.

   b) Determine the surface area of the tetrahedron, to the nearest tenth of a square inch.

   c) Determine the volume of the shape, to the nearest tenth of a cubic inch.

30. A single roll of hockey tape has an outside diameter of 5 in., has an inside diameter of $1\frac{1}{2}$ in., and is 1 in. thick.

   a) Name a personal referent that could be used to estimate the size of the roll of hockey tape. Use your referent to sketch the actual size of the roll of tape.

   b) Using the conversion rate 1 in. = 2.54 cm, determine the measures of the inner radius and the outer radius, each to the nearest hundredth of a centimetre.

   c) Determine the volume of tape in 4 rolls of tape, to the nearest cubic centimetre.

31. Use the diagram to answer the questions below.

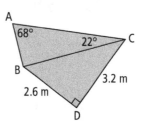

   a) Describe in words a possible strategy you could use to solve for the length of side AB.

   b) Determine the length of side AB, to the nearest tenth of a metre.

Chapter 4 Exponents and Radicals

4.1 Square Roots and Cube Roots

- A perfect square is the product of two equal factors. One of these factors is called the square root.
  36 is a perfect square: $\sqrt{36} = 6$ because $6^2 = 36$. The symbol for square root is $\sqrt{\ }$.

- A perfect cube is the product of three equal factors. One of these factors is called the cube root.
  -125 is a perfect cube: $\sqrt[3]{-125} = -5$ because $(-5)^3 = -125$. The symbol for cube root is $\sqrt[3]{\ }$.

- Some numbers are both perfect squares and perfect cubes.
  15 625 is a perfect square: $125^2 = 15\ 625$
  15 625 is a perfect cube: $25^3 = 15\ 625$

- You can use diagrams, prime factorization, or a calculator to solve problems involving square roots and cube roots. Prime factorization involves writing a number as the product of its factors.

Determine the cube root of 64.

    – Use a diagram.   – Use *prime factorization.*

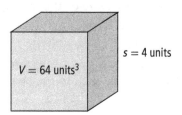

$s = 4$ units
$V = 64$ units^3

The edge lengths represent
the cube root: $(4)(4)(4) = 64$.

– Use a calculator.

C 64 **2nd** $\sqrt[x]{y}$ 3 = 4.

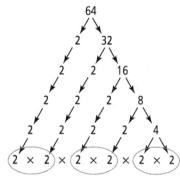

There are three equal groups of 4.
Therefore, the cube root of 64 is 4.

Example

Identify each number as a perfect square or a perfect cube.

a) 256   **b)** 3375

Solution

Method 1: Use Guess and Check

a) Perfect square:
Since $(13)(13) = 169$, you could try 14.
$14^2 = (14)(14) = 196$ Too low
$16^2 = (16)(16) = 256$ Correct!
Therefore, 256 is a perfect square.

Perfect cube:
Since 256 ends with a 6, you could try 6.
$6^3 = (6)(6)(6) = 216$ Too low
$7^3 = (7)(7)(7) = 343$ Too high
No whole number cubed results in a product of 256.
Therefore, 256 is not a perfect cube.

b) Perfect square:
Since 3375 ends with a 5, you could try numbers that end with a 5.
$55^2 = (55)(55) = 2025$ Too low
$65^2 = (65)(65) = 4225$ Too high
No whole number squared results in a product of 3375.
Therefore, 3375 is not a perfect square.

Perfect cube:
Since 3375 ends with a 5, you could try numbers that end with a 5.
$25^3 = (25)(25)(25) = 15\,625$ Too high
$15^3 = (15)(15)(15) = 3375$ Correct!
Therefore, 3375 is a perfect cube.

Method 2: Use Prime Factorization

a)

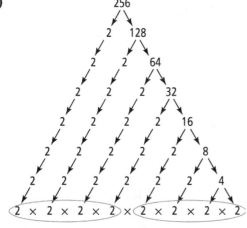

There are two equal groups of 2s.
Therefore, the square root of 256 is $(2)(2)(2)(2) = 16$.

b)

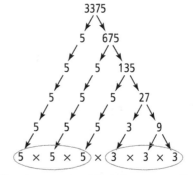

There is one group of 5s and one group of 3s.
Therefore, the cube root of 3375 is $(5)(3) = 15$.

Method 3: Use a Calculator

a) | C | 256 | √x | = | 16.
perfect square

| C | 256 | 2nd | $\sqrt[x]{y}$ | 3 | = | 6.349604
Since the cube root is not an integer, 256 is not a perfect cube.

b) | C | 3375 | √x | = | 58.09475
Since the square root is not a whole number, 3375 is not a perfect square.

| C | 3375 | 2nd | $\sqrt[x]{y}$ | 3 | = | 15.
perfect cube

A Practise

1. What is the value of each expression? Express the answers as integers or fractions.

   a) 9^2

   b) $(-15)^2$

   c) -25^2

   d) $\dfrac{4}{3^2}$

   e) $-\dfrac{5^2}{8}$

   f) $\left(\dfrac{-6}{7}\right)^2$

2. Evaluate. Express the answer as an integer or a fraction.

   a) 9^3

   b) $(-3)^3$

   c) -6^3

   d) $\dfrac{4^3}{8}$

   e) $\dfrac{-9}{3^3}$

   f) $\left(\dfrac{5}{7}\right)^3$

3. What is the value of each expression?

   a) $\sqrt{25}$

   b) $\sqrt{196}$

   c) $\sqrt{(49)(16)}$

   d) $\dfrac{18}{\sqrt{81}}$

   e) $\dfrac{\sqrt{64}}{12}$

   f) $\sqrt{\dfrac{64}{196}}$

   g) $\dfrac{\sqrt{16}}{\sqrt{144}}$

   h) $\sqrt{36x^2}$

   i) $\dfrac{\sqrt{49a^2}}{\sqrt{169b^2}}$

4. Evaluate.

   a) $\sqrt[3]{8}$

   b) $\sqrt[3]{27}$

   c) $\sqrt[3]{1728}$

   d) $\sqrt[3]{(64)(125)}$

   e) $\dfrac{\sqrt[3]{216}}{2}$

   f) $\dfrac{15}{\sqrt[3]{15\,625}}$

   g) $\sqrt[3]{\dfrac{8}{343}}$

   h) $\sqrt[3]{125y^3}$

   i) $\sqrt[3]{729a^3}$

⭐5. Identify each number as a perfect square, a perfect cube, or both. Support your answer using a diagram or a factor tree.

   a) 8

   b) 512

   c) 15 625

   d) 196

   e) 46 656

   f) 729

6. State whether each number is a perfect square, a perfect cube, both, or neither.

   a) 169

   b) 225

   c) 64

   d) 256

   e) 117 649

   f) 133 642

7. Determine if each number is a perfect square or a perfect cube using prime factorization. Explain the process.

   a) 16

   b) 27

   c) 1000

   d) 324

   e) 441

   f) 2917

8. Calculate.

   a) $\sqrt{289}$

   b) $\sqrt{529}$

   c) $\sqrt[3]{2744}$

   d) $\sqrt[3]{10\,648}$

   e) $\sqrt[3]{29\,791}$

   f) $\sqrt[3]{19\,683}$

9. Bill is designing a cube-shaped storage container to store his hockey equipment. The container will have a volume of 2.744 m^3. What will the dimensions of the container be?

10. Sharon plans to build a square patio in a sunny area in her yard. If the patio has an area of 529 ft^2, what is its side length?

B Apply

⭐11. Belle noticed that the water tap in the kitchen leaked. She decided to use a cylinder and collect the water drips for 24 h. She collected 5.88 cm^3 of water. Belle determined that at this rate her family would waste 2146.2 cm^3 of water per year. What would be the edge length of a cube that would contain this amount of water? Express the answer to one decimal place.

12. The Henderson family plans to build a square double garage. The floor plan shows that the garage will have an area of 576 ft^2. What are the side lengths of the garage?

13. If the area of John's square bedroom is 156.25 ft^2, what do the side lengths measure?

14. A right prism is shown. What would be the dimensions of a cube with the same volume?

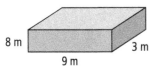

8 m   3 m
9 m

15. The surface area of two dice is 1452 mm^2. What is the volume of each die?

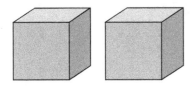

16. A grade 10 class collects scrap metal as a fundraiser. The students calculate that the scrap metal they collected occupies a volume of 238 m^3. If this metal were compressed into a cubic bale, what would its edge lengths be? Express the answer to the nearest tenth of a metre.

17. The Dice House is a zero carbon home designed by Sybarite, a British architecture firm. This cubic house has a volume of 729 m^3. What are the dimensions of the Dice House?

18. A sphere has the surface area shown. What is the length of the diameter of the sphere? Hint: $SA = 4\pi r^2$.

$SA = 803.84$ cm^2

C Extend

19. Given the equation $y = x^2 - 4$, determine the value of y when
  a) $x = 8$
  b) $x = 14$

20. Given the equation $y = x^2 - 4$, determine the value of x when
  a) $y = 32$
  b) $y = 525$

⭐**21.** Sonja owns a helium tank that holds 54 ft^3 of gas. She rents out the helium tank for parties and sells balloons with a 6-in. radius. How many balloons will a full helium tank inflate?

22. A sphere has a volume of 1296 cm^3. Determine the surface area of the sphere. Express the answer to the nearest square centimetre.
Hint: $V = \frac{4}{3}\pi r^3$.

23. Evaluate each square root.
  a)

$\sqrt{25}$	
$\sqrt{2.5}$	
$\sqrt{0.25}$	
$\sqrt{0.025}$	
$\sqrt{0.0025}$	
$\sqrt{0.00025}$	

  b)

$\sqrt{81}$	
$\sqrt{8.1}$	
$\sqrt{0.81}$	
$\sqrt{0.081}$	
$\sqrt{0.0081}$	
$\sqrt{0.00081}$	

  c) What can you conclude about the square root of decimal numbers?

D Create Connections

⭐**24.** Explain why $\sqrt{-25}$ has no solution and $\sqrt[3]{-27}$ has a solution.

25. a) What happens to the area of a square when you double the length of each side? triple the length of each side?

  b) What happens to the volume of a cube when you double the length of each edge? triple the length of each edge?

4.2 Integral Exponents

- A power with a negative exponent can be written as a power with a positive exponent.

  - $a^{-n} = \frac{1}{a^n}, a \neq 0$ $2^{-5} = \frac{1}{2^5}$ - $\frac{1}{a^{-n}} = a^n, a \neq 0$ $\frac{1}{2^{-5}} = 2^5$

- You can apply the above principle to the exponent laws.

Exponent Law	Example
Note that a and b are rational or variable bases and m and n are integral exponents.	
Product of Powers $(a^m)(a^n) = a^{m+n}$	$(3^{-2})(3^4) = 3^{-2+4}$ $= 3^2 \text{ or } 9$
Quotient of Powers $\frac{a^m}{a^n} = a^{m-n}, a \neq 0$	$\frac{x^3}{x^{-5}} = x^{3-(-5)}$ $= x^8$
Power of a Power $\left(a^m\right)^n = a^{mn}$	$(0.75^4)^{-2} = 0.75^{(4)(-2)}$ $= 0.75^{-8} \text{ or } \frac{1}{0.75^8}$
Power of a Product $(ab)^m = a^m b^m$	$(4z)^{-3} = \frac{1}{(4z)^3} \text{ or } \frac{1}{64z^3}$
Power of a Quotient $\left(\frac{a}{b}\right)^n = \frac{a^n}{b^n}, b \neq 0$	$\left(\frac{t}{3}\right)^{-2} = \left(\frac{3}{t}\right)^2$ $= \frac{3^2}{t^2} \text{ or } \frac{9}{t^2}$
Zero Exponent $a^0 = 1, a \neq 0$	$(4y^2)^0 = 1$ $-(4y^2)^0 = -1$

Example

Write each expression as a power with a single, positive exponent. Then, evaluate where possible.

a) $\left(\frac{0.4^{-2}}{0.4^2}\right)$ b) $(6^4)(6^{-2})$ c) $\left[(3x)^{-2}\right]^{-3}$

Solution

a) **Method 1: Subtract the Exponents**
Since the bases are the same, you can subtract the exponents.

$\left(\frac{0.4^{-2}}{0.4^2}\right) = 0.4^{(-2-2)}$
$= 0.4^{-4}$
$= 39.0625$

Method 2: Use Positive Exponents
Convert the negative exponent to a positive exponent. Then, add the exponents when multiplying.

$\left(\frac{0.4^{-2}}{0.4^2}\right) = \left(\frac{1}{0.4^2}\right)\left(\frac{1}{0.4^2}\right)$
$= \left(\frac{1}{0.4^{2+2}}\right)$
$= \left(\frac{1}{0.4^4}\right)$
$= 39.0625$

b) Method 1: Add the Exponents
Since the bases are the same, you can add the exponents.
$(6^4)(6^{-2}) = 6^{4 + (-2)}$
$\phantom{(6^4)(6^{-2})} = 6^2$
$\phantom{(6^4)(6^{-2})} = 36$

Method 2: Use Positive Exponents
Convert the negative exponent to a positive exponent. Then, subtract the exponents when dividing.
$(6^4)(6^{-2}) = (6^4)\left(\dfrac{1}{6^2}\right)$
$\phantom{(6^4)(6^{-2})} = \dfrac{6^4}{6^2}$
$\phantom{(6^4)(6^{-2})} = 6^{4-2}$
$\phantom{(6^4)(6^{-2})} = 6^2$
$\phantom{(6^4)(6^{-2})} = 36$

c) Method 1: Multiply the Exponents
Raise the power to the exponent. Then, multiply the exponents.
$\left[(3x)^{-2}\right]^{-3} = (3x)^{(-2)(-3)}$
$\phantom{\left[(3x)^{-2}\right]^{-3}} = (3x)^6$
$\phantom{\left[(3x)^{-2}\right]^{-3}} = 729x^6$

Method 2: Use Positive Exponents
Convert the negative exponent to a positive exponent. Convert twice. Then, multiply the exponents.
$\left[(3x)^{-2}\right]^{-3} = \left[\dfrac{1}{(3x)^2}\right]^{-3}$
$\phantom{\left[(3x)^{-2}\right]^{-3}} = \left[(3x)^2\right]^3$
$\phantom{\left[(3x)^{-2}\right]^{-3}} = (3x)^{(2)(3)}$
$\phantom{\left[(3x)^{-2}\right]^{-3}} = (3x)^6$
$\phantom{\left[(3x)^{-2}\right]^{-3}} = 729x^6$

Hint: When an expression has a coefficient and a variable, apply the exponent law to each one.
$(2b)^3 = (2^3)(b^3) = 8b^3$

A Practise

1. Write each expression with positive exponents.

   a) 4^{-2}

   b) $3x^{-3}$

   c) $(5x)^{-2}$

   d) $6a^{-3}b^{-2}$

   e) $-5a^{-4}$

   f) $-4a^4b^{-5}$

   g) $\left(\dfrac{2}{3}\right)^{-3}$

   h) $\dfrac{-3x^2}{y^{-4}}$

   i) $\dfrac{6a^{-3}}{b^4}$

2. Shelby rewrote the expression $\left(\dfrac{y^3}{4x^5}\right)^{-2}$ as $\dfrac{8x^{10}}{y^6}$. Is her answer correct? Justify your answer.

3. Simplify, then evaluate. Express your answers to four decimal places, if necessary.

   a) 1.4^{-3}

   b) $\left(\dfrac{-4^2}{2^3}\right)^{-3}$

   c) $\left[(2^{-2})(2^4)\right]^{-2}$

   d) $\left(\dfrac{-5^3}{5^3}\right)^{-3}$

   e) $\left(\dfrac{4}{4^3}\right)^{-3}$

   f) $\left(\dfrac{4^{-2}}{3^{-3}}\right)^{2}$

4. Simplify each expression by restating it using positive exponents only.

   a) a^4b^{-5}

   b) $\dfrac{-2}{a^3b^{-2}}$

   c) $\left[(p)^{-6}(p)^2\right]^{-3}$

   d) $\dfrac{12s^3}{4s^{-7}}$

   e) $(6x^{-4})^{-2}$

   f) $\left(\dfrac{t^{-3}}{t^5}\right)^{-2}$

   g) $\left[(n^3)(n^{-5})\right]^{2}$

   h) $(xy^{-3})^{-2}$

★5. Simplify each expression. State the answer using positive exponents.

a) $(6)^{-3}(6)$

b) $\dfrac{(-2)^{-6}}{(-2)^{-3}}$

c) $\dfrac{3^3}{3^{-2}}$

d) $\left(\dfrac{4^0}{4^{-2}}\right)^2$

e) $(6^{-4})^2$

f) $-(3^4)^{-3}$

g) $\left[(2^4)(2^{-7})\right]^{-3}$

h) $\left(\dfrac{3^3}{4^3}\right)^{-2}$

i) $(4a^{-3})^{-2}$

j) $-3\left[(2^4)(2^{-3})\right]^{-2}$

6. The students in a grade 10 class were investigating the algae growth rate on the surface of a local lake. When they began, 425 cm² of the surface area of the lake was covered with algae. The amount of surface area covered with algae doubles each month. The students modelled this situation using the formula $SA = 425(2)^n$, where SA is the surface area of the lake covered in algae after n months. If conditions remain constant, how much of the lake will be covered in algae

a) after 6 months?

b) after 2 years?

7. A biologist is monitoring the population growth of caribou in a national park. There were 1400 caribou in 2010. The caribou population increases at a growth rate of 1.04% per year. The growth rate can be modelled using the formula $P = 1400(1.04)^n$, where P is the projected population after n years. Assuming that the growth rate remains constant, what would be the estimated caribou population in 2014?

B Apply

8. A culture of bacteria in a lab contains 400 bacterium cells. The number of cells doubles every hour. This situation can be modelled by the equation $B = 400(2)^h$, where B is the estimated number of bacteria and h is the time in hours. How many bacteria were present

a) after 3 h?

b) after 24 h?

c) 3 h ago?

★9. Without using a calculator, evaluate $\left[((2^{-1})^2)^3\right]^{-1}$.

10. Kevin simplified $(2^3)(3^2)$ as 6^5. Is he correct? Justify your answer.

11. A radioactive element has a half-life of one month. The amount of the element remaining is given by the formula $A = 400\left(\dfrac{1}{2}\right)^n$, where n is the number of months. Today there are 400 g of the element.

a) How much will remain after 4 months?

b) How much was there a month ago?

★12. The formula $d = \dfrac{1}{2}gt^2$ can be used to determine how long it takes an object to fall a certain distance from rest. In the formula, d is the distance the object falls, in metres, g is the acceleration due to gravity at 9.8 m/s², and t is the time it takes to fall, in seconds. Express each answer to one decimal place.

a) From what height does a penny fall if it takes 12.4 s to reach the ground?

b) How long does a penny take to fall from a height of 28.5 m?

c) How long does a penny take to reach the ground from a height of 248 m?

13. The population of Earth reached 6.8 billion people in 2009. Assume that the population increases by a growth rate of 1.8% per year and that the rate remains the same. The rate of growth can be modelled using the formula $P = [(6.8)(10^9)](1.018)^n$, where P is the estimated population and n is the number of years. Determine the projected population

a) by the end of 2015

b) by the end of 2020

14. In 2010, there were approximately 34 million people living in Canada. Assume that Canada's overall population growth rate is 0.9% per year and that the growth rate remains constant. The population can be estimated using the formula $P = [(3.4)(10^7)](1.009)^n$, where P is the estimated population and n is the number of years. What is the projected population

a) in 2018?

b) in 2021?

C Extend

⭐**15.** Suppose you win the opportunity to receive a cash prize of $15 000 or double your money each year for a period of 25 years starting with an initial payment to you of $0.01. The value of your winnings can be determined using the formula $A = 0.01(2)^n$, where A is the payment at the end of n years.

a) What is the value of the payment you would receive after 3 years? after 10 years? after 25 years?

b) Which offer would you accept? Explain why.

c) If you received a cheque each year, how much money would you have received in total over the 25-year period?

16. The amount of sodium-24 remaining in a sample that started at 86 g can be represented by the equation $N = 86(0.5)^{\frac{t}{15}}$, where t is time, in hours. Determine the amount of sodium-24 remaining after each of the following time periods. Express the answers to two decimal places, if necessary.

a) after 30 h

b) after 90 h

c) after 120 h

17. Determine the value of x that makes each statement true.

a) $\left(\frac{4}{5}\right)^x = \frac{625}{256}$

b) $-3^x = -729$

c) $x^{-3} = \frac{27}{8}$

d) $2(6^x) = 432$

18. A scientist discovered a new isotope and called it mathodium-334. In the formula $A_f = A_i (3)^{-t}$, A_f represents the amount of the isotope remaining, A_i is the initial amount, in grams, and t is the time in days.

a) If a sample started at 85 g, how much would remain after 4 days? Express the answer to two decimal places.

b) The amount of mathodium-334 remaining after 6 h is 0.165 g. Calculate the amount of the original sample. Express the answer to two decimal places.

D Create Connections

19. Is $\left[(2^3)^4\right]^2$ equal to $\left[(2^4)^2\right]^3$? Justify your answer.

⭐**20.** What value of x makes the following statement true?

$2^x + 2^x + 2^x + 2^x = 256$

21. Without using a calculator, show that $2^2 + 2^3 + 2^4$ is not equal to $(2^2)(2^3)(2^4)$. Explain why the answers are not the same.

22. Describe a real-life situation in which a positive exponent and a negative exponent can be used to model a problem.

a) Give an example of what the positive exponent represents.

b) Give an example of what the negative exponent represents.

4.3 Rational Exponents

> ### **KEY IDEAS**

- A power with a negative exponent can be written as a power with a positive exponent.

$$- a^{-n} = \frac{1}{a^n}, a \neq 0 \qquad 9^{-1.3} = \frac{1}{9^{1.3}} \qquad - \frac{1}{a^{-n}} = a^n, a \neq 0 \qquad \frac{1}{2^{-3.2}} = 2^{3.2}$$

- You can apply the above principle to the exponent laws.

Exponent Law	Example
Note that a and b are rational or variable bases and m and n are integral exponents.	
Product of Powers $(a^m)(a^n) = a^{m+n}$	$\left(x^{\frac{3}{5}}\right)\left(x^{\frac{6}{5}}\right) = x^{\frac{3}{5} + \frac{6}{5}}$ $= x^{\frac{9}{5}}$
Quotient of Powers $\frac{a^m}{a^n} = a^{m-n}, a \neq 0$	$\frac{4s^{2.5}}{12s^{0.5}} = \frac{1}{3}s^{(2.5 - 0.5)}$ $= \frac{1}{3}s^2$ or $\frac{s^2}{3}$
Power of a Power $(a^m)^n = a^{mn}$	$(t^{3.3})^{\frac{1}{3}} = t^{(3.3)\left(\frac{1}{3}\right)}$ $= t^{1.1}$
Power of a Product $(ab)^m = a^m b^m$	$\left(8x^{\frac{1}{2}}\right)^{\frac{2}{3}} = (2^3)^{\frac{2}{3}}\left(x^{\frac{1}{2}}\right)^{\frac{2}{3}}$ $= 4x^{\frac{2}{6}}$ or $4x^{\frac{1}{3}}$
Power of a Quotient $\left(\frac{a}{b}\right)^n = \frac{a^n}{b^n}, b \neq 0$	$\left(\frac{x^3}{y^6}\right)^{\frac{1}{3}} = \frac{(x^3)^{\frac{1}{3}}}{(y^6)^{\frac{1}{3}}}$ $= \frac{x}{y^2}$
Zero Exponent $a^0 = 1, a \neq 0$	$(-2y^2)^0 = 1$ $-(2y^2)^0 = -1$

- A power with a rational exponent can be written with the exponent in decimal or fractional form. $\qquad x^{\frac{3}{5}} = x^{0.6}$

Example

Write each product or quotient as a power with a single positive exponent. Then, evaluate where possible.

a) $\left(7^{\frac{1}{2}}\right)(7^3)$ **b)** $\frac{9^{1.25}}{9^{\frac{3}{4}}}$ **c)** $(16x^6)^{\frac{1}{4}}$ **d)** $\left(\frac{3^{0.25}}{3^{\frac{3}{4}}}\right)^3$ **e)** $\left(\frac{27}{8}\right)^{-0.4}$

Solution

a) Since the bases are the same, you can add the exponents. Remember to determine the lowest common denominator when adding fractions.

$$\left(7^{\frac{1}{2}}\right)(7^3) = \left(7^{\frac{1}{2}}\right)\left(7^{\frac{6}{2}}\right)$$
$$= 7^{\left(\frac{1}{2} + \frac{6}{2}\right)}$$
$$= 7^{\frac{7}{2}}$$

b) Convert the rational exponents so both are fractions or decimal numbers. Then, since the bases are the same, you can subtract the exponents.

Method 1: Convert to Fractions

$$\frac{9^{1.25}}{9^{\frac{3}{4}}} = \frac{9^{\frac{5}{4}}}{9^{\frac{3}{4}}}$$

$$= 9^{\left(\frac{5}{4} - \frac{3}{4}\right)}$$

$$= 9^{\frac{2}{4}}$$

$$= 9^{\frac{1}{2}}$$

$$= 3$$

Method 2: Convert to Decimals

$$\frac{9^{1.25}}{9^{\frac{3}{4}}} = \frac{9^{1.25}}{9^{0.75}}$$

$$= 9^{(1.25 - 0.75)}$$

$$= 9^{0.5}$$

$$= 3$$

c) Raise each term to the exponent. Then, multiply the exponents.

$$(16x^6)^{\frac{1}{4}} = (16)^{\frac{1}{4}} x^{(6)\left(\frac{1}{4}\right)}$$

$$= 2x^{\frac{6}{4}}$$

$$= 2x^{\frac{3}{2}}$$

d) Method 1: Subtract the Exponents

Convert the rational exponents to fractions or decimal numbers. Since the bases are the same, you can subtract the exponents. Raise the result to the exponent 3. Then, multiply.

Convert to fractions:

$$\left(\frac{3^{0.25}}{3^{\frac{3}{4}}}\right)^3 = \left(\frac{3^{\frac{1}{4}}}{3^{\frac{3}{4}}}\right)^3$$

$$= \left[3^{\left(\frac{1}{4} - \frac{3}{4}\right)}\right]^3$$

$$= \left(3^{\frac{-2}{4}}\right)^3$$

$$= \left(3^{\frac{-1}{2}}\right)^3$$

$$= \left(3^{\frac{-3}{2}}\right)$$

$$= \frac{1}{3^{\frac{3}{2}}}$$

Method 2: Apply Power of a Power

Raise each power to the exponent 3. Next, convert the rational exponents to fractions or decimal numbers. Then, subtract the exponents of the resulting powers.

$$\left(\frac{3^{0.25}}{3^{\frac{3}{4}}}\right)^3 = \left(\frac{3^{\frac{3}{4}}}{3^{\frac{9}{4}}}\right)$$

$$= 3^{\frac{3}{4} - \frac{9}{4}}$$

$$= 3^{\frac{-6}{4}}$$

$$= \frac{1}{3^{\frac{3}{2}}}$$

e) Convert the bases to a single exponent. Then, raise the result to the exponent -0.4.

$$\left(\frac{27}{8}\right)^{-0.4} = \left[\frac{(3^3)}{(2^3)}\right]^{-0.4}$$

$$= \left[\left(\frac{3}{2}\right)^3\right]^{-0.4}$$

$$= \left(\frac{3}{2}\right)^{-1.2}$$

$$= \left(\frac{2}{3}\right)^{1.2}$$

A Practise

1. Use the exponent laws to simplify each expression. Where possible, compute numerical values.

   a) $\left(a^6\right)\left(a^{\frac{3}{2}}\right)$

   b) $\left(y^{\frac{1}{3}}\right)\left(y^{\frac{1}{2}}\right)$

   c) $\left(x^{0.4}\right)\left(x^{\frac{1}{2}}\right)$

   d) $\left(a^{0.2}\right)^3$

   e) $\left(x^{\frac{2}{3}}\right)^{-6}$

   f) $\left(81^{\frac{1}{4}}\right)^2$

   g) $\left(\dfrac{-64x^{\frac{3}{4}}}{27x^{\frac{1}{2}}}\right)^{\frac{1}{3}}$

   h) $\left(-5a^{\frac{1}{2}}\right)\left(2a^{\frac{3}{5}}\right)$

   i) $\left(256a^6\right)^{0.25}$

2. Use the exponent laws to simplify each expression. Leave your answers with positive exponents.

   a) $\left(a^{-2}\right)\left(a^{\frac{3}{4}}\right)$

   b) $\left(16^{-0.25}\right)^2$

   c) $\dfrac{\left(y^{\frac{2}{3}}\right)^{-2}}{\left(y^{\frac{1}{2}}\right)^{-4}}$

   d) $\left(a^{\frac{3}{4}}\right)^{-0.5}\left(a^2\right)^{-0.25}$

   e) $\left[\dfrac{(a^2b)}{(ab)^3}\right]^{-1.5}$

   f) $\left(\dfrac{25x^{-2}}{16x^{\frac{-1}{2}}}\right)^{-1.5}$

   g) $\left(4x^3\right)^{\frac{-1}{2}}\left(27y^2\right)^{\frac{1}{3}}$

   h) $\left(\dfrac{81x^{\frac{2}{3}}}{625y^{\frac{3}{5}}}\right)^{0.25}$

★ 3. Use the exponent laws to help identify a value for q that satisfies each equation.

   a) $\left(x^{\frac{2}{3}}\right)^q = x^{\frac{4}{3}}$

   b) $\left(x^{\frac{-2}{3}}\right)\left(x^q\right) = x^{\frac{-1}{6}}$

   c) $\dfrac{y^{\frac{2}{3}}}{y^q} = y^{\frac{11}{12}}$

   d) $\left(27x^2\right)^{\frac{1}{3}}\left(qx^2\right)^{\frac{-1}{2}} = \dfrac{3}{2x^{\frac{1}{3}}}$

   e) $\left(5^q\right)\left(-3^{-q}\right) = \dfrac{-125}{27}$

4. Evaluate without using a calculator. Leave the answers as rational numbers.

   a) $16^{\frac{3}{4}}$

   b) $-243^{\frac{2}{5}}$

   c) $8^{\frac{-5}{3}}$

   d) $\left(\dfrac{49}{9}\right)^{\frac{3}{2}}$

   e) $\left(\dfrac{125x^2}{8y^3}\right)^{\frac{2}{3}}$

   f) $\dfrac{5^{-2}}{25^{\frac{-3}{2}}}$

5. Evaluate using a calculator. Express the answers to four decimal places, if necessary.

   a) $\left(9^{-0.5}\right)^3$

   b) $\left(64^{\frac{1}{2}}\right)^3$

   c) $\left(3^{1.2}\right)\left(3^{2.4}\right)$

   d) $\dfrac{16^{\frac{2}{3}}}{16^{-0.2}}$

   e) $\left(\dfrac{3^{\frac{-1}{2}}}{81^{0.25}}\right)^2$

   f) $\left(\dfrac{8}{7^{\frac{1}{2}}}\right)^{\frac{5}{3}}$

6. Mid Lake, in Manitoba, is stocked with rainbow trout annually. The population grows at a rate of 11.5% per month. The number of trout stocked is given by the expression $623(1.115)^n$, where n is the number of months since the start of the trout season. Determine the number of trout after

   a) 3 months

   b) $7\frac{1}{2}$ months

   c) $3\frac{1}{2}$ months

   d) $6\frac{1}{2}$ months

B Apply

★ 7. For each solution, identify the step where an error was made. What is the correct answer? Compare your corrections with those of a classmate.

   a) $\dfrac{a^{\frac{2}{3}}}{a^{\frac{1}{4}}} = a^{\frac{2}{3}-\frac{1}{4}}$

   $= a^{-1}$

   $= \dfrac{1}{a}$

   b) $\left(16y^{-6}\right)^{-0.5} = (16)^{-0.5}\left(y^{-6}\right)^{-0.5}$

   $= 8y^3$

8. Karen has saved $1500 for college. She deposits this amount into a 3-year term deposit that earns 3.25% interest per year. The formula for calculating the value of her investment is $A = P(1 + i)^n$, where A is the amount of money at the end of the term, i is the interest rate as a decimal number, and n is the number of years the money is invested. How much will her investment be worth at the end of

   a) 3 years?

   b) $2\frac{1}{2}$ years?

9. A species of bacteria increases in number by 50% every 25 min. The growth of the bacteria can be modelled using the equation $N = 1000(1.5)^{\frac{t}{25}}$, where N is the number of bacteria after t min.

a) What does the value 1.5 in the formula represent? the value 1000?

b) How many bacteria are present after 1 h?

c) How many bacteria were present 30 min ago?

10. In June 2009, there were approximately 33.985 million people living in Canada. Assume that Canada's natural growth rate is 0.3% per year and that this growth rate remains constant. The natural growth rate represents the number of births and number of deaths in a population and does not take immigration and emigration into account. Canada's growth rate can be modelled using the formula $P = 33.985(1.003)^n$, where P is the population in millions and n is the number of years since 2009.

a) What is the projected population in 15.5 years? Express the answer to three decimal places.

b) What was Canada's population in March 2001?

☆**11.** Bismuth-214 has a half-life of approximately 20 min. The amount of bismuth-214 remaining in a sample that began at 28 g can be represented by the formula $A = 28(0.5)^{\frac{t}{20}}$, where A is the amount remaining after t min. Determine the amount of bismuth-214 remaining after each of the following periods of time. Express each answer to the nearest hundredth of a gram.

a) after 45 min

b) after 2 h

c) after $3\frac{1}{4}$ h

12. In the formula $C = 50(0.5)^{\frac{t}{3}}$, C is the remaining concentration of a particular medication in the bloodstream, in milligrams, and t is the time, in hours.

a) Determine the missing values in the table.

Time (t)	0	3	6	9	12
Concentration (C)					

b) Graph the data in part a). Let t represent the x-axis and C represent the y-axis.

c) If $C = 0.195$ mg, what is the value of t?

d) If $t = 42$ h, what is the value of C?

C Extend

13. Phosphorus-32 has a half-life of 14 days. If 2.56 g of a sample of phosphorus-32 remain after 70 days, what was the original mass of the sample? Use the formula $A_f = A_i(0.5)^{\frac{t}{14}}$, where A_f is the final amount, A_i is the initial amount, and t is the time in days.

14. Michelle invested money in a mutual fund. By the end of 3 years, she had lost 8% of the original value of her investment. Her account balance was $2672.57.

a) How much did Michelle originally invest? Use the formula $A_f = A_i(1 - r)^{\frac{t}{12}}$, where A_f is the final value of her investment, A_i is the original amount invested, r is the percent of the value lost, and t is the time, in months.

b) How much money did she lose in her investment?

D Create Connections

☆**15.** Solve for x using the exponent laws.
$$4^{\frac{1}{2}} + 4^{\frac{1}{2}} + 4^{\frac{1}{2}} + 4^{\frac{1}{2}} = 4^x$$

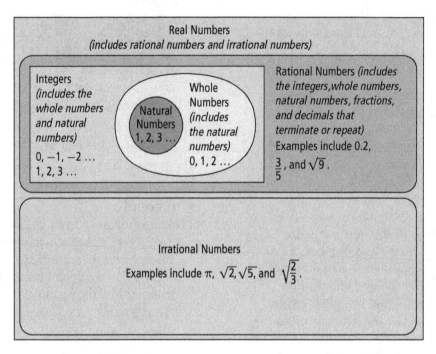

KEY IDEAS

- Rational numbers and irrational numbers form the set of real numbers.

- Radicals can be expressed as powers with fractional exponents.

$$\sqrt[n]{x^m} = x^{\frac{m}{n}}$$

The index of the radical has the same value as the denominator of the fractional exponent.

$$\sqrt[3]{10} = 10^{\frac{1}{3}} \qquad \sqrt[5]{7^3} = 7^{\frac{3}{5}}$$

- Radicals can be entire radicals such as $\sqrt{72}$, $\sqrt[5]{96}$, and $\sqrt[3]{\frac{54}{8}}$. They can also be mixed radicals such as $6\sqrt{2}$, $2\sqrt[5]{3}$, and $\frac{3\sqrt{2}}{2}$. You can convert between entire radicals and mixed radicals.

- You can order radicals that are irrational numbers using different methods:
  - Use a calculator to produce approximate values.
  - Express each irrational number as an entire radical.

Example

Convert each of the following as requested.
Express each power as an equivalent radical.

a) $32^{\frac{1}{2}}$ **b)** $16^{\frac{2}{3}}$ **c)** $(8x^3)^{\frac{1}{4}}$

Express each radical as a power with a rational exponent.

d) $\sqrt{6^3}$ **e)** $\sqrt[3]{5^2}$ **f)** $\sqrt[7]{8^3}$

Express each mixed radical as an entire radical.

g) $2.5\sqrt{4}$ **h)** $2\sqrt[3]{4}$ **i)** $-2\sqrt[5]{3}$

Express each entire radical as a mixed radical.

j) $\sqrt{112}$ **k)** $\sqrt[4]{96}$ **l)** $\sqrt{252}$

Solution

Write each power as a radical. Use the denominator of the exponent as the index.

a) $32^{\frac{1}{2}} = \sqrt{32}$ **b)** $16^{\frac{2}{3}} = \left(\sqrt[3]{16}\right)^2$ **c)** $(8x^3)^{\frac{1}{4}} = \sqrt[4]{8x^3}$

Write each radical as a power. Use the index as the denominator of the exponent.

d) $\sqrt{6^3} = 6^{\frac{3}{2}}$ **e)** $\sqrt[3]{5^2} = 5^{\frac{2}{3}}$ **f)** $\sqrt[7]{8^3} = 8^{\frac{3}{7}}$

> The index is 3. Convert the whole number 2 to a radical using the fraction $\frac{3}{3}$.
> $$2^{\frac{3}{3}} = \sqrt[3]{(2^3)}$$

Write each mixed radical as an entire radical.

g)
$$2.5\sqrt{4} = \sqrt{(2.5^2)}\sqrt{4}$$
$$= \sqrt{(2.5^2)(4)}$$
$$= \sqrt{(6.25)(4)}$$
$$= \sqrt{25}$$
$$= 5$$

h)
$$2\sqrt[3]{4} = \left(2^{\frac{3}{3}}\right)\left(\sqrt[3]{4}\right)$$
$$= \sqrt[3]{(2^3)(4)}$$
$$= \sqrt[3]{(8)(4)}$$
$$= \sqrt[3]{32}$$

i)
$$-2\sqrt[5]{3} = (-2)^{\frac{5}{5}}\left(\sqrt[5]{3}\right)$$
$$= \sqrt[5]{(-2^5)(3)}$$
$$= \sqrt[5]{(-32)(3)}$$
$$= \sqrt[5]{-96}$$

Express each entire radical as a mixed radical.

j)
$$\sqrt{112} = \sqrt{(16)(7)}$$
$$= \sqrt{16}\sqrt{7}$$
$$= 4\sqrt{7}$$

k)
$$\sqrt[4]{96} = \sqrt[4]{(2)(2)(2)(2)(6)}$$
$$= \sqrt[4]{(2^4)(6)}$$
$$= 2\sqrt[4]{6}$$

l)
$$\sqrt{252} = \sqrt{(36)(7)} \text{ or } \sqrt{252} = \sqrt{(4)(63)}$$
$$= \sqrt{36}\sqrt{7} \qquad\qquad = \sqrt{4}\left(\sqrt{(9)(7)}\right)$$
$$= 6\sqrt{7} \qquad\qquad = (2)(\sqrt{9})(\sqrt{7})$$
$$\qquad\qquad\qquad = (2)(3)(\sqrt{7})$$
$$\qquad\qquad\qquad = 6\sqrt{7}$$

A Practise

1. Express each power as an equivalent radical.

a) $5^{\frac{2}{3}}$

b) $8^{0.75}$

c) $6^{\frac{3}{5}}$

d) $81^{0.5}$

★e) $\frac{1}{9^{\frac{5}{3}}}$

f) $(x^3)^{\frac{1}{4}}$

g) $\left(a^{\frac{1}{3}}\right)^2$

h) $\left[\frac{\left(x^{\frac{1}{3}}\right)}{\left(y^{\frac{1}{3}}\right)}\right]^2$

2. Express each radical as a power.

a) $\sqrt[4]{3^3}$

b) $\sqrt[3]{(5t)^4}$

c) $\sqrt[3]{x^2}$

d) $\sqrt[5]{\frac{a^2}{b^3}}$

e) $\sqrt[3]{y^{\frac{5}{2}}}$

f) $\sqrt[a]{2^3}$

3. Evaluate each expression. State the result to four decimal places, if necessary.

a) $\sqrt{0.25}$

b) $(64)^{\frac{1}{3}}$

c) $3\sqrt{12}$

d) $\sqrt{\left(\frac{5}{4}\right)^2}$

e) $4(1.2)^{\frac{3}{4}}$

f) $\frac{\sqrt[3]{16}}{\sqrt{12}}$

4. Express each mixed radical as an equivalent entire radical.

★a) $4\sqrt{5}$

b) $3\sqrt{4}$

c) $5\sqrt{13}$

d) $6.2\sqrt{10}$

e) $3.3\sqrt{16}$

f) $\frac{1}{5}\sqrt{10}$

5. Express each mixed radical as an equivalent entire radical.

a) $3\sqrt[3]{5}$

b) $7\sqrt[3]{3}$

c) $5\sqrt[3]{6}$

d) $2\sqrt[4]{7}$

e) $\frac{1}{2}\sqrt[3]{5}$

f) $1.5\sqrt[4]{10}$

6. Express each entire radical as an equivalent mixed radical.

a) $\sqrt{32}$

b) $\sqrt{44}$

c) $\sqrt{90}$

d) $\sqrt{80}$

e) $\sqrt{360}$

f) $\sqrt{475}$

7. Express each entire radical as an equivalent mixed radical.

a) $\sqrt[3]{48}$

b) $\sqrt[3]{120}$

c) $\sqrt[3]{324}$

d) $\sqrt[4]{48}$

e) $\sqrt[4]{405}$

f) $\sqrt[4]{208}$

8. Order each set of numbers from greatest to least. Then, identify the irrational numbers.

a) $0.5\sqrt{2}$ $0.\overline{7}$ $\frac{3}{4}$ $\sqrt{0.49}$

b) $\frac{2}{3}$ $\sqrt[3]{0.343}$ $\sqrt{0.38}$ 0.62

9. Plot each set of numbers on a number line. Which of the numbers in each set is irrational?

a) $\sqrt[3]{435}$ $8.\overline{5}$ $4\sqrt{5}$ $\sqrt{64}$

b) $\frac{2\sqrt{85}}{3}$ $\sqrt[3]{216}$ $6\frac{9}{11}$ $3\sqrt{7}$

B Apply

10. Determine the diameter of a sphere that has a surface area of 320 cm^2. Use the formula $SA = 4\pi r^2$. Express the answer to three decimal places.

11. The volume of a cylinder is 312 cm^3 and its height is 6 cm. Determine the diameter of the cylinder. Use the formula $V = \pi r^2 h$. Express the answer to the nearest hundredth of a centimetre.

★12. There are approximately 1.3 billion km^3 of water on Earth. What would be the length of the edge of a cube that contained Earth's estimated total volume of water? Express the answer to the nearest kilometre.

13. In the formula $r = \sqrt[3]{\frac{3V}{4\pi}}$, r represents the radius of a sphere, in centimetres, and V is the volume of the sphere, in cubic centimetres. What is the length of the radius of a sphere with each of the following volumes? Express the answers to two decimal places.

a) 132 cm^3

b) 1896 cm^3

14. A pendulum has a length of 6 ft. The formula $T = \sqrt{\frac{4\pi^2 l}{32 \text{ ft/s}^2}}$ represents the period of the pendulum. In this formula, T is the period of the pendulum, in seconds, and l is the length of the pendulum, in feet. Calculate the period of the pendulum. Express the answer to two decimal places.

15. A cone has a volume of 27 489 cm3 and a height of 14 cm. Using the formula $V = \frac{1}{3}\pi r2h$, determine the diameter of the cone. Express the answer to the nearest centimetre.

16. Chemical equilibrium applies to chemical reactions that can occur in two directions. When a chemical reaction reaches equilibrium, the rate of the forward reaction is equal to the rate of its reverse reaction. In the formula $Q = \frac{C}{A^2B^3}$, Q represents the solutions at equilibrium, and A, B, and C are three chemicals involved in a chemical reaction. Express each answer to two decimal places.

   a) Determine the concentration of solution B if solution A has a concentration of 0.25 M, solution C has a concentration of 0.12 M, and the value of Q is 569.

   b) Determine the concentration of solution A if solution B has a concentration of 0.32 M, solution C has a concentration of 0.45 M, and the value of Q is 26.

17. The national arena of Sweden, the Ericsson Globe, is considered the largest hemispherical building in the world. The interior of the Ericsson Globe has a volume of 696 910 m³.

   a) Determine the diameter of the arena using the formula $r = \sqrt[3]{\frac{3V}{4\pi}}$, where r is the radius of the arena, in metres, and V is the volume of the arena, in cubic metres. Express the answer to one decimal place.

   b) Determine the surface area of the Ericsson Globe using the formula $SA = 4\pi r^2$, where SA represents the surface area in square metres. Express the answer to one decimal place.

★ 18. The surface area of a cylinder given its volume can be calculated using the formula $SA = 2\pi\left[h\left(\sqrt{\frac{V}{\pi h}}\right) + \left(\frac{V}{\pi h}\right)\right]$. Determine the surface area of a cylinder with height 26 m and volume of 26 465 m³. Express the answer to the nearest square metre.

C Extend
19. Without using a calculator, solve each of the following:

   a) $\sqrt{\sqrt{16}}$

   b) $\sqrt{\sqrt[3]{15\,625}}$

   ★c) $\sqrt{4 + \sqrt{19 + \sqrt{36}}}$

   ★d) $\sqrt[4]{13 + \sqrt[3]{22 + \sqrt[3]{125}}}$

20. Express as a power with a single rational exponent.

   ★a) $\sqrt[3]{\sqrt{7}}$ ★b) $\sqrt[4]{\sqrt[3]{5^2}}$

   c) $\sqrt[5]{\sqrt{\frac{1}{8}}}$ d) $\sqrt[4]{\sqrt[3]{\left(\frac{2}{5}\right)^6}}$

D Create Connections
21. Does the expression $\sqrt[4]{x^3}$ always have a solution? Explain your reasoning.

22. Does the expression $\sqrt[3]{x^4}$ always have a solution? Explain your reasoning.

23. Copy the table and add rows to fill in the information for the first 20 whole numbers.

Number	Square Root	Answer
1	$\sqrt{1}$	1

Use your calculator to determine each square root and copy all of the digits showing on the calculator.

   a) What do you notice about the square roots of numbers that are not perfect squares?

   b) Are the square roots of all non-perfect squares irrational? Explain.

Chapter 4 Review

4.1 Square Roots and Cube Roots

1. Which of the following numbers are perfect squares, perfect cubes, or both?
   a) 49   **b)** 343
   c) 484   **d)** 1728
   e) 1024   **f)** 15 625

2. Use prime factorization to evaluate
   ★**a)** $\sqrt{196}$ **b)** $\sqrt[3]{512}$

3. Calculate.
   a) $\sqrt{256}$ **b)** $\sqrt[3]{2197}$
   c) $\sqrt[3]{27\,000}$

4. What are the dimensions of the square?

$A = 361 \text{ cm}^2$

★**5.** Christina wants to replace the flooring in her bedroom with square tiles. Each tile measures 6 in. by 6 in. The area of the floor is 9 ft by 9 ft.
   a) How many tiles does Christina need?
   b) Each tile costs $1.38 including taxes. How much will the tiles cost?

4.2 Integral Exponents

6. Write as a power with a positive exponent.
   a) $\left(a^3\right)^{-2}$

   b) $\dfrac{(3.5)^3}{(3.5)^{-4}}$

   ★**c)** $\left(\dfrac{b^2}{b^{-5}}\right)^2$

7. Evaluate each expression. Express the answer to three decimal places, if necessary.
   a) $\left(3^2\right)^{-2}$

   b) $\left[\dfrac{5^2}{(2.5)^3(1.25)}\right]^3$

   c) $\left(0.5^2\right)^{-3}\left(2.8^2\right)^2$

8. A radioactive element has a half-life of one month. The formula for the amount of the element remaining is $A = m\left(\dfrac{1}{2}\right)^n$, where m is the mass of the element, in grams, and n is the number of months. How much of a 740-g sample of the element

   a) remains after 6 months? Express your answer to two decimal places.

   b) remains after 14 months? Express your answer to three decimal places.

   c) was there 4 months ago? Express your answer to the nearest gram.

9. Newfoundland has the highest population density of moose in North America. In 2009, there were approximately 135 000 moose on the island. Assuming a growth rate of 8.5%, this situation can be modelled using the formula $P = 135\,000(1.085)^n$, where P is the estimated moose population and n is the number of years since 2009. If the growth rate remains constant, how many moose will there be after
   a) 1 year?
   b) 2 years?
   c) 5 years?

10. **a)** Using the information in #9, how many moose will there be in 2020?

    b) Assume that the growth rate was the same before 2009. How many moose were there at the beginning of 2000?

4.3 Rational Exponents

⭐**11.** Simplify each expression. Express each answer with a positive exponent.

a) $(5^{-0.5})^{\frac{3}{4}}$

b) $\dfrac{2.8^{0.4}}{2.8^{\frac{-1}{2}}}$

c) $(27x^{-2})^{\frac{-2}{3}}$

12. Without using a calculator, Victoria incorrectly simplified the following expression. What errors did she make? Determine the correct answer.

$$(27x)^{\frac{-1}{3}}(9x)^{\frac{1}{2}} = (243x)^{\left(\frac{-1}{3} + \frac{1}{2}\right)}$$
$$= (243x)^{\frac{1}{6}}$$

⭐**13.** Without using a calculator, evaluate each expression.

a) $\dfrac{8^{\frac{5}{3}}}{4^2}$

b) $\dfrac{125^{\frac{2}{3}}}{5^{-1}}$

c) $\dfrac{9^{\frac{3}{2}}}{27^{\frac{1}{3}}}$

d) $\dfrac{8^{\frac{2}{3}}}{32^{\frac{4}{5}}}$

14. Evaluate each expression. Express each answer to four decimal places, if necessary.

a) $\left(20^{\frac{1}{4}}\right)\left(20^{\frac{2}{3}}\right)$

b) $(6^{-4})^{\frac{1}{3}}$

c) $\left(\dfrac{2.5^{\frac{3}{4}}}{2.5^{-0.5}}\right)^2$

d) $\dfrac{(25^3)}{(2^3)(10^2)}$

15. Jessica invested $1500 in an account that increases in value at a rate of 3.25% annually. The value of the account can be determined using the formula $A = 1500(1.0325)^t$, where A is the total value of the investment and t is the number of years. What is the value of Jessica's account at the end of three years?

16. The students in a grade 10 class are making T-shirts for a fundraiser. The cost of the ink needed to print T-shirts can be determined using the equation $C = 5.75n^{\frac{3}{4}} + 60$, where n is the number of T-shirts. Determine the cost of the ink needed to print 350 T-shirts.

17. Iodine-131 has a half-life of 8 days. Iodine-131 has medical uses such as treating people with an overactive thyroid. A patient is given 9.5 mg of iodine-131. How much would remain in the patient's body after 30 days? Use the formula $A = 9.5(0.5)^{\frac{t}{8}}$, where A is the amount remaining in the patient's body and t is the time, in days. Express the answer to the nearest thousandth of a milligram.

4.4 Irrational Numbers

18. Write each power as an equivalent radical.

a) $x^{\frac{2}{5}}$

b) $(16s^3)^{\frac{3}{5}}$

c) $\left(\dfrac{a^5}{7}\right)^{0.75}$

d) $(5a^4)^{\frac{-1}{3}}$

19. Express each radical as a power.

a) $\sqrt{x^5}$

b) $\sqrt[4]{5^2}$

c) $4\sqrt[5]{x^3}$

d) $\sqrt[3]{(4y)^4}$

20. Convert each mixed radical to an equivalent entire radical.

a) $4\sqrt{7}$

b) $6\sqrt{5}$

⭐c) $3\sqrt[3]{2}$

d) $-5\sqrt[3]{3}$

21. Express each entire radical as an equivalent mixed radical.

a) $\sqrt{252}$

b) $\sqrt[3]{384}$

c) $\sqrt[4]{48}$

d) $\sqrt[3]{405}$

22. Identify the irrational numbers in each set. Then, arrange the numbers from greatest to least.

a) $\sqrt[3]{216}$ $0.2\overline{3}$ $\dfrac{4\sqrt{5}}{2}$ $\sqrt{0.25}$

b) $\sqrt{0.81}$ $\sqrt[3]{32}$ $\dfrac{3\sqrt{25}}{4}$ $0.\overline{49}$

23. The volume of a sphere is given by the formula $V = \dfrac{4\pi r^3}{3}$, where r is the radius of the sphere.

a) What is the volume of a sphere with a radius of 25.4 cm? Express the answer to two decimal places.

b) Determine the radius of a sphere with a volume of 384.66 cm³. Express the answer to one decimal place.

Chapters 1–4 Cumulative Review

1. The orca is the motif for the 2010 Olympic gold medal. Assume that the image shows a reduction of 1:4. What is the diameter of the actual gold medal, to the nearest centimetre?

2. Determine possible dimensions for each area. Then, use your dimensions to calculate the area to the indicated equivalent.

a)
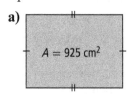
$A = 925$ cm²

$A = ?$ mm²

b)
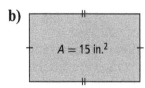
$A = 15$ in.²

$A = ?$ m²

c)
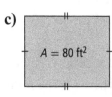
$A = 80$ ft²

$A = ?$ cm²

3. State whether each number is a perfect square, a perfect cube, both, or neither.

a) -1 b) 64 c) $19\,683$

d) 625 e) 7650

4. Identify the hypotenuse, opposite, and adjacent sides associated with each specified angle.

a) $\angle Z$

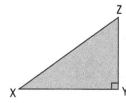

b) $\angle S$

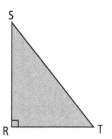

c) $\angle M$

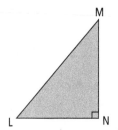

5. What is the reading represented on each measuring device? Estimate and then calculate each equivalent measurement in the other system (SI or imperial). Express the answer to the nearest tenth of a unit.

a) imperial ruler

b) SI caliper

6. Emma is planting a new lawn. The instructions on a 3-lb bag of grass seed say to apply 3 lb of seed per 1000 ft². The lawn has dimensions of 550 m².

    a) How many pounds of grass seed will Emma require? Express the answer to the nearest hundredth of a pound.

    b) How many bags of grass seed will she need to buy?

7. Draw and label a right triangle to show each ratio. Then, determine the measure of each angle, to the nearest degree.

    a) $\tan \beta = \frac{3}{2}$ **b)** $\tan \theta = \frac{1}{4}$

    c) $\sin A = \frac{4}{7}$ **d)** $\cos C = \frac{3}{5}$

8. What are the dimensions of a cube with volume 2197 cm³?

9. Calculate the surface area of each object, to the nearest hundredth of a unit.

a)

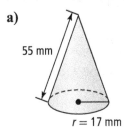

55 mm

$r = 17$ mm

b)

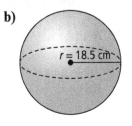

$r = 18.5$ cm

c)

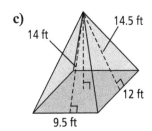

14 ft   14.5 ft

12 ft

9.5 ft

10. Jim is standing in front of a 75-m tall building. The angle of depression from the top of the building to Jim is 35°.

    a) How far is Jim from the building, to the nearest hundredth of a metre?

    b) Jim moves so that the angle of depression is now 40°. Did he move toward or away from the building? Explain your answer.

11. Evaluate each trigonometric ratio to four decimal places.

    a) $\cos 90°$ **b)** $\cos 67.2°$

    c) $\sin 18°$ **d)** $\tan 28°$

12. Write as a power with a positive exponent.

    a) $\left(x^{-5}\right)^3$ **b)** $\dfrac{b^4}{b^{-4}}$

    c) $\dfrac{(-5.6)^{-7}}{(-5.6)^{-2}}$

13. Stephen found a high wheel bike at an antique shop. The diameter of the front wheel is 54 in. and the diameter of the rear wheel is 18 in.

    a) How many times does the rear wheel rotate for each rotation of the front wheel? Give the answer as a ratio of front wheel rotations to rear wheel rotations. Write the ratio in lowest terms.

    b) How many times does the front wheel rotate when the bike travels 250 yd?

    c) Suppose Stephen cycles for $1\frac{1}{2}$ mi. How many rotations will the front wheel make?

14. There is a relationship between the mass of an organism and the mass of its brain. The estimated mass of an organism's brain can be modelled using the formula $E = 0.025b^{\frac{2}{3}}$, where E is the estimated brain mass, in kilograms, and b is the body mass, in kilograms.

    a) A bottlenose dolphin has a mass of 250 kg. What is the mass of its brain?

    b) The average mass of a human adult male is 70 kg. What is the approximate mass of a human brain?

15. Solve each triangle, to the nearest tenth of a unit.

a)

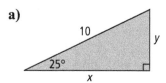

b)

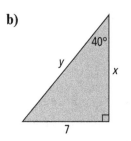

c)

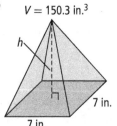

16. Determine the missing dimension for each of the following. Express the answer to the nearest hundredth of a unit, if necessary.

a) $V = 967.2$ cm³

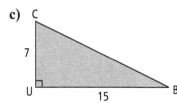

b) $V = 150.3$ in.³   **c)** $V = 2.6$ yd³

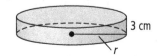

17. Evaluate each expression. Express the answer to four decimal places, if necessary.

a) $\left(9^{\frac{3}{5}}\right)\left(9^{0.6}\right)$ **b)** $-\left(2^{\frac{-1}{4}}\right)^{3}$

c) $\left(\dfrac{0.25^{0.25}}{0.25^{-3}}\right)^{2}$ **d)** $\left(\dfrac{4^{-2}}{6^{-3}}\right)^{\frac{1}{2}}$

18. Earth has a diameter of approximately 12 756 km. Earth's moon has a diameter of approximately 3475 km. Assume that they are both spheres.

a) Calculate the approximate surface area of Earth.

b) Calculate the approximate surface area of the moon.

c) How much greater is Earth's surface area than the moon's surface area? Express the answer as a percent.

19. Convert each measurement to the unit indicated.

a) 1 ft $2\frac{11}{16}$ in. to the nearest quarter of an inch

b) 8′2″ to the nearest quarter of a yard

c) 150 000 ft to the nearest tenth of a mile

d) 8 mi to the nearest foot

20. A right rectangular prism measures 16 cm by 8 cm by 4 cm. What would be the dimensions of a cube with the same volume?

21. Determine ∠ADB, to the nearest tenth of a degree.

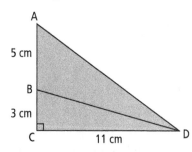

22. Express each entire radical as an equivalent mixed radical.

a) $\sqrt{54}$ **b)** $\sqrt{512}$

c) $\sqrt[3]{135}$ **d)** $\sqrt[4]{144}$

23. Write each power as an equivalent radical.

a) $x^{\frac{2}{7}}$ **b)** $(13t^{4})^{\frac{1}{5}}$

c) $\left(\dfrac{h^{2}}{12}\right)^{0.5}$

Chapter 4 Extend It Further

1. When a square sheet of paper is folded in half, its area is reduced by half. When folded again, the area is $\frac{1}{4}$ or 2^{-2} times as large. After the eighth fold, the area of the sheet of paper is 144 in.^{2}. What was the original size of the paper?

   A 256″ by 256″   **B** 192″ by 192″
   C 178″ by 178″   **D** 128″ by 128″

2. If $\sqrt{9^5}\, a^{-3} = 9$, what is the value of a?

   A 1   **B** 2
   C 3   **D** 9

3. If $a^{\frac{2}{3}} = 16$, determine the value of $\left(a^{\frac{2}{3}}\right)\left(a^{\frac{1}{6}}\right)$.

   A 4   **B** 6   **C** 8   **D** 32

4. If $3^{2b} = 49$, determine the value of 3^{-3b}.

   A $\frac{1}{3}$ **B** $\frac{1}{7}$
   C $\frac{1}{49}$ **D** $\frac{1}{343}$

5. Without using a calculator, determine which set of numbers is written in descending order.

   A $\sqrt[3]{3}, \sqrt[4]{5}, \sqrt{2}$
   B $\sqrt[3]{3}, \sqrt{2}, \sqrt[4]{5}$
   C $\sqrt[4]{5}, \sqrt[3]{3}, \sqrt{2}$
   D $\sqrt{2}, \sqrt[3]{3}, \sqrt[4]{5}$

6. Without using a calculator, determine which set of numbers is written in ascending order.

   A $(-3)^{42}, \left(\frac{1}{8}\right)^{-21}, (-5)^{28}, \left(\frac{1}{1024}\right)^{-7}$
   B $\left(\frac{1}{1024}\right)^{-7}, (-3)^{42}, (-5)^{28}, \left(\frac{1}{8}\right)^{-21}$
   C $\left(\frac{1}{8}\right)^{-21}, (-5)^{28}, (-3)^{42}, \left(\frac{1}{1024}\right)^{-7}$
   D $(-3)^{42}, (-5)^{28}, \left(\frac{1}{8}\right)^{-21}, \left(\frac{1}{1024}\right)^{-7}$

7. Express $(\sqrt{5})(\sqrt[3]{7})$ as a single radical.

8. If a and b are both irrational numbers, are all a^b also irrational? Explain.

9. Simplify $\dfrac{3^{n+2} - 3^{n+1}}{3^{n+3}}$.

10. In order to double the size of a spherical lollipop, by what percent must the radius be increased?

11. For what real values of n, if any, is each statement true?

    a) $\sqrt{n} = 8$
    b) $\sqrt{-n} = 8$
    c) $\sqrt{n} > 0$
    d) $\sqrt{n} = -8$
    e) $\sqrt{-n} = -8$

12. For what whole numbers n is $\sqrt{n}$ a rational number? Explain.

13. Solve for t if $512 = 4096^{-t}$.

14. Solve for x in $\sqrt{2009} = 2009\sqrt{x}$.

15. How many pairs of positive integers (a and b) satisfy $(2^a)^b = 2^{32}$? Justify your answer.

★16. James deposited $12 500 in a savings account. He earned $878.29 in interest after two years and nine months. What was the annual interest rate? Use the formula $A = P(1 + i)^n$, where A is the final value of his investment, P is the original amount invested, i is the interest rate, and n is time, in years.

Chapter 4 Study Check

Use the chart below to help you assess the skills and processes you have developed during Chapter 4. The references in italics direct you to pages in *Mathematics 10 Exercise and Homework Book* where you could review the skill. How can you show that you have gained each skill? What can you do to improve?

Big Idea	Skills	This Shows I Know	This Is How I Can Improve
Solve problems involving square roots and cube roots *pages 62–65, 78, 80–81, 83*	✓Determine square roots of perfect squares *pages 63–65, 78, 80, 83*		
	✓Determine cube roots of perfect cubes *pages 62–65, 78, 80–81*		
Solve problems involving integral and rational exponents *pages 66–73, 79, 81–83*	✓Apply the exponent laws to expressions with integral exponents *pages 66–69, 78, 81, 83*		
	✓Convert a power with a negative exponent to an equivalent power with a positive exponent *pages 66–69, 73, 76,78–79, 81*		
	✓Apply the exponent laws to expressions with rational exponents *pages 70–73, 78–79, 81–83*		
Solve problems involving irrational numbers, including radicals *pages 75–77, 79, 82–83*	✓Represent, identify, simplify, and order irrational numbers *pages 75–77, 79, 82–83*		
	✓Convert between powers and radicals *pages 75–77, 79, 82*		
	✓Convert between mixed radicals and entire radicals *pages 75–77, 79, 82–83*		

Organizing the Ideas

In the Venn diagram below, show examples of each type of real number. Use the intersections to show any common features of individual subgroups.

How can you use this Venn diagram to help show the similarities and differences between types?

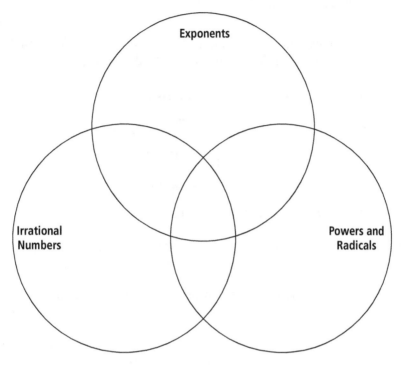

Study Guide

Review the types of problems you handled in Chapter 4. What do you need to remember to help you do similar problems?

Things to Remember		
Determining Square Roots and Cube Roots	Applying the Exponent Laws	Working With Irrational Numbers and Radicals

Chapter 5 Polynomials

5.1 Multiplying Polynomials

KEY IDEAS

- You can use the distributive property to multiply polynomials. Multiply each term in the first polynomial by each term in the second polynomial. Then, collect like terms.

- You can use algebra tiles to model algebraic expressions.

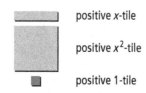

positive x-tile

positive x^2-tile

positive 1-tile

The same tiles not shaded represent negative quantities.

Example

Use the distributive property to determine the product of $(2a + 4)$ and $(a^2 + 5a + 7)$.

Solution

Multiply each term in the first polynomial by each term in the second polynomial.
$$(2a + 4)(a^2 + 5a + 7) = (2a)(a^2 + 5a + 7) + (4)(a^2 + 5a + 7)$$
$$= 2a^3 + 10a^2 + 14a + 4a^2 + 20a + 28$$

Collect the like terms and arrange them in descending order of the power of a.
$$= 2a^3 + 10a^2 + 4a^2 + 14a + 20a + 28$$
$$= 2a^3 + 14a^2 + 34a + 28$$

A Practise

1. Determine the product that each algebra tile model shows. Then, state the dimensions.

a)

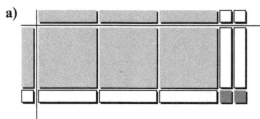

b)

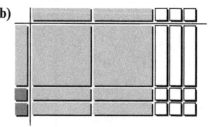

2. Determine each product using algebra tiles.

   a) $(x + 3)(x + 4)$

   b) $(x - 2)(x - 5)$

   c) $(2x - 1)(3x + 2)$

   d) $(4x + 3)(x + 2)$

   e) $(x - 4)^2$

   f) $(x - 3)(3x + 4)$

3. Multiply.

   a) $(x - 4)(2x + 4)$

   b) $(t + 5)(t + 4)$

   c) $(3w + 2)(2w - 9)$

   d) $(z + 2)(z - 2)$

   e) $(a + b)^2$

   f) $(5e + 5)(6e - 1)$

4. Match each binomial on the left with a trinomial on the right.

   a) $(x - 2)(x - 1)$ A $x^2 + 10x + 21$

   b) $(x + 5)^2$ B $x^2 - 8x + 16$

   c) $(x + 7)(x + 3)$ C $x^2 - x - 56$

   d) $(x + 6)(x - 2)$ D $x^2 - 7x + 12$

   e) $(x - 4)^2$ E $x^2 - 3x + 2$

   f) $(x - 8)(x + 7)$ F $x^2 + 11x + 10$

   g) $(x - 3)(x - 4)$ G $x^2 + 4x - 12$

   h) $(x + 1)(x + 10)$ H $x^2 + 10x + 25$

5. Choose the trinomial that is the product of the binomials.

   a) $(x + 2)(x - 3)$

      A $x^2 - x - 6$

      B $x^2 + x - 6$

      C $x^2 + x - 1$

      D $x^2 - x + 1$

   b) $(x - 4)(x - 1)$

      A $x^2 - 4x - 4$

      B $x^2 - 4x + 4$

      C $x^2 + 4x + 5$

      D $x^2 - 5x + 4$

   c) $(x + 5)^2$

      A $x^2 + 10x + 10$

      B $x^2 + 10x + 5$

      C $x^2 + 10x + 25$

      D $x^2 + 5x + 25$

   d) $(x - 6)(x + 3)$

      A $x^2 + 3x - 18$

      B $x^2 - 3x - 18$

      C $x^2 - 6x - 18$

      D $x^2 - 6x + 18$

   e) $(x - 7)^2$

      A $x^2 - 14x - 14$

      B $x^2 - 14x + 49$

      C $x^2 - x + 49$

      D $x^2 - 7x + 49$

   f) $(x + 1)(x + 10)$

      A $x^2 + 11x + 10$

      B $x^2 + 10x + 11$

      C $x^2 + x + 10$

      D $x^2 + x + 1$

6. Use the distributive property to determine each product.

   a) $(d + 3)(2d^2 + 5d - 2)$

   b) $(4s - 5)(s^2 - 9s - 1)$

   c) $k(5k^2 - k + 7)$

   d) $(3c + 6)(c^2 + 4c + 7)$

   e) $(5y^2 - y)(2y^2 + 2y - 6)$

   ☆f) $(r^2 - 5r - 3)(3r^2 - 4r - 5)$

7. Simplify.

   a) $4(5y + 3)(2y - 3)(3y + 1)$

   b) $(3a + 9) + (2a - 5)(4a - 7) + (6a + 3)$

   c) $(2d - e)(3d - 5e) + (6d + 5e)(d - 4e)$

   d) $(5n + 4)^2 - (2n + 7)(8n - 6)$

   e) $(3w^2 + w + 4)(2w^2 - 5w - 6)$

   ☆f) $2(4t + 5s)(2t - 3s) - (5t - s)$

8. Multiply. Then, combine like terms.

   a) $(3a + 7) + (4a - 3)(2a + 2)$

   b) $(b + 2)(3b + 6) + (b - 3)^2$

   c) $(2x - y)(x - 4y) + (x + y)(3x + y)$

   d) $4(6a + 2c)(a - 3c) - (a + 2c)^2$

   e) $(x^2 - 2x + 3)(2x^2 + 3x - 4)$

   f) $(4b - d)^2 - 2(2b + 3d)(b + d)$

B Apply

9. An error was made in each of the following solutions.

   • Write the step number that contains the error.

   • Determine the correct solution.

   a) $(4t - 5)(7t + 2) - (6t - 3)$

   Step 1: $4t(7t + 2) - 5(7t + 2) - (6t - 3)$

   Step 2: $28t^2 + 8t - 35t - 10 - 6t - 3$

   Step 3: $28t^2 + 8t - 35t - 6t - 10 - 3$

   Step 4: $28t^2 - 33t - 13$

   b) $x(2y^2 + y - 3) + x^2y$

   Step 1: $2xy^2 + xy - 3x + x^2y$

   Step 2: $2xy^2 + x^2y + xy - 3x$

   Step 3: $4x^2y + xy - 3x$

10. The width of a deck that surrounds a square wading pool is 2 m.

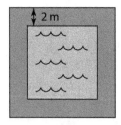

   a) Write a polynomial expression that represents the area of the pool and the pool deck.

   b) What is the area of the deck and the pool, if the pool has an area of 49 m²?

11. A mirror mounted horizontally on a wall has a width to height ratio of 5:2. The mirror frame adds 6 in. to the width and 4 in. to the height.

   a) Write a polynomial expression that represents the total area of the mirror, including the frame. Multiply and combine like terms.

   b) If the dimensions of the mirror are $5x$ by $2x$, calculate the total area when $x = 8$ in.

12. A diamond is drawn within a rectangle that has a width of $(x + 6)$ units and a length of $(2x + 4)$ units. The diamond touches the centre point of each side of the rectangle, as shown.

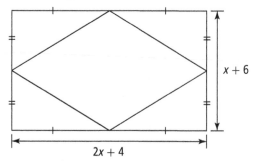

   a) Write an expression to represent the area of the diamond. Multiply and combine like terms.

   b) What is the relationship between the area of the diamond and the area of the rectangle?

C Extend

13. **a)** Write the expressions to calculate the area of the larger rectangle.

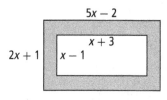

   b) Write the expression to determine the area of the smaller rectangle.

   c) Write the expression(s) for the area of the shaded region. Then, simplify.

14. An open-top box is made from a rectangular sheet of thin cardboard. The corner pieces are cut out as shown in the diagram. A metal corner piece reinforces the corner.

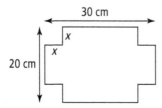

30 cm

x

x

20 cm

a) Write the expressions for the dimensions of the box.

b) Write the expression to calculate the volume of the box.

c) Simplify this expression.

D Create Connections

15. The diagram shows the first three rectangular prisms in a pattern.

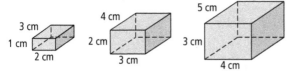

3 cm

1 cm

2 cm

4 cm

2 cm

3 cm

5 cm

3 cm

4 cm

a) Write the dimensions and the volume of the 4th prism.

b) Write the unsimplified expression that shows the volume of the nth prism.

c) Show two different ways to determine the volume of the 10th prism.

16. a) Choose three consecutive even numbers. Multiply the first and third numbers. Then, calculate the square of the middle number. Repeat this multiplication and squaring with several different groups of three consecutive even numbers. What pattern do you notice?

b) Let x represent your middle number. What algebraic expressions represent the first and last numbers?

c) Use algebraic multiplication to show that your pattern in part a) is always true.

17. a) Copy and complete the tables.

Table A	
Numbers	Total
6, 7	42
–	56
–	–
–	–
–	–

Table B				
Numbers				Total
5	25	15	2	42
–	36	–	2	–
7	–	–	–	72
–	–	–	–	–
–	–	–	–	–

b) Write two binomials and their equivalent trinomial to explain why the totals in Table A are equal to the totals in Table B.

18. Consider the following list of expressions.

$(4 \times 3) - (2 \times 1)$
$(5 \times 4) - (3 \times 2)$
$(6 \times 5) - (4 \times 3)$
$(7 \times 6) - (5 \times 4)$

a) If the least number in each group of four numbers is n, write the unsimplified expression that determines the difference of the products in each case.

b) Simplify the expression.

c) Show how the simplified expression matches the differences of the products.

5.2 Common Factors

- Factoring is the reverse of multiplying.

$5(x + 2) = 5x + 10$

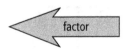

To find the greatest common factor (GCF) of a polynomial, find the GCF of the coefficients and variables.

- To factor a GCF from a polynomial, divide each term by the GCF.

- Polynomials can be written as a product of the GCF and the sum or difference of the remaining factors.

$$2m^3n^2 - 8m^2n + 12mn^4 = 2mn(m^2n - 4m + 6n^3)$$

- A common factor can be any polynomial, such as a binomial.

  $a(x + 2) - b(x + 2)$ has a common factor of $x + 2$.
  The final factored form of this polynomial is $(a - b)(x + 2)$.

Example

Write $12x^4y - 28x^3y^2 + 8x^2y^3$ in factored form.

Solution

The GCF of 12, 28, and 8 is 4.
The GCF of x^4y, x^3y^2, and x^2y^3 is x^2y.
So the GCF for the whole polynomial is $4x^2y$.
Mentally divide the polynomial by the GCF to determine the other factor.
So the polynomial in factored form is $4x^2y(3x^2 - 7xy + 2y^2)$. Note that this GCF is a monomial. A GCF *may* be a binomial.

A Practise

1. List the factors of each number in each pair. Then, identify the GCF.

   a) 10 and 15

   b) 24 and 36

   c) 16 and 48

   d) 40 and 60

   e) 18 and 45

   f) 14 and 24

2. List the prime factors of the coefficients and of the variables for each term.

   a) $6x^2$, $12x$

   b) $20c^2d^3$, $30cd^2$

   c) $4b^2c^3$, $6bc^2$

   d) $18xy^2z$, $24x^2y^3z^2$

   e) $5m^3n$, $20mn^2$

3. State the common prime factors and identify the GCF for each pair of terms in question 2.

4. Determine the GCF of the following sets of terms.

   a) $14a$, $21b$

   b) $-5n^2$, $-10n$

   c) $3rs$, $7t$

   d) $12f^2g^3$, $16fg^2$, $32f^3g^2$

   e) $-15d^2e^3$, $-30cd^2e$, $-45cde$

   f) $-18j^3k$, $27j^2kl$, $36j^2k^2l^2$

5. Identify the least common multiple for each of the following sets of numbers or terms.

   a) 16 and 20

   b) 15, 30, and 40

   c) $6x$ and $9x$

   d) $2t$, $3t^2$, and $4t^3$

   e) $4ab^3$, $6a^2b^2$, and $10a^3b$

   f) $8cde$, $14c^3de^2$, and $18c^2d^2e^3$

6. Factor the following polynomials. Then, use multiplication to check each answer.

   a) $6s + 30$

   b) $4t + 28$

   c) $5a - 5$

   d) $16r^2 - 12r$

   e) $7xy + 14xy - 49xz$

   f) $3c^3 - 9c^2 - 27d^2$

7. State the missing factor.

   a) $15w^2 - 5w = 5w ($_____$)$

   b) $4a^2 - 6a^3 = $ _____ $(2 - 3a)$

   c) $10x^2y^2 - 50xy = 10y ($_____$)$

   d) $2g^2 + 4g = 2g ($_____$)$

   e) $35x^2y + 15x^2y^2 + 5xy = $ _____ $(7x + 3xy + 1)$

   f) $2r^2 + 6r^3s - 4rs^2 = $ _____ $(r + 3r^2s - 2s^2)$

8. Identify the GCF for each pair of terms.

   a) $x(x - 6)$ and $4(x - 6)$

   b) $a(a + 3)$ and $-7(a + 3)$

   c) $d(d - 9)$ and $-6(d - 9)$

   d) $ab(b + 2)$ and $a^2b(b + 2)$

   e) $(x^2 + 2x)$ and $xy(x + 2)$

   f) $4m(n - 1)$ and $(2m^2n^3 - 2m^2n^2)$

9. Write each expression in factored form.

   a) $s(s + 5) - 2(s + 5)$

   b) $r(r - 7) - 4(r - 7)$

   c) $g(g + 6) + 9(g + 6)$

   d) $p^2 + 3p + 4p + 12$ (Hint: Group like terms to find a common factor.)

   e) $b^2 - 7b - 3b - 21$

   f) $r^2 - 3r + 2rs - 6s$

B Apply

★**10.** The Mount Baker girls' basketball team is planning a spaghetti dinner fund raiser. Table decorations will include floral centrepieces. The team decides to use roses, tulips, and daffodils. The local florist has 36 roses for $2.50 each, 48 daffodils for $1.70 each, and 60 tulips for $1.50 each.

   a) If each centrepiece is to have the largest possible number of each type of flower, with the same number of flowers in each centrepiece, how many of each type of flower will the centrepieces contain?

   b) To recover the money spent on the flowers, the centrepieces will be sold for the cost of the flowers. What will each centrepiece cost?

11. State whether each polynomial is factored fully and correctly. If it is not, write the correct and fully factored form.

   a) $12x - 6 = 3(4x - 2)$

   b) $-10w^2 - 10w = 10w(-w - 1)$

   c) $10c^4d - 20c^3d^2 + 15c^2d^2$
      $= 5c^2d(2c^2 - 4cd + 3d)$

   d) $x^2 + 2xy + 3x + 6y = x(x + 2y)$
      $+ 3(x + 2y)$

   e) $a^2 - 3ab - 2ab + 6b^2$
      $= (a - 2b)(a - 3b)$

   f) $t^2 - 4t + 5t - 5 = t(t - 4) + 5(t - 1)$

12. a) Write a polynomial with two terms that have a GCF of $4x$.

   b) Write a polynomial with two terms that have a GCF of $3rs$.

   c) Write a polynomial with two terms that have a GCF of $5m^2n^2$.

   d) Write a polynomial with three terms that have a GCF of ab.

   e) Write a polynomial with three terms that have a GCF of $2c^2d^2$.

   f) Write a polynomial with four terms that have a GCF of $2e$.

   g) Write a polynomial with four terms that have a common factor of $c + 4$.

13. The models show rectangles of algebra tiles. Answer the following questions for each rectangle.

   • What are the dimensions for each model?

   • Write an expression for each model, using your dimensions.

a)

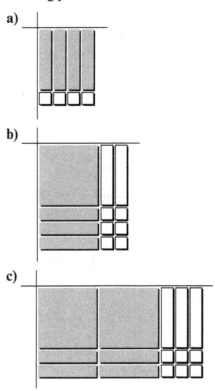

b)

c)

★**14. a)** The white rectangle in the diagram is centred within the larger rectangle. State the dimensions of the white rectangle.

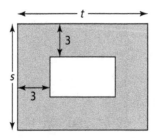

   b) If $t = 10$ cm and $s = 8$ cm, express the area of the white rectangle as a product of binomials.

15. You have two dishes of lasagna. One dish measures $6''$ by $15''$. The second dish measures $9''$ by $12''$.

   a) You want to cut the lasagna into equal-size servings with nothing left over. What is the largest size serving you can cut?

   b) Suppose there are 20 students in your class. What is the largest size square you can cut to ensure that each student receives at least one serving and all servings are of equal size?

C Extend

16. List the pairs of numbers less than 100 that have a GCF of 15 and a product of 2700. How do you know that you have all of the possible pairs?

17. A school receives a shipment of notebooks. The unopened and equal packages of notebooks are put into three stacks. The three stacks have 365, 525, and 595 notebooks, respectively. What is the largest possible number of notebooks in each package?

18. The diameter of the bottom tier of a three-tiered round cake is 6 cm greater than the diameter of the middle tier and 12 cm greater than the diameter of the top tier.

   a) Write an algebraic expression for the total top surface area of the three tiers.

   b) Multiply and then simplify.

19. Write a polynomial that satisfies the following clues:
   • It is a trinomial.
   • Each term has the same variable.
   • The exponents are odd integers.
   • The GCF is $8x$.
   • The greatest exponent is 5.
   • The coefficients in one term of the polynomial's factored form are 1, 2, and 3.

20. The greatest common factor of two numbers is 487. Both numbers are even. Neither is divisible by the other. What are the smallest two numbers they could be?

D Create Connections

21. a) Draw a diagram to illustrate the largest circle that can be contained within a square with side length s.

   b) Write an expression for the area of this circle. Use s as a variable in your expression.

   c) Write the expression for the area of the square not contained by the circle. Develop an appropriate polynomial. Then, factor the polynomial.

22. The height of a basketball thrown vertically can be modelled by the expression $v_0 t - 5t^2 + h_0$, where v_0 is the initial velocity of the basketball, t is the time, in seconds, that the ball is in the air, and h_0 is the initial height, in metres, of the ball.

   a) If the initial height of the ball is 2 m, and the initial velocity of the ball is 15 m/s, how long will the ball be in the air before it comes back down to its initial height?

   b) Factor the expression $15t - 5t^2$. At which times will the product be 0? Explain. Does this simplify the process for seeking the answer for part a)?

23. The height of a rectangular prism is $2x$. The width of the prism is 1 unit more than one and one half times the height.

   a) Determine the length of the prism if the volume is $30x^3 + 10x^2$.

   b) If the height is 6 cm, determine the width, length, and volume of the prism.

⟪ KEY IDEAS ⟫

- To factor a trinomial of the form $x^2 + bx + c$, first find two integers with
  – a product of c
  – a sum of b
  For $x^2 + 12x + 27$, find two integers with
  – a product of 27
  – a sum of 12
  The two integers are 3 and 9.
  Therefore, the factors are $x + 3$ and $x + 9$.

- To factor a trinomial of the form $ax^2 + bx + c$ (where b and c are integers), first factor out the GCF, if possible. Then, find two integers with
  – a product of $(a)(c)$
  – a sum of b
  Finally, write the middle term as a sum. Then, factor by grouping.
  For $8k^2 - 16k + 6$, the GCF is 2, so
  $8k^2 - 16k + 6 = 2(4k^2 - 8k + 3)$
  Identify two integers with
  – a product of $(4)(3) = 12$
  – a sum of -8
  The two integers are -2 and -6. Use these two integers to write the middle term as a sum. Then, factor by grouping.
  $2(4k^2 - 2k - 6k + 3) = 2(2k - 3)(2k - 1)$

- You cannot factor some trinomials, such as $x^2 + 3x + 5$ and $3x^2 + 5x + 4$, over the integers.

Example

Factor $6a^2 + 11a - 10$, if possible.

Solution

$\underline{6a^2} + \underline{11a} \underline{- 10}$	Ask: Are there two integers that when multiplied together equal -60 and when added together equal 11?
	Numbers that multiply to make 60.
	1, 60 4, 15
	2, 30 5, 12
	3, 20 6, 10
	Numbers that could add to make 11.
	4, 15
$6a^2 + 15a - 4a - 10$	Then, break up the middle term with these integers.
$3a(2a + 5) - 2(2a + 5)$	Factor by grouping.
$(3a - 2)(2a + 5)$	

A Practise

1. State the trinomial represented by each rectangle of algebra tiles. Then, determine the dimensions of each rectangle.

   a)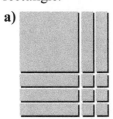

   b)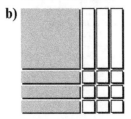

   c)

   d)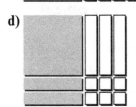

2. Use algebra tiles or a diagram to factor each trinomial.

   a) $2x^2 + 3x + 1$

   b) $3x^2 + 5x - 2$

   c) $6x^2 - 13x + 6$

   d) $2x^2 + 5x - 12$

   e) $4x^2 - 18x - 10$

   f) $3x^2 + 17x - 28$

3. If possible, identify integers with the given product and sum.

	Product	Sum
a)	12	8
b)	15	-3
c)	-4	-3

	Product	Sum
d)	24	-11
e)	-42	19
f)	12	-10

4. Factor, if possible.

   a) $y^2 + 8y + 12$

   b) $x^2 + 10x + 21$

   c) $a^2 - 19a + 90$

   d) $y^2 - 4y - 6$

   e) $m^2 - mn - 42n^2$

   f) $b^2 + 19b + 34$

5. Factor, if possible.

   a) $g^2 - 10g + 24$

   b) $n^2 - 15n + 26$

   c) $c^2 - 15c + 56$

   d) $s^2 - 7st + 10t^2$

   e) $f^2 - 6f + 12$

   f) $3v^2 + v - 2$

6. Factor, if possible.

   a) $2r^2 + 11r + 14$

   b) $2l^2 + 11l + 12$

   c) $3w^2 + 9w + 6$

   d) $10b^2 + 8b + 2$

   e) $y^2 + 5yz + 6z^2$

   f) $12a^2 + 19a + 4$

7. Factor, if possible.

   a) $2f^2 + 7f - 15$

   b) $r^2 + r - 110$

   c) $6b^2 + 6b - 3$

   d) $10m^2 - 17mn + 3n^2$

   e) $x^2 - x + 56$

   f) $9g^2 - 9gf + 2f^2$

   g) $6l^2 + 32l + 42$

   h) $5a^2 - 52a + 63$

B Apply

8. Determine at least two values of d that allow each expression to be factored.

    a) $a^2 + da + 6$

    b) $w^2 + dw - 15$

    c) $y^2 - dy + 18$

    d) $r^2 - dr - 14$

9. Determine two values of h that allow each expression to be factored.

    a) $6p^2 + hp - 1$

    b) $d^2 + hd + 8$

    c) $t^2 - ht + 56$

    d) $s^2 - hs - 20$

10. Determine two values of p that allow each expression to be factored.

    ☆**a)** $c^2 - pc - 10$

    b) $x^2 + pxy + 3y^2$

    c) $a^2 + pab + 14b^2$

    d) $v^2 - pvw + 35w^2$

11. Identify one value of r that will allow each expression to be factored.

    a) $10b^2 + 14b - r$

    b) $rs^2 + 19st + 3t^2$

    c) $d^2 - 8de + re^2$

    d) $5y^2 - 32y - r$

    e) $2x^2 - 11x - r$

    f) $3x^2 - 3x - r$

12. The penalty area on a soccer field can be represented by the trinomial $6x^2 - 2x - 48$.

    a) Factor the trinomial to determine a binomial that represents the width and the length of the area.

    b) The unit used for soccer fields is the yard. What are the dimensions of the area if $x = 12$ yd?

☆**13.** Determine the binomials that represent the width and length of each rectangle. Then, calculate the dimensions if $x = 12$ cm.

a)

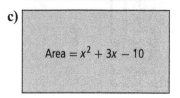

Area = $x^2 + 11x + 24$

b)

Area = $8x^2 + 6x - 2$

c)

Area = $x^2 + 3x - 10$

14. Carol throws a ball that will move through the air in a parabolic path due to gravity. The height, h, in feet, of the ball above the ground after t seconds can be modelled by the expression $h = -6t^2 + 27t + 15$.

    a) Write the formula in factored form.

    b) What is the height of the ball above the ground 4 s after it is thrown?

15. a) The area of a parallelogram is $A = x^2 + 13x + 42$. Determine the binomials that represent the height, h, of the parallelogram and the length, b, of its base. Then, calculate the dimensions of the parallelogram if $x = 18$ cm.

    b) Suppose the area of the parallelogram in part a) is $A = 6x^2 + 7x - 3$. What are the binomials that represent the height and length of the parallelogram? Determine the dimensions if $x = 18$ cm.

C Extend

☆**16.** The area of a rectangle can be represented by the expression $35 - 8x - 3x^2$, where x represents a positive integer. What are the possible values for the width and the length of the rectangle?

17. Determine one value of c that allows the trinomial $cy^2 + 36y - 18$ to be factored over the integers.

18. a) What shape might have an area represented by the expression $16s^2 - 48s + 36$?

    b) What in the expression indicates that shape?

    c) What are the factors?

19. The area of a certain shape can be represented by the expression $x^2 + 6x + 9$.

    a) Identify a possible shape.

    b) Write expressions for the possible dimensions of the shape you identified in part a).

    c) Suppose you have a second figure in the same shape as the shape you identified in part a) except that its area can be represented by the expression $4x^2 + 24x + 36$. Explain how you can use mental math to determine the dimensions of the second figure.

D Create Connections

20. A classmate is able to factor trinomials such as $n^2 + 7n - 44$ or $n^2 - 20n - 44$, but not trinomials such as $6n^2 + 13n - 5$ or $4n^2 - n - 3$. Explain the similarities and differences in factoring these two types of trinomials in sufficient detail that your classmate is then able to factor both types.

21. Write the completed statements after determining the answer in the blanks.

    a) When factoring a trinomial of the form $x^2 + bx + c$, such as $x^2 + 5x + 6$, one can ask, "What two integers have a sum of ____ and a product of ____?"

    b) The general form to show why part a) works, with each of m and n being any integer, is
    $$(x + m)(x + n) = x^2 + nx + \_\_ + mn$$
    $$= x^2 + (n + \_\_)x + mn$$

    c) Consider a trinomial of the form $ax^2 + bx + c$, such as $2x^2 + 13x + 15$. When factoring a trinomial of this form by grouping to break up the middle term, one can ask, "What two integers have a product of ____ and a sum of ____?"

    d) The general form to show why part c) works, with each of a, m, and n being any integer, is
    $$(ax + m)(x + n) = ax^2 + anx + \_\_ + mn$$
    $$= ax^2 + (an + \_\_)x + mn$$

22. A rectangular prism has the volume as shown.

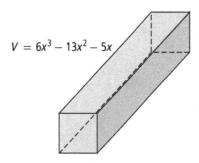

$V = 6x^3 - 13x^2 - 5x$

    a) Factor the expression that represents the volume to determine the length of each of the sides of the prism.

    b) If $x = 5$ cm, determine the lengths of the sides and the volume of the rectangular prism.

KEY IDEAS

- Some polynomials are the result of special products. When factoring, you can use the pattern that formed these products.

Difference of Squares:
The expression is a binomial.
The first term is a perfect square.
The last term is a perfect square.
The operation between the terms is subtraction.
The two binomial factors will be the square roots of the squares, connected by "+" and "−" signs.

$$x^2 - 25 = x^2 - 5$$
$$= (x - 5)(x + 5)$$

Perfect Square Trinomial:
The first term is a perfect square.
The last term is a perfect square.
The middle term is twice the product of the square root of the first term and the square root of the last term.
The trinomial is of the form $(ax)^2 + 2abx + b^2$ or $(ax)^2 - 2abx + b^2$.

$$x^2 + 16x + 64 = x^2 + 8x + 8x + 64$$
$$= x(x + 8) + 8(x + 8)$$
$$= (x + 8)(x + 8)$$

Example

Factor $y^2 + 28y + 196$, if possible.

Solution

$\underline{1}y^2 + \underline{28}y + \underline{196}$

$\sqrt{1} = 1$

$\sqrt{196} = 14$

$14 + 14 = 28$

This trinomial is a "perfect square." The first and last terms are squares, and the middle term is double the product of their square roots.

$y^2 + 14y + 14y + 196$
$y(y + 14) + 14(y + 14)$
$(y + 14)(y + 14)$
$(y + 14)^2$

A Practise

1. State the factors of the polynomial shown by each algebra tile model.

   a)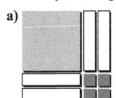

   b)

   c)

   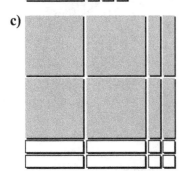

   d)

   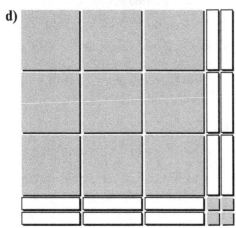

2. Solve.

   a) $(x + 5)(x - 5)$

   b) $(3r - 4)(3r + 4)$

   c) $5(w - 6)(w + 6)$

   d) $(2b - 7c)(2b + 7c)$

   e) $4(2x - 3y)(2x + 3y)$

   f) $2y(x + 3)(x - 3)$

3. Determine the product.

   a) $(y + 5)^2$

   b) $(3d + 2)^2$

   c) $(4m - 5p)^2$

   d) $2(e - 6f)^2$

   e) $3(2z - 4)^2$

   f) $(2x - 3y)^2$

4. Determine the missing terms that complete the factors or products.

   a) $n^2 - \underline{\quad} + 25 = (n - \underline{\quad})^2$

   b) $r^2 - \underline{\quad} = (r + \underline{\quad})(r - s)$

   c) $\underline{\quad} - 16d^2 = (3c - \underline{\quad})(3c + \underline{\quad})$

   d) $4s^2 + \underline{\quad} + 36 = (\underline{\quad} + \underline{\quad})^2$

   e) $4x^2 + \underline{\quad} + 4 = (2x + \underline{\quad})^2$

   f) $(4x - \underline{\quad})^2 = 16x^2 - \underline{\quad} + 4$

5. Factor each binomial, if possible.

   a) $a^2 - 100$

   b) $t^2 - 49$

   c) $x^2 + 4$

   d) $64 - h^2$

   e) $50g^2 - 72h^2$

   f) $9p^2 - 15r^2$

   g) $s^2 + 144$

   h) $72g^2 - 32h^2$

6. Factor each trinomial, if possible.

   a) $y^2 + 12y + 36$

   b) $x^2 - 6x + 9$

   c) $2z^2 + 12z + 18$

   d) $a^2 + 5a + 25$

   e) $144 - 48b - 4b^2$

   f) $9s^2 + 48s + 64$

   g) $25n^2 - 110n + 121$

   h) $5t^2 - 60t + 108$

7. Factor completely.

  a) $16d^2 - 64e^2$

  b) $27m^2 - 48$

  c) $-2k^2 - 24k - 72$

  d) $3c^3 + 51c^2 + 147c$

  e) $100a^2 - 25b^2$

  f) $s^3t - 18s^2t + 81st$

  g) $81g^4 - 16$

  h) $12lm^2 + 12lmn + 3ln^2$

B Apply

8. An error was made in factoring the following trinomials or binomials. Identify the error. Then, factor correctly.

  a) $4a^2 - b^2 = (2a - b)(2a - b)$

  b) $9x^2 + 6x + 1 = (3x + 1)(3x + 2)$

  c) $216 - 9y^2 = (16 - 3y)(16 + 3y)$

  d) $d^2 - 4e^2 = (d + 4e)(d - e)$

  e) $49 - 14h + h^2 = (h - 7)^2$

9. Determine the value(s) of c so that each trinomial is a perfect square.

  a) $w^2 + cw + 1$

  b) $9b^2 + cb + 16$

  c) $25 - cs + 36s^2$

  d) $16g^2 + cgh + 36h^2$

★10. The area of a rectangle can be represented by the trinomial $3x^2 + 24x + 48$.

Area $= 3x^2 + 24x + 48$

  a) Factor the trinomial completely.

  b) If the length of the rectangle is triple the width, use the factors in part a) to represent the length and width.

  c) If x represents 5 cm, what are the length and the width of the rectangle?

  d) Calculate the area of the rectangle and check your answer.

11. Using the difference of squares model, $a^2 - b^2 = (a - b)(a + b)$, use mental math to make the following calculations. Record your reasoning.

  a) $16^2 - 4^2$

  b) $7^2 - 27^2$

  c) $45^2 - 15^2$

  d) $113^2 - 13^2$

12. The diagram shows three concentric circles with radii r, $r + 3$, and $r + 5$.

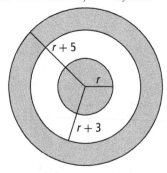

  a) Write an expression for the total area of the shaded regions.

  b) Factor this expression completely.

  b) If $r = 2$ cm, calculate the total area of the shaded regions. Give your answer to the nearest tenth of a square centimeter.

C Extend

★13. Factor $2r^5 - 4r^3 + 2r$ completely.

14. The volume of a rectangular prism is $x^3y + 16y^2 - 4x^2 - 4xy^3$.

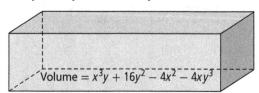

Volume $= x^3y + 16y^2 - 4x^2 - 4xy^3$

Determine expressions for the dimensions of the prism.

15. To determine the product of two numbers that differ by 6, square their average and then subtract 9.

a) Use this method to determine the following products.

(17)(23) = _____

(25)(31) = _____

b) Explain this method using a difference of squares.

16. The area of a square of side length a may be expressed as $A = 9b^2 - 12b + 4$. What is the area of a rectangle in terms of b if the length of the rectangle is $(a + 2)$ and the width of the rectangle is $(a - 2)$?

★**17.** Many road intersections use roundabouts to handle traffic flow. Some roundabouts contain a circular area with plants surrounded by a cement walkway.

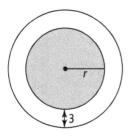

a) Write an expression that represents the area of the garden.

b) Write an expression that represents the area of the walkway and the garden. Then, expand that expression.

c) Using your answer from part a), write a simplified expression to determine the area of the walkway.

d) If $r = 8$ m, calculate the area of the walkway to the nearest tenth of a square metre.

D Create Connections

18. a) Continue the pattern to complete the table below.

$11^2 = 121$ $10 \times 12 = 120$

$12^2 =$ _____ $11 \times 13 =$ _____

$13^2 =$ _____ $12 \times 14 =$ _____

$14^2 =$ _____ $13 \times 15 =$ _____

_____   _____

b) How does the squared number compare with the product of the factors that are 1 less and 1 greater than the squared number?

c) Write and simplify algebraic expressions to show why this is the case.

19. Consider three squares having the dimensions shown.

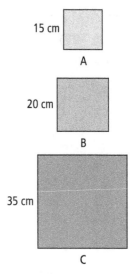

a) How much greater is the area of square C than the combined areas of square A and square B?

b) Explain how the answer can be calculated mentally.

5.1 Multiplying Polynomials

1. Draw an algebra tile diagram to model each product.

   a) $(x + 6)(x - 2)$

   b) $(s - 4)^2$

2. Determine the product and then combine like terms.

   a) $(a + 5)(a + 7)$

   b) $(y + 8)(y - 8)$

   c) $(2v + 4w)(5v + 6w)$

   d) $(2c - 1)(2c + 1)$

   e) $-2(r - 3s)(r + 3s)$

   f) $-(g + 4h)^2$

3. Multiply and then combine like terms.

   a) $(r + 4)(r^2 - 7r - 8)$

   ★**b)** $3p(4p - 5)(p - 7) - 5p(6p + 2)(2p - 8)$

4. Write a simplified expression to represent the area.

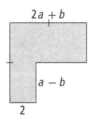

5. What expression represents the area of the white rectangle?

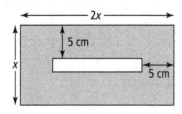

5.2 Common Factors

6. Determine the GCF of each set of terms.

   a) 30 and 45

   b) 84 and 112

   c) $72y$, 90, and $108y$

   d) $4d$ and $10d^2$

   e) $34a^2b$ and $51ab$

   f) $10rst$ and $15r^2s^2t^2$

7. Identify the LCM of the following pairs of numbers.

   a) 25 and 15

   b) 32 and 128

8. Identify the GCF of each set of terms.

   a) 18 and 27

   b) 13, 26, and 39

   c) $8ab^3$ and $12a^2b$

   d) $48xy^3z$ and $36x^2y^2z^4$

   e) $11m^6n^5$, $-22m^3n^9$, and $14m^5n^6$

9. Use algebra tiles or a diagram to factor each polynomial.

   a) $2x^2 + 4x$

   b) $x^2 + 3x$

10. Write an expression in fully factored form for the shaded area.

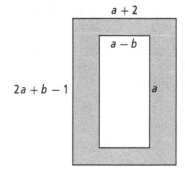

5.3 Factoring Trinomials

11. Use algebra tiles or a diagram to factor each trinomial.

   a) $x^2 + 2x - 8$

   b) $x^2 - 5x + 6$

   c) $2x^2 - 10x + 12$

   d) $4x^2 + 4x - 3$

12. Factor, if possible.

   a) $x^2 - 6x + 8$

   b) $x^2 - x - 20$

   c) $9x^2 - 12x - 5$

   d) $8x^2 - 10x - 2$

   e) $-6x^2 + 45x - 81$

   f) $-12x^3 + 2x^2 + 4x$

13. Given the volume of the rectangular prism as shown in the diagram, write the algebraic expressions that represent its dimensions. Then, calculate the dimensions of the rectangular prism if $x = 5$ cm.

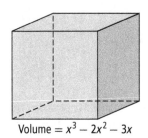

Volume = $x^3 - 2x^2 - 3x$

⋆14. The expression for a square field's area is as shown in the diagram. A fence borders the field, and also partitions it in half by running diagonally from corner to corner.

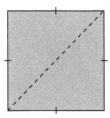

Area = $9x^2 - 42x + 49$

a) Write a factored and simplified expression to determine the perimeter of the field.

b) If $x = 20$ m, what is the length of the fence, to the nearest tenth of a metre?

5.4 Factoring Special Trinomials

15. Factor fully.

   a) $s^2 - 64$

   b) $d^2 - 121$

   c) $4h^2 - 25$

   d) $9n^2 - 81$

   e) $144 - 4b^2$

   f) $98c - 18cd^2$

16. Verify that each trinomial is a perfect square. Then, factor.

   a) $b^2 + 14b + 49$

   b) $144 + 24w + w^2$

   c) $16 - 24g + 9g^2$

   d) $64s^2 - 208st + 169t^2$

17. Factor fully.

   a) $81 - x^2$

   b) $10x^4y - 10y$

   c) $9x^2 + 30x + 25$

   d) $16x^2 - 100y^2$

   e) $x^4 - 16x^2 + 64$

   f) $-8x^2y - 24xy - 18y$

18. None of the following can be factored over the integers. In each case, explain why this is so.

   a) $s^2 - 12 - 36$

   b) $16m^2 + 25$

   c) $3y^2 - 30y + 25$

   d) $x^2 - 14x + 40$

Chapters 1–5 Cumulative Review

1. State the reading for point D on this imperial ruler as a mixed number in lowest terms. What is the distance from C to D? Show two ways to determine the answer.

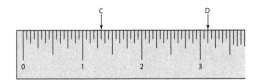

2. Calculate the area using the indicated unit. Round each answer to the nearest hundredth of a unit where appropriate.

a) unit: mm²

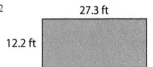

18 cm

10 cm

b) unit: m²

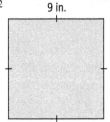

27.3 ft

12.2 ft

c) unit: cm²

9 in.

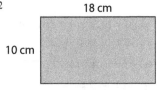

3. Triangles XYZ and RST are similar triangles. Calculate the lengths of the unknown sides.

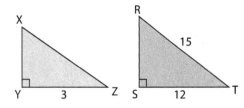

4. Calculate.

a) $\sqrt{169}$

b) $\sqrt[2]{(18)(8)}$

c) $\sqrt[3]{\dfrac{512}{27}}$

d) $\sqrt[3]{2744x^3}$

5. Determine the product and then combine like terms.

a) $(x + 4)(x + 2)$

b) $(b + 3)(b - 3)$

c) $(y - 8)(y + 8)$

d) $(4a + 7b)(2a - 3b)$

e) $-4(5x + 3y)^2$

f) $-(x + y)(x - y)$

6. What reading is shown on this imperial caliper? Name an object that could be this length.

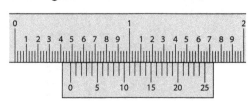

★7. Quentin wants to replace his shed. The current shed has a floor area of 11′ 8″ by 7′ 2″. The floor area of the shed Quentin wants to buy is 9.6 m². Which shed has the larger floor area? by what percent?

8. Draw and label a right triangle to illustrate each ratio. Then, calculate the measure of each angle to the nearest degree.

a) $\tan \beta = \dfrac{4}{3}$

b) $\tan \theta = \dfrac{2}{5}$

c) $\sin A = \dfrac{1}{3}$

d) $\cos X = \dfrac{7}{9}$

9. Simplify each expression. State the answer using positive exponents.

a) $[(-3x^{-7})(2x)]^3$

b) $\left[\dfrac{(5b)^2}{(4b)^{-2}}\right]^{-1}$

c) $\left[\dfrac{(-5)^{-1}}{(-5)^0}\right]^2$

d) $5[(6)^{-1}(6)^{-3}]^{-1}$

10. What is the circumference of the largest circle you could cut from a sheet of paper measuring 40 cm by 45 cm? What area of paper would you cut away? Round your answer to the nearest hundredth of a unit.

11. Calculate the volume, to the nearest hundredth of a unit, for each of the following.

a)

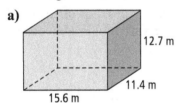

12.7 m
11.4 m
15.6 m

b)

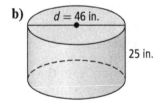

$d = 46$ in.
25 in.

c)

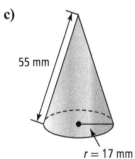

55 mm
$r = 17$ mm

d)

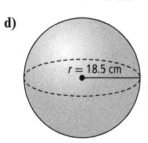

$r = 18.5$ cm

12. Evaluate each trigonometric ratio to four decimal places.

a) cos 30°

b) cos 48.6°

c) sin 90°

d) sin 45°

e) tan 72°

13. For each of the following, use the exponent laws to help identify a value for p that satisfies the equation.

a) $(x^p)^{\frac{-3}{2}} = x^6$

b) $\dfrac{b^p}{b^{-4}} = b^{\frac{3}{5}}$

c) $\left[\dfrac{16a^{-6}}{121}\right]^p = \dfrac{4}{11a^3}$

14. Factor the following polynomials.

a) $2x + 10$

b) $7z + 8z^2$

c) $a^3q + a^3r + a^3s$

d) $4m^5n - 12mn^3$

15. Kelsey wants to repaint her room. The walls are all 9′ high. The floor space measures 11′ 6″ by 10′ 9″. The room has one window measuring 4′ 6″ by 6′ and a door measuring 7′ by 3′.

a) Assuming that the room has no baseboards, what is the wall space Kelsey will need to paint?

b) Kelsey wants to apply two coats of paint. Each can of paint covers 32 m². How much paint will she need?

c) A can of paint costs $35.95. How much will it cost to paint the room?

16. A tree casts a shadow 11 m long. The angle measured to the top of the tree from the end of the shadow is 58°. What is the height of the tree? Express your answer to the nearest tenth of a metre.

17. From the beginning of 2001 to the beginning of 2009, the population of British Columbia increased at an average annual rate of 1.6%. This situation can be modelled with the equation $P = 3.9077(1.016)^n$, where P is the population, in millions, and n is the number of years since 2001.

   a) What do you think the number 3.9077 represents?

   b) Assuming the growth rate continues, what will be the population of British Columbia after 17.5 years?

   c) Assuming the growth rate was the same prior to 2001, what was the population of British Columbia at the beginning of 1997?

18. Factor, if possible.

   a) $x^2 + 6x - 27$

   b) $-2x^2 - 6x + 36$

   c) $-4x^2 + 30x - 14$

   d) $9x^2 + xy - 12y^2$

   e) $x^3 - 6x^2 - 7x$

19. Calculate the missing dimension for each. Where appropriate, round to the nearest hundredth of a unit.

   a) $V = 175.54 \text{ cm}^3$

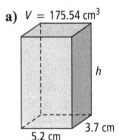

        h

        3.7 cm

     5.2 cm

   b) $V = 149.8 \text{ in.}^3$

     h

        7 in.

     7 in.

20. Solve for all unknowns for each triangle. Round your answers to the nearest hundredth of a unit.

   a) $\triangle ABC$, $BC = 5.3$ km, $\angle B = 90°$, and $\angle A = 52°$

   b) $\triangle DEF$, $\angle E = 90°$, $DE = 12$ m, and $EF = 16$ m

21. Express each radical as a power.

   a) $\sqrt[3]{4^5}$

   b) $\sqrt{(xt)^3}$

   c) $-2\sqrt[6]{a^{-5}}$

22. Convert each measurement to the unit specified.

   a) The distance from Banff to Medicine Hat is 227.8 mi. (kilometres).

   b) The height of the wooden roller coaster on the grounds of the Pacific National Exhibition in Vancouver is 75 ft (metres).

23. A right rectangular prism measures $20 \text{ cm} \times 7 \text{ cm} \times 8 \text{ cm}$. What is the radius of a sphere with the same volume? Round your answer to the nearest hundredth of a centimetre.

24. The angle of depression from the top of a 60-m lighthouse to a boat is 25°. Determine the distance from the base of the lighthouse to the boat to the nearest hundredth of a metre.

25. Convert each entire radical to an equivalent mixed radical.

   a) $\sqrt{200}$

   b) $\sqrt{1575}$

   c) $\sqrt[3]{128}$

   d) $\sqrt[4]{80}$

26. Determine two values of n that allow each polynomial to be a perfect square trinomial. Then, factor.

   a) $x^2 + nx + 36$

   b) $4x^2 + nx + 81$

Chapter 5 Extend It Further

For questions #1 to #5, choose the correct answer.

1. Simplify $(\sqrt{2} + \sqrt{6})(\sqrt{2} - \sqrt{6})$.

   A -8

   B -4

   C 4

   D 8

⭐**2.** The sum of the squares of 5 consecutive positive odd integers is 3685. What is the sum of the five numbers?

   A 121

   B 135

   C 147

   D 151

3. When $\frac{2}{5}$ is substituted into a polynomial, the expression is equal to zero. Which of the following is a factor of the polynomial?

   A $5x - 2$

   B $2x - 5$

   C $2x + 5$

   D $5x + 2w$

4. If x is a real number, what is the maximum value of $5 - (x - 7)^2$?

   A there is no maximum

   B 7

   C 5

   D 0

5. If x is a real number, what is the minimum value of the expression $(7 - x)^2 - 6$?

   A -6

   B 0

   C 6

   D there is no minimum

6. When $(6x^2 + kx + 13)$ is divided by $(3x - 4)$, the remainder is 1. Determine the value of k and the second factor.

7. Show that $(2m, m^2 - 1, m^2 + 1)$ is a Pythagorean triple, where m is an integer greater than 1.

⭐**8.** Calculate $\dfrac{2^{20} - 2^{16} + 15}{2^{16} + 1}$ without using a calculator.

9. Sammi simplified $\dfrac{x^2 - y^2}{(x + y)^2} = \dfrac{x - y}{x + y}$ by crossing out all the 2s. Even though her method was incorrect, show that she still has the right answer.

10. Identify the GCF and LCM of $a^2 - 6a + 9$ and $9 - a^2$.

11. Simplify $\dfrac{1 + a}{1 - \frac{1}{a^2}}$.

12. Without using a calculator, determine which is greater: $\sqrt{14} + \sqrt{12}$ or $\sqrt{15} + \sqrt{11}$.

13. $(x - 2)^2 - (x + 5)(x - 5) = A(x - 1) + B$. Solve for A and B.

14. Without using a calculator, explain how you can evaluate $\dfrac{2010}{(4321)(4319) - (4320)^2}$. What is the answer?

⭐**15.** If 1 is subtracted from the sum of the square of an odd number and the square of an even number, what is the greatest positive integer that will divide the difference?

16. Use the simplified expression for $\sqrt{(x + 1)^2 - (x - 1)^2}$ to evaluate $\sqrt{90\ 001^2 - 89\ 999^2}$. What is the value?

17. Determine all possible values of x for which $x^3 - x = 2009(x - 1)(x + 1)$.

Chapter 5 Study Check

Use the chart below to help you assess the skills and processes you have developed during Chapter 5. The references in italics direct you to pages in *Mathematics 10 Exercise and Homework Book* where you could review the skill. How can you show that you have gained each skill? What can you do to improve?

Big Idea	Skills	This Shows I Know	This Is How I Can Improve
Multiply polynomials using algebra tiles, diagrams, and algebra patterns *pages 86–89, 102, 104*	✓ Use algebra tiles to multiply binomials *pages 87, 102*		
	✓ Use the distributive property to multiply polynomial measurements *pages 87–89, 102*		
	✓ Apply binomial multiplication *pages 87–89, 102, 104*		
Determine factors of whole numbers and algebraic expressions *pages 90–103, 105–107*	✓ Identify the GCF and LCM of polynomials *pages 90–93, 102, 107*		
	✓ Factor polynomials using algebra tiles, using a table, and by modelling with a rectangle *pages 92–93, 95–97, 99–100, 102–103, 105–106*		
	✓ Factor polynomials using patterns such as the difference of two squares *pages 94, 98–101, 103, 105–107*		
	✓ Apply factoring to solve problems *pages 92–93, 96–97, 100–103, 107*		

Organizing the Ideas

In the Venn diagram below, show examples of factoring and multiplying. Be sure to represent these processes concretely, pictorially, and algebraically. How can you use this Venn diagram to show how factoring and multiplying are related?

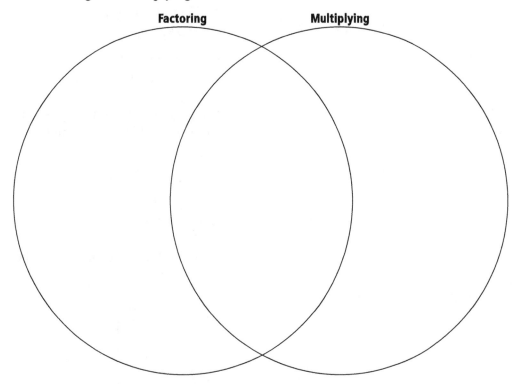

Factoring   **Multiplying**

Study Guide

Review the types of problems you handled in Chapter 5. What do you need to remember to help you do similar problems?

Things to Remember About Polynomials

Factoring   Multiplying

GCF and LCM   Concrete, Pictorial, Algebraic, and
                                   Special Patterns

Unit 2 Review

Multiple Choice

For #1 to #16, choose the best answer.

1. Which of the following numbers is *not* a perfect square?

   A 196

   B 625

   C 1000

   D 1600

2. The value of the expression $16^{-\frac{1}{2}}$ is

   A 4

   B $\frac{1}{4}$

   C $-\frac{1}{4}$

   D -4

3. Identify the irrational number.

   A $\sqrt{25}$

   B $\sqrt{10}$

   C $(\sqrt{5})^2$

   D $\frac{3}{4}$

4. The expression that represents the simplified form of the radical $-2\sqrt{24}$ is

   A $-8\sqrt{6}$

   B $-4\sqrt{6}$

   C $-12\sqrt{4}$

   D -24

5. The mixed radical $3\sqrt[3]{5}$ expressed as an entire radical would be

   A $\sqrt[3]{15}$

   B $\sqrt[3]{45}$

   C $\sqrt[3]{135}$

   D $\sqrt{45}$

6. Which equation best illustrates the use of the distributive property?

   A $2(3 + 3) = (2)(6)$

   B $3(7 - 4) = 9$

   C $4(7 + 5) = 4(5 + 7)$

   D $9(5 - 6) = (9)(5) - (9)(6)$

7. The trinomial $8m^2 - 19m + 6$ is the product of which two binomials?

   A $(8m - 3)(m - 2)$

   B $(4m - 3)(2m - 2)$

   C $(4m + 2)(2m + 3)$

   D $(m - 3)(8m - 2)$

8. What product does the algebra tile model show?

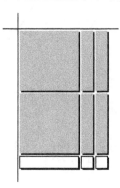

   A $2x^2 + 3x - 2$

   B $(2x + 1)(x - 2)$

   C $2x^2 + 4x - 2$

   D $(x + 2)(-1)$

9. Which expression represents the product of $(5a - 2)(3a^2 - 6a - 7)$?

   A $15a^3 - 17a^2 - 47a + 14$

   B $15a^3 - 30a^2 - 35a - 9$

   C $3a^2 - a - 9$

   D $15a^3 - 36a^2 - 23a + 14$

10. The greatest common factor in the set of terms $48x^3y^2(z-1)^3$ and $56x^2y^4(z-1)^2$ is

 A $8x^2y^2(z-1)$

 B $8x^2y^2(z-1)^2$

 C $4x^3y^4(z-1)^3$

 D $8x^3y^4$

11. One factor of the trinomial $x^2 - 19x - 20$ could be

 A $x - 5$

 B $x - 1$

 C $x + 1$

 D $x + 4$

12. Which of the following expressions shows the trinomial $12x^2 + 6x - 60$ written as a product of its prime factors?

 A $12(x - 6)(x + 10)$

 B $6(x + 2)(x - 5)$

 C $6(x - 2)(2x + 5)$

 D $2(3x - 6)(2x + 5)$

13. The expression $\frac{2a^6b^2c}{10a^2b^{-2}c}$ written in simplest form is

 A $5a^4b^4$

 B $\frac{a^4}{5}$

 C $\frac{a^4b^4}{5}$

 D $5a^8b^0c^2$

14. The algebra tiles in the diagram represent which expression?

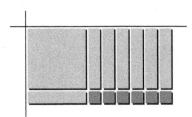

 A $(x^2 + 1)(x^2 + 6)$

 B $(x + 1)(x + 6)$

 C $x^2 + 7x - 6$

 D $(x - 1)(x + 6)$

15. When $\left(\frac{1}{2}r^2s^{-5}\right)\left(\frac{1}{4}r^3s^2\right)^{-1}$ is expressed in simplest form, the result is

 A $\frac{r^5}{8s^3}$

 B $\frac{2}{rs^7}$

 C $\frac{8s^3}{r^5}$

 D $\frac{1}{8r^6s^{10}}$

16. Which expression is equivalent to $\sqrt[3]{\frac{16a^6}{27}}$?

 A $\frac{4}{3}a^{\frac{1}{2}}$

 B $\frac{2a^2}{3}\sqrt[3]{2}$

 C $\frac{2a^3}{3}\sqrt[3]{2}$

 D $\frac{4a^3}{3}\sqrt[3]{\frac{1}{3}}$

Numerical Response

17. What must be the index of the radical to make the equation $\sqrt[?]{64} = \sqrt{16}$ true?

18. If the irrational numbers $\sqrt{12}$, $\sqrt[3]{12}$, $\sqrt[5]{4}$, and $\sqrt[4]{5}$ were placed on a number line, what would be their order from least to greatest?

19. What is the value of a when the expression $\left(8^{\frac{1}{2}}\right)^3$ is written in the simplified form $a\sqrt[i]{b}$?

20. The overall dimensions of the glass in one French door can be stated as $(2x - 1)$ by $(6x + 2)$. If $x = 25$ cm, what is the area of glass used in both doors?

21. Given the trinomial $x^2 + kx + 64$, what is the smallest positive value of k that would make the trinomial factorable over the integers?

22. What is the value of the missing factor, m, in the equality $25x^2 - 16 = (5x - m)(5x + m)$?

23. Use a calculator to determine the value of $32^{\frac{3}{5}}$.

24. Determine the value of -9^0.

25. When $(3x - 4)$ and $(-x + 6)$ are multiplied and expressed in the form $ax^2 + bx + c$, what is the value of b?

26. What is the value of r that would make the equation $\left(\dfrac{a^{-2}b}{a^2 b^{-1}}\right)^{-r} = \dfrac{a^2}{b}$ true?

27. Determine two values of k that allow each polynomial to be a perfect square trinomial. Then, factor.

  a) $a^2 + ka + 9$

  b) $y^2 + ky + 144$

  c) $16d^2 + kd + 64$

  d) $49r^2 + kr + 100$

28. Find three values of k such that the trinomial $6x^2 + kx + 15$ can be factored over the integers.

29. Determine one value of c that allows the trinomial $cy^2 + 36y - 18$ to be factored over the integers.

30. The expression $144 - 72s + 9s^2$ represents the area of a square. The variable s represents a positive integer. What are the possible values for the perimeter of the square?

31. The volume of a pyramid with a square base is $4x^3 - 12x^2 + x$. If the height of the pyramid is $3x$, what is the side length of the base expressed in terms of x?

Extended Response

32. A new Internet service is launched to allow subscribers to download and share music online. The growth in the number of people who signed up in the first four months can be modelled by the equation $U = 1(26.7)^t$, where U is the number of users and t is the number of months since the service started.

  a) Using the model equation, how many people subscribed to the service in the first four months of release?

  b) If the subscription pattern continued according to this model, how many subscribers would there be after five months?

  c) Could the number of subscribers continue to grow at this rate for one year? Explain.

33. The partial solution for the multiplication of two polynomials is shown.

  $(5a - 3)(4a + 7)$
  $= 5a(4a + 7) - 3(4a + 7)$
  $= 20a^2 + 7 - 12a + 7$
  $= 8a^2 + 14$

  a) Identify and explain the error in the solution for the polynomial multiplication.

  b) Provide a correct product for the multiplication.

  c) Verify your solution for the product by substituting $a = 2$.

34. Demonstrate algebraically the complete factorization of the following trinomials.

  a) $x^2 + 8x + 16$

  b) $x^2 + 8x + 15$

  c) $3y^2 - 6y - 24$

  d) $2a(b - 7) - 5(b - 7)$

  e) $x^2 - 121$

  f) $64x^2 - 196y^2$

35. The algebra tiles in the diagram represent the multiplication of two binomials.

a) Write an expression that represents each binomial.

b) Complete the diagram to represent the product of the two binomials.

c) Express the product of the two binomials in simplified form.

36. The length of one edge of a cube is represented by $2k - 1$.

a) Write an expression in simplest form for the volume of the cube.

b) A smaller cube with a side length of $k + 1$ is removed from the larger cube. Write an expression in simplified form for the volume that remains.

37. Determine the area of the shaded region. Express the answer in simplest form.

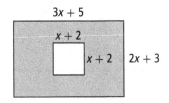

38. Consecutive integers are integers that follow each other in order.

a) Would it be possible to factor $ax^2 + bx + c$ if the values of a, b, and c were positive consecutive integers?

b) Find three consecutive integers for a, b, and c that would make the trinomial $ax^2 + bx + c$ have binomial factors.

39. Factor $2r^5 - 4r^3 + 2r$ completely.

40. The Golden Ears Bridge in British Columbia, which opened in 2009, spans the Fraser River.

a) Factor the expression $20x^2 - 97x - 15$ to find the binomials that represent the length and width of the bridge.

b) Calculate the length and width of the bridge if $x = 40$ m.

41. You have been asked to factor the expression $84ab^2 - 54abc + 6ac^2$.

a) What is the first step when factoring this expression?

b) What are the factors?

42. a) Consider the following three factored differences of squares.

$9x^2 - 9 = (3x + 3)(3x - 3)$
$16m^2 - 64 = (4m - 8)(4m + 8)$
$36d^2 - 100 = (6d - 10)(6d + 10)$

In each case, is the product of the factors the original expression?

b) Are these differences of squares factored correctly? Explain.

c) If your answer to part b) is no, factor the expressions correctly.

d) Suggest a guideline to follow in cases of this type to ensure that the difference of squares expression has been factored completely.

43. a) Rewrite the polynomial $3y^2 + cy - 12$, replacing the variable c with an integer so that it is possible to remove a common factor from the rewritten polynomial.

b) What do we know about the integer that replaces the variable c?

Chapter 6 Linear Relations and Functions

6.1 Graphs of Relations

- When comparing two quantities, straight lines are used to indicate a constant change in the relationship. Curves are used when the rate of change is not constant. Horizontal lines are used if one quantity is not changing relative to a change in the other quantity.

Example

Travel guides often provide climate information, such as the graph shown here. Travellers can use this information to plan their trips.

a) What might the curves represent? Can you think of more than one explanation? What would the points on the curves represent for each of your explanations?

b) What assumptions can you make about the climate and location based on the shapes of the curves?

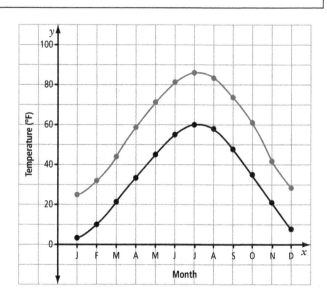

Solution

a) There are several possible explanations for having two curves:
- Both lines could represent temperatures for the *same* location. The upper curve would represent the average high temperature and the lower curve would represent the average low temperature. The dots on the curve would represent the average high and low temperature for each month.
- The curves could represent the average monthly temperatures for two *different* locations. Again, the dots would represent the average temperature for the month in each location.
- The curves could represent the record high and low temperatures in a single location, or compare record temperatures in two locations. The points on the curve would represent the record temperatures each month. But this explanation is unlikely. It is doubtful that the record temperatures would follow such a consistent pattern, represented by a smooth curve.

b) We can make several assumptions about the location from the shapes of the curves:
  - If the curves represent two locations, the shapes and curves are similar enough that the two locations are probably both in the same area or in a similar climate zone. The location represented by the lower curve would be in a cooler location, perhaps further north or at a higher elevation.
  - Considering that the highest temperatures occur in July, the location(s) are in the northern hemisphere.
  - The slopes of the curves show a significant difference between winter and summer temperatures. But the differences are not extreme, as they might be in many places on the Canadian prairies. The average temperature curves here would be steeper. Similarly, in locations on the west coast, such as Victoria, British Columbia, where there is a more moderate climate, the curves would be flatter.

A Practise

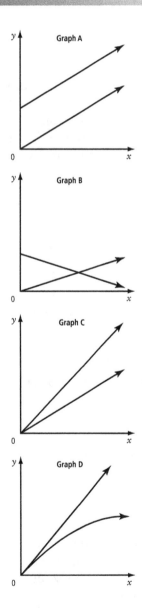

1. Describe in words how each of the following situations can be drawn on a graph where time is on the horizontal axis and distance is on the vertical axis.

  a) walking at a slow, constant rate away from the school

  b) running at a constant rate toward the school

  c) walking quickly away from the school, but constantly slowing the rate

  d) standing still a distance from the school

  e) running away from the school at a constant rate, and then suddenly turning around and walking toward the school at a constant rate

  f) walking away from the school to a point, and then walking in a perfect circle around the school, all the while keeping a constant pace

2. For the pairs of lines in each graph

  a) state what is similar

  b) state what is different

  c) give a real-life scenario that could be represented by the graph

⭐**3.** For each scenario, draw a graph that is appropriate to the context, representing the activity in relation to time. Label the axes and provide a scale, if possible.

a) eating a bowl of cereal for breakfast

b) reading a novel from start to finish

c) washing a load of laundry

d) flying from Calgary to Edmonton

4. a) Give two scenarios in which you would use only line segments to represent the relation.

b) Give two scenarios in which you would use only curves to represent the relation.

5. A student is drawing a graph, plotting time, t, in relation to cost, C, as shown. On his first attempt, the student produced a curve. After reconsidering the graph, he changed it to produce a line segment.

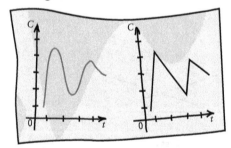

a) Explain the similarities that you see between the two relations.

b) Why might the student have made this change?

B Apply

⭐**6.** The directions for cooking a particular type of rice say to add 1 cup of rice to 2 cups of boiling water, and then simmer the rice until the water is absorbed. Graph the cooking process from the time the pot is put on the stove, to the time the rice is cooked. Hint: Put time along the horizontal axis, and choose what will be represented on the vertical axis.

⭐**7.** In long track speed skating, skaters race around an oval track. Skaters start the race at the beginning of a long straightaway. They then race around the track for a number of laps, finishing near the end of the straightaway on which they started the race. Create a graph showing time versus distance from the finish line for a skater who skates at a constant pace for 2 laps. Explain why the symmetry occurs in your graph.
Hint: Draw a diagram of this situation and trace the path of a skater.

8. Kari drew the distance-time graph below to represent a scenario described by their teacher:
- time A to B: drive away from home accelerating to 50 km/h
- time B to C: continue away from home driving at 50 km/h
- time C to D: continue away from home accelerating to 100 km/h
- time D to E: continue away from home driving at 100 km/h
- time E to F: continue away from home decelerating to 0 km/h
- time F to G: spend 30 minutes in the mall
- time G to H: drive straight home at 40 km/h

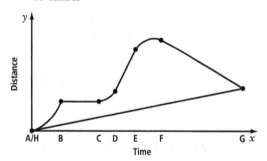

a) For sections that you think are drawn incorrectly, state what you think is wrong. Then, draw the graph correctly.

b) Draw a speed-time graph for the scenario.

9. Les is the marketing manager at Noble Leather Goods in Winnipeg, Manitoba. His company is considering a new line of belts. Les's boss has asked him to present the business model for the new line. Les produced a simple model for cost (amount of money paid out) and revenue (amount of money received) relative to the number of belts made and sold. The graph shows his predictions for the first batch of belts to be produced.

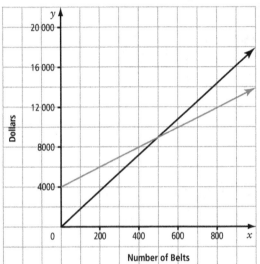

a) Les forgot to label the lines on his graph. Which of the lines represents revenue and which represents cost? Explain.

b) What is the initial cost (the amount of money to start the production)?

c) How many belts does the company have to make and sell to break even (revenue exactly equals cost)?

d) What are the cost and revenue at the breakeven point?

e) What is the predicted profit (the difference between revenue and cost) if the company makes and sells 1000 belts?

f) How much would the company lose if, after setup, management decide not to produce any of these belts?

g) What is the projected selling price of one belt?

C Extend

10. Use the graph below to discover or verify facts regarding the relationship between temperatures measured in Celsius and those measured in Fahrenheit.

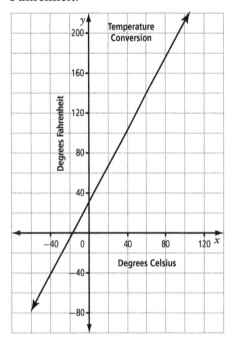

D Create Connections

11. Supply and demand is a model that economists use to show how prices are determined for goods and services. This graph represents this model. The point where the two curves intersect represents where supply is equal to demand. Many factors affect the location and steepness of the curves, and where they intersect. Research supply and demand and try to determine three of these factors.

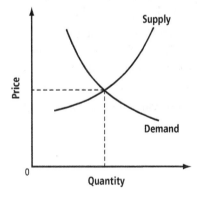

KEY IDEAS

- Relations can be represented in a variety of ways. You can use words, equations, tables of values, ordered pairs, or graphs.

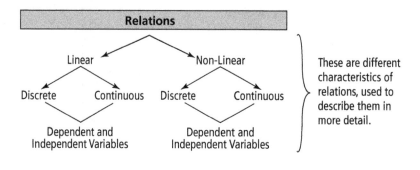

Example

Consider the following two relations:

a) Amir's height above the water after springing from a diving board

b) the cost for downloading music from a site that charges $1.25 per song

For each relation, decide
- if it is linear or non-linear
- if it is discrete (made up of values that are not connected on a graph) or continuous (made up of values that are connected by a line on a graph)
- what the dependent and independent variables are
- the best way to represent it (words, an equation, an ordered pair, a table of values, or a graph)

Solution

a) Amir's height above the water is non-linear over time. His height increases when he springs from the board, and then decreases as he plunges toward the water.

The data for this relation is continuous because for every instant of time that Amir is in the air there is a corresponding positive height above the water.

Amir's height above the water depends on how long he has been in the air. So, time is the independent variable and height is the dependent variable.

A graph is the best means of representing this situation. The dependent variable is always on the y-axis, so height is on the y-axis and time is on the x-axis.

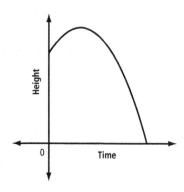

b) The cost per song is constant, so this is a linear relationship.

This is a discrete relation because you cannot purchase part of a song. Each additional song purchased results in a unique purchase price.

The cost for the songs depends on the number of songs you download. So, the independent variable is number of songs, and the dependent variable is cost.

You could represent this relationship with a series of ordered pairs, a table of values, or a graph. Each would be clear. The equation $C = 1.25(n)$, where C is the cost and n is the number of songs downloaded, is probably most effective in this case. This equation makes it easy to determine the cost of any number of downloads.

A Practise

1. Convert each relation to a set of ordered pairs and a graph

a)

x	2	3	5	8	12
y	0	2	4	6	8

b)

a	10	8	6	4	2
b	2	4	6	8	10

★2. Convert each relation to an equation and a table with 4 pairs of values. Is the relation discrete or continuous? Explain why.

a) the cost of buying concert tickets priced at $23.00 each

b) two positive numbers whose product is 24. Hint: Don't forget decimals. How would your answer change if you considered whole numbers only?

3. Given the following tables of values, determine which relations are linear and which are non-linear. Describe each relation in words.

a)

x	−3	−2	−1	0	1	2	3
y	6	2	0	0	2	6	12

b)

x	−3	−2	−1	0	1	2	3
y	−5	−3	−1	1	3	5	7

c)

x	−3	−2	−1	0	1	2	3
y	6	5	4	3	2	1	0

d)

x	−3	−2	−1	0	1	2	3
y	3	2	1	0	−1	−2	−3

★4. Determine if each formula is linear or non-linear by representing it in any of the other forms of a relation. Indicate which variable is independent, and which is dependent.

a) the area, A, of a circle with radius r: $A = \pi r^2$

b) the perimeter, P, of an equilateral triangle with side s: $P = 3s$

c) the number of diagonals, d, of a polygon with n sides: $d = \dfrac{n(n-3)}{2}$

5. Predict which of the following are linear relations. Use a graphing calculator or graphing software to check your prediction.

a) $y = \pi x$

b) $y = \dfrac{x}{9}$

c) $y = x\sqrt{x}$

d) $y = (x + 1)(x - 1)$

B Apply

6. A video store charges $4.50 to rent a new release movie. The store's owner wants to put up a poster to make it easy for customers to determine the cost of renting multiple movies.

   a) Name the independent and dependent variables in this situation.

   b) Describe the pricing policy in words.

   c) Write an equation to represent the cost of renting 1 through 5 movies.

   d) Show a set of ordered pairs for renting 1 through 5 movies.

   e) Make a table of values that shows the cost of renting 1 through 5 movies.

   f) Make a graph for renting 1 through 5 movies. Does it make sense to show the cost of renting zero movies?

   g) From the 5 ways you represented the relation, which do you think would be the best way for the owner to present the information on the poster? Explain.

7. A pizza restaurant sells 4 sizes of pizza: 8 in., 10 in., 12 in., and 14 in. All the pizzas are round and the size is the pizza's diameter.

   a) Make a table of values comparing diameter to the area of the pizza.

   b) Which is the independent variable?

   c) Graph the four ordered pairs.

   d) Is this data linear or non-linear?

   e) Is this data continuous or discrete?

8. The pizza restaurant owner from question 7 charges $10 for his 8 in. pizza. He wants to price the others so that the relation between the *area* of the pizza and the price is linear.

   a) What are the radii of the four different pizzas?

   b) Determine the areas of the four pizzas, rounded to the nearest square inch. Hint: Remember that $A = \pi r^2$.

   c) What is the price per square inch of the 8 in. pizza?

   d) What should the owner charge for each of the other pizzas, rounded to the nearest $0.10?

   e) Do you think it is a good idea for the restaurant owner to price his pizzas this way?

   f) Is the relation between the area of the pizza and the price linear or non-linear? discrete or continuous?

   g) Is the relation between the diameter of the pizza and the price linear or non-linear?

★9. Jogging is usually defined as running at approximately 10 km/h, or 6 min/km.

   a) Is this a linear or non-linear relation?

   b) Make one table of values with time in hours versus distance for running up to 5 hours. Make another table of values with distance versus time in minutes for running up to 8 km. Which table gives a better representation of jogging speed?

   c) What would be the independent variable for graphing a jogging speed of 10 km/h?

   d) Make a graph for jogging 10 km at a 6 min/km.

   e) Is your graph continuous or discrete? Why?

10. The advertising manager for a small Alberta computer company believes that in any given month there is a linear relation between the amount of money spent on advertising, a, and the number of computers sold, n. In September, the company spent $8000 on ads and sold 12 000 computers. Then, in October, it increased the advertising budget to $20 000 and sold 18 000 units.

a) Set up a grid and plot the two points in the question. Hint: Determine the independent and dependent variables to decide what each axis represents. Mark both axes from 0 to 40 000.

b) Draw a line through your two points and use the graph to predict the number of computers the company would sell if the advertising budget were increased to $40 000.

c) How much would the company need to spend on ads to sell 21 000 units?

d) How many computers would the company sell if it did no advertising?

C Extend

11. The length from your wrist to your elbow is approximately the same as the length of your foot. Measure 5 of your friends' arms and feet to determine if this is true.

a) Place this data in a table of values.

b) Graph the 5 pairs of data.

c) In this question, which measurement is independent? dependent?

d) Is the data linear or non-linear?

e) Is the data discrete or continuous?

12. When grocery shopping, the costs of many items can be represented by a linear relationship.

a) List 5 grocery items having costs that are linear in nature.

b) What is the dependent variable in all of these examples?

c) Are your examples discrete or continuous?

d) Name one item from a grocery store for which the cost would always be discrete. Name one for which the cost would always be continuous.

e) Name a grocery item that may have non-linear pricing structure.

★**13.** Make a table of values for each of the following using $x = \{0, 1, 2, 3, 4, 5\}$.

- $y = 3x(x - 2)$
- $y = 5(x - 2)$
- $y = \dfrac{(x - 2)}{2}$

Predict whether each equation is a linear function by considering whether the y-value is increasing or decreasing by a constant amount. Then, graph each equation using technology and explain how the graphs support your predictions.

D Create Connections

14. When looking at a given relation, describe a way that you can predict whether the relation is linear or non-linear if the relation is

a) an equation

b) a table of values

c) a set of ordered pairs

d) a graph

e) given in words

15. When you are graphing a relation, is there a simple way to decide whether to connect the data points to make the graph continuous or to leave the points discrete? Discuss with a classmate, and then explain in your own words.

<< **KEY IDEAS** >>

- The domain of a relation is the set of all numbers for which the independent variable is defined.

- The domain of a relation may also be described as:
  – the set of first coordinates in a set of ordered pairs
  – the possible values in the first column of a table of values
  – the possible values on the horizontal axis of a graph.

- The range of a relation is the set of all numbers for which the dependent variable is defined.

- The range of a relation may also be described as:
  – the set of second coordinates in a set of ordered pairs
  – the possible values in the second column of a table of values
  – the possible values on the vertical axis of a graph.

- The domain and range can be expressed in different ways.

Words	All integers equal to or greater than -2 and less than or equal to 3
Number Line	$\xleftarrow{\quad}\!\!\bullet\!\!-\!\!\bullet\!\!-\!\!\bullet\!\!-\!\!\bullet\!\!-\!\!\bullet\!\!-\!\!\bullet\!\!\xrightarrow{\quad}$ $-2\ -1\ \ 0\ \ \ 1\ \ \ 2\ \ \ 3$
Interval Notation	$[-2, 3]$
Set Notation	$\{n \mid -2 \leq n \leq 3, n \in I\}$
A List	$\{-2, -1, 0, 1, 2, 3\}$

Example

The annual ecoENERGY for Vehicles Awards, administered by Natural Resources Canada's Office of Energy Efficiency, are presented for the most fuel-efficient vehicles for the current model year. One popular midsized car has a 77 L fuel tank. Its fuel efficiency is listed as 7.0 L/100 km in the city, and 5.5 L/100 km on the highway.

a) State the domain for the distance this car can travel for both city and highway driving. Express the domains in words and in set notation.

b) State the range of the fuel tank.

c) Draw one graph with two consumption lines on it: one for city driving and another for highway driving. Provide appropriate labels and scaling for the axes.

d) What does the portion of the graph between the two lines represent?

Solution

a) For city driving, the vehicle can travel 100 km for every 7.0 L of fuel. On a full tank of fuel it can travel $\frac{77}{7} \times 100$, or 1100 km. So, the domain of distance travelled for city driving is from 0 km, if the car is simply left idling, to 1100 km, or $\{d \,|\, 0 \le d \le 1100\}$. For highway driving, the vehicle can travel 100 km for every 5.5 L of fuel. On a full tank of fuel it can travel $\frac{77}{5.5} \times 100$, or 1400 km. So, the domain of distance travelled for highway driving is from 0 km to 1400 km, or $\{d \,|\, 0 \le d \le 1400\}$.

b) The range of the fuel tank is from 0 L to 77 L of fuel, or $\{L \,|\, 0 \le L \le 77\}$.

c) The independent variable, plotted on the x-axis, is distance driven. The dependent variable, plotted on the y-axis, is the amount of fuel used.

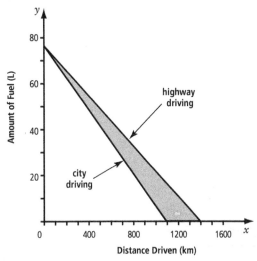

d) The shaded area between the two lines represents all of the possible distances and litres of fuel consumed by a mixture of city and highway driving, if the car is always kept within the predicted consumption rates.

A Practise

1. Draw a number line to represent each set of numbers. Hint: On a number line a solid dot means that the value is part of the set and an open circle means that the value is not part of the set.

   a) $\{-2, 0, 2, 4, 6, 8, 10\}$

   b) $\{x \,|\, x < 5\}$

   c) your age from grade 1 until now

   d) all the factors of 15

   e) the square roots of all perfect squares from 1 to 100

   f) $(-3, 4]$

2. For each relation, state the domain and range.

   a) buying less than 5 cans of soup that cost $0.38 each

   b) listing all coin names from $0.01 to $2.00 and their value

   c) the squares of numbers 1 through 10

   d) the cost for you and up to 5 of your friends to attend a concert at $35.00 per ticket

   e) the granola bars you can buy with a $10.00 bill, at $1.50 per bar

---

3. Give the domain and range of each graph. Use both set notation and interval notation.

a)

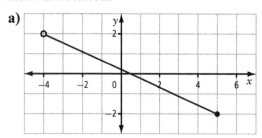

b)

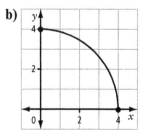

c)

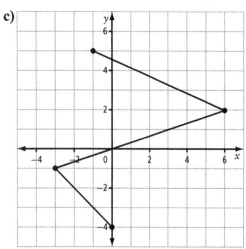

d)

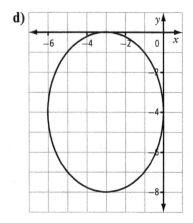

e)

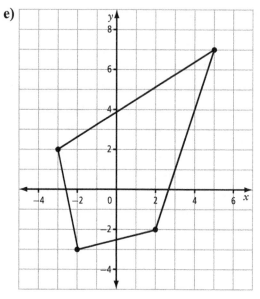

f)

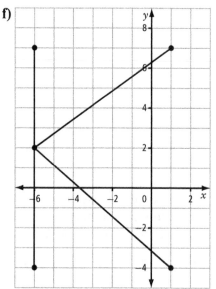

★**4.** The cost, C, of filling up a car with gasoline and buying an $8.00 car wash can be expressed by the equation $C = 0.92n + 8.00$, where n is the number of litres of gasoline purchased. The car has a gas tank capacity of 40 L.

a) What is the domain of this equation?

b) What is the range of costs for this problem?

c) Which is the independent variable? Explain why.

B Apply

5. The table presents the internal temperatures that particular foods must reach in order to achieve the specified doneness and be considered safe to eat.

Food	Internal Temperature
Beef, veal, and lamb—medium-rare	63 °C (145 °F)
Beef, veal, and lamb—medium	71 °C (160 °F)
Beef, veal, and lamb—well done	77 °C (170 °F)
Pork (pieces and whole cuts)	71 °C (160 °F)
Poultry—pieces	74 °C (165 °F)
Poultry—whole	85 °C (185 °F)
Egg dishes	74 °C (165 °F)

a) State the range of temperatures for safe cooking of the foods in the table.

b) Is it better to use set notation or a list for the range, considering the context of the information?

c) What would be the danger of using either set notation or a list for the temperatures?

6. Draw a graph with each domain and range in the table. The graph can be made up of line segments or curves. Hint: Remember that a round bracket means that the value is not part of the set, while a square bracket means that the value is part of the set.

	Domain	Range
A	(−3, 5)	(1, 5)
B	(−3, 5]	[1, 5)
C	[−3, 5]	[1, 5]
D	[−3, 5)	(1, 5]

7. The domain of a relation is given as (−8, 6), while its range is $\{y \mid -4 \leq y < 5\}$. Set up a grid with the x-axis and y-axis marked from −10 to 10. Draw a rectangle that the relation would lie within when graphed. When drawing the rectangle, use a solid line if the graph could be on it, and a dashed line if the graph only comes up to it, but does not include it.

8. Which among the items listed could have a domain or range of either [−12, ∞) or (−∞, 0]? Hint: Remember that ∞ is used when there is no end point.
   - a line
   - a line segment
   - a ray
   - an oval

C Extend

9. Draw a graph of any relation that has

   a) an identical domain and range

   b) only one domain element

   c) only one range element

10. Does a relation always need a domain? Explain.

D Create Connections

11. Create a relation where the range is $\{0 \text{ cm} \leq y \leq 20 \text{ cm}\}$.

12. In professional sports, there are many relationships that have an independent and dependent connection. For example, the players in a golf tournament represent a domain, and the scores they post for each round or for the tournament are the range. Provide two or more different examples, stating what the domain and range would be for each example.

6.4 Functions

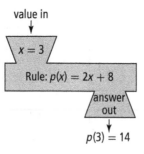
Example

To distinguish between relations and relationships that are functions, and those that simply relate in an input/output manner, you must consider all the possibilities of the domain. If it is possible to have more than one output for one unique input, the relation is not a function.

Carefully consider the relationships listed in the table. State whether the relation is a function or not, and explain why. Sketch a graph of a function and a non-function from the questions. Show how the vertical line test supports your answer.

Relationship	Domain Input	Range Output
a) Working for $8/h	Hours worked in one week	Amount earned in that week
b) Putting footwear on before leaving the house	Choosing a pair of shoes	Leaving with something on your feet
c) Baking bread	Temperature of the oven	Height loaf rises
d) Studying for a math exam	Number of hours	Mark on exam
e) Squaring a number, and then adding 3	Any number you choose	Example: 28

Solution

a) Function: it can be represented by $E(n) = 8(n)$, where E is earnings, and n is the number of hours worked. Each unique number of hours worked generates only one amount of money earned. This is supported by the vertical line test. Any vertical line, such as the one shown, will pass through one and only one point on the graph.

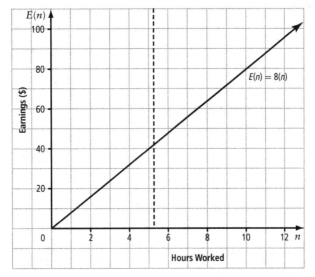

b) Function: you could wear runners, sandals, or any other footwear, and you would have something on your feet. Having footwear on produces only one output.

c) Not a function: the loaf may rise the same amount using different oven temperatures. Also, baking at the same temperature could produce a loaf of different heights.

d) Not a function: you could have studied for 3 hours for several exams and received different marks on some or all of them. The vertical line test shows that this is not a function because the vertical line at $x = 3$ passes through the mark received in both Math and French.

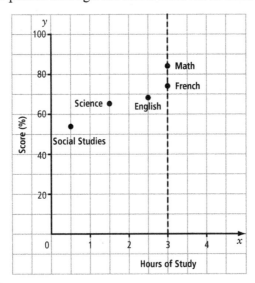

e) Function: for $S(n) = n^2 + 3$, both 5 and −5 produce 28. It is still a function if two different inputs produce the same output. It is not a function only if one input produces more than one output.

A Practise

⭐**1.** For each relation, state whether it is a function. For those that are not functions, indicate where or explain why it is not a function. Where possible, use the vertical line test as part of your explanation.

a) (1, 3) (2, 4) (3, 5) (4, 3) (2, 1)

b) (5, 1) (4, 1) (3, 1) (2, 1) (1, 1)

c) (9, 3) (4, 2) (1, 1) (9, −3) (4, −2) (1, −1)

d)

Name	Shoe Size
Andrew	10
Nathan	11
Joel	12
Aaron	13
Simeon	12

e)

Name	Sibling
Anika	Jared
Anika	Joel
Anika	Nathan
Carolyn	Aaron
Carolyn	Simeon

f)

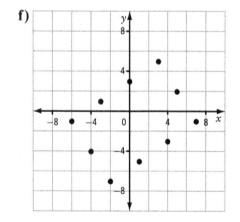

g)

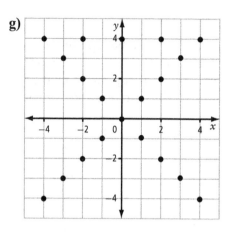

2. The formula for calculating the value of $500.00 deposited into an account earning 8% compounded annually for n years is $A = 500(1 + 0.08)^n$. Write this formula using function notation.

3. Anika is helping her parents make plans for her grandparents' 50th wedding anniversary. The cost for the banquet is given by the function $W(p) = 26p + 1200$, where W is the cost in dollars, and p is the number of people attending. Write this function as a formula in two variables.

4. If $z(a) = -3a + 7$, determine the following:

a) $z(-3)$

b) $z(2)$

c) a, if $z(a) = 7$

5. If $t(n) = 5 + (n - 1)(4)$, determine the following:

a) $t(1)$

b) $t(20)$

c) n if $t(n) = 41$

B Apply

★**6.** For a single membership to FITFIT Health Club, you pay a $55 initiation fee upon enrollment and then $35 a month. The cost of belonging to the club is represented by the function $P(m) = 35m + 55$.

  a) What is the independent variable in this relation and what does it represent?

  b) What would it cost for you to belong to this health club for one year?

  c) After how many months of membership would you have spent $1000?

  d) The cost of belonging to one of FITFIT's competitors is represented by the function $P(w) = 10w + 100$, where w represents the number of weeks you are enrolled. Which club would be cheaper to belong to for one year?

7. For each function, calculate $f(5)$.

  a) $f(x) = 3x - 6$

  b) $f(x) = -2x + 11$

  c) $f(x) = \dfrac{(x + 5)}{2}$

  d) $f(x) = \frac{1}{4}(3 - x)$

8. Determine the value of x for the functions in question 7, when $f(x) = -15$.

9. Graph the following functions for the given domain. For what x-value does the graph go through $(x, 7)$?

  a) $g(x) = 3x - 5$, for the domain $\{-5, -4, -3, -2, -1, 0, 1, 2, 3, 4, 5\}$

  b) $h(x) = -2x + 7$, for the domain $\{-5, -4, -3, -2, -1, 0, 1, 2, 3, 4, 5\}$

  c) $j(x) = 7(x - 4)$, for the domain $\{-5, -4, -3, -2, -1, 0, 1, 2, 3, 4, 5\}$

C Extend

10. Graphing calculators or software can find many function values quickly. Enter the function $f(x) = 3x - 11$ into either of these technologies. Determine the smallest value of x that produces

  a) a prime number

  b) a multiple of 8

  c) a number larger than 100

  d) the largest negative number

11. A science teacher asks students to write an equation to represent the temperature, T, measured in °C, of a liquid cooling on a laboratory table. The equation is to be in the form $T(m) = (A)m + (B)$, where m is the number of minutes since the liquid was placed on the table. Determine the values for A and B so that the equation produces the values in the chart.

Time (min)	Temperature (°C)
4	74
7	62
13	38
16	26

D Create Connections

12. Using the Internet, find the addresses in Canada associated with the following postal codes:

  • V0B 2P0

  • R2J 3E7

  • T0H 2P0

  a) Are any of these postal codes and the address(es) associated with them a function? Explain.

  b) Use the Internet to search your own postal code. Is your postal code and address a function? Explain.

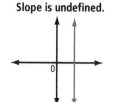

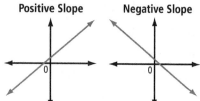

KEY IDEAS

-
  Positive Slope Negative Slope Slope is 0. Slope is undefined.

- The slope of a line is the ratio of the rise to the run.

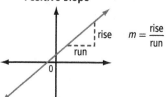

Positive Slope

$m = \dfrac{\text{rise}}{\text{run}}$

- The slope of a line can be determined using two points on the line, (x_1, y_1) and (x_2, y_2).

$m = \dfrac{y_2 - y_1}{x_2 - x_1}, x_2 \neq x_1$

- If you know one point on the line, you can use the slope to find other points on the line.

- The slope gives the average rate of change.

Time (s)	Distance (m)
1	4
2	7
3	10
4	13
5	16
6	19
7	22

Time (s)	Distance (m)
1	4
3	10
5	16
7	22

Rate of change $= \dfrac{\Delta d}{\Delta t}$

Rate of change $= \dfrac{3}{1}$

The average rate of change is 3 m/s.

Rate of change $= \dfrac{\Delta d}{\Delta t}$

Rate of change $= \dfrac{6}{2}$

Rate of change $= \dfrac{3}{1}$

The average rate of change is 3 m/s.

Example

Use two methods to determine the slope of each of the following
line segments:

- A(−4, 1) and B(1, 6)
- C(3, 5) and D(6, −3)
- E(−3, −4) and F(4, −4)

Solution

Method 1: Graph each line segment. Then, for each segment, connect the two endpoints by
drawing a right triangle.

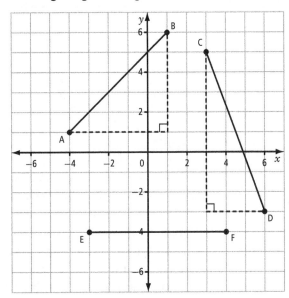

Slope, m, is equal to $\frac{\text{rise}}{\text{run}}$. Determine the *rise* by counting the units along the height
of the triangle, and the *run* by counting the units along the base of the triangle.

For AB:
$$m = \frac{5}{5}$$
$$= 1$$

For CD:
$$m = \frac{-8}{3}$$

For EF:
$$m = \frac{0}{7}$$
$$= 0$$

Method 2: Use the slope formula, $m = \frac{y_2 - y_1}{x_2 - x_1}$, $x_2 \neq x_1$.

Substitute values to determine each slope.

For AB:
$$m = \frac{(6 - 1)}{(1 - (-4))}$$
$$= \frac{5}{5}$$
$$= 1$$

For CD:
$$m = \frac{(-3 - 5)}{(6 - 3)}$$
$$= \frac{-8}{3}$$

For EF:
$$m = \frac{(-4 - (-4))}{(4 - (-3))}$$
$$= \frac{0}{7}$$
$$= 0$$

A Practise

1. Create a three-column table with the headings Positive Slope, Negative Slope, and Zero Slope. Place each line segment in the diagram in the appropriate column.

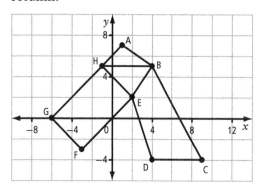

2. Determine the slope of each line segment in the diagram.

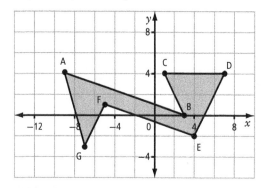

3. A 45° line has a slope of +1 or −1. Use the slope formula to determine the slope of a line passing through each pair of points. Is the line steeper or less steep than 45°?

a) (3, 5), (1, 4)   b) (6, 5), (1, −3)

c) (2, −3), (−2, 6)   d) (−4, 5), (−1, 4)

4. Graph a line from each given point back to the origin. Determine the slope of each line.

a) (4, −2)   b) (−3, 0)

c) (7, 3)   d) (−2, −5)

5. For each given point and slope, calculate what the next ordered pair *to the right* of the point will be. If possible, try to do this mentally, without graphing. The first one is done for you.

Given Point A(x, y)	Slope	Next Point to the Right of A
(3, 5)	$-\frac{1}{2}$	(5, 4)
(3, 5)	$\frac{2}{3}$	
(−3, 7)	$\frac{3}{7}$	
(2, −5)	$-\frac{4}{1}$	
(0, −4)	$\frac{5}{4}$	

B Apply

6. Building codes and safety concerns dictate slopes in structures. According to Canadian building codes, a wheelchair ramp cannot have a slope greater than $\frac{1}{12}$. When designing a mall, an architect has designed a central courtyard that is 84 cm higher than the corridor approaching it. How far away will a wheelchair ramp have to begin, in metres, if it is to have the steepest allowable slope?

7. Phoebe has asked her mother to help her save money for a vacation. At the end of each work week, Phoebe gives her mother the same amount of money to hold for her. At the beginning of last year, Phoebe had given her mother $255.00. At the end of the current year, the total had risen to $1035.00. Determine the average rate of change in her vacation savings. What does the number represent?

★**8.** Snowcoach rides on the Columbia Icefields travel from a side moraine onto the glacier via a road that is constantly shifting due to ice movement and melting. The road is the steepest passenger route in the world, at a 32% grade.

   a) If the elevation increase on this road is 130 m from start to finish, what would be the horizontal distance travelled (referred to as the shortest run)?

   b) State the slope of the road in terms of $\frac{\text{rise}}{\text{run}}$.

   c) Use the Internet to research how long the actual road is.

9. On the first day of school in September, Jodi measured the length of her hair. She found that her longest hair was 36 cm. At the end of the school year, in June, Jodi measured her hair again. Her longest hair at this time was 48.5 cm. What is the average rate of change of hair length per month?

10. Adult fingernails grow at a yearly rate of change. Lee Redmond set a Guinness world record when she grew her nails for about 29 years without cutting them. Added together, her nails were 8.65 m long. Assuming that she grew her nails for exactly 29 years, what was the average rate of change in her nails' length, per month, to the nearest centimetre?

C Extend

11. In 1981, the population of Saskatoon, Saskatchewan, was 154 210. In 2006, its population had grown to 202 340. Determine the average annual rate of growth and, assuming this rate of growth will continue, project Saskatoon's population in 2021. Research the most recent population of Saskatoon that you can, and see if it matches your projection.

★**12.** A business wants to decide whether employees should use their own vehicle for company business or use a rental car. An employee uses a rental company that charges a daily rate plus a mileage charge, with no free kilometres.

	Trip A	Trip B
Days	3	3
Distance Driven (km)	425	680
Rental Charge	$301.25	$365.00

   a) Determine the rate the car rental company charges per kilometre.

   b) Determine the daily rate for a car rental.

   c) Determine if it would be cheaper for the company to pay employees $0.50/km to use their own car.

   d) Will your answer for part c) ever change if the trip is always 3 days long? Explain.

D Create Connections

13. Slope is defined as rise over run. Draw three different positive-sloped line segments on a piece of graph paper, with each one steeper than the previous. Make sure your lines go through ordered pairs that you can identify. For each segment, calculate the slope and then calculate the fraction $\frac{\text{rise}}{\text{run}}$. Explain why, as the line gets steeper, it becomes more apparent why the fraction is in the form $\frac{\text{rise}}{\text{run}}$.

14. Graph a series of lines that start at the origin and have the slope ratios found in the table. Notice that the numerator (rise) is consecutive even numbers and the denominator (run) is consecutive prime numbers. If you kept this pattern going, would you ever draw a line with a slope of 0? Explain.

Rise	2	4	6	8	10	12	14	16	18
Run	2	3	5	7	11	13	?	?	?

Chapter 6 Review

6.1 Graphs of Relations

1. Darlene goes to the grocery store. She buys milk, granola, deli ham, bananas, and bread.

   a) Draw a map of a grocery store and label the locations of the five items. Draw a dashed line representing the route Darlene would take to pick up these items.

   b) What units would best be used to describe Darlene's speed and time as she walks around the store?

   c) Draw a graph of Darlene's speed versus time from the time she enters the store until the time she leaves. Be sure to consider any stops she makes or time she spends waiting for service. On your graph, explain each section and label the point on the graph at which each item is picked up.

2. Serge and Colette plan to bike from Banff, Alberta to Castle Mountain along the Bow Valley Parkway. The graph shows the elevation change over the distance of their route.

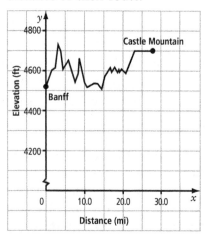

   a) Choose two 5-mile sections of the graph, and describe what the riding might be like in these sections.

   b) Which 5-mile section is the easiest? most difficult? Explain your choice.

6.2 Linear Relations

3. For each of the following scenarios, would the graph of the relation be discrete or continuous? Explain.

   a) the number of tickets written by a police officer

   b) time on the ice during a hockey game for one player

   c) number of characters used in a text message

4. Insurance for Priority Mail International parcels is calculated according to this table.

Fee	Insured Amount (not over)
$1.75	$50
$2.25	$100
$2.75	$200
$4.70	$300
$5.70	$400
$6.70	$500
$7.70	$600
$8.70	$675 max

   a) Assign a variable to each quantity. Which is independent and which is dependent?

   b) Is this relation linear or non-linear? Explain.

   c) Graph the relation. Note that one fee charge covers a range of insured amounts.

6.3 Domain and Range

5. State the domain and range of each relation.

   a) {(3, −7), (5, 5), (3, −4), (0, 0), (3, 11)}

   b) All the factors of 10. The answers when the factors are divided back into 10.

6. Change from the given notation to the other notation for each domain given.

Set Notation	Interval Notation
$\{x \mid 3 < x < 7\}$	
	$[-5, 0]$
$\{x \mid -13 \le x < 27\}$	
	$(-\infty, 5]$

7. Provide the domain and range of each relation in set notation.

a)

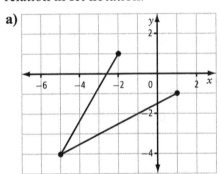

b)

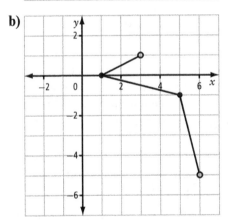

6.4 Functions

8. Consider the function $f(x) = 2x^2 - 2x + 1$.

a) Calculate $f(0)$.

b) Calculate $f(-1)$.

c) Calculate $f(3)$.

d) Considering that $f(-2)$ and $f(3)$ result in the same value, is $f(x)$ still a function? Explain.

e) Graph $f(x)$. Does the function pass the vertical line test?

9. The formula for the volume of a cube is $V = s^3$. The formula for the volume of a sphere is $V = \frac{4}{3}\pi r^3$.

a) Write each formula in function notation.

b) Complete the table for a sphere that fits exactly inside the given cube.

Side Length of Cube	Volume of Cube	Volume of Sphere
10 cm		
20 cm		
30 cm		
40 cm		

6.5 Slope

10. Find the slope between pairs of points. Before calculating, predict if the slope will be positive, negative, zero, or undefined.

a) P(11, 3), Q(2, 8)

b) M(−6, 0), N(0, 8)

c) J(−3, 5), K(−2, −7)

11. Jordan kept track of all his training distances while bike riding one week in July. His goal was to ride farther each day to build endurance.

	July Date	Distance (km)
Monday	4	60
Tuesday	5	80
Wednesday	6	110
Thursday	7	120
Friday	8	100

a) Plot this data on a graph.

b) Calculate the slopes of the four line segments that connect these points.

c) What does the slope represent?

d) What does a negative slope mean?

Chapters 1–6 Cumulative Review

1. This ruler shows imperial units. State the reading for point D on this ruler as a mixed number in lowest terms. What is the distance from C to D? Show two ways to determine the answer.

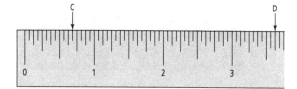

2. What are the dimensions of a cube that has a volume of 17 576 cm³?

3. Multiply and then combine like terms.
   a) $(a - 2)(a^2 + 7a + 4)$
   b) $3b(4b - 2)(b + 3) - b(4b + 8)(3b - 1)$

4. What reading is shown on this metric caliper? Name an object that could be this length.

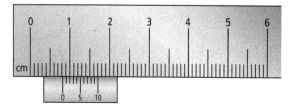

5. Jasmine is planning a family reunion. She rents a hall for $200 for the evening. She estimates that she will need $10 per person to pay for food and entertainment. Consider the relationship between the cost of the evening and the number of people in attendance.
   a) Is this a linear or non-linear relationship? Explain how you know.
   b) Assign a variable to represent each quantity in the relation. Which variable is the dependent variable? Which is the independent variable?

c) Create a table of values for the following number of guests: 0, 10, 20, 30, 40, 50, and 100.

d) Is the data discrete or continuous? Explain how you know.

e) Is this relation a function? Explain how you know.

f) Graph the relation.

6. Triangles ABC and ADE are similar. If AC = 5 cm, BC = 3 cm, and DE = 9 cm, determine the length of CE.

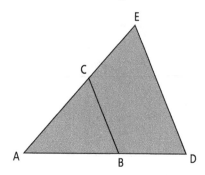

7. Lucy wants to invest in a guaranteed investment fund (GIF) that pays 6% interest per year, compounded monthly. To guarantee her interest rate, she must keep her money in the account for three years. This relationship can be modelled by the equation $A = P\left(1 + \frac{0.06}{12}\right)^{36}$, where P is the principal (money invested) and A is the amount of money after a certain length of time.

   a) If Lucy invests $1500, how much money will she have after three years?

   b) How much interest has Lucy earned in three years?

   c) If Lucy reinvests the original principal plus the interest she earned, and leaves it in the GIC for another three years, how much will the investment be worth?

8. The average centre-to-centre distance from Earth to the moon is 384 403 km. It takes the moon 27.32 days to orbit Earth. In this time it will have travelled approximately 2 455 260 km.

   a) Draw and label a diagram of Earth and the path of the moon.

   b) How far does the moon travel along its orbit in one day, to the nearest hundredth of a kilometre?

   c) What is the speed of the moon's orbit, to the nearest hundredth of a kilometre per hour? Hint: Use the formula, speed = distance/time.

9. Calculate the volume and surface area of the following prisms, to the nearest hundredth of a unit.

   a)

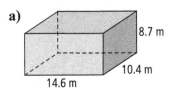

8.7 m
10.4 m
14.6 m

   b)

$d = 38$ in.
7 in.

   c)

8.7 mm
1.4 mm

   d)

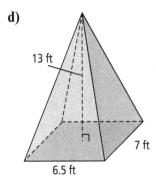

13 ft
7 ft
6.5 ft

   e)

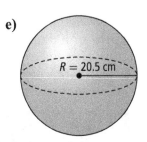

$R = 20.5$ cm

10. Draw and label a right triangle to illustrate each ratio. Then, calculate the measure of each angle to the nearest degree.

   a) $\tan \beta = \frac{9}{2}$ **b)** $\tan \theta = \frac{1}{6}$

   c) $\sin A = \frac{8}{9}$ **d)** $\cos X = \frac{2}{7}$

11. Use the exponent laws to simplify each expression. Leave your answers with positive exponents.

   a) $(x^4)\left(x^{-\frac{3}{4}}\right)$ **b)** $(16^{-0.25})^5$

   c) $\dfrac{(k^{-3})^{\frac{1}{4}}}{\left(k^{\frac{2}{3}}\right)^{-5}}$ **d)** $\left(8p^3\right)^{-\frac{1}{3}}\left(p^{-\frac{4}{3}}\right)$

12. Factor the following polynomials.

   a) $3x(x - 5) + 9(x - 5)$

   b) $4yz - 2y + 10z - 5$

   c) $14a^2b^2 - 21ab$

   d) $12x^3y - 9x^2y + 3xy$

13. Factor completely.

   a) $x^2 - x - 56$

   b) $-4x^2 + 16x - 48$

   c) $6m^2 + 7mn + 2n^2$

   d) $35s^2 + 59s + 18$

14. Factor completely.

   a) $c^2 - 121$

   b) $1 - 81y^4$

   c) $27h^2 - 147$

   d) $y^2 + 4y + 4$

   e) $121 - 110x + 25x^2$

15. An advertising company wants to put this picture on the front of a Banff brochure. The picture needs to be enlarged to 4 in. by 6 in. Is this possible? Explain, using measurements and ratios.

16. A ladder truck is needed for the fire department to reach the top of a building. If the ladder is 89 ft long and the top of the building is 56 ft higher than the bottom of the ladder, determine the angle of the ladder. Give your answer to the nearest degree.

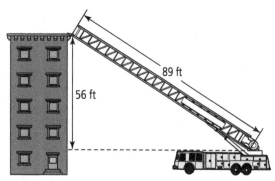

17. Write each power as an equivalent radical.

a) $c^{\frac{4}{3}}$

b) $(18t^3)^{\frac{2}{5}}$

c) $\left(\frac{m^2}{12}\right)^{0.25}$

18. A balloonist is flying at an altitude of 1456 m. She measures her angle of depression to the landing spot to be 19.5°. If she begins her descent at that moment in a straight diagonal line, how far away, to the nearest hundredth of a kilometre, is she from her landing site?

19. Give the domain and range of each relation. Use words, interval notation, and set notation.

a)

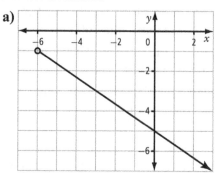

b)

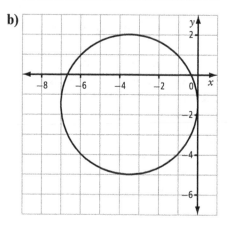

20. Solve for all unknown sides and angles for each. Round your answers to the nearest hundredth of a unit.

a) For ΔDEF, AB = 12 km, ∠B = 90°, and ∠A = 52°.

b) For ΔDEF, ∠E = 90°, DF = 18 m, EF = 11 m.

21. Use the slope formula to determine the slope of the line passing through each pair of points.

a) (−2, 6) and (12, 18)

b) (3, −5.6) and (−0.7, 1.8)

Chapter 6 Extend It Further

1. Point $(4, -1)$ is one endpoint of the diameter of a circle with centre $C(-3, 4)$. What are the coordinates of the other point?

   A $(-11, 8)$ **B** $(-11, 7)$

   C $(-10, 9)$ **D** $(-9, 9)$

2. Points $(5, 0)$, $(3, 8)$, and $(-1, 4)$ are three vertices of a parallelogram. The fourth vertex is in quadrant II. What are its coordinates?

   A $(-1, 11)$ **B** $(-3, 7)$

   C $(-3, 12)$ **D** $(-4, 12)$

3. A linear function, f, includes the ordered pairs $(-3, 2)$ and $(3, 6)$. What is $f(-1)$?

   A $3\frac{1}{3}$ **B** $2\frac{2}{3}$

   C $1\frac{1}{3}$ **D** $1\frac{1}{6}$

4. What is $g(3)$ if g is a linear function, where $g(1) = 2$ and $g(-1) = 8$.

   A 6   **B** 4

   C 0   **D** -4

5. If $f(x)$ means the reciprocal of x, what is the value of x that satisfies $f(x) = f(2) + f(3) + f(6)$?

   A 6   **B** 3

   C 2   **D** 1

★6. Two sides of a triangle are 12 cm and 19 cm. The length of the third side is a natural number, x. The perimeter of the triangle is represented by $T(x)$. Determine the domain and range.

7. Show that $(-3, 0)$, $(0, 6)$, and $(0, -1.5)$ are the vertices of a right triangle.

8. If $g(x) = 10x + 2009$, determine the domain for which $g(x) \geq 0$.

9. A function is defined to be $f(ab) = f(a) + f(b)$. If $f(3) = x$ and $f(4) = y$, what is the value of $f(144)$ in terms of x and y?

10. What is the ordered pair of real numbers, (x, y), that satisfy $y = 6x - 12$, but do not satisfy $\frac{y}{x-2} = 6$?

★11. Draw the line $4x - 3y + 12 = 0$ using the domain $\{x \mid -4 \leq x \leq 2\}$. Calculate the area of the shape bounded by the line and the two axes.

12. Determine the slope of the straight line joining the two given points.

   a) (a, b) and (ma, mb), where $m \neq 1$

   b) (a, b) and (b, a)

13. Consider the lines in the figure.

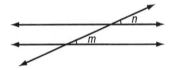

   a) Measure the angle m to the nearest degree, using a protractor. Create triangles and measure sides. Express the slope of the line as rise over run.

   b) Explain why angle n has the same properties as angle m.

14. A circle has a radius of 5 units. $P(x, y)$ is a point on the circle.

   a) Use a compass to construct the circle with $(0, 0)$ as the centre.

   b) If $x = 3$, find the value(s) of y.

   c) If $y = -4$, find the value(s) of x.

   d) Each point (x, y) on this circle is represented by the equation $x^2 + y^2 = 25$. Is this a relation or a function?

Chapter 6 Study Check

Use the chart below to help you assess the skills and processes you have developed during Chapter 6. The references in italics direct you to pages in *Mathematics 10 Exercise and Homework Book* where you could review the skill. How can you show that you have gained each skill? What can you do to improve?

Big Idea	Skills	This Shows I Know	This Is How I Can Improve
Make and explain graphs of data *pages 114–121, 134*	✓ Graph a set of data *pages 114–116, 120–121, 134*		
	✓ Interpret a graph of data *pages 114–121, 134*		
Identify, describe, and represent linear relations in a variety of ways, and determine and apply the characteristics of linear relations *pages 118–126, 130–136, 138–139*	✓ Represent relations in a variety of ways *pages 118–121*		
	✓ Justify whether or not a given relation is linear *pages 118–121, 134, 136*		
	✓ Differentiate between discrete and continuous data *pages 118–121, 134, 136*		
	✓ Identify the independent and dependent variables in a relation *pages 118–121, 124, 129, 134, 136*		
	✓ Determine and express the domain and range of a relation *pages 122–126, 134, 138–139*		
	✓ Determine and classify slopes of line segments *pages 131–132, 135, 138*		
	✓ Calculate and apply slope to solve problems and graph linear relations *pages 132–133, 135, 139*		

Big Idea	Skills	This Shows I Know	This Is How I Can Improve
Identify and explain the differences between relations and functions, and apply function notation to linear functions *pages 118–129, 135*	✓ Sort relations into functions and non-functions *pages 126–129, 135–136, 139*		
	✓ Apply function notation to determine range and/or domain values for a given function *pages 118–126, 135, 139*		
	✓ Apply function notation to graph linear functions *pages 127–129, 135–136, 139*		

Organizing the Ideas

In the concept definition map below, indicate the key characteristics of linear relations and functions. Show how to tell a linear relation from a non-linear relation. Show how function notation is used.

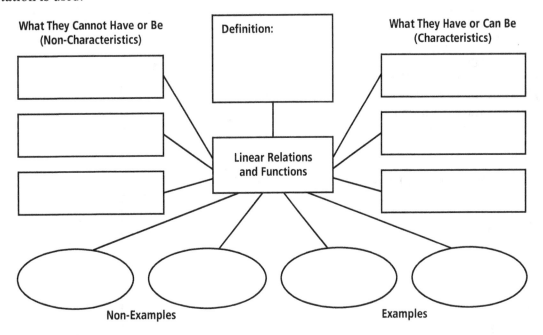

Study Guide

Review the types of problems you handled in Chapter 6. What do you need to remember to help you do similar problems? Use a file card to write a series of brief notes outlining what you need to remember about:
- graphs
- linear relations and functions
- function notation
- applications of slope

Chapter 7 Linear Equations and Graphs

7.1 Slope-Intercept Form

- The slope-intercept form of a linear equation is
  $y = mx + b$, where m represents the slope and
  b represents the y-intercept.

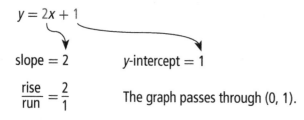

slope = 2 y-intercept = 1

$\dfrac{\text{rise}}{\text{run}} = \dfrac{2}{1}$ The graph passes through (0, 1).

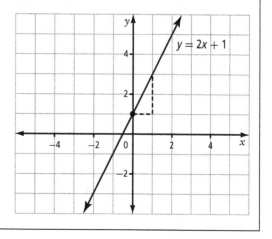

Example

Consider the given graph.
  a) What is the slope of the line?
  b) What is the y-intercept?
  c) What is the equation of the line in
    slope-intercept form?

Solution

a) Using the points (0, 3) and (1, 1), the
   slope is

$$m = \frac{\text{rise}}{\text{run}}$$
$$m = \frac{y_2 - y_1}{x_2 - x_1}$$
$$m = \frac{1 - 3}{1 - 0}$$
$$m = \frac{-2}{1}$$
$$m = -2$$

The slope is −2.

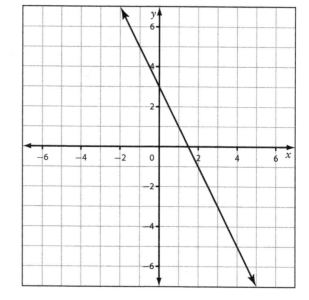

b) The line crosses the y-axis at the point (0, 3). Therefore, $b = 3$.

c) Substitute the values $m = -2$ and $b = 3$ into the slope-intercept form of an equation.
   $y = mx + b$
   $y = -2x + 3$

A Practise

1. What are the slope and y-intercept of each line?

   a) $y = \frac{1}{2}x - 2$

   b) $y = -4x + 3$

   c) $y = x$

   d) $y = 0.75x + 3.5$

★2. Convert each of the following into slope-intercept form. Then, state the slope and y-intercept.

   a) $x + y = 7$

   b) $y - 4x = 12$

   c) $5x + 2y = 10$

   d) $x - 3y - 12 = 0$

3. Given the slope and y-intercept, write an equation of the line in slope-intercept form.

   a) $m = 4; b = -1$

   b) $m = -\frac{1}{2}; b = 7$

   c) $m = \frac{2}{3}; b = -2$

   d) $m = 0.5; b = 0$

   e) $m = -5; b = 1$

   f) $m = 1; b = \frac{4}{5}$

4. Draw the graph of each line using the slope and y-intercept. Use graphing technology to check your graphs.

   a) $y = 2x + 5$

   b) $y = 3x - 1$

   c) $y = x + 6$

   d) $y = -x$

   e) $x - 3y - 9 = 0$

   f) $y + 4 = 5x$

5. What are the slope and y-intercept of each line? Write the equation of each line in slope-intercept form.

   a)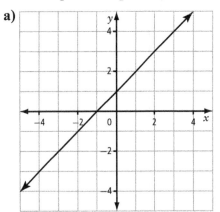

   b)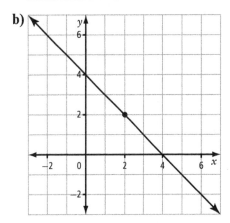

   c)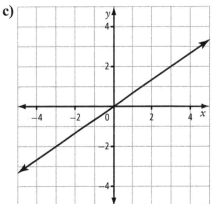

d)

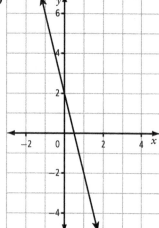

e)

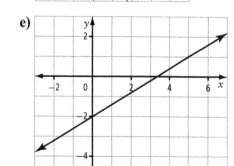

f)

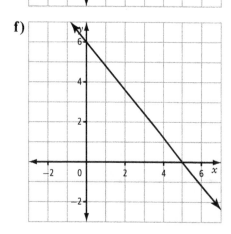

6. An equation of a line is $y = \frac{1}{2}x + b$. What is the value of b if the line passes through the given point?

a) $(12, 8)$ **b)** $\left(-3, \frac{1}{2}\right)$

7. An equation of a line is $y = mx - 8$. What is the value of m if the line passes through the given point?

a) $(4, 0)$ **b)** $(-3, 4)$

B Apply

8. Mr. Wong's class is holding a raffle to raise money for earthquake relief efforts. The class buys a pair of Edmonton Oilers hockey tickets for $250 as the prize. The raffle tickets are going to be sold for $2 each.

   a) Write a linear equation to represent the money raised based on the ticket sales, x, and the cost of the prize.

   b) What is the slope of the line? What does it represent?

   c) What is the y-intercept? What does it represent?

   d) How many tickets does the class need to sell if they want to raise $300.00?

9. The Rabbit Hill Snowboard and Ski Resort is sponsoring a freestyle snowboard competition. Each competitor pays an entry fee of $75. The winner gets $600.

   a) Write a linear equation, in slope-intercept form, to show the relationship between the number of contestants, x, and the money generated from the competition, y.

   b) How much money will organizers make if 5 contestants enter? 15? 25?

   c) How many competitors need to enter for the organizers to break even?

10. Ernesto needs to rent a paint sprayer. His friend Daniela rented one and paid $15/h plus a fixed charge. Daniela could not remember the fixed charge, but remembered that she rented the sprayer for 4 hours and paid $85.

   a) What is the fixed charge?

   b) Write an equation in slope-intercept form to represent the cost, y, for x hours to rent a paint sprayer.

   c) What is the y-intercept? What does it represent?

   d) Describe the graph.

★11. The following table relates the number of litres left in a car's fuel tank to the distance travelled.

Distance (km)	Fuel (L)
0	60
50	56
100	52
150	48
200	44

a) Draw a graph of the relation.

b) What is the slope of the line? What is the y-intercept?

c) Write the equation in slope-intercept form.

d) What does the y-intercept represent?

e) After how many kilometres will the tank be empty?

12. The cost of printing programs for the school play, y, is a fixed charge of $200 for the artwork, plus $0.25 for each program.

a) Build a table of values to represent the cost of printing 50, 100, 150, 200, and 250 programs.

b) Draw a graph of the relation.

c) What is the slope? What does it represent?

d) What is the y-intercept? What does it represent?

e) Write the equation in slope-intercept form.

f) How many programs can be printed if the school wants to spend $350 on programs?

C Extend

★13. The following table shows the linear relationship between temperatures in degrees Celsius and temperatures in degrees Fahrenheit.

°C	°F
−50	−58
−10	14
5	41
20	68

a) Sketch the graph of the line through the points.

b) What is the slope?

c) What is the y-intercept? What does it represent?

d) Write the equation in slope-intercept form, where x represents degrees Celsius and y represents degrees Fahrenheit.

e) Write the inverse of your equation in part d), where x is replaced with y, and y is replaced with x. Write this equation in slope-intercept form.

f) Calculate the conversions using your graph or equation.

$-40\,°C = $ _____ °F

$100\,°F = $ _____ °C

$0\,°C = $ _____ °F

14. Maureen is hosting a party and needs to choose a hall. Clarksdale Hall charges $200 for hall rental and $12/person for food and drinks. Lane Hall charges $320 for hall rental and $10.50/person for food and drinks. Use linear equations to determine the number of people that would make the costs for both halls the same.

D Create Connections

15. Given the linear equation $4x - y + 12 = 0$,

a) graph the line by building a table of values

b) graph the line by using the slope and y-intercept of the line

c) Which method do you prefer? Explain.

KEY IDEAS

- The general form of a linear equation is $Ax + By + C = 0$, where A, B, and C are real numbers, and A and B are not both zero. By convention, A is a whole number.

- To graph an equation in general form, determine the intercepts, then draw a line joining the intercepts; or convert to slope-intercept form.

- To determine the x-intercept, substitute $y = 0$ and solve. To determine the y-intercept, substitute $x = 0$ and solve.

- A sketch of a linear relation may have one, two, or an infinite number of intercepts. A line that represents an axis has an infinite number of intercepts with that axis. A horizontal or vertical line that does not represent an axis has only one intercept.

Equation	x-Intercept(s)	y-Intercept(s)	Graph
$x + 2y - 3 = 0$	$x + 2y - 3 = 0$ $x + 2(0) - 3 = 0$ $x = 3$	$x + 2y - 3 = 0$ $(0) + 2y - 3 = 0$ $2y = 3$ $y = 1.5$	
$x = 5.3$	$x = 5.3$	no y-intercept	
$3y = 0$	infinite number of x-intercepts	$3y = 0$ $y = 0$	

Example

Consider the linear equation $y = -\frac{3}{2}x - 3$, which is in slope-intercept form.

a) Write the equation in general form, $Ax + By + C = 0$.
b) How many intercepts will this graph have? Explain how you know.
c) Sketch the graph using the x-intercept and y-intercept.
d) Explain how the equation $3x + 6 = 0$ differs from the linear equation in part a). Predict how this difference will be reflected in the graph of the line. Sketch the graph to check your prediction.
e) Explain how the equation $2y + 6 = 0$ differs from the linear equation in part a). Predict how this difference will be reflected in the graph of the line. Sketch the graph to check your prediction.

Solution

a)
$$y = -\frac{3}{2}x - 3$$
$$(2)y = (2)\left(-\frac{3}{2}x - 3\right) \qquad \text{Multiply by 2 to get rid of the fraction.}$$
$$2y = -3x - 6$$
$$2y + 3x + 6 = -3x + 3x - 6 + 6 \qquad \text{Move all terms to one side of the equal sign.}$$
$$3x + 2y + 6 = 0$$

b) This equation has both an Ax-term and a By-term, which means that it can be solved in terms of both x and y. Hence, the equation has two intercepts.

c) Determine the x-intercept and y-intercept and draw a line passing through the two.

To determine the x-intercept, replace y with 0, and solve for x.
$$3x + 2y + 6 = 0$$
$$3x + 2(0) + 6 = 0$$
$$3x + 0 + 6 = 0$$
$$3x + 6 = 0$$
$$3x + 6 - 6 = 0 - 6$$
$$3x = -6$$
$$\frac{3x}{3} = \frac{-6}{3}$$
$$x = -2$$
The x-intercept is $(-2, 0)$.

To determine the y-intercept, replace x with 0 and solve for y.
$$3x + 2y + 6 = 0$$
$$3(0) + 2y + 6 = 0$$
$$0 + 2y + 6 = 0$$
$$2y + 6 = 0$$
$$2y + 6 - 6 = 0 - 6$$
$$2y = -6$$
$$\frac{2y}{2} = \frac{-6}{2}$$
$$y = -3$$
The y-intercept is $(0, -3)$.

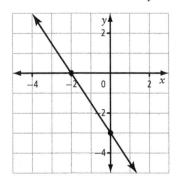

d) The equation $3x + 6 = 0$ is in general form, but has no By-term. Since the equation cannot be solved in terms of y, there is no y-intercept. This graph must be a vertical line passing through the x-intercept.

$$3x + 6 = 0$$
$$3x + 6 - 6 = 0 - 6$$
$$3x = -6$$
$$\frac{3x}{3} = \frac{-6}{3}$$
$$x = -2$$

The x-intercept is $(-2, 0)$.

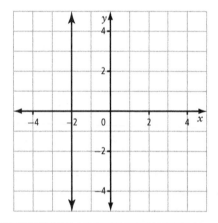

e) The equation $2y + 6 = 0$ is in general form, but has no Ax-term. Since the equation cannot be solved in terms of x, there is no x-intercept. This graph must be a horizontal line passing through the y-intercept.

$$2y + 6 = 0$$
$$3y + 6 - 6 = 0 - 6$$
$$2y = -6$$
$$\frac{2y}{2} = \frac{-6}{2}$$
$$y = -3$$

The y-intercept is $(0, -3)$.

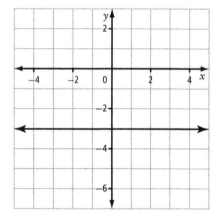

A Practise

1. Write each equation in the general form, $Ax + By + C = 0$.

a) $y = \frac{1}{3}x + 5$ **b)** $y = \frac{-2}{7}x$

c) $y = \frac{1}{8}$ **d)** $y = -0.2x + 1.2$

2. Determine the intercepts of each line. Graph each line.

a) $2x - y - 8 = 0$ **b)** $9x - 4y = 0$

c) $5x - 20 = 0$ **d)** $8y + 4 = 0$

★**3.** For each line, state the domain and range, slope, and any intercepts. Then, write the equation in general form.

a)

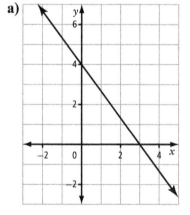

b)

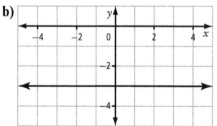

B Apply

4. Write an equation in general form for each.

   a) a line that does not have an x-intercept

   b) a line that has an infinite number of intercepts

   c) a line that does not have a y-intercept

   d) a line for which both the x-intercept and y-intercept are 0

   e) a line for which the x-intercept and y-intercept are the same, but are not 0

5. Determine the missing value, A, B, or C, in the following linear equations.

   a) $6x - By + 1 = 0$, for the line that passes through the point $(-1, 5)$

   b) $Ax + y - 10 = 0$, for the line that passes through the point $(3, -2)$

   c) $9x - 5y + C = 0$, for the line that passes through the point $(0, 0)$

★6. Josef is training for a race. His training consists of swimming and mountain biking. The table shows the number of calories burned per minute for a person of Josef's body mass.

Activity	Calories Per Minute
Swimming	14
Biking	12

   a) Write a linear equation to show the number of minutes Josef would need to swim, x, and the number of minutes he would need to bike, y, to burn 4200 calories.

   b) What are the intercepts of the line? What do they represent?

   c) What are the graph's domain and range?

   d) Suppose Josef bikes for 2 hours. How long would he need to swim to burn 4200 calories?

7. Jaden plants trees for the British Columbia government during the summer. The table shows how many trees she can plant per minute under different conditions.

Conditions	Number of Trees Planted Per Minute
Ideal	5
Rocky muskeg	2

   a) If Jaden planted 2250 trees in one day, write an equation, in general form, showing the number of minutes she planted trees under ideal conditions, x, and the number of minutes she planted trees under rocky muskeg conditions, y.

   b) For the linear equation, what are the slope, intercepts, and domain and range?

   c) If Jaden planted trees under rocky muskeg conditions for 125 minutes, how long did she spend planting trees under ideal conditions?

C Extend

8. Graph the following on the same coordinate plane.
   Line 1: $2x + 10 = 0$
   Line 2: $4x - 5y + 30 = 0$
   Line 3: $3x - 21 = 0$
   Line 4: $-8x + 10y + 30 = 0$
   Calculate the area of the region formed by their intersection.

D Making Connections

9. Write the coordinates of two points on a line that satisfies each given condition. Then, write the equation of each line in general form.

   a) a line rises from left to right

   b) a line is horizontal

   c) a line falls from left to right

   d) a line is vertical

7.3 Slope-Point Form

- For a non-vertical line through the point (x_1, y_1) with slope m, the equation of the line can be written in slope-point form as $y - y_1 = m(x - x_1)$.

  A line through $(-2, 5)$ has a slope of 3.

  The slope-point form of the equation of this line is

  $y - y_1 = m(x - x_1)$

  $y - 5 = 3[x - (-2)]$

  $y - 5 = 3(x + 2)$

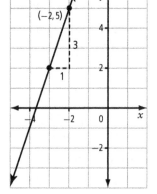

- An equation written in slope-point form can be converted to either slope-intercept form or general form.

- Any point on a line can be used when determining the equation of the line in slope-point form.

Example

Consider a line passing through the points $(-4, 5)$ and $(6, 0)$.
  a) Write the equation of this line in slope-point form.
  b) Rewrite the equation in part a) in slope-intercept form.
  c) Rewrite the equation in part a) in general form.
  d) Sketch the graph.

Solution

a) Determine the slope.

$m = \frac{y - y_1}{x - x_1}$

$m = \frac{0 - 5}{6 - (-4)}$

$m = \frac{-5}{10}$

$m = \frac{-1}{2}$

Use either point $(-4, 5)$ or $(6, 0)$ to replace the point (x_1, y_1). Replace m with $\frac{-1}{2}$.

Using point $(-4, 5)$:

$y - y_1 = m(x - x_1)$

$y - 5 = \frac{-1}{2}(x - (-4))$

$y - 5 = \frac{-1}{2}(x + 4)$

Using point $(6, 0)$:

$y - y_1 = m(x - x_1)$

$y - 0 = \frac{-1}{2}(x - 6)$

$y = \frac{-1}{2}(x - 6)$

The slope-point form of the equation of the line passing through the points $(-4, 5)$ and $(6, 0)$ is $y - 5 = \frac{-1}{2}(x + 4)$ or $y = \frac{-1}{2}(x - 6)$.

b) The slope-point form can be changed to the slope-intercept form by solving for y.

For point $(-4, 5)$:

$$y - 5 = \frac{-1}{2}(x + 4)$$

$$y - 5 = \frac{-1}{2}x - 2$$

$$y - 5 + 5 = \frac{-1}{2}x - 2 + 5$$

$$y = \frac{-1}{2}x + 3$$

For point $(6, 0)$:

$$y = \frac{-1}{2}(x - 6)$$

$$y = \frac{-1}{2}x + 3$$

The slope-intercept form of the equation passing through the points $(-4, 5)$ and $(6, 0)$ is $y = \frac{-1}{2}x + 3$. The result is the same, regardless of which of the two points is used.

c) The slope-point form can be changed to general form.

$$y - 5 = \frac{-1}{2}(x + 4)$$

$$y - 5 = \frac{-1}{2}x - 2$$

$$2(y - 5) = 2\left(\frac{-1}{2}x - 2\right)$$

$$2y - 10 = -x - 4$$

$$2y - 10 + 4 = -x - 4 + 4$$

$$2y - 6 = -x$$

$$2y - 6 + x = -x + x$$

$$x + 2y - 6 = 0$$

The general form for the equation of the line passing through the points $(-4, 5)$ and $(6, 0)$ is $x + 2y - 6 = 0$.

d) Plot the points $(-4, 5)$ and $(6, 0)$ and draw a line passing through them. Or, plot the y-intercept, $(0, 3)$, and draw a line passing through it with a slope of $\frac{-1}{2}$.

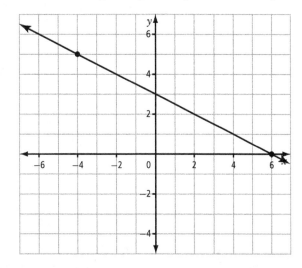

A Practise

1. Identify the slope and a point on each line.

   a) $y + 7 = 4(x - 3)$ **b)** $y - 5 = \frac{1}{3}(x + 5)$

   c) $y = -2(x - 6)$ **d)** $y + 1 = x - 3$

2. Rewrite the following in slope-intercept form, $y = mx + b$, and general form, $Ax + By + C = 0$.

   a) $y - 3 = \frac{2}{3}(x + 1)$ **b)** $y + 4 = -2(x - 1)$

   c) $y = \frac{3}{4}(x - 4)$ **d)** $y - 1 = 3(x + 6)$

3. From the information given, write the equation of the line in slope-point form, slope-intercept form, and general form.

   ☆**a)** $(-1, -5)$; $m = \frac{4}{3}$

   b) $\left(\frac{-1}{2}, -3\right)$; $m = 1$

   c) $(1, 4)$; $m = -1.5$

   ☆**d)** $(-5, -8)$ and $(-7, -9)$

   e) $(-1, -2)$ and $(3, 0)$

4. Write an equation in slope-point form for each graph.

   a)
   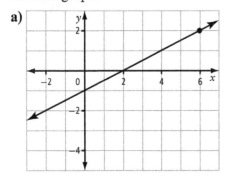

   b)
   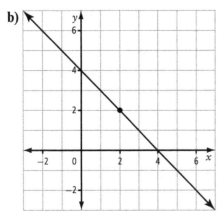

c)
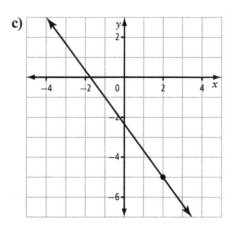

B Apply

5. Write the equation of each line in slope-point form. Then, convert each equation to general form.

   a) slope of 0 and passing through $(-3, 1)$

   b) same slope as $y = 2x + 2$ and passing through $(-1, 8)$

   ☆**c)** same slope as $5x + 2y - 10 = 0$ and passing through $(-1, 4)$

   d) same y-intercept as $3x - y - 1 = 0$ and passing through $(2, -6)$

   e) x-intercept of -5 and y-intercept of 3

   f) same slope as $3x + 2y + 6 = 0$, with an x-intercept of 0

☆6. Show that the point $(-2, -6)$ lies on the line that has an x-intercept of 10 and a y-intercept of -5.

7. A rectangle has vertices A$(-3, 4)$, B$(-3, -1)$, C$(4, -1)$, and D$(4, 4)$. Plot the points on a grid and draw the rectangle. Then, draw the two diagonals and write an equation in general form for each.

8. Use graphing technology to identify the x-intercept and y-intercept of the line $2x - 3y + 12 = 0$. Use algebra to verify your answer.

9. Consider the linear equation $8x + ky - 6 = 0$. If the line passes through the point $(1, -2)$, what is the value of k?

10. Compare the following five lines to the line graphed below.

Line 1: $x + y + 3 = 0$
Line 2: $2x + 3y + 6 = 0$
Line 3: $2x - 3y + 18 = 0$
Line 4: $4x - 6y - 9 = 0$
Line 5: $2x - y + 2 = 0$

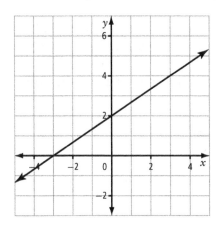

a) Which line(s) have the same slope as the graphed line?

b) Which line(s) have the same y-intercept as the graphed line?

c) Which line(s) have the same x-intercept as the graphed line?

11. The annual cost of operating a snowmobile depends on the distance driven plus a fixed cost, which includes maintenance, depreciation, and trail fees. The cost is $4000 for 1200 miles driven and $5625 for 2500 miles driven.

a) Sketch a line showing the relationship between distance and cost.

b) Calculate the slope of the line. What does the slope represent?

c) Determine the y-intercept. What does it represent?

d) Write an equation in general form for the cost of operating a snowmobile.

e) Use your equation to determine the cost of operating the snowmobile for 900 miles.

C Extend

12. A candle is lit at 1400 hours. At 1600 hours, it is 16 cm tall. At 2030 hours, it is 4.75 cm tall.

a) Write a linear equation, in general form, with the points representing (hours, height).

b) Use the equation to determine the rate at which the candle burns per hour and its height at 1400 hours.

c) What does the slope of the line represent?

d) What does the y-intercept represent?

13. The following lines pass through the sides of a triangle:

$2x + 3y - 18 = 0$
$5x + y + 7 = 0$
$3x - 2y - 14 = 0$

Determine the vertices of the triangle.

14. Consider the linear equation $\frac{x}{-8} + \frac{y}{6} = 1$.

a) Write the equation in general form.

b) What are the x- and y-intercepts? How do they relate to the original form of the equation?

c) Predict the x- and y-intercepts of the equation $\frac{x}{3} - \frac{y}{5} = 1$. Verify your answer.

D Create Connections

15. In 2001, the pollution in a local lake was measured at 4.5 parts per million. In 2010, the level had decreased to 1.4 parts per million.

a) Write an equation in slope-point form, showing the relationship between time, x, and the pollution rate, y.

b) If the decrease in pollution continues at the same rate, in what year should the pollution level be 0 parts per million?

KEY IDEAS

- Parallel lines have the same slope and different intercepts. Vertical lines are parallel to each other, as are horizontal lines, if they have different intercepts.

- Perpendicular lines have slopes that are negative reciprocals of each other. A vertical line with an undefined slope and a horizontal line with a slope of zero are also perpendicular.

- The properties of parallel and perpendicular lines can give information about the slopes. Knowing the slopes can help you develop an equation.

A line perpendicular to $y = 5x + 7$ has the same y-intercept.

The line $y = 5x + 7$ has a slope of 5 and a y-intercept of 7.

The perpendicular line has a slope of $-\frac{1}{5}$ and a y-intercept of 7. So, the equation of the perpendicular line is $y = -\frac{1}{5}x + 7$.

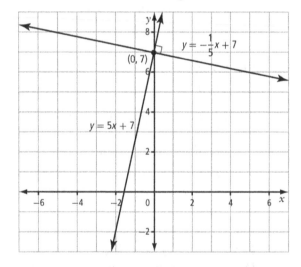

Example

a) Write an equation, in slope-intercept form, for the line that has a y-intercept of -4 and is parallel to the line $5x + 3y - 6 = 0$. Graph the lines using graphing technology.

b) Write the equation, in slope-intercept form, for the line that has a y-intercept of -4 and is perpendicular to $5x + 3y - 6 = 0$. Graph the lines using graphing technology.

c) Write the equations for the lines you created in parts a) and b) in general form.

Solution

a) Since the new line is parallel to the line
$5x + 3y - 6 = 0$, the two lines have the same slope.
Determine the slope of $5x + 3y - 6 = 0$ by rewriting it in
slope-intercept form, $y = mx + b$.

$$5x + 3y - 6 = 0$$
$$5x + 3y - 6 + 6 = 0 + 6$$
$$5x + 3y = 6$$
$$5x - 5x + 3y = -5x + 6$$
$$3y = -5x + 6$$
$$\frac{3y}{3} = \frac{-5x}{3} + \frac{6}{3}$$
$$y = \frac{-5x}{3} + 2$$

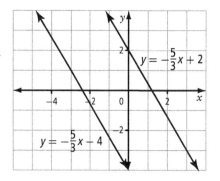

The slope of the first line is $\frac{-5}{3}$.
Since the second line has the same slope and a y-intercept of -4, the equation for the
second line is $y = \frac{-5}{3}x - 4$.

b) A perpendicular line has a slope that is the
negative reciprocal of the slope of the first line.
Since the slope of the first line is $\frac{-5}{3}$, the slope
of the perpendicular line is $\frac{3}{5}$. So, the equation
of the perpendicular line running through $(0, -4)$
is $y = \frac{3}{5}x - 4$.

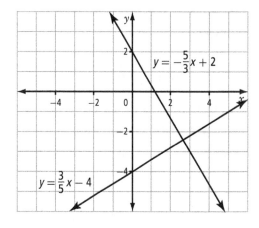

c) Rewrite the equations from part a) and b) in general form.

Parallel line: $y = \frac{-5}{3}x - 4$

Multiply each term by 3.

$$3y = 3\left(\frac{-5}{3}x - 4\right)$$
$$3y = -5x - 12$$

Bring all the terms to one side of the
equal sign.
$$3y + 5x + 12 = -5x + 5x - 12 + 12$$
$$5x + 3y + 12 = 0$$
The equation in general form is
$5x + 3y + 12 = 0$.

Perpendicular line: $y = \frac{3}{5}x - 4$.

Multiply each term by 5.

$$5y = 5\left(\frac{3}{5}x - 4\right)$$
$$5y = 3x - 20$$

Bring all the terms to one side of the
equal sign.
$$5y - 3x + 20 = 3x - 3x - 20 + 20$$
$$-3x + 5y + 20 = 0$$
The equation in general form is
$3x - 5y - 20 = 0$.

A Practise

1. Given the slopes of two different lines, determine whether the lines are parallel, perpendicular, or neither.

   a) $m_1 = \frac{1}{2}$; $m_2 = -2$

   b) $m_1 = \frac{3}{4}$; $m_2 = \frac{6}{8}$

   c) $m_1 = \frac{-1}{4}$; $m_2 = 4$

   d) $m_1 = -0.5$; $m_2 = 2$

   e) $m_1 = 1$; $m_2 = -1$

   f) $m_1 = \frac{1}{4}$; $m_2 = 0.25$

2. For each given line, state the slope of a line that is parallel and the slope of a line that is perpendicular.

   a) $y = -3x - 4$

   b) $y = x$

   c) $4x + y - 4 = 0$

   d) $8y - 7 = 0$

   e) $5x - 2y + 3 = 0$

3. The following are slopes of parallel lines. Determine the value of n.

   a) $2, \frac{n}{2}$ **b)** $-3, \frac{6}{n}$

   c) $\frac{2}{n}, \frac{4}{5}$ **d)** $\frac{-n}{3}, \frac{-2}{4}$

4. The following are slopes of perpendicular lines. Determine the value of r.

   a) $3, \frac{r}{6}$ **b)** $\frac{r}{9}, \frac{-3}{5}$

   c) $\frac{9}{2}, \frac{4}{r}$ **d)** $\frac{-1}{2}, \frac{r}{4}$

5. Write the general form of the equation of a line that is parallel to the given line and passes through the given point.

   a) $5x + y + 8 = 0$; $(2, -3)$

   b) $y = \frac{-1}{3}x + 2$; $(-4, 0)$

   c) $y + 2 = -(x + 1)$; $(-2, 6)$

6. Write the general form for the equation of a line that is perpendicular to the given line and passes through the given point.

   a)
   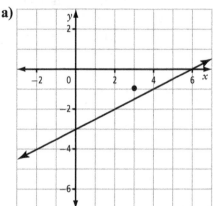

   b)
   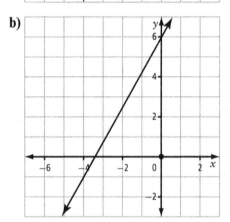

   c)
   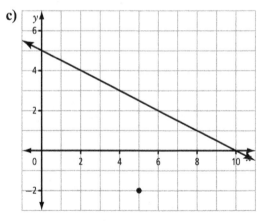

B Apply

7. Consider lines $x - 2y + 10 = 0$ and $y = \frac{1}{2}x + 5$.

a) What are the slopes of the lines?

b) Are the lines parallel? Explain your answer.

8. Write the general form for the equation of a line passing through the given point and running parallel to the line.

a)

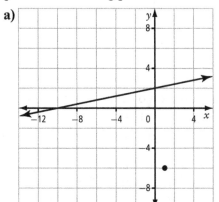

b)

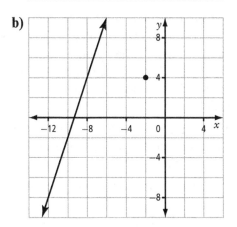

9. Write the equation of a line that is perpendicular to the y-axis and has a y-intercept of 15.

10. Given three points, determine whether or not the points are vertices of a right triangle. Explain.

a) M(1, 1), N(−2, 5), C(3, −2)

b) D(2, 4), F(−2, 2), G(5, −2)

★11. Consider the linear equation $4x + y - 11 = 0$.

a) Write an equation of a line parallel to the given line. How many such equations can be written?

b) Write an equation of a line perpendicular to the given line. How many such equations can be written?

12. Write the equation of the line perpendicular to $x - 12y + 15 = 0$ and having the same y-intercept as $7x + 4y - 12 = 0$.

13. Sketch the graph of a line parallel to the line $3x + 6y - 7 = 0$ and passing through the origin.

C Extend

14. The line passing through A(−2, 3) and B(0, 4) is perpendicular to the line passing through C(k, 4) and D(1, −6). What is the value of k.

15. What is the value of k if the lines $x - 2y + 6 = 0$ and $kx + 8y + 1 = 0$ are parallel?

16. For what value of k are the lines $3kx - 7y - 10 = 0$ and $2x + y - 7 = 0$ perpendicular?

★17. Determine the value(s) of k for which the lines $kx - 2y - 1 = 0$ and $8x - ky + 3 = 0$ are

a) parallel

b) perpendicular

18. Write the equation of a line that passes through the point of intersection of the lines $5x + y - 11 = 0$ and $2x + 3y - 7 = 0$ and is

a) parallel to the x-axis

b) perpendicular to the line $2x - y + 4 = 0$

D Making Connections

19. Write the equations of lines that form the sides of a square or a rectangle so that no sides are vertical or horizontal lines.

7.1 Slope-Intercept Form

1. For each line, state the slope and y-intercept. Then, write the equation of the line in slope-intercept form.

a)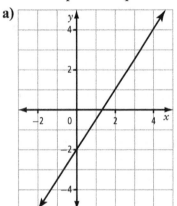

b)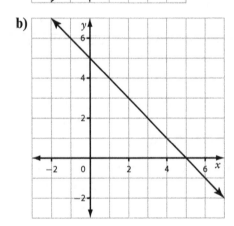

c)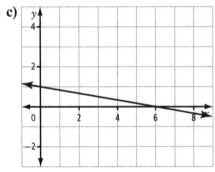

d)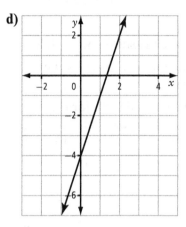

2. The equation of a line is $y = \frac{1}{3}x + b$. What is the value of b if the line passes through the point $(-3, 7)$?

★3. The equation of a line is $y = mx - 8$. Determine the value of m if the line passes through the point $(-2, 6)$.

4. Mandy's hockey team is trying to raise $850 to attend a tournament. The team has raised $500. They plan to raise the remainder of the money by collecting plastic 4-L milk jugs, which they redeem for $0.25 per jug.

   a) Write a linear equation to represent this situation, where y is the money they have raised.

   b) Graph the line for the equation in part a).

   c) State the slope and y-intercept of the line. What does each of these represent?

   d) Determine from the graph how many jugs the team must collect to raise enough money to attend the tournament. Verify your answer algebraically.

7.2 General Form

5. Express each equation in general form.

   a) $y = \frac{-1}{2}x - 9$

   b) $\frac{x}{-3} + \frac{y}{2} = 1$

   c) $y + 2 = -(x + 1)$

6. Determine the intercepts of each line. Then, graph each line.

   a) $2x + y - 4 = 0$

   b) $5x - 4y + 20 = 0$

7. Bamboo is the fastest growing plant on Earth. On average, it can grow 60 cm/day, depending on the soil and climatic conditions. Under less than ideal conditions, the growth rate averages 10 cm/day.

   a) Write an equation, in general form, that represents the number of days of growth for ideal conditions, x, and the number of days of growth under less than ideal conditions, y, needed for a bamboo plant to reach a height of 42 m.

   b) What are the intercepts? What do they represent?

   c) What are the domain and range?

   d) If it takes 55 days for a bamboo tree to reach 42 m under ideal conditions, how many days would it take to reach this height under less than ideal conditions?

7.3 Slope-Point Form

8. A line has a slope of 2 and passes through the point $(-6, -5)$. Write the equation of the line in slope-point form and in general form.

9. A line has an x-intercept of $\frac{-1}{2}$ and a y-intercept of 4. Write the equation of the line in slope-point form and in general form. Verify your answer using graphing technology.

⭐10. Robyn is skiing with friends at Marmot Basin in Jasper, Alberta. When he is at the top of Marmot Peak, which has an elevation of 8570 ft, he notes that the temperature is 3 °F. When he skis to the base, where the elevation is approximately 5570 ft, the temperature is 12 °F.

   a) Assuming that the temperature change is constant as the altitude changes, write a linear equation in slope-point form showing the relationship between altitude, x, and temperature, y.

   b) Use the equation to determine the temperature at the base of Eagle Chair, where the elevation is approximately 6500 ft.

7.4 Parallel and Perpendicular Lines

11. State whether each set of lines is parallel or perpendicular.

   a) $6y + 2x - 4 = 0$
      $y = 3x + 12$

   b) $y = \frac{4}{3}x - 17$
      $9y - 12x + 8 = 0$

   c) $-9y = 3x - 12$
      $12y - 4x = 14$

12. Write the equation of a line, in general form, that runs perpendicular to $2x - y + 8 = 0$ with a y-intercept of 6.

⭐13. A line runs through $(-1, 3)$ and $(2, 1)$ and has an x-intercept of -4. Write the equation of the line perpendicular at the x-intercept.

14. Explain how the following lines are related.

   Line 1: $-2x = 3y$

   Line 2: $y = \frac{-2}{3}x - 11$

   Line 3: $8x + 12y + 7 = 0$

   Line 4: $y - 6 = \frac{-4}{6}(x + 5)$

1. What are the slope and y-intercept of each line?

   a) $y = -7x + 10$ **b)** $9x + 2y - 15 = 0$

2. Calculate the following areas to the indicated SI unit. Express your answers to the nearest tenth of a square unit.

   a) the area of a rectangle 18 in. by 11 in., in square centimetres

   b) the area of a rectangle 15.5 ft by 40 ft, in square metres

3. Julie is biking to the grocery store. She is going to pick up her friend Fong, who lives about halfway the store. Julie starts off, but when she is about halfway to Fong's house, she realizes that she forgot her money. She returns home, finds her wallet, and then starts off again. Julie stops at Fong's house and they ride the rest of the way together. At the store, the girls meet their friend Zoe. The three decide to go to a juice bar, which is in the opposite direction from Julie's home. Julie and Fong walk their bikes because Zoe does not have hers with her. They buy a juice, then Julie suddenly remembers that she has frozen food in her shopping bag and has to leave. She jumps on her bike and rides straight home. Draw a distance–time graph for Julie's journey.

4. Calculate.

   a) $\sqrt{64}$ **b)** $\sqrt[3]{729}$

   c) $\sqrt[3]{27\,000}$

5. Factor completely.

   a) $x^2 + 13x + 12$ **b)** $6m^2 - 9mn + 3n^2$

   c) $15x^2 + 2xy - 1y^2$ **d)** $2s^2t - 2st - 12t$

   e) $c^2 - 81$ **f)** $x^4 - 25x + 144$

   g) $1 - 16y^4$ **h)** $28h^2 - 847f^2$

6. Multiply and then combine like terms.

   a) $3(5n + 6)(2n - 3) + (n - 2)^2$

   b) $(4s^2 + 2s - 3)(-2s^2 + 5s + 1)$

7. Estimate the perimeter of the figure. Express your answer in appropriate SI units.

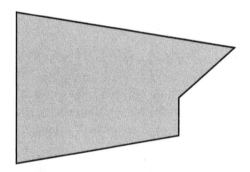

8. Fuel efficiency is the amount of gas it takes a vehicle to drive a certain distance. A truck has a fuel efficiency of 0.138 L/km. Consider the relationship between the amount of gasoline consumed, in litres, and the distance the truck travels, in kilometres.

   a) Assign variables to represent each quantity in the relation. Identify the dependent variable and the independent variable.

   b) Assume that the truck drives for 250 km. Create a set of ordered pairs for the relation.

   c) Is the relation continuous or discrete? Explain.

   d) Graph the relation.

   e) Is the relation linear or non-linear? Explain.

9. What are the x-intercept and y-intercept of each line? Sketch the lines.

   a) $x = -7$

   b) $12x - 3y - 6 = 0$

10. Niobium is a radioactive element. A certain type of niobium has a half-life of 1 min. The formula for the amount of niobium remaining is $A = 900\left(\frac{1}{2}\right)^n$, where n is the number of minutes. Consider a 900-g sample of this element.

  a) How many grams remain after 10 minutes? Answer to the nearest tenth of a milligram. Hint: There are 1000 mg in a gram.

  b) How many grams were there 12 min ago? Answer to the nearest tenth of a kilogram.

11. State the missing factor.

  a) $4ab^2c^3 + 18a^3c = (?)(2b^2c^2 + 9a^2)$

  b) $5s - 20s^2 = (5s)(?)$

  c) $9xyz^2 - 6x^2y = (3xy)(?)$

12. Solve for all unknowns. Round your answer to the nearest hundredth of a unit.

  a) $\triangle ABC$, $BC = 8.4$ km, $\angle B = 90°$, and $\angle A = 27°$

  b) $\triangle DEF$, $\angle E = 90°$, $DE = 6.1$ m, $EF = 9.1$ m

13. Use slope-point form to write an equation of a line through each point with the given slope. Express each answer in slope-intercept form and in general form.

  a) $(-5, 4)$ and $m = -3$

  b) $(-3, 2)$ and $m = -\frac{1}{2}$

14. In the figure, $\triangle ADB$ and $\triangle BCE$ are similar triangles. Calculate the length of AC. Round your answer to the nearest tenth of a centimetre.

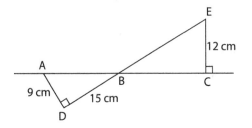

15. Evaluate each expression. Express the answers with positive exponents.

  a) $\left(x^{\frac{1}{5}}\right)\left(x^{-\frac{1}{3}}\right)$

  b) $(81h^8)^{-\frac{3}{4}}$

  c) $\dfrac{8^{\frac{3}{4}}}{8^{-\frac{2}{5}}}$

  d) $\left(\dfrac{x^{-3}}{0.25x^{-6}}\right)^3$

16. In the following paragraph, convert each imperial unit to an equivalent SI unit.

  Mount Edziza, in northwestern British Columbia, is Canada's highest volcano at 9144 ft. Its summit comprises an ice-filled bowl, or caldera, which stretches for almost a mile. But some people argue that Edziza is not Canada's highest volcano. They say that Mount Silverthrone, also in British Columbia, is higher at 9400 ft. But since Silverthrone's peaks are always covered by snow and ice, it is difficult to determine if they are, in fact, volcanic rock.

17. Calculate the surface area of each to the nearest hundredth of a centimetre.

  a) a cone with a radius of 8.5 cm and slant height of 29.2 cm

  b) a square-based pyramid 41-cm-wide that has a slant height of 72 cm

  c) a sphere with a diameter of 5.0 cm

  d) a cylinder with a diameter of 11 cm and a height of 7 cm

  e) a rectangular prism with a height of 2.3 cm, a length of 3.7 cm, and a width of 1.8 cm

18. A plane is at a cruising altitude of 10 000 m. It begins its descent to the airport at an angle of depression of 8°. What is the horizontal distance of the plane to the airport, to the nearest tenth of a mile?

19. Express each power as an equivalent radical.

  a) $3^{\frac{2}{3}}$

  b) $16^{0.5}$

  c) $\left(\dfrac{y^3}{x^5}\right)^{\frac{3}{2}}$

20. Give the domain and range of each relation. Use words, interval notation, and set notation to describe each.

a)

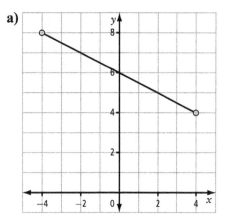

b)

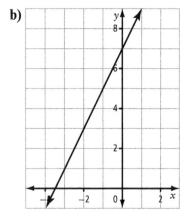

21. Chloe is flying her kite. She lets out 500 ft of string. Chloe's hand holding the kite is 5 ft from the ground. The angle of elevation from Chloe's hand to the kite is 50°. How high is Chloe's kite from the ground, to the nearest tenth of a metre?

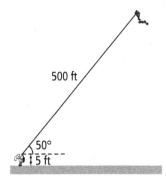

22. A box is sitting on four identical cylinders. Calculate the volume of the composite object, in cubic metres. Round to the nearest hundredth of a cubic metre.

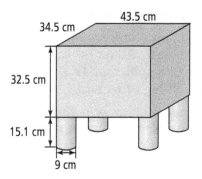

23. Determine the slope of each.

a)

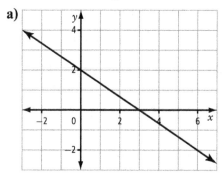

b)

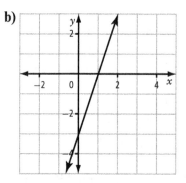

24. A wooden wedge is used to prop open a door. The wedge is 7 cm long, 5 cm high, and 2 cm deep. If the bottom of the door is 2.5 cm from the floor, what percent of the volume of the wedge is under the door?

25. Write an equation of a line through (8, 0) and perpendicular to $2x + 4y + 10 = 0$.

⭐**1.** Which point on the line $2x + 5y = 10$ is closest to the origin?

A $x = \frac{17}{20}, y = \frac{33}{20}$ **C** $x = \frac{20}{23}, y = \frac{50}{23}$

B $x = \frac{17}{23}, y = \frac{33}{23}$ **D** $x = \frac{20}{29}, y = \frac{50}{29}$

2. For what value of k does the point $(-1, 5)$ lie on the graph of the equation $4x - 2ky = 3$?

A $\frac{-3}{10}$ **C** $\frac{7}{10}$

B $\frac{-7}{10}$ **D** $\frac{3}{10}$

3. For the linear equation $y = -2x + 5$, what is the decrease in y that results when x is increased by 1?

A 5   **C** 3

B 4   **D** 2

⭐**4.** Prove that the midpoint, M, of the hypotenuse of a right triangle is equidistant from the three vertices.

5. Points $(2, 1)$ and $(-2, 4)$ lie on the graph of $Ax + By = 10$.

a) Identify the values of A and B.

b) Point $(2010, s)$ also lies on the graph. Determine the value of s.

6. Describe the effect on the graph of $y = mx + b$ when

a) the coefficient of x increases

b) the coefficient of x decreases

c) the constant term increases

d) the constant term decreases

7. Water freezes at 0 °C, or 32 °F. Water boils at 100 °C, or 212 °F.

a) Use these two points to write an equation relating Celsius and Fahrenheit.

b) Use the equation you created in part a) to convert −40 °C to degrees Fahrenheit.

8. A 10-km taxi ride costs $9.75. At the same rate, a 22-km ride costs $18.75.

a) Write an equation to represent the distance travelled, x, and the cost of the fare, y.

b) What does the y-intercept represent?

9. Consider the equation of each line in slope-intercept form: $y = mx + b$. Replace the question marks with $=$, $>$, or $<$.

a) $m ? 0, b ? 0$

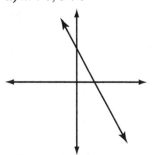

b) $m ? 0, b ? 0$

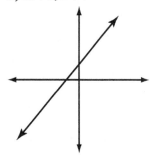

10. Consider the equation of each of the lines in question 9 in general form: $Ax + By + C = 0$. Replace the question marks with $=$, $>$, or $<$.

a) $A ? 0, B ? 0, C > 0$

b) $A > 0, B ? 0, C ? 0$

Chapter 7 Study Check

Use the chart below to help you assess the skills and processes you have developed during Chapter 7. The references in italics direct you to pages in *Mathematics 10 Exercise and Homework Book* where you could review the skill. How can you show that you have gained each skill? What can you do to improve?

Big Idea	Skills	This Shows I Know	This Is How I Can Improve
Relate the various forms of linear relations (slope-intercept, general, and slope-point) to their graphs *pages 142–145, 147–155, 157–160, 162–163*	✓ Given a graph of a linear relation, determine the slope and *y*-intercept *pages 142–145, 148, 152–153, 158–159, 162–163*		
	✓ Graph linear relations with and without technology *pages 143–145, 147–149, 151, 154–155, 157–159, 163*		
	✓ Change a linear relation given in one form to another form (e.g., slope-intercept to general form, point-slope form to slope-intercept form, point-slope form to general form) *pages 143–145, 147–155, 158–160, 163*		
Use the characteristics of a linear relation to determine the equation of the related linear relation *pages 150, 152–157, 159, 161–163*	✓ Given a graph, determine the equation of the relation *pages 152–153, 156–157*		
	✓ Determine the equation of a relation when given one of the following: a graph, the slope and *y*-intercept, two points on the line, the slope and one point on the line *pages 150, 152–153, 157, 159, 161, 163*		
	✓ Determine the equation for a relation given a point and the equation of a line parallel *or* perpendicular to the given line *pages 154–157, 159, 162*		
Apply linear equations to model and solve problems *pages 144–145, 149, 153, 157–159, 163*	✓ Use a linear relation to model a real-life situation *pages 144–145, 149, 153, 157–159, 163*		

Organizing the Ideas

Use the Venn diagram below to compare and contrast the three forms of the equation for a linear relation.

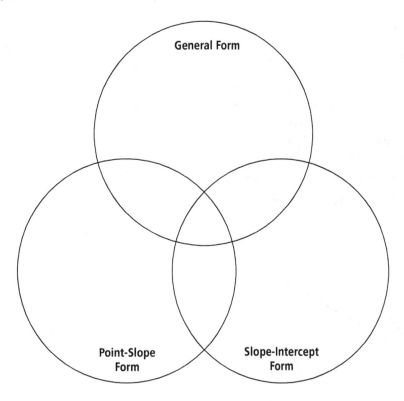

Study Guide

Review the types of problems you handled in Chapter 7. What do you need to remember to help you do similar problems?

Things to Remember

Graphing Linear Equations

Writing Equations

Changing From One Form of the Equation for a Relation to the Other

Applying Linear Equations to Solve Problems

Multiple Choice

For #1 to 12, choose the best answer.

1. A particular model of hybrid automobile has a fuel economy of 4.6 L/100 km for city driving. Another vehicle in the same size class, but which runs only on gasoline, has a fuel economy of 8.7 L/100 km in the city. Which of the following is a possible graph comparing the rates of fuel consumption for the two vehicles?

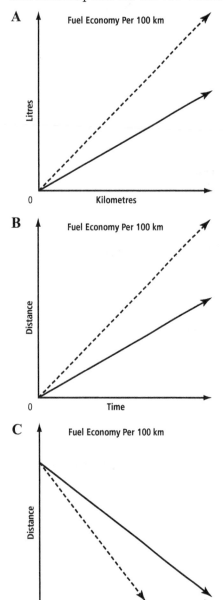

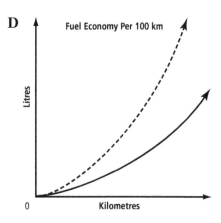

2. Which of the situations below could be represented by the following graph?

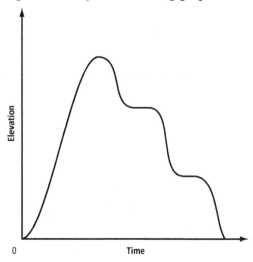

A Steven rolls a ball down the stairs of his home.

B Samantha takes the bus to a shopping mall up on a hill. After spending the entire day at the mall, she takes the bus home. The bus makes two stops before reaching Samantha's stop.

C DeeJay takes a chair lift to the top of a ski hill and rides her snowboard to the bottom, stopping twice to rest for a short period of time.

D An airplane flies from Vancouver to Winnipeg, with short stopovers in Edmonton and Saskatoon.

3. Given the set of ordered pairs {(5, 1), (3, 1), (1, 2), (−1, 2)}, which is a true statement regarding the domain or range?

A domain [5, −1]

B range [1, 2]

C domain $\{x \mid -1 \le x \le 5, x \in R\}$

D range $\{y \mid y = 1, 2\}$

4. Which of the following relations does not represent a function?

A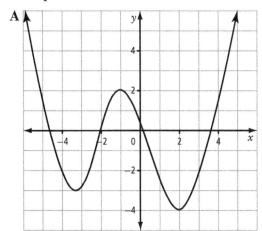

B

x	y
−3	−9
−2	−7
−1	−5
0	−3
1	−1
2	1
3	3

C $x = y^2$

D {(−2, 5), (−1, 5), (0, 5), (1, 5), (2, 5)}

5. A line with a positive slope would pass through which pair of points?

A (−5, −2), (3, −6)   B (−3, 4), (−5, 2)

C (2, 5), (2, 2)   D (4, 7), (6, 7)

6. Which of the following lines would have a slope that is undefined?

A $y = 3$

B $x = 3$

C $y = 0$

D $x = -y$

7. A line passing through the point (−3, 7) has a slope of $-\frac{3}{5}$. Which of the following ordered pairs represents another point on the line?

A (−5, 12)

B (2, 4)

C (3, −7)

D (7, −3)

8. The slopes of two lines are $-\frac{2}{9}$ and $\frac{k}{6}$. Which of the following values of k would make the two lines perpendicular?

A −27   B 1

C 18   D 27

9. What is the slope of the line defined by the equation $3x - 4y = 16$?

A 3   B $\frac{4}{3}$

C $\frac{3}{4}$ D −4

10. Which of the following is true when referring to the domain and range of $y = -2x + 5$?

A The domain refers to all possible values of y, and the range refers to all possible values of x.

B The domain refers to all possible input values, and the range refers to the resulting output values.

C The range refers to all possible independent values, and the domain refers to the possible dependent values.

D The range refers to functions, and the domain refers to relations.

11. Which representation of a linear relation matches the following table of values?

x	y
1	−3
2	−1
3	1
4	3

A $y = 2x - 5$

B

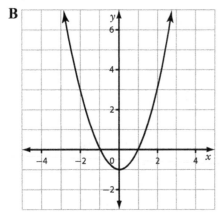

C $\{(1, -3), (2, 1), (3, -1), (4, 3)\}$

D The x-values go up by 1.

12. Which of the following graphs has a slope of $\frac{2}{3}$ and a y-intercept of −2?

A

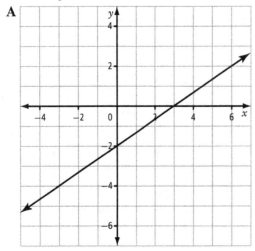

B

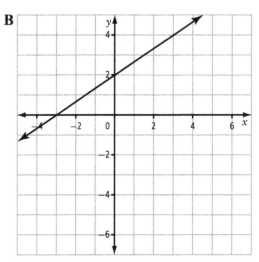

C

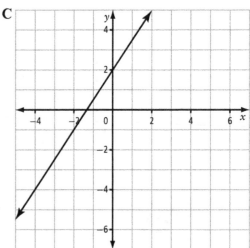

D

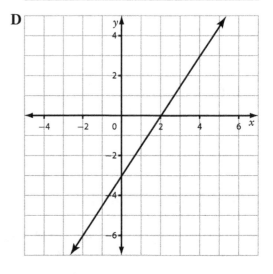

Numerical Response

13. A local band used to charge $2000 for a concert that sold 200 tickets. The band has become more popular, so it now charges $5000 for 350 tickets. What is the rate of change in the price per ticket?

14. What is the slope of the line defined by $y + 2 = 3(x - 4)$?

15. A line passing through the point $(-1, 5)$ has a slope of -3. What is the value of b when the equation is written in the form $y = mx + b$?

16. Given the linear relation $d(t) = \frac{1}{2}t + 5$, what is the value of t when $d(t) = 15$?

17. Given $f(x) = -3x + 15$, determine $f(-2)$.

18. What is the x-intercept of the linear relation in the graph?

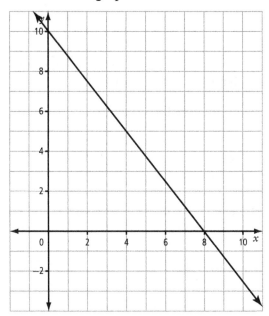

Extended Response

19. A line passes through the points $(-3, 5)$ and $(2, -3)$. Write the equation of this line in the form $Ax + By + C = 0$.

20. Students are selling chocolate bars to raise money for their band program. The relationship between the number of bars sold, x, and the profit, y, in dollars, can be represented by the equation $25x - 10y - 1500 = 0$.

   a) Rewrite the equation in slope-intercept form.

   b) What is the value of the slope? What does it represent?

   c) What is the value of the y-intercept? What does it represent?

   d) How many chocolate bars must the students sell in order for the fundraiser to pay off expenses?

21. A line passes through the point $(2, -5)$ and is parallel to the line $3x + 2y + 8 = 0$.

   a) Express the equation of the line in slope-intercept form.

   b) Rewrite the equation in the form $Ax + By + C = 0$.

   c) Describe two methods of graphing the line from the general form of the equation, without first rewriting it in slope-intercept form.

22. Michelle is downloading music from an online music store. She pays $0.49 for every song she downloads.

   a) Create a table of values to represent the cost of downloading 5 songs.

   b) Is the relation a function or a non-function? Explain your choice.

   c) Write an equation that relates the number of songs downloaded to the cost.

   d) Is this relation discrete or continuous? Explain your reasoning.

Chapter 8 Solving Systems of Linear Equations Graphically

8.1 Systems of Linear Equations and Graphs

≪ KEY IDEAS ≫

- Systems of linear equations can be modelled numerically, graphically, or algebraically.

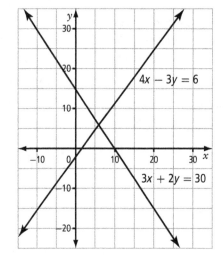

x	y
3	7
5	11
7	15
9	19
11	23

$4x - 3y = 6$

$3x + 2y = 30$

$6a + 2b = 0$
$2a + 5b = -13$

- The solution to a linear system is a pair of values that occurs in each table of values, an intersection point of the lines, or an ordered pair that satisfies each equation.

- One way to solve a system of linear equations is to graph the lines and identify the point of intersection on the graph.

- A solution to a system of linear equations can be verified using several methods:
  - Substitute the value for each variable and evaluate the equations.
  - Create a graph and identify the point of intersection.
  - Create tables of values and identify the pair of values that occurs in each table.

Example

Consider the system of linear equations $y = 3x + 2$ and $2x - y = -4$.
  a) Rewrite the equations in slope-intercept form.
  b) Use technology to graph the equations together and identify the point of intersection.

Solution

  a) Rearrange each equation into slope-intercept form by isolating y. Identify the y-intercept and slope to draw the graph.

$y = 3x + 2$ is in slope-intercept form already.

$$2x - y = -4$$
$$2x - y + y = -4 + y$$
$$2x = -4 + y$$
$$2x + 4 = -4 + y + 4$$
$$2x + 4 = y$$
$$y = 2x + 4$$

The y-intercept is 2. The slope is 3.   The y-intercept is 4. The slope is 2.

- Using the **Y=** screen of your calculator, enter $y = 3x + 2$ as Y1 and $y = 2x + 4$ as Y2. Set the viewing window as **X** [3, 5, 1] and **Y** [−2, 12, 2]. The graph of the two lines will appear in the form shown. Use the 2nd/Calc/Intersect functions to identify the ordered pair at the point of intersection of the two lines. The point of intersection (2, 8) is the solution to the linear system.

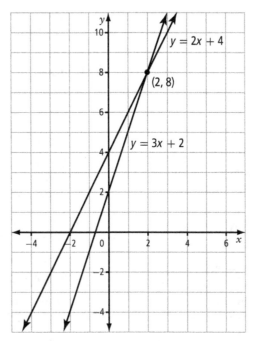

A Practise

1. Rewrite the equations in slope-intercept form. Then, use technology to graph each pair of equations and determine the point of intersection.

   a) $x + y = 6$
   $2x - 3y = 2$

   b) $x - 4y = -2$
   $y = -x - 5$

   c) $3x + 4y = 0$
   $2x - 2y + 14 = 0$

2. Determine graphically whether each given point is a solution to the system of linear equations.

   a) $y = 4x - 9$
   $y = -2x + 3$
   $(2, -1)$

   b) $x + y = 7$
   $3x - 2y = -3$
   $(2, 5)$

3. For each pair of tables of values, determine two equations in slope-intercept form. Then, use technology to graph the equations and identify the point of intersection.

   a)

x	0	−1	2	3
y	5	7	1	−1

x	0	−2	1	4
y	2	3	1.5	0

   b)

Time (s)	0	2	5	10
Distance (m)	0	7	17.5	35

Time (s)	0	2	4	10
Distance (m)	10	13	16	25

⭐**4.** Solve each system of linear equations by creating a table of values and graphing with pencil and graph paper. Then, verify you solution for each case.

a) $y = 8x - 3$
$y = 2x + 3$

b) $x - y = -2$
$4x + y = 12$

c) $y = \frac{1}{2}x - 6$
$3x - y = -4$

B Apply

5. Alan has $10 and saves $0.50 each day. Vanessa has $5 and saves $1 each day.

a) Create a system of linear equations to model the amount of money, M, in dollars, that each of Alan and Vanessa has in terms of days, d.

b) Use a graph to determine when Alan and Vanessa will have the same amount of money. How much money will each of them have on that day?

⭐**6.** Two large tanks of oil are being drained. The first tank contains 125 m³ of oil and is being emptied at a rate of 2.5 m³ per minute. The second tank contains 80 m³ of oil and is being drained at a rate of 1 m³ per minute.

a) Create a system of linear equations to model the amount of oil, A, remaining in each tank in terms of time, t.

b) Graph the equations together to identify the point of intersection.

c) What does the point of intersection mean in the context of the problem?

d) Use your graph to determine which tank will be empty first.

7. A theatre production sold tickets at a price of $15 for adults and $10 for children. The total revenue from the sale of 69 tickets was $900.

a) Write a system of linear equations to model revenue from ticket sales, where a is the number of adults' tickets sold and c is the number of children's tickets sold.

b) Rewrite the equations in slope-intercept form.

c) Graph the equations together and determine the point of intersection.

d) Explain the meaning of the point of intersection in the context of the problem.

C Extend

8. 200 L of oil in a cylindrical tank are being transferred to a second container that is empty. The oil is being pumped at a rate of 8 L per minute.

a) Write an equation to model the volume, V, in litres, of oil in each tank in terms of time, t, in minutes.

b) Graph the two equations together and determine the point of intersection.

c) What is true about the volumes of oil in both tanks at this point?

d) How long will it take to empty the first tank?

e) Does the shape of the second container affect your answers?

9. The graph represents a system of linear equations.

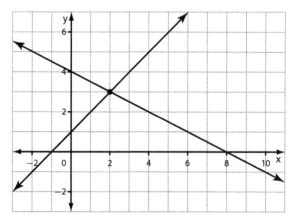

For each line, determine the

a) x-intercept

b) y-intercept

c) slope

d) point of intersection with the other line

e) equation

10. Mr. Darwal told his students that his daughter was getting married. When the students expressed surprise that he had a daughter old enough to be engaged, Mr. Darwal said: "Our ages have a sum of 62 and half of my age is one year more than my daughter's age."

a) Create a system of linear equations for the relationship between the two ages.

b) Solve the system graphically to determine the ages of Mr. Darwal and his daughter.

11. When an airplane is flying with a tailwind, the plane's speed is equal to its airspeed plus the speed of the wind. When a plane is flying into a headwind, its speed is equal to its airspeed minus the speed of the wind. Suppose that the airspeed of an airplane is 180 km/h and that the wind speed is 30 km/h.

a) Create a system of linear equations to model the distance, d, that the plane travels in terms of time, t, when the aircraft is flying with the wind and when it is flying against the wind.

b) What is the point of intersection of the two lines representing these equations?

c) How much farther can the airplane travel in 4 h with a 30-km/h tailwind than with a 30-km/h headwind?

⭐**12.** At what point will a line that passes through (1, 1) and (4, 7) intersect a second line that passes through (1, 6) and (3, 0)? Solve algebraically.

13. To convert temperatures expressed in degrees Celsius, C, to temperatures expressed in degrees Fahrenheit, F, you can use the equation $F = \frac{9}{5}C + 32$. To convert temperatures from the Fahrenheit scale to the Celsius scale, you can use the equation $C = \frac{5}{9}(F - 32)$. At what point are temperatures on the two scales equal?

14. Ferdinand lives in the mountains and rides his bicycle to and from school in the valley. Over level ground, Ferdinand rides at an average speed of 20 km/h. He travels at twice that speed coming down the mountain, and pedals back up the trail at half that speed. It takes Ferdinand a total of 1 hour to complete a ride to and from school.

a) Write a system of linear equations to model Ferdinand's ride in each direction in terms of distance travelled, d, in kilometres and time, t, in hours.

b) Use graphing technology to solve your system. What does the point of intersection represent?

c) Assuming that Ferdinand rides at a constant speed in each direction, how long does it take for him to travel from home to school? from school to home?

d) How far from school does Ferdinand live?

D Create Connections

15. Is it possible for two lines to have no point of intersection? Explain.

16. You are starting a website creation company. Your start-up costs are $200. For each website you create you must pay a fee of $25. If you charge customers $50 each to create a website for them, how many customers will it take for you to break even?

⭐**17.** For the parallelogram shown, determine the values of x and y.

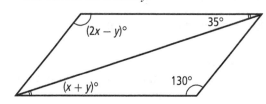

8.2 Modelling and Solving Linear Systems

Example

Sean is comparing the costs that two computer repair companies charge for home visits. Company A charges a rate of $45 per hour. Company B charges a flat rate of $50, plus $25 per hour for labour.

a) Create a system of linear equations to model the rates that both companies charge.

b) Solve the system of linear equations graphically. Explain what the solution represents.

Solution

a) Let h represent the number of hours for a home visit and let C represent the cost, in dollars. For Company A, the equation to express its rate is $C = 45 \times h$. For Company B, its rate may be modelled by the equation $C = 50 + 25 \times h$. These two equations form a linear system.

b) Use technology to graph the equations.

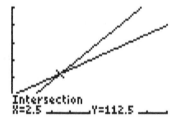

The point of intersection is (2.5, 112.5). This indicates that the charges of the two companies are equal, at $112.50, when 2.5 hours of labour are needed for a computer repair.

A Practise

1. Model each situation using a system of linear equations.

   a) Shandra is three times as old as Cory. In four years she will be twice as old as Cory will be.

   b) One vehicle has 5 L of fuel in its tank and is being filled at a rate of 0.9 L/s. A second vehicle has 3 L of fuel in its tank and is being filled at a rate of 1.2 L/s.

$\star$**2.** The sum of two numbers is 168. Their difference (subtracting the second number from the first) is 18.

   a) The table shown has x- and y-values adding to 168. Calculate the difference between x and y and put these values in the table. If you want the difference to be 18, what inferences can you make about the size of x and the size of y?

x	y	$x - y$
30	138	-118
50	118	
70	98	
80	88	
90	78	
100	68	

   b) Create a system of equations to model the relationships between the two numbers.

   c) Rewrite the equations in slope-intercept form.

   d) Graph the equations to determine the intersection point.

   e) Does the intersection point confirm the inferences you made using the table in part a)?

3. Josee invests a total of $15 000 in two different investments. The first amount is put into a long-term account that pays interest at a rate of 6.5% per year. The second amount is put into a short-term account earning interest at a rate of 5% per year. Josee's investments earn a total of $885 in interest in one year.

   a) Write equations to represent the total amount invested and the total interest earned.

   b) Rewrite the equations in slope-intercept form.

   c) Use technology to graph the two equations and determine the point of intersection. Explain how this point relates to the investments.

B Apply

$\star$**4.** A chemist wants to make 5 L of bromine solution with 32% concentration. The chemist has two available bromine solutions of concentrations 40% and 25%. She needs to determine the amount of each solution to mix to obtain the final amount in the desired concentration.

   a) Write an equation to express the final amount of solution.

   b) Write a second equation using the concentrations and amounts of the available solutions.

   c) Rewrite the equations in slope-intercept form, if necessary, and graph them using technology.

   d) Use the point of intersection to determine the amount of each bromine solution that the chemist needs to use.

5. A rectangle with a perimeter of 72 m has a length that is three times its width.

   a) Create a table of values for each equation and determine five ordered pairs to satisfy each equation.

$l = 3w$

w					
l					

$2l + 2w = 72$

w					
l					

   b) Plot the ordered pairs on graph paper with axes labelled w and l. Connect each set into a line, and estimate the intersection point of the lines.

   c) Check your estimate using technology.

   d) Explain the meaning of the point of intersection.

6. A food company wants to produce 0.5-kg bags of a mixture of cashews and peanuts to sell for $5.00. The company pays $12/kg for cashews and $3/kg for peanuts. The company needs to determine the amount of each to put into the bags to at least break even.

  a) Create an equation for the amount of cashews, c, and peanuts, p, in each bag. Create a second equation for the total cost of the different nuts and the mixture.

  b) Rewrite the equations in the form $y = mx + b$ and graph them on a graphing calculator.

  c) Solve the system of linear equations.

7. Aircraft are landing and taking off on parallel runways at a busy airport. On its approach, one aircraft descends from an altitude of 1200 m to an altitude of 500 m in 35 s. During the same time, a departing aircraft climbs from an altitude of 200 m to an altitudes of 1250 m.

  a) Write a system of linear equations to model the altitudes of the aircraft.

  b) When are the aircraft at the same altitude? What is that altitude?

C Extend

8. The highest point in Alberta is Mount Columbia. The highest point in Saskatchewan is Cypress Hills. Their elevations are related by the system of linear equations $a - s = 2279$ and $a + s = 5215$, where a is the height, in metres, of Mount Columbia above sea level, and s is the height, in metres, of Cypress Hills above sea level.

  a) Explain the meaning of each equation.

  b) Rewrite each equation to isolate the variable s.

  c) Graph the equations together and determine the heights of Mount Columbia and Cypress Hills.

9. Janna and Jordan are planning a birthday party and are comparing prices from two restaurants. Both restaurants have a flat rate for renting a banquet hall for a maximum of 100 guests, as well as a set meal price per guest.

  a) The prices that the restaurants charge can be modelled by the equations $C = 175 + 20n$ and $C = 100 + 22.5n$. Explain what each equation means.

  b) Graph the equations together and determine the point of intersection.

  c) For how many guests is the first restaurant the less expensive choice? For how many guests is the second restaurant the less expensive choice? Express each answer as a range of values.

☆**10.** The tables of values model the relationship between time and distance for two drivers who are travelling from Calgary in the same direction but who leave at different times.

Driver A

Time (h)	0	1	2	5	6
Distance (km)	0	75	150	375	450

Driver B

Time (h)	0	1	2	3	6
Distance (km)	0	0	95	190	475

  a) Which driver left one hour later than the other?

  b) Which driver is travelling at a faster rate?

  c) What happens when 6 h have elapsed?

  d) Plot the points in the tables of values on graph paper, using time and distance axes, and estimate the number of hours it takes for the drivers to travel the same distance.

D Create Connections

11. A boat travels 50 km along a river in 2.5 h when it is moving downstream with the current at a constant speed. When moving upstream against the current, it takes 4 h for the boat to cover the same distance.

a) Write equations to model the travel of the boat in each direction, using s for the constant speed of the boat and c for the constant speed of the current, each in kilometres per hour.

b) Rewrite the equations and graph them together to determine the point of intersection.

c) What does the point of intersection indicate about the boat's travel on the river?

★**12.** The graph shows the change in volume of water in two tanks over time. V represents volume, in litres, and t represents time, in minutes.

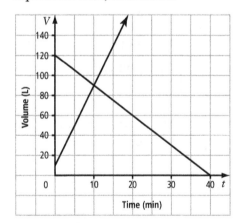

a) How much water is in each tank at $t = 0$?

b) What is different about how the volume of water is changing in the two tanks?

c) When do the tanks have the same volume of water and how much water is that?

d) At what rate is the volume of water changing for each tank?

e) Determine a system of linear equations to express the relationship between volume and time that matches the graphs.

13. The graph shows the charges, C, in dollars, of two appliance repair companies, A and B, in terms of hours of labour, t.

a) What is the point of intersection of the lines on the graph?

b) Which company charges less if a repair takes several hours?

c) Create a system of linear equations to match the graphs shown.

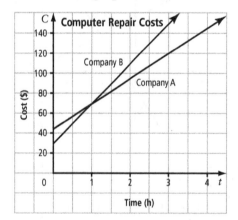

14. Create a problem or situation that could be modelled by each linear system.

a) $C = 100 + 18.5t$
$C = 75 + 20t$

b) $a + b = 900$
$0.05a + 0.045b = 74$

c) $y = x + 8$
$5x + 9y = 100$

15. Create a problem involving a system of linear equations that has a solution of (3, 24).

« **KEY IDEAS** »

- A system of linear equations can have one solution, no solution, or an infinite number of solutions.

- Before solving, you can predict the number of solutions for a linear system by comparing the slopes and y-intercepts of the equations.

Intersecting Lines	Parallel Lines	Coincident Lines
one solution	no solution	an infinite number of solutions
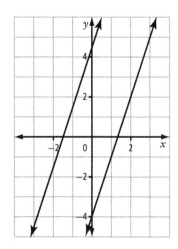		
different slopes	same slope	same slope
y-intercepts can be the same or different	different y-intercepts	same y-intercept

- For some linear systems, reducing the equations to lowest terms and comparing the coefficients of the x-terms, y-terms, and constants may help you predict the number of solutions.

Consider the system of linear equations
$3x - y - 4$ and $6x - 2y = -9$.
Rewrite the equations in slope-intercept form.

$y = 3x - 4$ and $y = 3x + \frac{9}{2}$

The lines both have a slope of 3. Since they have different y-intercepts, the lines are parallel. Parallel lines have no intersection, so this system of linear equations has no solution.

Graphing the equations together shows that the lines are parallel and will not generate any solutions.

Example

Four students are going to type the same lengthy essay. Shonna begins first. Anna and Kristian start together, a short time later, and type at an equal speed that is faster than Shonna's rate. James begins last and types at the same speed as Shonna. If the number of words typed by each student as a function of time could be represented by a linear equation, how many solutions would there be for each system of linear equations?

a) Shonna and Anna

b) Anna and Kristian

c) Shonna and James

Solution

a) Although Anna started to type after Shonna did, Anna types more quickly. In time, Anna will catch up to and pass Shonna in terms of the number of words typed. There will be one point at which the numbers of words typed by Shonna and Anna are equal. Therefore, there is one solution.

b) Since Anna and Kristian start at the same time and are typing at the same speed, they will have typed the same number of words at all times. Therefore, there is an infinite number of solutions.

c) James is typing at the same speed as Shonna, but because he started typing after she did, he will never catch up. Therefore, there is no solution.

A Practise

1. Predict the number of solutions for each system of linear equations. Justify your answers.

a) $y = 4x - 1$
$y = 4x + 7$

b) $y = 3x + 5$
$y = -3x + 5$

c) $x + 2y = 7$
$5x + 10y = 35$

d) $y = 2x + 3$
$y = 2x - 7$

e) $2y = \frac{x}{2} + 3$
$3y = \frac{3x}{2} + \frac{9}{2}$

2. One equation of a linear system is $2x - 3y = 8$. Write a second equation so that the linear system will have

a) no solution

b) one solution

c) an infinite number of solutions

3. The four lines on the graph intersect to produce parallelogram ABCD. Indicate the number of solutions for each system of linear equations.

a) AB and CD   **b)** AC and BD

c) AB and AC   **d)** BD and CD

e) AD and BC

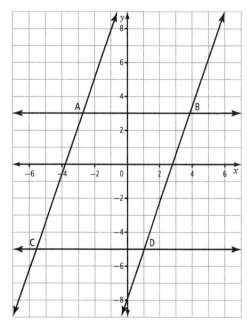

4. Graph each system of linear equations and indicate the number of solutions.

a) $6x + 2y = 10$
$y = -3x - 1$

b) $x + y = 9$
$x - y = 9$

c) $3y = x + 6$
$6y - 2x = 12$

5. Explain in words a method to correctly predict the number of solutions of a system of linear equations simply by looking at the equations.

6. A line is defined by the equation $7x - 3y = 12$. Determine the equation of a second line such that the system of linear equations has

a) no solution

b) an infinite number of solutions

c) one solution

B Apply

7. A real estate company is comparing the projected earnings, E, of several of its sales representatives. Projected earnings are based on current earnings plus a percent of sales, s, of each employee.

Employee	Current Earnings ($)	Percent of Sales (s)
Jocelyn	1200	3.00
Mario	1000	4.50
Kendra	2000	3.00
Pavel	2000	3.00

Write a linear equation for the projected earnings of each sales representative. For which pair(s) of sales representatives could you create a system of linear equations that has

a) no solution?

b) an infinite number of solutions?

c) one solution?

8. Service charges of two cell phone companies consist of a flat rate (a constant) and a rate per minute of use. If C represents the total cost and m represents the rate per minute, use values of your choice to create a system of linear equations that expresses the service charges of the companies where the system has

a) one solution

b) no solution

c) an infinite number of solutions

9. Two students are using graphing technology to solve the system of linear equations $y = \frac{3}{5}x + \frac{5}{2}$ and $y = \frac{2}{3}x$. The graphing calculator viewing window is set at X [0, 10, and 1] and Y [−2, 10, 1]. Antonio says that the system has no solution. Ling says it has one solution.

a) Which student is correct? Why?

b) How could the system of linear equations be solved without actually graphing the equations?

C Extend

10. The Gold Coast Fishery pays fishers $1.25/kg for Coho salmon and has a $40 processing fee. The Salmon House pays fishers $1.00/kg for Coho salmon and charges $25 for processing.

a) Determine a system of linear equations to model the earnings, E, in dollars, for fishers in terms of kilograms, k, of salmon delivered.

b) Predict the number of solutions to the system.

c) For what range of k-values should a fisher bring his or her salmon catch to Gold Coast Fishery? to The Salmon House?

d) How would your answer to part c) change if The Salmon House raised its rate to $1.25/kg to match its competitor?

11. Given the system of linear equations $3x - 5y = 30$ and $6x - 10y = C$, for what value(s) of C is there

   a) no solution?

   b) an infinite number of solutions?

12. Given the system of linear equations $2x + 6y = 12$ and $Ax + 3y = 6$, for what value(s) of A is there

   a) an infinite number of solutions?

   b) one solution?

13. Two 20-storey office towers are under construction. The first building is being erected at a rate of 2 storeys every 6 weeks. The height of each storey is 15 ft. Construction of the second tower began 4 weeks after the first. It is going up at a rate of 1 storey every 2 weeks. Each storey has a height of 12 ft.

   a) Determine a system of linear equations to model construction of the towers where h is the height of each building, in feet, and w is the number of weeks since construction first started.

   b) Predict the number of solutions to the system of linear equations.

   c) What is the solution to the linear system? What does the solution represent?

D Create Connections

★14. Consider the statement "Determine two natural numbers having a sum of 20 and a difference of 10."

   a) If a system of linear equations can model the statement, how many solutions will the system have?

   b) Compare the statement "Determine two natural numbers that have a sum of 10 and a difference of 20." If a system of linear equations can model this statement, how many solutions will the system have?

   c) Graph each system of linear equations to confirm your answers for parts a) and b).

   d) Why are the answers for parts a) and b) different?

15. There is an international dragon boat festival each year in Vancouver. Competitive racing takes place on False Creek over a course that is 500 m in length. Information about four dragon boats part way through one race is shown in the table of values.

Boat	Current Distance (m)	Current Speed (m/s)
A	220	3.1
B	206	3.4
C	198	3.6
D	230	3.2

Represent the data for each pair of boats using a system of linear equations, assuming that each boat continues at its current speed. What is the solution to each system? What does the solution represent?

   a) A and C   b) A and D

   c) B and D

16. The volume of water, V, in two different pools as they are being filled is given by the equations $V = 150 + 32.5t$ and $V = 175 + 35t$, where V is measured in litres and t is time, in minutes. Eva says that one pool has less water to start with and is filling more slowly, so the system of linear equations has no solution. Vince says that the lines have different slopes and must intersect, so there is one solution. Who is correct? Justify your answer.

17. A linear system of equations can be described in general as $ax + by = c$ and $dx + ey = f$, where coefficients $a, b, c, d, e, f \in I$. What is the relationship between the coefficients in the two equations such that the system has

   a) no solution?

   b) an infinite number of solutions?

Chapter 8 Review

8.1 Systems of Linear Equations and Graphs

1. Verify, without graphing, whether the given point is a solution for the system of linear equations.

   a) $y = 4x + 9$ and $y = -3x - 5$, $(-2, 1)$

   b) $5x - 3y = 17$ and $2x + 2y = 11$, $(4, 1)$

2. Use technology to solve each system of linear equations. Round your answer to two decimal places, if necessary.

   a) $y = \frac{3}{4}x - 3$
   $y = -\frac{2}{5}x + 1$

   b) $5x + 6y = -35$
   $3x + 8y = 10$

3. The lines on the graph form a system of linear equations.

   a) State the solution of the system.

   b) Determine the equation of each line in slope-intercept form.

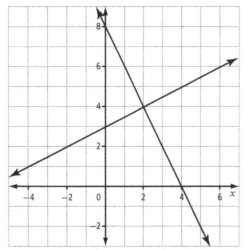

4. A cyclist is riding along a trail. Her distance travelled can be represented by the equation $d = 20t + 15$. A second cyclist's distance on the same trail is given by the equation $d = 25t + 5$. In both equations, d is distance, in kilometres, and t is time, in hours.

   a) Graph the system using technology to determine the solution for the system of linear equations.

   b) Explain what the solution represents in the context of the situation.

8.2 Modelling and Solving Linear Systems

5. Model each situation with a system of linear equations.

   a) One long distance phone plan charges $0.50/min with no sign-up fee. A second plan charges a $25 sign-up fee plus $0.25/min.

   b) A box contains 23 coins consisting of dimes and quarters. There is a total of $3.35 in the box.

   c) A bus leaves Regina, heading west at 85 km/h. A car leaves Regina 1 h later at 100 km/h, also heading west.

6. Jenny needs to rent a car for the day. The graph shows the daily cost, C, of renting a vehicle from each of two companies in terms of distance driven, d, in kilometres.

   a) How can you use the graph to determine the basic cost of a rental car (excluding distance charges) and the distance charge per kilometre for each company?

   b) Jenny thinks she will drive about 100 km. Which company should she choose?

   c) Under what circumstances should Jenny choose DirectCar?

   d) How does the point of intersection of the lines relate to the decision about which company to choose?

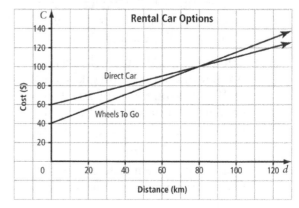

★7. A load of 12.5 m³ of grain is being dumped from a truck into a bin at a rate of 1.4 m³ per minute.

  a) Write an equation to express the volume of grain in the truck and a second equation to represent the volume of grain in the bin, both in terms of time. In the equations, let V represent volume, in cubic metres, and let t represent time, in minutes.

  b) Graph the system of linear equations.

  c) Determine the point of intersection and explain its meaning in the context of the problem.

8. A desktop computer begins downloading an 885-megabyte (MB) file at 35 MB/s. At the same time, a laptop begins downloading a 1450 MB file at a rate of 60 MB/s.

  a) Create a system of linear equations for the amount, A, of each file still to be downloaded, in terms of time, t, in seconds.

  b) Graph the equations together and determine the point of intersection of the lines.

  c) Explain the meaning of the point of intersection in the context of the downloading of files to the two computers.

9. The sum of Bill's age and Nancy's age is 45. In three years, Bill will be three times as old as Nancy was four years ago.

  a) Create a system of linear equations to represent the relationship between Bill's age and Nancy's age.

  b) Solve the system graphically to determine how old Bill and Nancy are today.

8.3 Number of Solutions for Systems of Linear Equations

10. Predict the number of solutions for each system of linear equations. Justify your answers.

  a) $y = 3x + 7$ and $y = 3x - 7$

  b) $x - 2y = -5$ and $4x - 8y = -20$

  c) $y = -6x + 1$ and $y = 6x + 1$

11. Without graphing, determine the number of solutions to the system of linear equations $2x - 5y = 18$ and $10y = 4x + 13$.

12. Which pair(s) of lines in the graph has (have)

  a) exactly one solution?

  b) no solution?

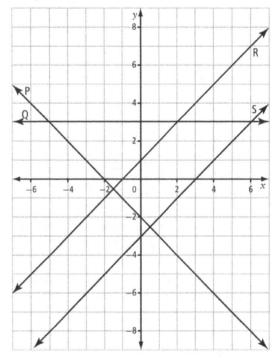

13. The South Edmonton Pet Shop has several parrots and dogs for sale. There are a total of 24 heads and 82 legs in the display cages.

  a) Write a system of linear equations to represent the number of parrots, p, and the number of dogs, d, for sale.

  b) Determine the solution to this system graphically.

  c) Explain why this system of linear equations would have no solution if the total number of legs is changed from 82 to 83.

  d) Why is your answer to part c) not related to the slopes of the two lines?

Chapters 1–8 Cumulative Review

1. Estimate the perimeter of the figure in an appropriate SI and imperial unit.

2. The infield of a baseball field is covered with a tarp to protect it from rain when the field is not in use. The tarp covers a square area that measures 30 m on each side. Determine the area of the tarp in square yards. Round your answer to the nearest tenth of a square yard.

3. Draw right $\triangle$JKL in which $\angle$K is the right angle.
   a) Label the leg opposite to $\angle$J and the leg adjacent to $\angle$J and the hypotenuse.
   b) State the tangent, sine, and cosine ratios of $\angle$J.

4. Which numbers are perfect squares? perfect cubes? both perfect squares and perfect cubes?
   a) 1024
   b) -8
   c) 216
   d) 1
   e) 4096
   f) 169

5. Simplify. Then, combine like terms.
   a) $2(-5n + 4)(3n - 2) + (n - 5)^2$
   b) $(6s^2 + s - 2)(-s^2 + 3s + 6)$

6. During the 2010 Olympic Winter Games, a zip line was erected over Robson Square in downtown Vancouver. The line stretched across a distance of 170 m at a height of six storeys. Create a speed–time graph for the following scenario:

   Rebecca decides to take a ride on the zip line and climbs to the top of the tower. After climbing into safety gear, she jumps from the tower and accelerates to a speed of 11 m/s within the first 10 s of the ride. Rebecca stays at this top speed for another 10 s, until the line starts to curve upward and begins to slow her down. Rebecca lands at the opposite tower 30 s after she began her ride.

7. Write the equation of the line with each slope and y-intercept.
   a) slope is $-\frac{2}{5}$, y-intercept is $(0, -3)$
   b) slope is 0, y-intercept is $(0, 12)$

8. For each system of linear equations, explain how you could verify whether the given point is a solution. Is the given point a solution?
   a) $y = x - 7$ and $y = -3x + 1$, $(2, -5)$
   b) $12x + 4y = 12$ and $-3x + 4y = 12$, $(3, -6)$

9. From 2006 to 2009, the population of Calgary increased at an average annual rate of 4.85%. This growth can be modelled using the formula $P = (1\,079\,310)(1.0485)^n$, where P is the estimated population and n is the number of years since 2006. Assume that the city's rate of growth is constant.
   a) What will be the population of Calgary in 2015?
   b) What was the population in 1988, the year that Calgary hosted the Olympic Winter Games?

10. Determine the measure of angle θ in each triangle. Express your answer to the nearest tenth of a degree.

a)

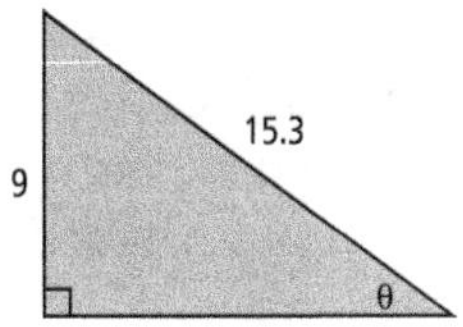

b)

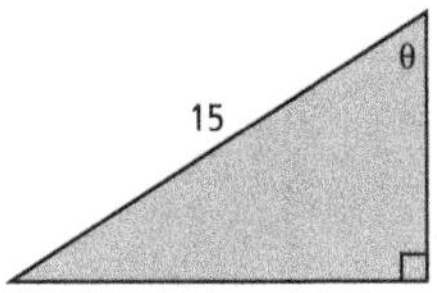

c)

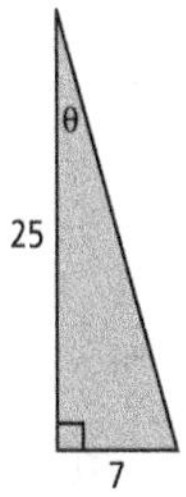

11. The population of a small college grows at a constant rate of 89 students per year. The college had 3420 students in 2006. Consider the relationship between the total number of students at the college and time, in years.

a) Assign variables to represent each quantity in the relation. Identify the dependent variable and the independent variable.

b) Is the graph of the relation linear or non-linear? Explain.

c) Write a formula to represent the relation.

d) How many students will the college have in 2017?

e) Use the formula to determine the year in which the college had 1017 students.

12. Solve each system of linear equations by graphing.

a) $y + 3x = 4$ and $4y - x = 3$

b) $y = \left(\frac{1}{3}\right)x - 5$ and $y = -\left(\frac{3}{2}\right)x + 6$

13. For each object, the surface area is given. Calculate the missing dimension to the nearest hundredth of a unit.

a) A cone has a surface area of 314.5 cm^2 and a radius of 8.5 cm.

b) A right pyramid has a surface area of 4080 cm^2 and a square base with area 1156 cm^2.

c) A sphere has a surface area of 245 cm^2.

14. Identify the GCF of each set of terms.

a) $12ab^2$ and $42ab$

b) $18x^3y^2$ and $108xy^4$

c) $13p^3q^5$, $-26p^5q^3$, and $3p^2q^2$

15. State the intercepts of each line as ordered pairs. Then, write the equation of each line in general form.

a)

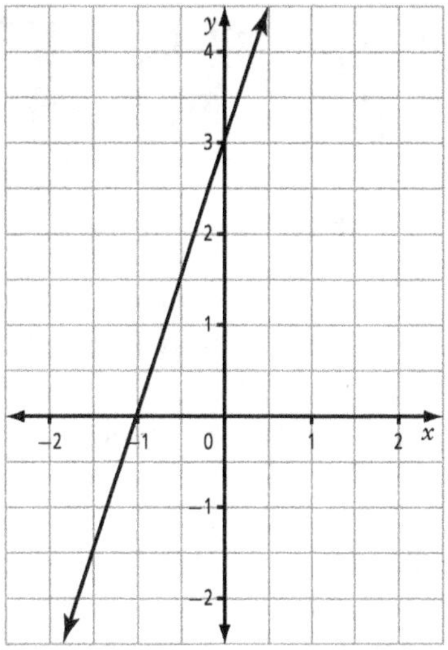

b)

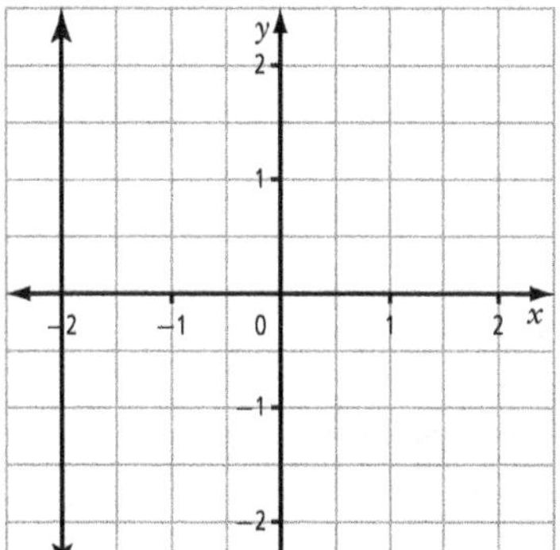

16. What reading is shown on this SI caliper? Name an object that could be this length.

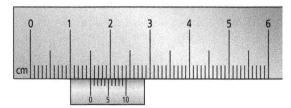

17. A bongo drum has a diameter of $6\frac{1}{2}$ in. A second, smaller drum has a diameter of $5\frac{3}{8}$ in. Both drums are $\frac{7}{8}$ in. deep. What is the minimum amount of hide to cover only the tops and lateral surfaces of the drums? Express your answer to the nearest square inch.

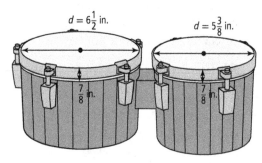

$d = 6\frac{1}{2}$ in. $d = 5\frac{3}{8}$ in. $\frac{7}{8}$ in. $\frac{7}{8}$ in.

18. A boy at an amusement park is standing at a distance of 7 m away from a bouncy castle. He is looking up to the top at an angle of 40°. How high is the castle, to the nearest hundredth of a metre?

19. Evaluate each expression. Express the answers with positive exponents.

a) $\left(x^{\frac{1}{4}}\right)\left(x^{\frac{-3}{2}}\right)$

b) $(64h^9)^{\frac{-3}{2}}$

c) $\dfrac{12^{\frac{3}{5}}}{12^{\frac{-2}{7}}}$

d) $\left(\dfrac{x^{-2}}{0.125x^{\frac{-1}{3}}}\right)^4$

20. Factor completely.

a) $c^2 - 144$

b) $1 - 256y^4$

c) $54h^2 - 486f^2$

d) $x^4 - 13x + 36$

21. A relation is given by the formula $m = 9.3p - 4.7$. If the domain of the relation is $[-3, 18]$, what is the range?

22. Use slope-point form to write an equation of a line through each point with the given slope. Express each answer in slope-intercept form and in general form.

a) $(-4, 1)$ and $m = -2$

b) $(5, 9)$ and $m = \frac{1}{3}$

23. Factor completely.

a) $x^2 + 3x - 54$

b) $3x^2 + 8x - 3$

c) $20m^2 - 14mn + 2n^2$

d) $12x^2 + 16xy - 3y^2$

e) $3s^2t + 3st - 36t$

24. Consider two tanks of water. One tank, which holds 100 L, drains at a rate of 5 L per minute. The function $T(w) = 100 - 5w$ describes this draining pattern. The second tank holds 120 L of water and drains at a rate of 6 L per minute. The function $H(w) = 120 - 6w$ models the tank's draining pattern.

a) What does the variable w represent in each function?

b) Determine $T(4)$ and $H(4)$. Explain your answer.

c) Determine the value of w if $T(w) = 25$. Explain your answer.

d) Identify the domain and range of both functions.

25. Calculate the volume of each object, to the nearest hundredth of a unit.

a) A cylinder has a radius of 25 ft and height equal to its diameter.

b) A cone has a height of 24 cm and diameter 14.5 cm.

c) A rectangular pyramid has a base measuring 22 ft by 24 ft and a height of 28 ft.

d) A sphere has a radius of 14.1 cm.

26. A plane takes off from Calgary International Airport in the direction of Nose Hill Park at an angle that is to be kept constant until the aircraft passes the hill. At takeoff, the plane is a horizontal distance of 7.7 km from the peak of the hill, which is 1230 m in height. The pilot wants to clear the peak by 200 m. What is the angle of elevation of the plane to the nearest degree?

27. Police can estimate the speed of a car by the length of the skid marks made when the driver braked. The formula is $v = \sqrt{30df}$, where v is the speed of the vehicle, in miles per hour; d is the length of the skid marks, in feet; and f is the coefficient of friction. What was the speed of a vehicle if the length of the skid marks is 90 ft and the coefficient of friction is 0.9?

28. Write the equation of a line that passes through the point (9, 0) and is parallel to the line $2x + 6y - 7 = 0$.

29. Graph each line, given a point on the line and its slope.

   a) $(-2, 3)$, $m = -\frac{2}{3}$

   b) origin, $m = \frac{3}{5}$

   c) $(5, -6)$, $m =$ undefined

   d) $(7, 1)$, $m = 0$

30. Write an equation of a line that passes through $(-3, -4)$ and is perpendicular to the line $6x + 7y - 5 = 0$.

31. How many solutions does each linear system have? Justify your answers.

   a) $x + 4y = 7$
   $\quad y = -\frac{x}{4} + 9$

   b) $5x - 2y = 16$
   $\quad 6x - 2y = 16$

   c) $-7x - 3y = 5$
   $\quad -14x - 6y = 10$

32. Justin has 14 coins in his pocket. Some are quarters and the rest are dimes. Justin has a total of $2.90.

   a) Write a system of linear equations to model the situation.

   b) How many of each type of coin does Justin have?

33. Convert each measurement to the unit indicated.

   a) The distance from Fort St. John, BC, to Prince George, BC, is 297 miles. (kilometres)

   b) Lake Athabasca is the largest and deepest lake in both Alberta and Saskatchewan. It has a maximum depth of 124 m. (feet)

34. A container in the shape of a cylinder measures 6.6 cm in diameter and 12.1 cm in height. A box of 24 containers is arranged in four rows of six cans each. How much empty space is in the box, to the nearest hundredth of a cubic centimetre?

35. A house is sighted from a taller building that is 30 m in height. From the top of the taller building, the angle of depression to the bottom of the house is 40°. How far is the house from the building, to the nearest hundredth of a metre?

36. Express each radical as an equivalent power.

   a) $\sqrt{(18x)^5}$

   b) $\sqrt[3]{7^2}$

   c) $\sqrt{z^{\frac{4}{5}}}$

   d) $\sqrt{\frac{a^2}{b^2}}$

37. Verify that each trinomial is a perfect square. Then, factor.

   a) $16s^2 - 24s + 9$

   b) $108s^3 + 108s^2 + 27s$

   c) $225 - 120y + 16y^2$

1. Zeno's paradox of Achilles' race with the tortoise was an impossible problem to solve at the time. The paradox states that Achilles gives the tortoise a head start of 100 units but runs at a speed 10 times as fast. Using an arbitrary speed for the tortoise, plot a distance–time graph on the same grid for each of Achilles and the tortoise. Then, determine the distance where Achilles catches up to the tortoise. Compare your answer with that of another person using a different speed. What do you notice?

2. Determine the values of m and n so that the system of linear equations $4x + 3y = 6$ and $2x + (m - 4)y = n + 1$ has

   a) no solution

   b) an infinite number of solutions

3. The sum of the digits of a two-digit number is 10. If the digits are reversed, the number decreases by 18.

   a) Write a system of linear equations to model the information.

   b) Represent the linear system graphically.

   c) What is the number?

4. Consider the rectangle shown.

   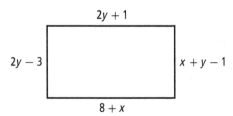

   a) Write a system of linear equations to represent the length and width of the rectangle.

   b) Represent the linear system graphically.

   c) Calculate the area of the rectangle.

5. Points (0, 0), (0, 6), and (4, 0) are three vertices of a trapezoid. The intersection of a vertical line passing through (4, 0) and a line passing through (0, 6) provides the coordinates of the last vertex. The area of the trapezoid is 15 square units.

   a) Determine the coordinates of the last vertex.

   b) Write the system of linear equations that gives the same intersection.

6. Given $Ax + 3Bx + 2A + B = 8 - x$

   a) Write a system of equations.

   b) Solve for A and B.

7. Determine the perimeter of the equilateral triangle.

   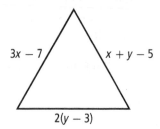

8. The ratio of the number of English books to Math books in the school library is $7:2$. After six English books are borrowed, the ratio of English books to Math books becomes $5:2$. How many books were there initially?

9. If $4^{2y + x - 3} = 1$ and $5^{x - 2y} = 25$, what is the value of $16^{3y}2^{2x}$?

10. If $x + y = 4$ and $x - y = 1$, what is the value of $2^{x^2 - y^2}$?

11. If $2009x + 2009y = 2010(x + y)$, $xy \neq 0$, what is the value of $\frac{x}{y}$?

Chapter 8 Study Check

Use the chart below to help you assess the skills and processes you have developed during Chapter 8. The references in italics direct you to pages in *Mathematics 10 Exercise and Homework Book* where you could review the skill. How can you show that you have gained each skill? What can you do to improve?

Big Idea	Skills	This Shows I Know	This Is How I Can Improve
Create and graph systems of linear equations with two variables to model and solve problems *pages 170–185, 187–188*	✓ Create graphs of systems of linear equations with and without technology *pages 170, 173–177, 180–183, 185, 188*		
	✓ Determine and verify the solution to a system of linear equations *pages 171–177, 180–184, 188*		
	✓ Interpret information provided by a graph of a system of linear relations *pages 172, 174, 177, 179, 182–183*		
	✓ Explain why systems of linear equations can have different numbers of solutions and identify the number of solutions for a given system *pages 178–181, 183, 187–188*		

Organizing the Ideas

Use the table below to compare solving linear equations with solving systems of linear equations.

Linear Equations Comparison Chart			
Characteristics	**Solving Equations**	**Solving Systems of Equations**	
Tables			Similarities
			Differences
Graphs			Similarities
			Differences
Possible Number of Solutions			Similarities
			Differences
Interpreting Results			Similarities
			Differences

Study Guide

Review the types of problems you handled in Chapter 8. What do you need to remember to help you do similar problems?

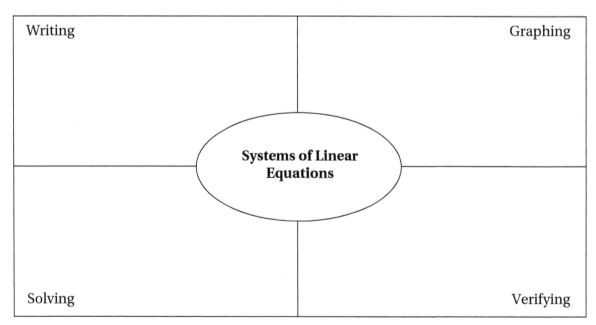

Chapter 9 Solving Systems of Linear Equations Algebraically

9.1 Solving Systems of Linear Equations by Substitution

⟪ KEY IDEAS ⟫

- You can solve systems of linear equations algebraically using substitution.
  - Isolate a single variable in one of the two equations.
  - Where possible, choose a variable with a coefficient of 1 or -1.
  - Solve the linear system.

    $5x + y = 11$ (Equation 1)
    $2x + 3y = 7$ (Equation 2)

  - Isolate the variable y in Equation 1 since its coefficient is 1.

    $$5x + y = 11$$
    $$5x + y - 5x = 11 - 5x$$
    $$y = 11 - 5x$$

  - Substitute the expression for y in Equation 2.

    $$2x + 3y = 7$$
    $$2x + 3(11 - 5x) = 7$$
    $$2x + 33 - 15x = 7$$
    $$33 - 13x = 7$$
    $$-13x = 7 - 33$$
    $$-13x = -26$$
    $$\frac{-13x}{-13} = \frac{-26}{-13}$$
    $$x = 2$$

  - Substitute the solution for the first variable into one of the original
    equations. Solve for the remaining variable.

    $$5x + y = 11$$
    $$5(2) + y = 11$$
    $$10 + y = 11$$
    $$10 + y - 10 = 11 - 10$$
    $$y = 1$$

    The solution to the system is $x = 2$ and $y = 1$.

  - Check your answer by substituting into both original equations.

$5x + y = 11$	$2x + 3y = y$
$5(2) + 1 = 11$	$2(2) + 3(1) = y$
$10 + 1 = 11$	$4 + 3 = 7$
$11 = 11$	$7 = 7$

    Therefore, $x = 2$ and $y = 1$ is the correct solution.

Example

Ryan bought 3 tickets and 6 hot dogs at an Edmonton Rush lacrosse game. The total cost of his purchases was $153. His friend Carrie bought 1 ticket and 3 hot dogs and spent $54. What was the price of a single ticket? What was the price of a hot dog?

Solution

Let T represent the price of a ticket.
Let D represent the price of a hot dog.
Write an equation that represents Ryan's purchases.
$3T + 6D = 153$ (Equation 1)
Write an equation that represents Carrie's purchases.
$1T + 3D = 54$ (Equation 2)
Isolate a variable in one of the equations. Isolate T in Equation 2.

$$1T + 3D = 54$$
$$T + 3D - 3D = 54 - 3D$$
$$T = 54 - 3D$$

Substitute this expression for T into Equation 1. Solve for D.

$$3T + 6D = 153$$
$$3(54 - 3D) + 6D = 153$$
$$162 - 9D + 6D = 153$$
$$162 - 3D = 153$$
$$162 - 162 - 3D = 153 - 162$$
$$-3D = -9$$
$$\frac{-3D}{-3} = \frac{-9}{-3}$$
$$D = 3$$

Therefore, the cost of a hot dog is $3. Substitute the cost of a hot dog into one of the equations. Solve for T.

$$T + 3D = 54$$
$$T + 3(3) = 54$$
$$T + 9 = 54$$
$$T + 9 - 9 = 54 - 9$$
$$T = 45$$

Therefore, the cost of a ticket is $45.
Verify by substituting 45 for T and 3 for D into each equation.

$3T + 6D = 153$	$T + 3D = 54$
$3(45) + 6(3) = 153$	$45 + 3(3) = 54$
$135 + 18 = 153$	$45 + 9 = 54$
$153 = 153$	$54 = 54$

Therefore, $T = 45$ and $D = 3$ is the correct solution.
The cost of a ticket is $45 and the cost of a hot dog is $3.

A Practise

1. Solve the following linear systems of equations by substitution.

   a) $x = y + 2$
   $x + y = 25$

   b) $y = 4x$
   $x - y = 33$

   c) $y = 18 - 2x$
   $3x + y = 17$

   d) $x - 2y = 8$
   $3x + y = 3$

   e) $2x + 5y = 5$
   $8x - y = 41$

   f) $\frac{1}{2}x - y = -2$
   $x + y = 5$

⋆2. Solve the following system of linear equations by isolating x. Then, solve by isolating y. Which method do you prefer? Explain why.

   $2x - y = -5$
   $5x + y = -2$

⋆3. Determine algebraically if the point $(2, 4)$ is the solution to the system $3x - y = 2$ and $x + y = 5$. Explain your answer.

B Apply

4. Seventy-five hundred fans attended a rock concert. Ticket prices were $60 for adults and $35 for students. If the total revenue from ticket sales was $300 000, how many students attended the concert?

5. Meredith invested $4000 in the stock market. She used some of the money to buy stock worth $2.50 a share and invested the rest in a stock worth $4.50 a share. If Meredith purchased a total of 1280 shares, how many shares of each type did she buy?

⋆6. Joel's hockey team collected a total of 900 aluminum cans and plastic bottles for recycling. The team received 10¢ for each can and 25¢ for each bottle. If the team received a total of $145.20, how many cans did they bring in?

7. Canada won 26 medals at the 2010 Winter Olympic Games, including 7 silver medals. The number of gold medals was 4 more than twice the number of bronze medals. How many gold medals did Canada win?

8. A satellite radio station plays 108 new wave and hip-hop songs in a 6-hour time slot. If the station plays 5 times as many new wave songs as hip-hop songs, how many songs of each type does the station play in 1 hour? What assumption(s) did you make?

9. The sum of Jane's age and Tim's age is 40. Four years from now, Jane's age will be 6 years less than twice Tim's age at that time. How old are Jane and Tim now?

10. A bag contains a total of 71 marbles, 14 of which are red. Each remaining marble is either black or white. If the number of black marbles is 3 less than 3 times the number of white marbles, how many marbles are black?

11. Your neighbourhood music store is having a sale. You spend a total of $81.50 to buy 5 music videos and 4 compact discs. Your friend spends a total of $42.25 to buy 3 videos and 1 compact disc. All music videos cost the same amount, and all compact discs cost the same amount.

    a) What is the price for one video?

    b) What is the price for one CD?

12. Teams in the girls' school basketball league are awarded 2 points for a win and 1 point for a loss. At the end of the season, Team A has 36 points and Team B has 24 points. Deborah, the league statistician, notices that the record of Team A is the reverse of the record of Team B: the number of Team A's wins equals the number of Team B's losses, while the number of Team A's losses is the same as the number of Team B's wins. What is the win-loss record of each team?

13. A student is given the following problem.

> A vending machine in the school cafeteria accepts only $1, $2, and 25¢ coins. When it was emptied, the machine contained 125 coins, 45 of which were loonies. If the total value of the coins was $184, how many coins of each type were in the machine?

The student wrote the following system of linear equations to solve the problem.

Let T represent the number of $2 coins.
Let Q represent the number of 25¢ coins.
$T + Q + 45 = 125$
$27 + 0.25Q = 184$

Will this linear system provide the correct solution? If so, solve it. If not, write a correct system and solve it.

14. In which step is the first error made in the partial solution of the linear system $3x + y = 2$ and $2x + 5y = 23$?

Step 1: $2x + 5(-3x + 2) = 23$

Step 2: $2x - 15x + 2 = 23$

Step 3: $-13x = 21$

Step 4: $x = \frac{13}{21}$

Correct the error and determine the solution.

C Extend

★**15.** Mandy drove from Prince George to Kamloops, a distance of approximately 400 km. It took her 4.5 hours to complete the trip. For part of the trip, she drove at an average speed of 80 km/h. For the remaining part, she travelled at an average speed of 100 km/h. For what distance did she drive at the higher speed?

16. $3x + 2y = 2$ and $4x + 5y = 12$ form a linear system in which part of the solution is $x = -2$. Determine the y-value of the solution.

17. Consider the system of linear equations $5x - 4y = 0$ and $x + 3y = 15$.

a) Without solving the system, determine whether there is one solution, an infinite number of solutions, or no solution. Explain your thinking.

b) If there is one solution, in which quadrant will the lines intersect? Show how you determined your answer.

18. Use a substitution method to solve this system of linear equations involving three variables.

$2x - y + 2z = -7$
$4x - 3y + 4z = -33$
$-x + y + z = -3$

D Create Connections

19. Consider the system of linear equations $x - 2y = 10$ and $3x - y = 0$.

a) Solve the system by graphing.

b) Solve the system by using substitution.

c) How are the methods similar? How are they different?

d) Which method do you prefer for solving this system of equations? Explain.

« **KEY IDEAS** »

- A table can help you organize information in a problem. This can help you to determine the equations in a linear system.
  - You can solve a linear system by elimination.
    $3x + 2y = 2$
    $4x = 12 - 5y$

  - If necessary, rearrange the equations so that like variables appear in the same position in both equations. The most common form is $ax + by = c$.
    $3x + 2y = 2$ (Equation 1) $4x = 12 - 5y$ (Equation 2)
    $4x + 5y = 12 - 5y + 5y$
    $4x + 5y = 12$

  - Determine which variable to eliminate. If necessary, multiply one or both equations by a constant to eliminate the variable by addition or subtraction.

    Eliminate the variable y.

  - The lowest common multiple of 2 and 5 is 10. Multiply Equation 1 by 5 and multiply Equation 2 by 2 so that the coefficients of the terms involving y add to zero.
    $5(3x + 2y) = 5(2)$ $2(4x + 5y) = 2(12)$
    $15x + 10y = 10$ $8x + 10y = 24$

    Subtract the second equation from the first equation to eliminate y.
    $15x + 10y = 10$
    $\underline{-(8x + 10y = 24)}$
    $\qquad 7x = -14$

  - Solve for the remaining variable.
    $\frac{7x}{7} = \frac{-14}{7}$
    $x = -2$

  - Solve for the second variable by substituting the value for the first variable into one of the original equations.
    $3x + 2y = 2$
    $3(-2) + 2y = 2$
    $-6 + 2y = 2$
    $-6 + 6 + 2y = 2 + 6$
    $2y = 8$
    $\frac{2y}{2} = \frac{8}{2}$
    $y = 4$

  - Check your solution by substituting each value into both original equations.
    $3x + 2y = 2$ $4x = 12 - 5y$
    $3(-2) + 2(4) = 2$ $4(-2) = 12 - 5(4)$
    $-6 + 8 = 2$ $-8 = 12 - 20$
    $2 = 2$ $-8 = -8$
    The solution is $x = -2$ and $y = 4$.

Example

The Fête au Village is an annual festival in Legal, Alberta, to celebrate the French culture of Legal's pioneers. Two popular events are the tug o' war and the demolition derby. A tug o' war team consists of 8 people. The entry fee is $20 per team. Each demolition derby team has 2 members. The entry fee is $100 per team. If a total of 94 people enter both events and $1660 is collected in fees, how many teams are entered in each event?

Solution

Let W represent the number of teams entered in the tug o' war.
Let D represent the number of teams entered in the demolition derby.
Write an equation that represents the total number of people entered in both events.
$8W + 2D = 94$ (Equation 1)

Write an equation that represents the total entry fees collected.
$20W + 100D = 1660$ (Equation 2)

Solve the system by elimination.
Eliminate variable W.

The lowest common multiple of 8 and 20 is 40. Multiply Equation 1 by 5 and multiply Equation 2 by 2.

$5(8W + 2D) = 5(94)$ $\qquad$ $2(20W + 100D) = 2(1660)$
$40W + 10D = 470$ $\qquad\qquad$ $40W + 200D = 3320$

Subtract Equation 1 from Equation 2.

$$\begin{array}{r} 40W + 200D = 3320 \\ -(40W + 10D = 470) \\ \hline 190D = 2850 \end{array}$$

Solve for D.
$$\frac{190D}{190} = \frac{2850}{190}$$
$$D = 15$$

Substitute $D = 15$ into Equation 1. Solve for W.
$$8W + 2D = 94$$
$$8W + 2(15) = 94$$
$$8W + 30 = 94$$
$$8W + 30 - 30 = 94 - 30$$
$$8W = 64$$
$$\frac{8W}{8} = \frac{64}{8}$$
$$W = 8$$

Check the answer by substituting $D = 15$ and $W = 8$ into both equations.

$8W + 2D = 94$ $\qquad\qquad$ $20W + 100D = 1660$
$8(8) + 2(15) = 94$ $\qquad$ $20(8) + 100(15) = 1660$
$64 + 30 = 94$ $\qquad\qquad$ $160 + 1500 = 1660$
$94 = 94$ $\qquad\qquad\qquad$ $1660 = 1660$

Therefore, there are 8 teams entered for the tug o' war and 15 teams entered for the demolition derby.

A Practise

1. Solve, using elimination.

   a) $2x - y = -5$
      $5x + y = -2$

   b) $4x + 2y = 6$
      $4x - 3y = 1$

   c) $3x + 7y = 17$
      $2x - 3y = -4$

   d) $2x - 3y = 20$
      $2x + 2y = 12$

   e) $7x + 2y = 3$
      $4x - 3y = -48$

2. Rearrange the terms of the equations to the form $ax + by = c$.

   a) $x + 3y = -1$
      $2x + 4y - 12 = 0$

   b) $3y = -2x + 1$
      $4x = 2y + 10$

   c) $3x - 5 = 2y$
      $4y - 1 - 5x = 0$

   d) $x - 3y = -4$
      $4x + 2y - 12 = 0$

   e) $2y = -3x - 9$
      $3y + 2x - 9 = 0$

3. Solve the equations in question 2 by elimination.

4. Solve the following systems of linear equations by the elimination method.

   a) $y = \frac{1}{2}x + 2$
      $x + y = 5$

   ☆ b) $\frac{1}{2}x - \frac{1}{3}y = 1$
      $x + \frac{1}{4}y = 2$

   c) $\frac{2}{3}x + \frac{1}{5}y = -2$
      $\frac{1}{3}x - \frac{1}{2}y = -7$

5. Solve the following systems of linear equations by the elimination method. For each system, explain the result and determine the solution by another method.

   a) $x + 3y = -1$
      $2x + 6y + 2 = 0$

   b) $3x - 2y = 5$
      $-6x + 4y = 1$

B Apply

Solve problems 6 to 14 by the elimination method. Check your answers.

6. Mrs. Chan's Math class contributed $2 coins and $1 coins to an earthquake relief fund. The number of $1 coins contributed was 8 less than 5 times the number of $2 coins contributed. If the class raised a total of $160, how many coins of each type were collected?

7. A sports club charges an initiation fee and a monthly fee. At the end of 5 months, Christelle had paid a total of $170. Her friend, Keaton, had paid $295 at the end of 10 months. What is the initiation fee and what is the monthly fee?

8. Huyen paid $124 to rent a car for 3 days and drove a total distance of 160 km. When she rented the same car for 5 days and drove 400 km, it cost Huyen $240. What was the rental charge per day and what was the charge per kilometre?

9. Robyn wishes to invest $660 so that the income from an investment paying interest at 10% per annum is equal to the interest from a bond paying 12% annual interest. How much should Robyn invest at each rate?

10. A 500-space parking lot is filled with motorcycles and passenger cars, with only one vehicle in each space. How many motorcycles and cars are there if the total number of tires on the parked vehicles is 1650?

11. General admission tickets to the Calgary Zoo cost a total of $109 for a group of 4 adults and 3 children. Tickets for a group of 2 adults and 5 children cost a total of $93. What is the cost for one adult ticket? What is the admission price for one child?

12. John lives 1.2 miles from his school. Each morning, he walks the entire distance in a time of 24 min. On his return each afternoon, John runs part of the way so that it takes him only 15 min to reach home. If John runs twice as fast as he walks, how far does he run on his way home from school?

13. The Golden Ears Bridge is a toll bridge across the Fraser River in British Columbia. It connects Pitt Meadows and Maple Ridge on the north side to Langley and Surrey on the south side. The regular toll for passenger cars is $3.95. The fee is reduced to $2.80 if a vehicle is equipped with an electronic transponder to pay the toll automatically. One day, 8200 cars crossed the bridge. If the total of the tolls paid was $30 032.50, how many vehicles had a transponder?

☆**14.** Shanice purchased a total of 50 oranges and granola bars as a snack for the girls' soccer team. Oranges cost $2.40 per dozen and granola bars cost $3.25 for a 5-bar box. If Shanice paid a total of $19, how many boxes of granola bars did she buy?

C Extend

15. Cashews and peanuts are mixed together and sold by the pound. You can buy 3 lb of peanuts and 4 lb of cashews for $14.90. You can also buy 5 lb of peanuts and 2 lb of cashews for $12.70. What is the price per pound of each of cashews and peanuts?

☆**16. a)** The sum of the digits of a two-digit number is 14. The number formed by reversing the digits is 36 more than the original number. What is the original number?

   b) The sum of the digits of a two-digit number is 11. If the digits are reversed, the second number is 9 more than the original number. What is the original number?

17. For what values of m and n is (2, 5) the solution of the linear system $mx + y = 19$ and $nx - 2y = -6$?

18. Using the equation $2x + y = 3$, write a second equation to form a linear system that has
   a) an infinite number of solutions
   b) no solution
   c) one solution

19. If (2, −5) and (−5, −2) both satisfy the equation $Ax + By = -29$, what is the value of A?

D Create Connections

20. Consider the system of linear equations $3x + 4y = 1$ and $5x - 3y = -8$.

   a) Solve the system by substitution.

   b) Solve the system by elimination.

   c) Which method do you prefer? Explain.

   d) What do you need to consider when choosing whether to use the substitution method or the elimination method to solve a system of linear equations?

9.3 Solving Problems Using Systems of Linear Equations

<< **KEY IDEAS** >>

- Systems of linear equations can be solved
  - graphically
  - algebraically by substitution or elimination

Method	Advantages	Disadvantages
Graphical	• provides a visual that can show how two variables relate • can be done with or without a graphing calculator • can result in an accurate and quick solution when using a graphing calculator	• can be time-consuming • may not provide an exact solution
Algebraic	• allows for an exact solution relatively quickly • can be done using more than one method (substitution and elimination)	• does not provide any visual insight into how the two variables relate • can result in an incorrect answer due to a minor arithmetic error

- It may be better to use a graphical approach to solve linear equations when you wish to see how the two variables relate, such as for cost analysis and speed problems.

- It may be better to use an algebraic approach when
  - you need only the solution (intersection point)
  - it is unclear where to locate the solution on a coordinate plane

Example

An aircraft travels 5432 km from Montreal to Paris in 7 h with a tailwind and returns in 8 h against the wind. Determine the wind speed and the speed of the aircraft in still air. What assumption(s) are you making?

Solution

Assume that the wind speed and the aircraft's speed in still air are constant throughout both trips.
Let W represent the wind speed.
Let A represent the aircraft's speed in still air.

Organize the information about distance, D, aircraft groundspeed, S, and time, T.

	D (km)	S (km/h)	T (h)
With a tailwind	5432	$A + W$	7
Against the wind	5432	$A - W$	8

Write a system of linear equations from the information in the chart.
$D = ST$
$5432 = (A + W)(7)$
$5432 = (A - W)(8)$

Choose a method to solve the system. For example, use the algebraic method involving elimination.

Expand each equation using the distributive property.
$5432 = 7A + 7W$
$5432 = 8A - 8W$

Choose a variable to eliminate. Eliminate the variable W by multiplying the first equation by 8 and the second equation by 7.
$8(5432) = 8(7A + 7W)$
$7(5432) = 7(8A - 8W)$

Rewrite the first equation so the like variables in the equations line up. Then, add the equations.
$$\begin{array}{r} 43\,456 = 56A + 56W \\ +\ 38\,024 = 56A - 56W \\ \hline 81\,480 = 112A \end{array}$$

$81\,480 = 112A$
$\dfrac{81\,480}{112} = \dfrac{112A}{112}$
$727.5 = A$

Substitute $A = 727.5$ into the first equation and solve for W.
$$5432 = 7A + 7W$$
$$5432 = 7(727.5) + 7W$$
$$5432 = 5092.5 + 7W$$
$$5432 - 5092.5 = 5092.5 - 5092.5 + 7W$$
$$339.5 = 7W$$
$$\dfrac{339.5}{7} = \dfrac{7W}{7}$$
$$48.5 = W$$

Verify the solutions by substituting $W = 48.5$ and $A = 727.5$ into both original equations.

$5432 = 7(A + W)$	$5432 = 8(A - W)$
$5432 = 7(727.5 + 48.5)$	$5432 = 8(727.5 - 48.5)$
$5432 = 7(776)$	$5432 = 8(679)$
$5432 = 5432$	$5432 = 5432$

Therefore, the wind speed was 48.5 km/h and the aircraft's speed in still air was 727.5 km/h.

A Practise

1. Solve each system of linear equations by an algebraic method. Verify your answer graphically.

   a) $x - 2y = 10$
   $3x - y = 0$

   b) $3x + 2y = 6$
   $3x - 5y = -15$

   c) $5x + 4y = 2$
   $2x - 3y = 10$

   d) $3x - 2y = 10$
   $4x + y = -5$

   e) $2x + 4y = 12$
   $\frac{x}{5} + 3y = 17$

2. Solve each system of linear equations by a method of your choice. Leave any non-integer answers in fraction form. Explain your choice of method.

   ☆**a)** $2x - 5y = -18$
   $8x - 13y = -58$

   b) $5x = y$
   $-x + 3y = 3$

   c) $\frac{1}{3}x + \frac{1}{2}y = -\frac{1}{2}$
   $\frac{1}{5}x - \frac{1}{3}y = \frac{8}{5}$

B Apply

To solve the following problems, write a system of equations and use a method of your choice to solve the system.

3. The perimeter of a rectangular field is 6400 m. Two times the width is 40 m more than the length. Determine the dimensions of the field.

4. Jimal plans to invest $12 000 in two types of bonds which yield 9% and 11% annually. If he wants to earn a total of $1200 annually, how much should Jimal invest in each type of bond?

5. A boat travelling against a current took 3 h to travel 36 mi. Travelling with the current, the boat took 2 h for the return trip. Determine the speed of the boat in still water.

6. Liam paid a total of $27 for 6 tennis balls and 8 golf balls. Jessica paid $43.50 for 14 tennis balls and 10 golf balls at the same store. What is the price of a tennis ball?

☆7. During the winter, Mason feeds his horse a daily diet of hay and a mixture of grain. The total weight of the hay and grain is 20 pounds. He recently ordered enough grain at $2.10/lb and hay at $0.08/lb to last 60 days and paid a total of $702.00. How much hay and how much grain does Mason feed his horse per day?

8. Raymark's basketball team scored a total of 93 points in its last game. A total of 49 baskets were made, consisting of free throws worth 1 point each, field goals worth 2 points each, and three-point shots worth 3 points apiece. If the team made 11 free throws, how many field goals and three-point shots did it make?

9. Devon has a summer job planting trees. He is paid $0.07 per tree when planting in ideal conditions and $0.30 per tree for planting in rocky or muskeg regions. One day, Devon planted 1750 trees and earned $180.00. How many trees did he plant in rocky or muskeg areas?

10. During a 20-day period, Tom spent 70 hours mountain biking and swimming. He burned 860 calories per hour when he swam and 730 calories per hour when he rode his bike. If Tom burned a total of 54 350 calories, how many hours did he spend doing each activity?

11. Diobel operates a student painting company with a crew of five painters. They are paid at two different rates—an hourly wage for outdoor work and an hourly wage for indoor work. During one week, Diobel's payroll was $3060 for 180 hours of indoor work and 20 hours of outdoor work. The following week, her payroll was $3555 for 15 hours of indoor work and 185 hours of outdoor work. What is a painter's pay per hour for indoor work? for outdoor work?

12. Company A rents cars at a price of $25 per day and 15 cents per kilometre. Company B charges a daily rental fee of $30 and 10 cents per kilometre.

   a) Create a system of linear equations relating the cost of a rental (y dollars) to the distance driven (x kilometres).

   b) How many kilometres do you have to drive for the total rental charges of Company A and Company B to be equal?

13. Hockey teams are awarded 2 points for winning a game and 1 point for tying a game by the end of regulation time. The Vancouver Giants have 26 points this season. Three times the number of ties is 1 more than the number of wins the Giants have.

   a) Write a system of linear equations to represent the situation.

   b) How many wins do the Giants have?

C Extend

14. A car averages 8.5 L/100 km in city driving and 6.4 L/100 km in highway driving. In a trip that covered a distance of 720 km, the car used 55.7 L of fuel.

   a) How far was the car driven in the city?

   b) How much fuel did the car consume in city driving?

15. Two snowmobile riders start at the same point heading in opposite directions, but leave at different times and travel at different speeds. The first rider leaves at 1:00 p.m. and travels east. The second rider leaves at 3:00 p.m., travelling west at a speed 15 km/h faster than the first rider. At 6:00 p.m., the riders are 365 km apart. What is the speed of each snowmobile rider? What assumption are you making?

16. A 95% sulfuric acid solution needs to be diluted with 60% solution to obtain a 70% solution. If 2700 mL of the new solution is required, how much of the 95% solution is needed?

☆**17.** On a multiple choice test with 5 possible answers for each question, students are penalized 0.2 points for each incorrect answer. If the test consisted of 76 questions and a student achieved a score of 58, how many questions did the student answer correctly? What assumption are you making?

18. The lines that enclose a triangle can be represented by graphs of the equations $x = -4$, $y = 3x + 4$, and $y = -2x + 9$. Use a system of linear equations to determine the area of the triangle.

D Create Connections

19. Create a system of linear equations.

   a) Solve your system using a method of your choice.

   b) Explain your method of choice. What did you consider when making your choice?

   c) Try solving your system by another method. Which method do you prefer? Explain.

Chapter 9 Review

9.1 Solving Systems of Linear Equations by Substitution

1. Solve each system of equations by substitution.

   a) $2x + 3y = 11$
   $5x - y = -15$

   b) $3m - n = 5$
   $5m - 2n = 8$

   c) $3a + b - 7 = 0$
   $5a + 2b - 13 = 0$

   d) $z - 1 = -3w$
   $11 - 5w = 3z$

2. Determine the number of solutions for each system of equations. Identify the answers for the systems that have one solution.

   a) $2x + y = 6$
   $y - 8 = -2x$

   b) $3x + y = 1$
   $6x + 2y = 2$

   c) $2x + y = -4$
   $x + 2y - 6 = 0$

   d) $7x + 4y = -9$
   $2y - 6 = 0$

3. The world's longest suspension bridge, in Kobe, Japan, and the Capilano Bridge in Vancouver have a combined length of 2129 m. The bridge in Kobe is 74 m longer than 14 times the length of the Capilano Bridge. What is the length of each bridge?

4. A hockey team offers players two annual salary packages. Package A includes a base salary plus $1000/goal. Package B includes a base salary of $30 000 less than the base salary in package A plus $1500/goal. How many goals must be scored for the packages to pay the same amount?

☆5. A board 180 cm long is cut into two pieces such that 3 times the length of the larger piece is 85 cm longer than 4 times the length of the smaller piece. How long are the two pieces of board?

6. Green Health Food store makes quarter-pound and half-pound veggie burgers. One month they sold 3 times as many half-pound burgers as quarter-pound burgers. If the total vegetable mixture used was 378 pounds, what was the total number of burgers sold that month?

9.2 Solving Systems of Linear Equations by Elimination

7. Solve using elimination.

   a) $7x - 4y = 26$
   $3x + 4y = -6$

   b) $5x = 5 - 2y$
   $23 + 3x = 4y$

   c) $\frac{x}{3} + \frac{y}{2} = \frac{1}{6}$
   $-6y + 8 = -x$

   d) $8x + 2y = -10$
   $3y + 2x = 5$

   e) $5 - 3(y - x) + y = 13$
   $2(x + y) - 3x + 5y = 10$

☆8. Wade pays a monthly charge for his cell phone plus a charge per text message sent. In January, when he sent 300 text messages, his bill was $63. Wade missed his February payment, so in March he paid $142.50 for 675 text messages and a $12.00 late fee charge.

   a) What is Wade's monthly cell phone charge?

   b) What is the cost per text message sent?

9. For what values of m and n is $(5, -3)$ the solution to the system of linear equations $mx + ny = -11$ and $2mx - 3ny = 8$?

10. For which system of linear equations is $(-1, 1)$ a solution?
   a) $5x + 6y = 1$
   $5x + 2y = -3$
   b) $3x + 4y = 1$
   $5x - 3y = -8$
   c) $7x - 3y = 10$
   $6x + 5y = -1$

11. Yasmin invested $2100 in high-yield investments. Part of the $2100 was invested at 7% per annum and part at 10% per annum. After 1 year the total interest earned was $166.50. How much did Yasmin invest at each rate?

12. The perimeter of a tennis court is 69 m. The length is 13 m longer than the width. What are the dimensions of the tennis court?

13. The Alberta ski resorts at Marmot Basin in Jasper and Sunshine Village in Banff have a total of 193 runs. If the number of runs at Sunshine is 64 more than half the number of runs at Marmot, how many runs are there at each resort?

9.3 Solving Problems Using Systems of Linear Equations

14. You are given this system of linear equations:

$2x - y = 9$ and $x - \frac{1}{2}y = -5$.

   a) Solve the system graphically and algebraically.

   b) Use the graphs of these two lines to explain the solution.

15. Michele competed in a running–swimming race of total length 16.5 km. If Michele ran at a speed of 12 km/h and swam at a speed of 3 km/h, how far did she run if she completed the race in 105 min?

★**16.** Avatar works at an electronics store. He is paid a fixed weekly wage and a commission on his sales. One week, his sales totalled $15 500 and his take-home pay was $1015. The following week, his sales were $9800 and his pay was $844. What is Avatar's fixed wage and what is his commission rate?

17. Xan rides her bike from home to school in 15 min. If she increases her speed by 5 km/h, she reduces her travel time by 5 min. How far from school does Xan live?

18. Two kayakers paddled downstream on the North Saskatchewan River. They travelled 15 miles in 90 minutes. The return trip took 165 minutes. What was the speed of the current in miles per hour?

19. Mackenzie paid $187.50 for 2 concert tickets and 2 T-shirts. Awet paid $408.75 for 5 tickets and 3 T-shirts. What was the cost of a concert ticket?

20. The cost of electricity is charged by usage as measured in kilowatt-hours (kWh). For usage under a fixed amount of kilowatt-hours, the cost is 6.25¢/kWh. For usage for any amount over the fixed amount, the cost is 8¢/kWh. One month Mrs. Richelieu paid $92.25 for using 1350 kWh of electricity. At what number of kilowatt-hours of usage does the rate increase?

21. The total weight of Marvel's truck and a full load of recyclable asphalt is 45.5 tons. At the waste recycling centre, Marvel is charged $17 per ton for the asphalt and a service fee of $1.50 per ton based on the weight of her truck. If Marvel pays $564.25 to dump a full load of asphalt, what is the weight of Marvel's truck?

Chapters 1–9 Cumulative Review

1. For each system of linear equations, explain how you could verify whether the given point is a solution. Is the given point a solution?

   a) $y = 2x - 12$
   $y = -3x + 13$
   $(5, -2)$

   b) $4x + y = 7$
   $-x + 2y = -5$
   $(1, 3)$

2. A semicircular window of radius 14 in. is to be laminated with a sun block coating. The coating costs 12 cents per square centimetre. What is the cost to laminate the window?

3. Write each trigonometric ratio in lowest terms.

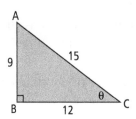

   a) sin A   b) sin C   c) cos A
   d) cos C   e) tan A   f) tan C

4. What is the value of each expression? Express your answers as integers or fractions.

   a) 4^3

   b) -25^2

   c) $(-7)^2$

   d) $-\dfrac{3^3}{5}$

   e) $\dfrac{3}{4^3}$

   f) $\left(\dfrac{-1}{5}\right)^3$

5. Multiply. Then, combine like terms.
   a) $6(-2n + 3)(5n - 2) + (2n - 3)^2$
   b) $(4s^2 + 2s - 3)(-s^2 - s + 5)$

6. Describe a possible scenario for the following graph.

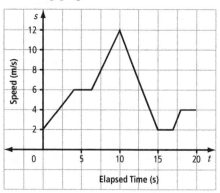

7. Solve each system of linear equations graphically. Verify your solution.

   a) $y = -x - 4$
   $y = -3x + 8$

   b) $2x + y = -6$
   $-x + 2y = 3$

   c) $y = -2x - 5$
   $y = -3x - 4$

8. Determine the measure of each angle θ to the nearest tenth of a degree.

   a)
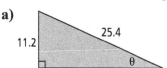

   b)

   c)
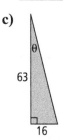

9. What are the slope and y-intercept of each line?

   a) $y = -5x + 8$

   b) $3x - 7y - 10 = 0$

10. Calculate the surface area of each object. Round your answer to the nearest hundredth of a unit.

   a) A right cone has a circular base with a radius of 18 cm and slant height of 29.3 cm.

   b) A right cone having a circular base has a slant height of 12 in. and a diameter of 5 in.

   c) A pyramid has a square base with sides 54 cm and a slant height of 74 cm.

   d) A sphere has a diameter of 31 cm.

11. For each line, state the domain, range, intercepts, and slope. What is the equation of each line in general form?

   a)

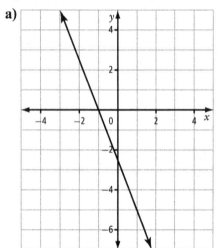

   b)

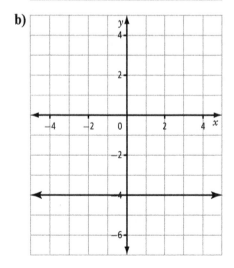

12. Identify the greatest common factor of each set of terms.

   a) $18a^3b^2$ and $8ab^3$

   b) $27x^4y^2$ and $63xy^4z$

   c) $19p^4q$, $-9pq^6$, and $81p^3q^3$

13. Bees maintained by beekeepers in Alberta produce about 13 million kilograms of honey per year. Suppose the average price of honey is \$10.98 per kilogram. Consider the relationship between the total amount of money each beekeeper receives and the number of kilograms of honey the beekeeper sells.

   a) Is this relationship linear or non-linear?

   b) Assign a variable to represent each quantity in the relation. Which variable is the dependent variable? Which is the independent variable? How do you know?

   c) Honey production in Alberta is 90 kg per hive. Create a table of values for the relationship.

   d) Are the data discrete or continuous? Explain how you know.

   e) Graph the relationship.

14. Determine whether each linear system has no solution, one solution, or an infinite number of solutions.

   a) $y = \frac{2}{5}x + 9$
      $y = \frac{5}{2}x + 9$

   b) $2x - 6y + 17 = 0$
      $-2x + 6y + 17 = 0$

   c) $-5x - 8y = 12$
      $10x + 16y = -24$

15. What reading is shown on this SI caliper? Name an object that could be this length.

16. Solve by substitution.

   a) $y = 3x - 2$
      $x + y = 6$

   b) $3x - 2y = 10$
      $4x + y = -5$

17. Determine the measure of each side length x. Express your answer to the nearest tenth of a unit.

   a)

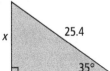

   b)

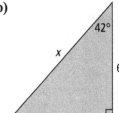

   c)

18. Evaluate each expression. Use positive exponents to express the answers.

   a) $(x^5)(x^{\frac{-2}{5}})$

   b) $(256^{-0.25})^3$

   c) $\dfrac{(z^3)^{\frac{3}{2}}}{(z^{\frac{1}{4}})^2}$

   d) $(125p^3)^{\frac{-1}{3}}\,(p^{\frac{-3}{2}})$

   e) $\left[\dfrac{x^{-3}}{(xy)^5}\right]^{-25}$

   f) $\left[\dfrac{x^{-3}}{0.16(y^{-6})}\right]^{-\frac{3}{4}}$

19. Factor completely.

   a) $4x^2 + 7x - 2$

   b) $x^2 - 9x + 18$

   c) $-24m^2 + 42mn - 9n^2$

   d) $35x^2 - 11xy - 6y^2$

   e) $12s^2t + 24st - 288t$

20. Solve using elimination.

   a) $2x + y = 6$
      $x + y = 2$

   b) $y = 5 - 3x$
      $4x + 3y = 20$

21. Read the following paragraph about Lake Athabasca. Convert each measurement to the unit specified.

   Lake Athabasca is the largest and deepest lake in both Alberta and Saskatchewan and the eighth largest in Canada. The lake is 283 km (miles) in length and has a maximum width of 31 miles (kilometres). The average depth of the lake is 20 m (feet). The surface elevation is 700 ft (metres).

22. Calculate the missing dimension in each of the following. Round each answer to the nearest hundredth of a unit.

   a) A cylinder has a volume of 1 ft³ and a height of 0.7 ft.

   b) A right cone has a circular base with a radius of 35 cm and a volume of 7500 cm³.

   c) A square-based pyramid has a height of 91 cm and a volume of 5.7 m³.

   d) A sphere has a volume of 3476 cm³.

23. Order each set of numbers from least to greatest. Then, identify the irrational numbers.

   a) $\frac{4}{9}$, 0.77..., $\sqrt{82}$, $\sqrt[3]{634}$

   b) $\sqrt[5]{67}$, $\sqrt{289}$, $14\frac{1}{3}$, $\sqrt[4]{1296}$

24. A relation is given by the formula $t = 6.3s - 5.8$. If the domain of the relation is $[-2, 12]$, what is the range?

25. Use slope-point form to write an equation of a line through each point with the given slope. Express each answer in slope-intercept form and in general form.

a) $(-2, -1)$ and $m = -3$

b) $(3, -9)$ and $m = \frac{3}{4}$

26. Factor completely.

a) $c^2 - 169$

b) $81 - 16y^4$

c) $175h^2 - 1008f^2$

d) $x^4 - 41x^2 + 100$

27. Twyla is collecting pledges as she prepares to enter a 20-km charity run. She donates $40 of her own money and collects pledges of $20 each. The function $P(n) = 20n + 40$ represents the total amount of money that Twyla raises.

a) Determine an appropriate domain and range. Then, use a table of values to graph the function.

b) Determine the value for $P(9)$. Explain the meaning of your answer.

c) Awards are presented to students who raise more than $520. How many pledges must Twyla collect to receive an award?

d) Explain why this situation depicts a function.

28. Write the equation of a line that passes through $(-2, 0)$ and is parallel to $5x - 4y + 8 = 0$.

29. Verify that each trinomial is a perfect square. Then, factor.

a) $9s^2 - 54s + 81$

b) $16s^3 + 96s^2 + 144s$

c) $256 - 160y + 25y^2$

30. Use the figure below to answer the following questions.

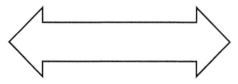

a) What is the perimeter of the figure in centimetres? in millimetres?

b) What is the perimeter of the figure in inches?

c) Is it necessary to measure all the sides of the figure three times to answer parts a) and b)? Explain.

31. You are standing 15 ft from a three-storey building observing a worker on the roof. The angle of elevation of your line of sight to the top of the worker's head is 62°. If your eyes are 5.1 ft from the ground and the building is 27 ft high, how tall is the worker?

32. Express each entire radical as an equivalent mixed radical.

a) $\sqrt{40}$

b) $\sqrt{18}$

c) $\sqrt[3]{108}$

d) $\sqrt[4]{162}$

33. Determine the slope of each line.

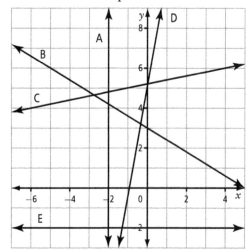

Chapter 9 Extend It Further

For #1 to #4, choose the best answer.

1. $Ax + By = C$ and $Dx + Ey = F$, where $\frac{A}{D} = \frac{B}{E} = \frac{C}{F}$. The system of linear equations has

    A one solution

    B two solutions

    C an infinite number of solutions

    D no solution

2. $Ax + By = C$ and $Dx + Ey = F$, where $\frac{A}{D} = \frac{B}{E} \neq \frac{C}{F}$. The system of linear equations has

    A one solution

    B two solutions

    C an infinite number of solutions

    D no solution

3. If $18x + 54y = 26$, what is the value of $19x + 57y$?

    A $27\frac{1}{9}$

    B $27\frac{4}{9}$

    C $28\frac{1}{6}$

    D $29\frac{2}{5}$

4. The point $(2, -6)$ lies on the graph of $3x + ky + 2 = 0$. The point $(m, 4)$ also lies on the graph. What is the value of m?

    A $\frac{-22}{9}$

    B $\frac{-3}{7}$

    C $\frac{-22}{7}$

    D $\frac{7}{3}$

5. Determine (x, y) such that $123x + 321y = 345$ and $321x + 123y = 543$.

6. What is the ordered pair of real numbers (x, y) for which $x + y = 80$ and $x^2 - y^2 = 80$?

7. At an aquarium, if hoses M and N are both used, it takes 4 h 48 min to fill a giant fish tank. If only hose M is used for the first 2 h, it takes another 3 h and 36 min to fill the tank. How long does it take to fill the entire tank if only hose N is used from the start?

8. Let $m = \frac{1}{x}$ and $n = \frac{1}{y}$ to solve for x and y in the following system of linear equations.

    $\frac{6}{x} - \frac{4}{y} = -5$

    $\frac{9}{x} + \frac{8}{y} = 26$

9. The cost of postage, C, in dollars, to mail a parcel is given by $C = a + bn$, where a and b are constants and n is the parcel's weight, in kilograms. If C equals \$8.05 when n is 1.5 kg and C equals \$20.74 when n is 6.2 kg,

    a) Determine the constants a and b.

    b) What is the cost of postage for a parcel that weighs 4.2 kg?

10. Robert and Maggie are running on a 400-m circular track. Starting at the same place and running in the same direction, Robert runs 1.5 laps when Maggie is completing her first lap. If they ran in opposite directions, Robert and Maggie would have met each other after 25 s. What is Robert's speed, in metres per second?

11. A six-digit number of the form $a2b407$ is divisible by 33. Identify all the possible solutions for the number.

12. If $(x + a)(x + b) = x^2 - 3x + 1$, calculate $(a + 1)(b + 1)$.

Chapter 9 Study Check

Use the chart below to help you assess the skills and processes you have developed during Chapter 9. The references in italics direct you to pages in *Mathematics 10 Exercise and Homework Book* where you could review the skill. How can you show that you have gained each skill? What can you do to improve?

Big Idea	Skills	This Shows I Know	This Is How I Can Improve
Solve a system of linear equations algebraically *pages 191–198, 203–204, 207, 209*	✓ Solve systems using substitution *pages 191–194, 198, 203, 209*		
	✓ Solve systems by writing equivalent equations or using a table to eliminate a variable *pages 195–198, 203–204, 207*		
Solve problems that involve systems of linear equations *pages 199–202, 204–205, 209*	✓ Select an algebraic method to solve a given problem *pages 199–202, 204–205, 209*		
	✓ Solve algebraically using substitution or elimination *pages 201–202, 204*		

Organizing the Ideas

How can you use this diagram to help you use systems of equations to solve problems? Draw an enlargement of this organizer on a fresh sheet of paper. Insert notes to help remind you of when a problem needs a system to help you solve it, how to decide which method to use, and an example of each method.

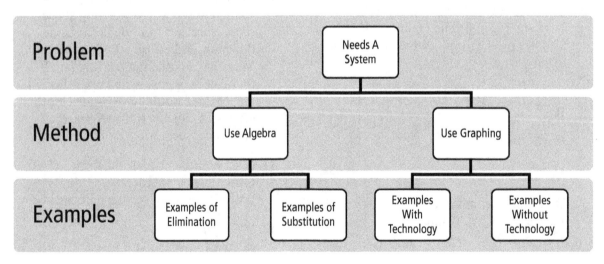

Study Guide

Review the types of problems you handled in Chapter 9. What do you need to remember to use each method to do similar problems?

Things to Remember

Elimination Method

Things to Remember

Substitution Method

Multiple Choice

For #1 to #16, choose the best answer.

1. Which ordered pair represents the solution to the system of linear equations?

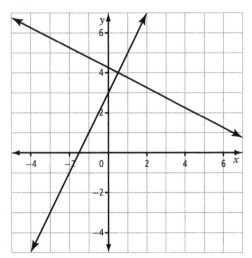

   A $\left(\frac{1}{2}, 4\right)$

   B $\left(\frac{5}{2}, 3\right)$

   C $\left(-1\frac{1}{2}, 0\right)$

   D $(0, 3)$

2. The solution to the linear system given by $3x - 5y = 10$ and $2x + 3y = 12$, rounded to the nearest tenth, is

   A $(4, 1)$

   B $(4.7, 0.8)$

   C $(30, -16)$

   D $(4.7, -0.8)$

3. The solution to the linear system represented by $4x - 3y + 12 = 0$ and $2x + 5y - 20 = 0$ is

   A the y-intercepts of the graphs

   B the x-intercepts of the graphs

   C the point $(10, -3)$

   D the point $(4, 0)$

4. Which graph shows the solution to the system of linear equations represented by $y = -\frac{1}{3}x + 4$ and $y = 4x - 1$?

   A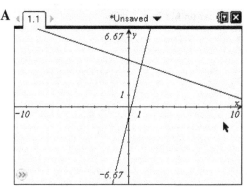

   B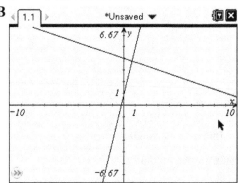

   C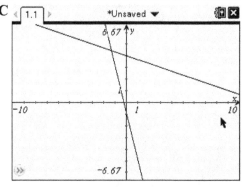

   D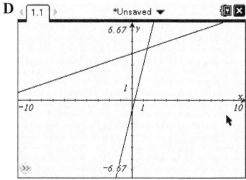

5. The Math department is selling school supplies to raise money to buy new calculators for students. Pencils are $2 each and pads of sticky notes are $5 each. Suppose that 500 items are sold and $1870 is raised. Which system of linear equations can be used to determine the number of pencils, p, and the number of note pads, g, that were sold?

A $p + g = 500$
  $p + g = 1870$

B $p + g = 500$
  $2p + 5g = 1870$

C $2p + 5g = 500$
  $p + g = 1870$

D $2p + 5g = 500$
  $2p + 5g = 1870$

6. How many solutions are there for the system of linear equations $2x - y = 12$ and $4x + 20 = 2y$?

A zero

B one

C two

D an infinite number

7. Janine wants to solve the following system of linear equations algebraically.

$$5x + 3y = 21$$
$$3x - 5y = 15$$

Which calculation is a possible process to determine the correct solution?

A Multiply both equations by 3. Then, subtract the equations.

B Multiply the top equation by 5 and the bottom equation by 3. Then, subtract the equations.

C Multiply the top equation by 5 and the bottom equation by 3. Then, add the equations.

D Multiply the top equation by 3 and the bottom equation by 5. Then, add the equations.

8. For which system is $(1, 0)$ a solution?

A $6x + y = -1$
  $2x + y = 2$

B $x - y = -1$
  $x + y = 1$

C $4x + 3y = 4$
  $2x - 5y = 2$

D $3x - y = 10$
  $5x + 3y = 2$

9. The graph of three lines is shown.

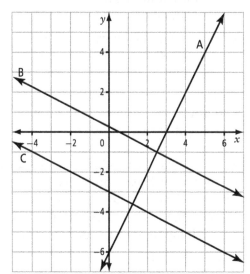

Which pair of lines represents a system of equations with no solution?

A A and C

B A and B

C B and C

D all pairs have a solution

10. The Manitoba Children's Museum is located at The Forks, in the heart of downtown Winnipeg. Two seniors and five children would pay $47.50 for admission. Three children and one senior would pay $27.25 for tickets. Which statement about admission prices is true?

A A child's ticket costs $6.25.

B A senior's ticket costs $6.25.

C A senior's ticket costs $6.80.

D A child's ticket costs $6.82.

11. Amanda has $50 and earns $10 per hour. John has $30 and earns $15 per hour. Amanda creates a system of linear equations to model the amounts of money they each could earn. When she graphs the lines, Amanda determines the point of intersection to be (4, 90). Which conclusion about the point of intersection is true?

A Amanda will always have more money than John.

B John will always have more money than Amanda.

C Amanda and John will make the same amount of money after working 90 hours.

D If Amanda and John both work 4 hours, they will have the same amount of money.

12. Taylor wants to use substitution to solve the system of linear equations $5x - y - 12 = 0$ and $x - 4y + 9 = 0$. Which equation is a possible first step to determining the correct solution?

A $y = -5x + 12$

B $y = 5x + 12$

C $x = 4y - 9$

D $x = 4y + 9$

13. The solution to the system of linear equations represented by $12x - 6y = -11$ and $6x + 18y = 47$ is

A $\left(-\frac{1}{3}, \frac{49}{18}\right)$

B $\left(-\frac{19}{60}, \frac{6}{5}\right)$

C $\left(\frac{1}{3}, \frac{5}{2}\right)$

D $\left(\frac{46}{3}, -\frac{5}{2}\right)$

14. Melody is trying to solve the following system of linear equations by using substitution.

$$4x - y - 18 = 0$$
$$x + 2y - 9 = 0$$

Her partial solution is as follows.

Step 1: $4x - y - 18 = 0$
$2y - 9 = x$
Step 2: $4(2y - 9) - y - 18 = 0$
Step 3: $8y - 9 - y = 18$
Step 4: $y = \frac{27}{7}$

In which step did Melody make her first error?

A Step 1

B Step 2

C Step 3

D Step 4

15. The Environment Club in your school held a recycling drive to raise money. The club collected a total of 1965 1-L and 2-L milk containers and raised $456.15. If the refund is 10 cents for a 1-L container and 25 cents for a 2-L container, how many containers of each type did the students collect?

A 324 1-L containers, 128 2-L containers

B 124 1-L containers, 128 2-L containers

C 1731 1-L containers, 234 2-L containers

D 234 1-L containers, 1731 2-L containers

16. Which one of the following systems is *not* a system of linear equations?

A $x = -y + 2$
$2x + y = 0$

B $x + y = 10$
$2x + 2y = 20$

C $3x + y = 11$
$3x + y = 10$

D $x^2 + y = 10$
$2x - y = 6$

Numerical Response

17. Frank is 3 years older than twice Dolores's age. If the sum of their ages is 51, how old is Dolores?

18. What is the x-coordinate of the solution to the linear system represented by $x - 4y = 13$ and $x + y - 18 = 0$?

19. Cody has $2.20 in dimes and quarters. If Cody has 13 coins in total, how many dimes does he have?

20. If the system of linear equations represented by $4x + 3y = 7$ and $12x + ky = 21$ has an infinite number of solutions, what is the value of k?

21. Joseph wants to solve the system of linear equations $6x + 5y = -28$ and $x + y = 11$ by elimination. By what value could he multiply the second equation and then subtract the two equations to eliminate the y-variable?

Extended Response

22. The diagrams represent a system of linear equations.

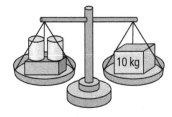

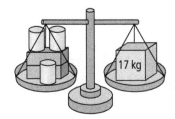

a) Write the system of linear equations that the diagrams model.

b) Algebraically determine the mass of each cylinder and rectangular block.

23. Determine the exact values for the solutions to each linear system.

a) $\frac{2}{3}x + \frac{3}{2}y = -1$

$\frac{1}{4}x - y = \frac{1}{2}$

b) $2x - y = -\frac{1}{10}$

$-x + \frac{2}{5}y = 1$

24. The Steier family drove 880 km in 10 hours to attend a family reunion. On the highway, they drove at an average speed of 100 km/h. In the city, their average speed was 60 km/h. If x represents the time spent on the highway and y represents the driving time in the city, the situation could be modelled by the linear system $x + y = 10$ and $100x + 60y = 880$.

a) Which algebraic method would you choose to solve the system? Explain your reasoning.

b) Solve the linear system to determine how many hours the family drove on the highway and how many hours they drove in the city.

c) Verify your solution to the linear system by graphing.

25. In geometry, two angles are supplementary if their sum is 180°. Eric measures two supplementary angles and concludes that one angle is 12° less than three times the other angle.

a) Write a system of linear equations involving two variables that could be used to determine the measures of the two angles.

b) Which algebraic method would you choose to solve the system? Explain your reasoning.

c) Solve the linear system to determine the measures of the two angles.

26. The points $(5, 2)$ and $(2, -7)$ lie on the line $Ax - By = 13$. Algebraically determine the values of A and B.

Mathematics 10 Practice Final Exam

For each multiple choice question, identify the correct letter. For each numerical response question, record your answer.

Sports
Sports often involve mathematics. Apply your mathematical knowledge and skills to solve problems related to sports.

Use this information to answer #1.

A beginning skier practises by making turns around flags on a ski hill. The flags are spaced 2 m apart.

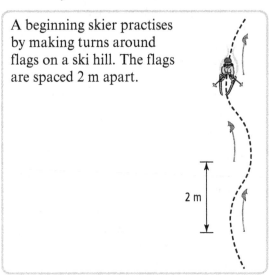

2 m

1. If there are 8 flags, what is the approximate distance that the skier travelled, to the nearest foot?

   A 42 ft　　　　**B** 46 ft
   C 48 ft　　　　**D** 52 ft

2. A trail map for a wall in the ski patrol office is $8\frac{1}{2}$ ft long. If 7 in. of white border needs to be cut off, what is the final length of the trail map?

   A 7′11″　**B** 7′5″　**C** 87″　**D** 84″

Use this information to answer #3.

A ski hill has a slope of $\frac{7}{20}$.

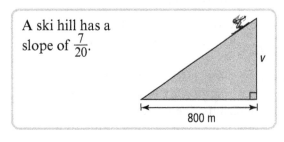

800 m

3. What is the vertical distance, v?

   A 40 m　　　　**B** 110 m
   C 280 m　　　　**D** 320 m

Use this information to answer #4.

A krumkake is a Norwegian cookie sold in ski resorts. It is baked in a krumkake iron and then rolled around a wooden cone. The cone has a diameter of 2 in. and a slant height of 6 in. The cookie covers only the lateral surface and not the circular base of the cone.

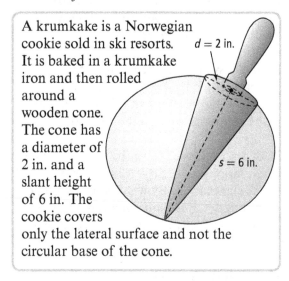

$d = 2$ in.

$s = 6$ in.

4. What is the minimum amount of cookie dough needed to cover the lateral surface of the cone, to the nearest square inch?

   A 19 in.²　　　**B** 21 in.²
   C 29 in.²　　　**D** 30 in.²

Use this information to answer #5.

At a winter sports event, one ice sculpture shaped like a hemisphere has a radius of 2.8 m.

$r = 2.8$ m

5. What is the volume of the ice sculpture, to the nearest cubic metre?

   A 46 m³　　　　**B** 49 m³
   C 92 m³　　　　**D** 98 m³

Use this information to answer #6 to 8.

Freestyle skiers train by skiing up a specially constructed ramp toward a jump. The ramp can be lengthened, creating two right triangles.

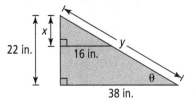

Use this information to answer #10.

Circles are painted into the ice surface of a rink for a curling bonspiel.

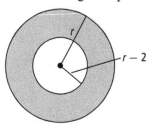

6. What is the height of the short ski ramp, x, to the nearest inch?

   A 6 in.   B 9 in.

   C 14 in.   D 16 in.

7. What is the measure of $\angle\theta$, to the nearest degree?

   A 30°   B 35°   C 55°   D 60°

Numerical Response

8. What is the length of the long ramp, y, to the nearest inch?

Use this information to answer #9.

Satellites transmit sports events around the world. When a satellite is h kilometres above Earth, the time, t, in minutes, that it takes to complete one orbit is given by the formula $t = \dfrac{\sqrt{(6370 + h)^3}}{6024}$.

9. How long would it take a satellite that is 28 km above Earth to orbit our planet twice? Express the answer to the nearest minute.

   A 66 min   B 85 min

   C 132 min   D 170 min

10. Which algebraic expression represents the surface area of the shaded region?

    A $4\pi r$ B $4\pi(r-1)$

    C $\pi(4r^2 - 4)$ D $\pi(4r^2 - r + 40)$

Use this information to answer #11 and 12.

The manager of a snack bar in the ski chalet used a table of values to determine how many people (p) need to buy each of two types of sausages for the costs (C) of the sausages to be equal.

p	C_1	C_2
0	4.00	5.00
1	3.50	4.25
2	3.00	3.50
3	2.50	2.75
4		
5		

Numerical Response

11. How many customers for sausages are needed for the costs to be the same?

12. Which system of equations represents the table of values?

    A $C_1 = \dfrac{-1}{2}p - 4$ B $C_1 = \dfrac{-1}{2}p + 4$

    　$C_2 = \dfrac{-3}{4}p - 5$ 　$C_2 = \dfrac{-3}{4}p + 5$

    C $C_1 = \dfrac{1}{2}p - 4$ D $C_1 = \dfrac{1}{2}p + 4$

    　$C_2 = \dfrac{3}{4}p - 5$ 　$C_2 = \dfrac{3}{4}p + 5$

Use this information to answer #13 and 14.

The cross-country ski team stores ski waxes in a box.

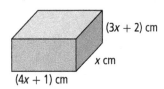

$(3x + 2)$ cm
x cm
$(4x + 1)$ cm

13. What is the simplified expression for the volume of the box?

A $x(4x + 1)(3x + 2)$

B $7x^2 + 3x^3$

C $(3x^3 + 2x)(4x + 1)$

D $12x^3 + 11x^2 + 2x$

Numerical Response

14. If $x = 20$ cm, what is the volume of the box, to the nearest tenth of a cubic metre?

Use this information to answer #15.

Short track speed skaters train on an oval ice rink.

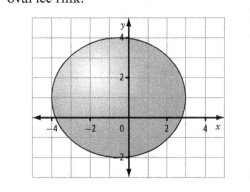

15. What are the domain and the range of the oval?

A domain: $x = -4, 3$; range: $y = 4, -2$

B domain: $[-4, 3]$; range: $[4, -2]$

C domain: $\{x \mid -4 \le x \le 3; x \in R\}$; range $\{y \mid -2 \le y \le 4; y \in R\}$

D domain: $\{-4, 3\}$; range: $\{4, -2\}$

Connections

Many of the concepts that you study in mathematics are related and can help you solve different kinds of problems. Connect the concepts and skills you have learned to solve the following problems.

16. Which graph of a relation is *not* a function?

A
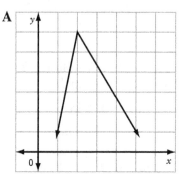

B
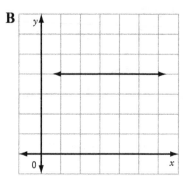

C
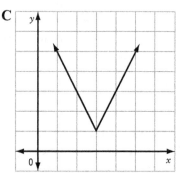

D
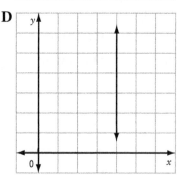

17. The general form of a line is given as $3x + 6y + 12 = 0$. What are the intercepts?

A The x-intercept is -4. The y-intercept is -2.

B The x-intercept is -3. The y-intercept is -6.

C The x-intercept is 3. The y-intercept is 6.

D The x-intercept is 4. The y-intercept is 2.

Use this information to answer #18 and 19.

The factor tree shows the prime factorization of x.

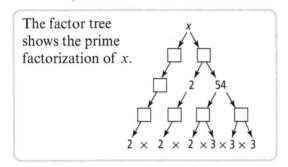

$2 \times 2 \times 2 \times 3 \times 3 \times 3$

18. What is the value of $x^{\frac{1}{3}}$?

A 2 **B** 3 **C** 6 **D** 9

Numerical Response

19. What is the value of x?

20. Simplify, then evaluate $\left[\left(\frac{3}{4}\right)^{-5} \div \left(\frac{3}{4}\right)^{3} \right]^{-1}$.

A $\frac{1}{\left(\frac{3}{4}\right)^{8}}$ **B** $\frac{3}{4}$ **C** $\frac{9}{16}$ **D** $\frac{1}{10}$

Use this diagram to answer #21.

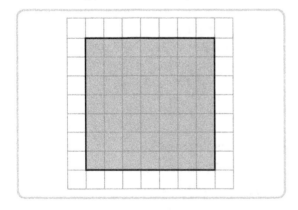

21. Which of the following square roots of perfect squares is represented by the shaded region?

A 2 **B** 5 **C** 7 **D** 9

Numerical Response

22. If $p(x) = 2x^3 + x^2 - 5x + 3$, what is the value of $p(-2)$?

Use this key to interpret the algebra tile models in #23.

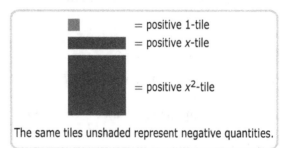

= positive 1-tile

= positive x-tile

= positive x^2-tile

The same tiles unshaded represent negative quantities.

23. Which model represents the product of $(x + 4)(x + 2)$?

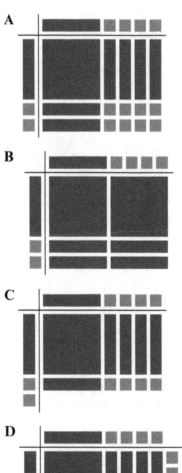

24. Given the linear equation $y = 2x + 7$, which of the following statements is correct?

 A The linear function $f(x) = 2x + 1$ is parallel to $y = 2x + 7$.

 B The line joining $(-2, 3)$ and $(0, 4)$ is parallel to $y = 2x + 7$.

 C The slope of a line perpendicular to $y = 2x + 7$ is $m = -2$.

 D The y-intercept of $y = 2x + 7$ is 2.

25. Amelie simplified $(x + a)(x + b)$, where a and b are > 0, to the form $x^2 + mx + n$. Which statement about m and n is true?

 A $m < 0$ and $n > 0$

 B $m < 0$ and $n < 0$

 C $m > 0$ and $n < 0$

 D $m > 0$ and $n > 0$

Use this number line to answer #26.

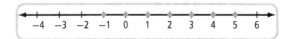

26. Which of the following correctly describes the number line?

 A $\{n \mid -1 \leq n \leq 5, n \in R\}$

 B $\{n \mid -1 < n < 5, n \in I\}$

 C $[-1, 5], n \in I$

 D $\{-3, -2, -1, 0, 1, 2, 3, 4, 5\}$

Use this number line to answer #27.

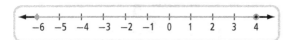

27. Which of the following correctly describes the number line?

 A $-6 < x < 4$

 B $-6 \leq x < 4$

 C $[-6, 4]$

 D $(-6, 4)$

28. What is $\sqrt{48}$ as an equivalent mixed radical?

 A $4\sqrt{6}$ **B** $4\sqrt{3}$ **C** $4\sqrt[3]{3}$ **D** $2\sqrt{3}$

29. What is $(3a^2)^3 (4a^3)^0$ simplified?

 A $9a^6$ **B** $27a^6$ **C** $36a^8$ **D** $108a^9$

30. Which ordered pair represents $f(7) = -3$?

 A $(-7, 3)$ **B** $(-3, 7)$

 C $(3, 7)$ **D** $(7, -3)$

31. What is the equation $y = \frac{x}{7} - 6$ expressed in general form?

 A $x - 7y - 6 = 0$

 B $x - 7y - 42 = 0$

 C $7x - y - 6 = 0$

 D $7x - 7y - 42 = 0$

32. Which expression represents $(4x - 5)^2$ expanded and simplified?

 A $16x^2 + 25$

 B $16x^2 - 25$

 C $16x^2 + 40x + 25$

 D $16x^2 - 40x + 25$

Use this information to answer #33.

Melanie expanded and simplified
$(x - 2)(x^2 + 4x + 4)$. Her work was
as follows:
$(x - 2)(x^2 + 4x + 4)$
$= x(x^2 + 4x + 4) - 1(x^2 + 4x + 4)$ Step 1
$= x^3 + 4x^2 + 4x - x^2 + 4x + 4$ Step 2
$= x^3 + 3x^2 + 8x^2 + 4$ Step 3
$= x^3 + 11x^2 + 4$ Step 4

33. Melanie has errors in

 A Step 1 and Step 2

 B Step 1 and Step 4

 C Step 1, Step 2, and Step 3

 D Step 1, Step 3, and Step 4

34. Which set of numbers has rational numbers only?

A $\frac{-1}{2}$ 6.9 $\sqrt{25}$

B $\frac{1}{2}$ -6 $\frac{\sqrt{3}}{2}$

C -3 $4.\overline{17}$ $4.121\,314\,15...$

D $\sqrt{11}$ $3\sqrt{7}$ π

Use this information to answer #35 to 37.

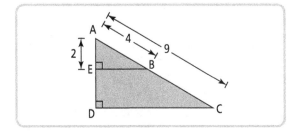

Numerical Response

35. What is the length of side AD, to the nearest tenth?

Numerical Response

36. The exact length of side EB can be written in the form $x\sqrt{y}$. What is the value of y?

37. The ratio for $\cos \angle B$ is

A $\frac{\sqrt{20}}{42}$ **B** $\frac{2}{4}$ **C** $\frac{\sqrt{3}}{2}$ **D** $\frac{4}{\sqrt{12}}$

38. A right pyramid fits exactly into a cube with edge length 5 cm. Suppose that the dimensions of the solids are doubled. By what factor would the volumes of the pyramid and the cube increase?

A 2   **B** 4   **C** 6   **D** 8

Business

It is challenging to set up and operate a business that can compete successfully in the global market. Managing a business involves many skills, including mathematics skills. Use the concepts and skills you have learned to solve business-related problems.

Use this information to answer #39 and 40.

Safe Transport has a fleet of delivery trucks. Two trucks leave the truck yard at the same time. Truck A travels north at 40 km/h and Truck B travels east at 60 km/h.

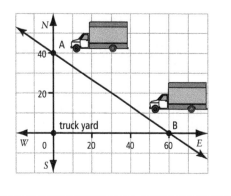

Numerical Response

39. How far apart are the two trucks after 1 h, to the nearest kilometre?

40. The shortest distance from a point to a line can be determined by drawing a perpendicular line. If the slope of the line shown is $\frac{-2}{3}$, what is the equation of the perpendicular line through the point at the truck yard?

A $y = \frac{-2}{3}x + 20$ **B** $y = \frac{-3}{2}x + 20$

C $y = \frac{3}{2}x + 20$ **D** $y = x + 20$

Use this information to answer #41.

The U Move company's daily revenue can be represented by the function $R(t) = 210t - 550$, where t represents the number of trucks rented.

41. To ensure U Move earns daily revenue, what is the minimum number of trucks that must be rented?

A $\{t \mid t \geq 3, t \in I\}$ **B** $\{t \mid t > 3, t \in R\}$

C $\{t \mid t \leq 3, t \in R\}$ **D** $\{t \mid t < 3, t \in I\}$

Use this information to answer #42.

The owner of U Move decided to expand the truck yard. He purchased three smaller square fields, each with area *A*, and two larger square fields, each with area *B*.

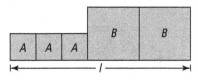

42. Which simplified radical represents length *l*?

A $5\sqrt{AB}$ B $5\sqrt{A} + B$

C $3\sqrt{A} + 2\sqrt{B}$ D $\sqrt{3A + 2B}$

Use this information to answer #43 and 44.

U Move sends out a flyer advertising cardboard boxes.

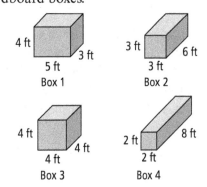

Box 1

Box 2

Box 3

Box 4

The dimensions of the storage compartment in a U Move truck are shown.

43. The correct order of the boxes from least to greatest volume is

A 1, 2, 3, 4   B 2, 1, 3, 4

C 4, 2, 1, 3   D 4, 3, 2, 1

44. If only one type of box is used to fill the truck, which one will waste the least amount of space?

A Box 1   B Box 2

C Box 3   D Box 4

Use this information to answer #45.

A truck repair business uses a laser beam security system.

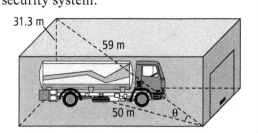

Numerical Response

45. What angle does the laser beam form with the garage floor, to the nearest degree?

Written Response

You will need one sheet of grid paper.

Use this information to answer #46a) and b).

Marmot Basin ski resort in Jasper, Alberta, has the longest high-speed quad chair in the Canadian Rockies. The Canadian Rockies Express takes skiers up a vertical height of 600 m in 8 min.

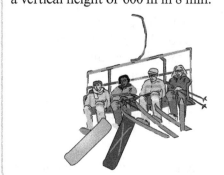

46. a) Assume that the quad chair moves at a constant speed. What is the rate of change for height and time?

b) Sketch the shape of the graph representing the relationship between height and time.

Use this information to answer #46c).

Jim is on a flat part of the ski hill looking up at the chairlift passing overhead.

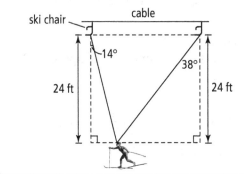

c) How far apart are the chairs, to the nearest foot? Justify your answer mathematically.

Use this graph to answer #47.

Kelly is driving home from a figure skating event. The graph represents changes in speed during the trip.

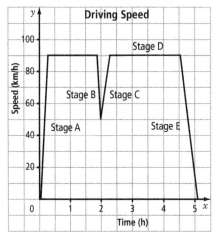

47. Describe a possible reason for the changes in speed at each stage.

Use this information to answer #48.

A company introduces a new product, B_2, which it expects will sell well. The company plans to discontinue selling an older product, B_1, over a short period of time. Assume that the daily sales of both products are constant. The situation can be represented using a system of linear equations.

B_1: $3m + \frac{3}{2}P = 6$

B_2: $P = 3m - 1$

In the equations, P represents profit, in thousands of dollars, and m represents the number of months of sales.

48. a) Solve the system graphically. Label the lines as B_1 and B_2.

b) Verify your solution algebraically.

c) After how many months can product B_1 be discontinued?

d) Explain the meaning of the y-intercept for B_2.

Use this information to answer #48e).

In his first attempts, the business manager records the following systems of equations to represent the two products.

Trial 1

B_1: $\frac{-3}{2}m = -3P + 4.5$

B_2: $2m - 4P = -6$

Trial 2

B_1: $3m = \frac{6}{5}P + 2$

B_2: $\frac{1}{5}P = \frac{1}{2}m - \frac{2}{3}$

e) The manager realizes that these systems of equations do not provide the needed solutions. Explain how many solutions each system has. Give a reason why the solutions cannot be applied to new product sales.

Answers
Chapter 1 Measurement Systems

1.1 SI Measurement

1. **a)** Example: The perimeter is estimated to be 10 cm or 100 mm. The circumference is estimated to be 12 cm or 120 mm.
   b) The perimeter is 12 cm or 120 mm. Using 3.14 as the value of pi, the circumference is 12.56 cm or 125.6 mm.
   c) Example: width of a fingernail

2. **a)** 5.2 cm; 52 mm
   b) 1.84 cm; 18.4 mm

3. **a)** No. Kilometres are the appropriate units to measure long distances. 1850.75 km
   b) No. Millimetres are more appropriate units to measure a short length. 42 mm
   c) Yes. Centimetres are commonly used to measure the circumference of a bicycle tire.

4. **a)** 31.9 km
   b) Example: length of 12 city blocks

5. Stefan runs twice the length, l, of the track plus a distance equal to the circumference of a circle having a diameter of 50 m.

   Let x represent the distance that Stefan runs.

   $x = 2l + \pi d$
   $x = 2(150 \text{ m}) + 3.14(50 \text{ m})$
   $x = 457 \text{ m}$

   Stefan runs a distance of 457 m.

   Vishaal runs twice the length of the track plus a distance equal to the circumference of a circle having a diameter of 50 m plus 20 dm.

   Convert 20 dm to metres.

   $20 \text{ dm} = 2 \text{ m}$

   The diameter of the circle is 50 m + 2 m, or 52 m.

   Let y represent the distance that Vishaal runs.

   $y = 2l + \pi d$
   $y = 2(150 \text{ m}) + 3.14(52 \text{ m})$
   $y = 463.28 \text{ m}$

Vishaal runs a distance of 463.28 m, a distance that is 6.28 m farther than Stefan runs.

6. **a)** 0.4 mm
   b) Example: Millimetres are appropriate units to measure short lengths such as the length of a flea.

7. **a)** The scale rate is $\frac{1.5 \text{ cm}}{15 \text{ km}}$, which is equivalent to $\frac{1.5 \text{ cm}}{1\,500\,000 \text{ cm}}$. This simplifies to the ratio $\frac{1}{1\,000\,000}$.
   b) Example: The park is estimated to be 90 km in length by 50 km in width.
   c) On the map, the length of the park is approximately 8.9 cm and the width of the park is approximately 5.4 cm. Let x represent the length of the park.

   Set up a proportion:

   $\frac{8.9 \text{ cm}}{x \text{ km}} = \frac{1.5 \text{ cm}}{15 \text{ km}}$
   $x = 89 \text{ km}$

   The length of the park is 89 km.

   Let y represent the width of the park.

   Set up a proportion:

   $\frac{5.4 \text{ cm}}{x \text{ km}} = \frac{1.5 \text{ cm}}{15 \text{ km}}$
   $x = 54 \text{ km}$

   The width of the park is 54 km.

   d) The map's distance from Waskesiu to the South Gate is approximately 4.1 cm. Let z represent the distance.

   Set up a proportion:

   $\frac{4.1 \text{ cm}}{z \text{ km}} = \frac{1.5 \text{ cm}}{15 \text{ km}}$
   $z = 41 \text{ km}$

   The distance from Waskesiu to the South Gate is approximately 41 km or 41 000 m.

8.

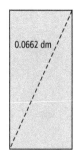

0.0662 dm

length : width = 15 : 7

Let x represent the scale factor. So, $7x$ represents the width of the newspaper page and $15x$ represents its length.

Convert 0.0662 dam to centimetres.

1 dam = 1000 cm

$\left(\frac{1000 \text{ cm}}{1 \text{ dam}}\right)(0.0662 \text{ dam}) = 66.2 \text{ cm}$

The length of the diagonal is 66.2 cm.

Use the Pythagorean theorem to solve for x:

$(7x)^2 + (15x)^2 = (66.2)^2$

$49x^2 + 225x^2 = 4382.44$

$274x^2 = 4382.44$

$x^2 = 15.9943$

$x \approx 4$

Therefore, the width is $(4)(7) = 28$ cm and the length is $(4)(15) = 60$ cm.

The dimensions of the newspaper page are 60 cm by 28 cm.

9. a) The largest area is obtained when a square-shaped field is formed. To obtain the largest square field, one field will be the smallest allowable area, which is 1 ha. This field will have dimensions of 100 m by 100 m. The larger square field shares a side with the 100 m by 100 m square field. So, 1600 m – 300 m or 1300 m of fencing are available to form the sides of the square. Therefore, the larger square field will be 325 m by 325 m.

b) 115 625 m²

10. a) polar radius: ≈ 1.25 cm; equatorial radius: ≈ 2.9 cm; oblateness of the ellipse: ≈ 0.57

b) approximately 0.003 35

c) The oblateness of a sphere is zero, which is close to the oblateness of Earth.

11. a) Example: Tukani first measures the length of the metre stick as it appears in the photograph. Then, he measures the height of the wall as it appears in the photograph using the first length as a referent. The number of these lengths that equal the height of the wall represent the wall's height, in metres.

b) Examples may vary.

c) Example: waist height of a person standing against the wall

1.2 Imperial Measurement

1. a) Estimate: 5 cm by 3 cm

b) length: 2″; width: 1″

c) Example: The width of a fingernail is a referent that can be used. Centimetres are an appropriate unit of length to measure the rectangle and the width of a fingernail is approximately 1 cm.

2. a) 15″

b) 2716′

c) 2.5 mi

3. a) $3\frac{3}{16}″$; Example: caterpillar

b) 4.052″: Example: computer mouse

4. Examples may vary.

5. a) Let x represent the number of inches of snowfall. The value of x is 10 times the depth of the melted snow (i.e., the water).

$x = \left(1\frac{1}{2}\right)(10)$

$x = \left(\frac{3}{2}\right)(10)$

$x = \frac{30}{2}$

$x = 15$

15″ of snow fell in the 12-h period. To determine the snowfall per hour, divide 15″ by 12.

$15″ \div 12 = \frac{15″}{12}$

$= 1\frac{1}{4}″$

The average snowfall per hour was $1\frac{1}{4}″$.

b) Multiply 36 in. by 10: (36 in.)(10) = 360 in. The amount of snow in an average season is 360 in. To find the average number of inches of snow falling each week, divide 360 by 24 (i.e., the number of weeks in six months):

$$\frac{360 \text{ in.}}{24} = 15 \text{ in.}$$

The average snowfall per week is 15″.

6. a) The scale ratio is $\frac{1}{15}$.

b) The length of the scale drawing is 48″ and the width is 25.6″.

7. a) Convert 32 500 yd into miles.
1 mi = 1760 yd

Use unit analysis:

$$(32\ 500 \text{ yd})\left(\frac{1 \text{ mi}}{1760 \text{ yd}}\right) = 18.466 \text{ mi}$$

Convert 78 000 yd into miles.

1 mi = 1760 yd

Use unit analysis:

$$(78\ 000 \text{ yd})\left(\frac{1 \text{ mi}}{1760 \text{ yd}}\right) = 44.318 \text{ mi}$$

The total distance Josephine travelled is 18.466 mi + 44.318 mi, or 62.784 mi.

To find the distance that Marcus drove, use the Pythagorean theorem:

Let d equal the number of miles driven.

$$d = \sqrt{18.466^2 + 44.318^2}$$

$$d = 48.011$$

Therefore, Marcus drove 48.011 mi.

Let t_1 represent the time for Josephine to drive 62.784 mi. Time is equal to distance divided by rate of speed.

$$t_1 = \frac{\text{distance}}{\text{speed}}$$

$$t_1 = \frac{62.784 \text{ mi}}{60 \text{ mph}}$$

$$t_1 = 1.0464 \text{ h}$$

Therefore, Josephine will reach the destination in 1.0464 h.

Let t_2 represent the time for Marcus to drive 48.011 mi. Time is equal to distance divided by rate of speed.

$$t_2 = \frac{\text{distance}}{\text{speed}}$$

$$t_2 = \frac{48.011 \text{ mi}}{45 \text{ mph}}$$

$$t_2 = 1.0669 \text{ h}$$

Therefore, Marcus will reach the destination in 1.0669 h.

Josephine will arrive before Marcus.

b) To find how much sooner Josephine arrives, subtract: 1.0669 h − 1.0464 h = 0.0205 h. Josephine will arrive 0.0205 h or (0.0205)(60) = 1.23 min before Marcus. Rounding that value to the nearest minute, Josephine will arrive 1 min before Marcus.

8. Estimate examples: 60 000 s; 1000 min; 20 h. Calculated times: 63 360 s; 1056 min; 17 h 36 min

9. a) MN = 40 mm, PQ = 55 mm. The difference is 15 mm.

b) 11 pieces of MN and 8 pieces of PQ

10. a) Five 12′ boards laid end to end cover a length of 60′. Therefore, a deck with dimensions of 60′ by 10′ will consist of five sections of boards, with each section measuring 12′ by 10′. To determine how many rows of boards are needed per section, first convert the width of 10′ to inches: 10′(12 in. per ft) = 120 in. Since each board is 8 in. wide, the number of rows of boards to cover a width of 120 in. is: $\frac{120 \text{ in}}{8 \text{ in}} = 15$. Therefore, 15 boards are required in each of five sections, for a total of 75 boards to build the deck.

b) Since a space of $\frac{1}{4}$ in. must be left between rows of boards, one board in each section will need to be trimmed along its entire length in order to fit. With 15 boards, there are 14 spaces. The total width of these spaces is $(14)\left(\frac{1}{4} \text{ in}\right)$ or $3\frac{1}{2}$ in. For the last board to fit, the board will need to be trimmed by this amount.

The wastage will be $3\frac{1}{2}$ in. along the entire length of the deck. To determine the wastage in square inches, first convert 60′ to inches: 60′(12 in. per ft) = 720 in. Therefore, in square inches, the wastage is

$(720 \text{ in.}) \left(3\frac{1}{2}\text{in.}\right) = 2520$ sq in.

11. a) 186.56 yd; 170.59 m
b) 1509.44 yd; 1380.23 m

12. a) 46 cubic yards
b) $10 752.50

13. a) 37.5 mi
b) 2.2 yd
c) 0.9375 mi
d) 3.75 chains
e) 1980 ft

1.3 Converting Between SI and Imperial Systems

Note: Because of rounding, some answers may vary.

1. a) Estimate: 2 in.

b) Estimate: $1\frac{1}{2}$in.

2. a) $2\frac{1}{4}$in.

b) $1\frac{5}{8}$in.

3. a) 64 mm

b) $2\frac{1}{2}''$

c) The conversion should be the same as the measurement. But, because of loss of accuracy in measuring, the two may not be exactly the same.

4. a) 107.95 mm   **b)** 42.19 km
c) 94.0′   **d)** 414.5 cm

5. Units chosen for the conversion may differ.
a) 4.05 yd or 12.14′
b) 12.0 m
c) 826.77″ or 68.9′
d) 975.36 cm or 9.75 m
e) 42.98′ or 14.33 yd

6. a) The length of the swim is 1.5 km. To find the length of the run, multiply 1.5 km by $6\frac{2}{3}$.

Let l represent the length of the run in kilometres.

$= (1.5 \text{ km}) \left(6\frac{2}{3}\right)$

$l = \left(\frac{3}{2}\text{ km}\right)\left(\frac{20}{3}\right)$

$l = 10$

The length of the run is 10 km.

To find the length of the bike ride, multiply 10 km by 4. The length of the ride is 40 km.

b) 1 mi = 1.609 km

Let x represent the number of miles in 1.5 km.

Set up a proportion:

$\frac{x \text{ mi}}{1.5 \text{ km}} = \frac{1 \text{ mi}}{1.609 \text{ km}}$

$x = 0.9$

The length of the swim is 0.9 mi.

Let y represent the number of miles in 10 km.

$\frac{y \text{ mi}}{10 \text{ km}} = \frac{1 \text{ mi}}{1.609 \text{ km}}$

$y = 6.2$

The length of the run is 6.2 mi.

Let z represent the number of miles in 40 km.

$\frac{z \text{ mi}}{40 \text{ km}} = \frac{1 \text{ mi}}{1.609 \text{ km}}$

$z = 24.9$

The length of the bike ride is 24.9 mi.

c) The total distance of the competition, in kilometres, is 1.5 km + 10 km + 40 km = 51.5 km. The total distance of the competition, in miles, is 0.9 mi + 6.2 mi + 24.9 mi = 32 mi

7. a) Peace River
b) approximately 4578 km
c) 3.9 times longer

8. a) Convert 2 yd to metres. Since 1 yd = 0.9144 m, 2 yd = 2(0.9144 m) or 1.8288 m.
Convert 1.75 yd to metres.

1 yd = 0.9144 m

Let x represent the number of metres in 1.75 yd.

Set up a proportion:

$$\frac{1 \text{ yd}}{0.9144 \text{ m}} = \frac{1.75 \text{ yd}}{x \text{ m}}$$

$$x = 1.6$$

Therefore, 1.75 yd = 1.6 m.

Convert 45 in. to centimetres.

1 in. = 2.54 cm

Let y represent the number of centimetres in 45 in.

Set up a proportion:

$$\frac{1 \text{ in.}}{2.54 \text{ cm}} = \frac{45 \text{ in.}}{y \text{ cm}}$$

$$y = 114.3 \text{ cm.}$$

Therefore, 45 in. = 114.3 cm.

Convert 60 in. to centimetres.

1 in. = 2.54 cm

Let z represent the number of centimetres in 60 in.

Set up a proportion:

$$\frac{1 \text{ in.}}{2.54 \text{ cm}} = \frac{60 \text{ in.}}{z \text{ cm}}$$

$$z = 152.4$$

Therefore, 60 in. = 152.4 cm.

b) Using the width of 114.3 cm, find the area of fabric in square metres by first converting 114.3 cm to 1.143 m.
Let A_1 represent the area of the fabric in square metres.

$$A_1 = l \times w$$

$$A_1 = (1.143 \text{ m})(1.829 \text{ m})$$

$$A_1 = 2.09 \text{ m}^2$$

So, the amount of fabric Molly will buy if she chooses the first width is 2.09 m².

Using the width of 152.4 cm, find the area of fabric in square metres by first converting 152.4 cm to 1.524 m.

Let A_2 represent the area of the fabric in square metres.

$$A_2 = l \times w$$

$$A_2 = (1.524 \text{ m})(1.6 \text{ m})$$

$$A_2 = 2.44 \text{ m}^2$$

The two areas are not equal. More material is needed if using the wider fabric. Therefore, Molly should choose the material with the narrower width to have a lesser amount left over.

9. a) 12 000
   b) 34 km, assuming the torch was carried the same distance each of the 106 days from October 30 until February 12

10. Convert 25 mi to kilometres.
   1 mi = 1.609 km
   Let x represent the number of kilometres in 25 mi.

   Set up a proportion:

   $$\frac{1 \text{ mi}}{1.609 \text{ km}} = \frac{25 \text{ mi}}{x \text{ km}}$$

   $$x = 40$$

   There are 40 km in 25 mi. Therefore, Savario has travelled (240 km – 40 km) or 200 km in 2.5 h (4:30 p.m. to 7:00 p.m.).

   Let s represent Savario's rate of speed. Speed is distance divided by time.

   $$s = \frac{\text{distance}}{\text{time}}$$

   $$s = \frac{200 \text{ km}}{2.5 \text{ h}}$$

   $$s = 80 \text{ km/h}$$

   Savario's speed is 80 km/h.

   Let t represent the time to travel the remaining 40 km. Time is distance divided by rate of speed.

   $$t = \frac{\text{distance}}{\text{speed}}$$

   $$t = \frac{40 \text{ km}}{80 \text{ km/h}}$$

   $$t = 0.5 \text{ h}$$

   Therefore, Savario will arrive in Brandon at 7:30 pm.

11. a) No. A maximum speed limit of 80 km/h is approximately 50 mph.
   b) approximately 68 mph
   c) approximately 28 min
   d) Example: One mile is approximately 1.6 km. Multiplying 53 mi by 1.5 is about 80 km, which means that multiplying 53 by 1.6 is more than 80 km. Therefore, the cousins are driving over the posted maximum speed limit of 80 km/h.

12. a) 1105.92 mm^2 or ≈ 1.7142 sq in.

b) $0.057\ 6 \text{ mm}^2$ or $0.000\ 089\ 28$ sq in.

13. a) Let H_g represent your predicted adult height if you are a girl. To find your height in inches, first convert the height of each parent into inches:

father's height: 6 ft = 6(12 in.) = 72 in.

mother's height: 5ft 5in. = 5(12 in.) + 5 in. = 65 in.

Use these values in the appropriate formula.

$$H_g = \frac{(\text{father's height} - 5'' + \text{mother's height})}{2}$$

$$H_g = \frac{(72'' - 5'' + 65'')}{2}$$

$$H_g = 66''$$

Therefore, your predicted adult height is 66 inches or 5 ft 6 in.

If you are a boy, let H_b represent your predicted adult height. To find your height in inches, use the same values calculated above for your parents' heights and use the formula for boys:

$$H_b = \frac{(\text{father's height} + 5'' + \text{mother's height})}{2}$$

$$H_b = \frac{(72'' + 5'' + 65'')}{2}$$

$$H_b = 71''$$

Therefore, your predicted adult height is 71 in. or 5 ft 11 in.

b) In SI units, change the 5 in. in the formula to 12.7 cm. Use the father's and mother's heights in centimetres.

14. Example: 5 yd: $5 \text{ yd} \left(\frac{3 \text{ ft}}{1 \text{ yd}} \right) = 15$ ft;

$$15 \text{ ft} \left(\frac{30.48 \text{ cm}}{1 \text{ ft}} \right) = 457.2 \text{ cm}$$

Chapter 1 Review
1.1 SI Measurement

1. a) Predictions may vary.

b) Using a can with a diameter of 6 cm, the circumference is 18.84 cm. So, the number of rotations to cover 2 m or 200 cm would be 200 ÷ 18.81 or 10.6 rotations.

c) Answers may vary.

2. 5.4 cm

3. Example: Follow these steps to read a caliper:

Step 1. Read the value on the fixed scale that is located exactly at or just to the left of the zero on the moving scale.

Step 2. Identify the next line on the moving scale that aligns with a line on the fixed scale. Read the value on the moving scale.

Sample diagram:

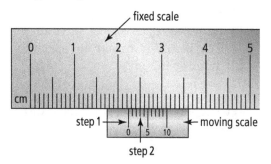

The reading for the SI caliper in this example is 2.23 cm. (2.2 + 0.03 = 2.23)

4. 1 h is equal to (60 min/h)(60 s/min) = 3600 s.

Let x represent Montgomery's speed in metres per hour.

Set up a proportion:

$$\frac{100 \text{ m}}{9.78 \text{ s}} = \frac{x \text{ m}}{3600 \text{ s}}$$

$$x = 36\,809.8$$

Montgomery's speed is 36 809.8 m/h.

Change 36 809.8 m to kilometres.

Let y represent the number of kilometres.

Set up a proportion:

$$\frac{1000 \text{ m}}{1 \text{ km}} = \frac{36\,809.8 \text{ m}}{y \text{ km}}$$

$$y = 36.8$$

The runner's speed is 36.8 km/h.

5. Convert 6 318 138.7 m to kilometres.

Let x represent the radius of Earth, in kilometres.

Set up a proportion:

$$\frac{1000 \text{ m}}{1 \text{ km}} = \frac{6\,318\,138.7 \text{ m}}{x \text{ km}}$$

$$x = 6318.14$$

The radius of Earth is 6318.14 km.

Find the circumference, C, of Earth by multiplying the radius by 2π.

$C = 2\pi r$
$C = 2(3.14)(6318.14 \text{ km})$
$C = 39\,677.9 \text{ km}$

Find the speed, s, of the waves in kilometres per second by multiplying the circumference by 7.

$s = 7(39\,677.9)$
$s = 277\,745.38 \text{ km/s}$

The radio waves travel at a speed of 277 745.38 km/s. Convert this speed to kilometres per hour.

$1 \text{ h} = (60 \text{ min/h})(60 \text{ s/min}) = 3600 \text{ s}$

Let x represent the distance the radio waves travel in 1 h or 3600 s.

Set up a proportion:
$$\frac{277\,745.38 \text{ km}}{1 \text{ sec}} = \frac{x \text{ km}}{3600 \text{ sec}}$$
$$x = 999\,883\,358.1$$

So, the speed of the radio transmission is 999 883 358.1 km/h.

1.2 Imperial Measurement

6. Example estimate: 8″ by 10″; actual measurement: $8\frac{1}{4}$″ by $10\frac{5}{16}$″

7. 3.04 in./h

8. Determine if the ratio $\frac{4}{6}$ is equivalent to the ratio $\frac{16}{20}$. Since the ratios are not equivalent, an enlargement of this size would result in distortion or omission. Any ratio equivalent to $\frac{4}{6}$, such as $\frac{16}{24}$ or $\frac{20}{30}$, would work. To obtain an equivalent ratio, multiply the numerator and the denominator of $\frac{4}{6}$ by the same number.

9. a) Seven platforms, assuming that there is a platform at the top of the tower; 203 rungs, assuming that 29 rungs are needed between each platform
   b) 228 steps; 30 steps are needed to reach each of 7 platforms (29 ladder rungs plus 1 step onto each platform) and

three steps need to be taken across each of the 6 platforms below the top (18 steps); Assume that no steps are taken across the platform at the top of the tower.

10. a) Since the walls are 10 feet high, the 4′ by 10′ sheets would be the most suitable.
    b) Find the perimeter, P, of the room:
    $P = 2l + 2w$
    $P = 2(20') + 2(15')$
    $P = 70'$
    The perimeter of the room is 70′.
    Since the width of each sheet of drywall is 4′, divide 70 by 4: $\frac{70}{4} = 17.5$. So, 17.5 sheets are needed for the walls.

    The ceiling is 20′ by 15′, so for calculating the number of sheets that are 4′ by 10′, assume that the ceiling is 20′ by 16′. Then 2(4) or 8 sheets would be needed for the ceiling.

    Add the number of sheets needed for the walls and ceiling, and subtract $2\left(\frac{1}{3}\right)$ or $\frac{2}{3}$ of a sheet for the two doors, and subtract $\frac{1}{4}$ sheet for the one window: $17.5 + 8 - \frac{2}{3} - \frac{1}{4} = 24\frac{7}{12}$ or 24.583 sheets.

    Finally, find 5% of 24.583 and add to 24.583. Then, round to the next highest number of whole sheets: $(5\%)(24.583) = 1.229$. So, $24.583 + 1.229 = 25.812$ or 26 sheets are needed.

1.3 Converting Between SI and Imperial Systems

11. a) 98.48 m
    b) 62.76 mph
    c) 899 ft

12. a) 205.4 km/h   b) 127.7 mph

13. a) Answers may vary.
    b) Matt (439 km versus 365.2 km for Bethany)

14. a) 1 h 43 min
    b) 2099.7 m; 6888.9 ft

15. Convert 6318.1387 km to miles.

Let x represent the radius of Earth, in miles.

Set up a proportion:

$$1 \text{ mi} = 1.609 \text{ km}$$

$$\frac{1 \text{ mi}}{1.609 \text{ km}} = \frac{x \text{ mi}}{6318.1387 \text{ km}}$$

$$x = 3926.749$$

The radius of Earth is 3926.749 mi.

If the shuttle orbits Earth once in 1 h at the rate of 25 500 mph, the distance covered is 25 500 mi, which is represented as the circumference of the larger circle in the diagram. Find the radius, r, of a circle with circumference 25 500 mi.

$$C = 2\pi r$$

$$r = \frac{C}{2\pi}$$

$$r = \frac{25\,500}{2(3.14)}$$

$$r = 4060.51$$

The radius of the shuttle's orbit is 4060.51 mi.

To find the shuttle orbit's distance above Earth, subtract the radius of Earth from 4060.51 mi.: 4060.51 mi − 3926.749 mi. = 133.76 mi.

Convert 133.76 mi to kilometres.

$$1 \text{ mi} = 1.609 \text{ km}$$

Set up a proportion.

Let x represent the number of kilometres above Earth at which the shuttle is orbiting.

$$\frac{1 \text{ mi}}{1.609 \text{ km}} = \frac{133.76 \text{ mi}}{x \text{ km}}$$

$$x = 215.22$$

The shuttle is orbiting 133.76 mi or 215.22 km above Earth.

16. a) 357
 b) 180 cm
 c) 574.4
 d) 70.866 in.

e) Example: A length of 1 in. is approximately 2.5 cm. Dividing 180 cm by 2.5 is equivalent to dividing 360 cm by 5. The answer is 72 in., which is a reasonable approximation of the calculated length.

Chapter 1 Cumulative Review

1. Estimates:
 a) 13 cm   **b)** 16 cm

2. The perimeter of the figure in part a) is 13.2 cm, or 5.2 in. The perimeter of the figure in part b) is 17.3 cm, or 6.48 in. Inches are an appropriate imperial unit to measure the perimeter of figures of this size.

3. a) 1.52 mm   **b)** 450 ft
 c) 74.98 km   **d)** 22.23 cm

4. a) 3.1 cm
 b) $1\frac{7}{32}$ in.
 c) Examples: erasers, magnets, buttons

5. a) approximate; 626 ft $\frac{1}{5}$ in. is equal to 190.809 88 m
 b) 1 cm : 41.48 m

6. a) 3.12 cm; Example: eraser
 b) Estimate: $1\frac{1}{4}$ in.
 c) 3.12 cm $\left(\frac{1''}{2.54 \text{cm}}\right) \approx 1.228$ in.

7. 5959 m = 19 551 ft; 6050 m = 19 849 ft; 300 m = 984 ft

8. a) 1 : 2 500 000
 b) 25
 c) Estimate: 72.5 km

9. a) No. The ratio of the photograph's width to length is 2 : 3. The ratio of the frame's width to length is 3 : 4. Because the ratios are not equal, the photograph cannot be enlarged proportionally to fit the frame without cropping.
 b) 10″ by 15″

10. 7.96 cm

11. a) $101\frac{1}{4}$ sq ft

b) 68

c) Assume that Jeremy cannot buy a fraction of a laminate. The area of each laminate is $\left(4\frac{1}{2}\text{ft}\right)$ $\left(4\frac{1}{2}\text{ft}\right)$ = 1.5 ft^2. To cover the floor, Jeremy needs 68 pieces of laminate. The area of the total laminate is (68 pieces)(1.5 ft^2/piece) = 102 ft^2. Therefore, it will cost (102 ft^2)($4.59/ft^2) = $468.18 to cover the room.

12. a) The Grand Canyon is deeper by approximately 828.8 m.

b) Methods may vary.

13. a) $23\frac{1}{2}''$, to the nearest quarter of an inch

b) Example: The length of the larger semicircle is approximately $\frac{(3.14)(20)}{2} \approx$ 30 cm. The total length of the smaller semicircle and the length of the two ends is approximately the same as the perimeter of the larger semicircle. Therefore the perimeter of the figure is approximately 60 cm. A length of 1 in. is approximately 2.5 cm. Dividing 60 cm by 2.5 is equivalent to dividing 240 cm by 10. The answer is 24 in., which is a reasonable approximation of the calculated length.

Chapter 1 Extend It Further

1. C

2. C

3. B

4. A

5. D

6. a) 26 mi 386 yd

b) 42 195 m or 138 441 ft

7. 5

8. approximately 14.2 yd

9. George is taller by 3.8 mm.

10. 3 ft 2.5 in.

11. cost before tax: $51.60

Chapter 2 Surface Area and Volume

2.1 Units of Area and Volume

1. **a)** 154.84   **b)** 0.46
   c) 0.08   **d)** 32.29
2. **a)** Example: 25 cm by 20 cm; 50 000
   b) Example: 3 ft by 5 ft; 13 935.5
3. **a)** 16 387.1 cm^3 **b)** 690 233.1 cm^3
4. **a)** 0.03
   b) Convert the dimensions to inches.
   1 cm $\approx$ 0.3937 in.
   $[25(0.3937)][16(0.3937)][7(0.3937)]$
   $= (9.8425)(6.2992)(2.7559)$
   $= 170.865\,458\,3$
   ≈ 170.87 in.^{3}
5. 1.3 m^3
6. **a)** 7.8 m^2 **b)** 1 can
7. $135.48
8. 817.5 m^2
9. 8.75 ft^3
10. **a)** Convert the dimensions of the room
    to metres. Since 1 yd = 0.9144 m,
    $1 \text{ ft} = \frac{0.9144}{3} = 0.3048$ m.
    Use proportional reasoning to convert
    6 m into feet and 10 m into feet.
    $\frac{l}{6} = \frac{1}{0.3048}$
    $l = \frac{6}{0.3048}$
    $l = 19.685$
    6 m is approximately 19.685 ft.
    $\frac{w}{10} = \frac{1}{0.3048}$
    $w = \frac{10}{0.3048}$
    $w = 32.8084$
    10 m is approximately 32.8084 ft.
    Calculate area in square feet:
    $A = lw$
    $A = (19.685)(32.8084)$
    $A = 645.833\,354...$
    To the nearest tenth, the area is
    approximately 645.8 ft^2.

b) Convert 4 in. to feet. Since 12 in. = 1 ft,
$\frac{4}{12} = \frac{1}{3}$ ft.
The area of each strip is given by:
$A = l\,w$
$A = (4)\left(\frac{1}{3}\right)$
$A = 1.\overline{3}$
The area of each strip is approximately
1.3 ft^2.

c) The manager needs 12% more than the
area of the room. That is 1.12 times the
area of the room:
$(1.12)(645.833\,354... = 723.333\,356\,48...$
Since each strip has an area of $1.\overline{3}$ ft^2,
divide $\frac{723.333\,356\,48}{1.3} = 542.5$ strips.
Since it is not possible to buy part of a
strip, the manager should buy 543 strips
of hardwood.

11. 203 km^2
12. **a)** 3 cm   **b)** 9 in. by 9 in.
13. **a)** 122 cm   **b)** 4 ft
14. The radius of the barrel is $\frac{23.5}{2}$ in. or
    11.75 in. To convert inches to centimetres,
    multiply the measurement by $\frac{2.54 \text{ cm}}{1 \text{ in.}}$
    Determine the volume of the barrel in
    cubic centimetres:
    $V = \pi r^2 h$
    $V = \pi \left[\left(\frac{11.75}{1}\right)\left(\frac{2.54}{1}\right)\right]^2 \left(\frac{34}{1}\right)\left(\frac{2.54}{1}\right)$
    $V = 241\,660.501\,724$
    To express in cubic metres, divide by
    1 000 000 to obtain 0.24 m^3.
    The volume of the barrel is approximately
    0.24 m^3.

15. a) $V = lwh$

$$V = \left(\tfrac{19}{12}\right)\left(\tfrac{11}{12}\right)\left(\tfrac{34}{12}\right)$$

$V = 4.112\,268\,2$

$V \approx 4.1$

Each bag holds about 4.1 ft^2.

b) 1 yd = 3 ft;
1 yd^3 = 3 ft $\times$ 3 ft $\times$ 3 ft = 27 ft^3
The 10-yd^3 dumpster will hold (10)(27)
= 270 ft^3. The 15-yd^3 dumpster will hold
(15)(27) = 405 ft^3. If each volunteer
collects 4.1 ft^3 of litter, that is a total of
(80)(4.1) = 328 ft^2. The 10-yd^3 dumpster
is too small. Amy should rent the 15-yd^3
dumpster.

16. a) 0.5 mi; 0.8 km   **b)** 0.6 km^2
c) 1.5 mi; 2.4 km   **d)** 9 times as large
e) 3 times as long

17. a) 101 277 000 ft^2 **b)** 9 408 941 m^2
c) 941 ha

18. Example: **a)** I prefer to measure rooms in
imperial units.

b) Consider a room with dimensions 12 ft
by 10 ft. To convert the dimensions to
metres, recall that 1 ft = 0.3048 m.
Multiply (12)(0.3048) = 3.6576 and
(10)(0.3048) = 3.048. A room that is
12 ft by 10 ft is approximately 3.7 m
by 3 m.

c) For a quick estimate, it is reasonable to
use 1 ft $\approx$ 0.3 m.

19. Example: **a)** I prefer to measure my
electronic equipment using SI units.

b) Consider a computer screen with
dimensions 40 cm by 35 cm. To convert
the dimensions to inches, recall that
1 cm = 0.3937 in.
Multiply (40)(0.3937) = 15.748 and
(35)(0.3937) = 13.7795. A computer
screen that measures 40 cm by 35 cm is
approximately 15.7 in. by 13.8 in.

c) For a quick estimate, it is reasonable to
use 1 cm $\approx$ 0.4 in.

2.2 Surface Area

1. a) 3232 cm^2 **b)** 27.9 m^2
   c) 2827.43 cm^2 **d)** 753.98 in.^{2}
   e) 6.99 m^2

2. a) 600 in.^{2} **b)** 13 273.23 cm^2
   c) 3242.12 cm^2 **d)** 3.14 ft^2

3. 5 in.

4. 3689 ft^2

5. a) Since the diameter is 1.2 m, the radius
is 0.6 m. Substitute values into the
formula for surface area of a cylinder:
$$SA = 2\pi r^2 + 2\pi rh$$
$$4 = 2\pi(0.6)^2 + 2\pi(0.6)h$$
$$4 = 0.72\pi + 1.2\pi h$$
$$4 - 0.72\pi = 1.2\pi h$$
$$\frac{4 - 0.72\pi}{1.2\pi} = h$$
$0.461\,032\,95\ldots = h$
The height of the cylinder is
approximately 0.46 m.

b) 2.59 in.   **c)** 1.47 cm
d) 22.1 ft

6. a) 6872.23 cm^2
b) The base of the composite object is a
right prism with no top.
Calculate the surface area of the prism:
$SA_{\text{prism}} = lw + 2lh + 2wh$
$SA_{\text{prism}} = (10)(18) + 2(10)(38) + 2(18)(38)$
$SA_{\text{prism}} = 2308$
The top of the composite object is a
right pyramid with no base.
Calculate the surface area of the right
pyramid:
$SA_{\text{pyramid}} = 2\left[\tfrac{1}{2}(10)(15)\right] + 2\left[\tfrac{1}{2}(18)(13)\right]$
$SA_{\text{pyramid}} = 384$

The combined surface area is 2308 +
384 = 2692. The total surface area of
the composite object is 2692 m^2.

7. a) 16 596 mm^2 **b)** 15 936 mm^2

8. 509 904 364 km^2

9. a) 1.7 m   **b)** 5.5 m^2
   c) 4.1 m^2

10. 25 cm

11. 6300 cm^2

12. 104.7 ft^2

13. 36 cm

14. Use the circumference of the base to determine the radius.

$C = 2\pi r$

$r = \dfrac{C}{2\pi}$

$r = \dfrac{12}{2\pi}$

$r = \dfrac{6}{\pi}$

Use the Pythagorean relationship to determine the slant height of the cone.

$s^2 = r^2 + h^2$

$s^2 = \left(\dfrac{6}{\pi}\right)^2 + 6^2$

$s = \sqrt{\left(\dfrac{6}{\pi}\right)^2 + 6^2}$

$s = 6.296\,631\,05...$

Calculate the surface area of the cone:

$SA = \pi r^2 + \pi rs$

$SA = \pi\left(\dfrac{6}{\pi}\right)^2 + \pi\left(\dfrac{6}{\pi}\right)(6.296\,631\,05...)^2$

$SA = 49.2$

The surface area of the mandrel is approximately 49.2 in.^{2}.

15. a) 3.2 m   **b)** $l = \sqrt{\dfrac{SA}{6}}$

16. a) 3.2 ft   **b)** 2.3 ft

c) No. Construction requires some cutting, so some material will be unusable or unavailable. The surface area of a manufactured object will be less than the surface area of the sheet of aluminum.

17. a) 7.3 m   **b)** 117 m^2

18. a) $SA = \dfrac{1}{2}\pi d^2 + \pi dh$

b) $SA = \dfrac{C^2}{2\pi} + Ch$

c) Answers will vary. Example:
Suppose a homeowner wants to paint a rain barrel. It is easier to determine the diameter of the barrel than the radius, since it is difficult to locate the centre of the barrel. The homeowner would use the formula in part a).
Suppose an arborist needs to wrap the trunk of a tree to protect it from pests. Since it is clearly undesirable to cut the tree to measure its diameter or radius, the arborist would measure the circumference and use the formula in part b).

2.3 Volume

1. a) 4647.12 in.^{3} **b)** 41.47 m^3
c) 2572.44 cm^3 **d)** 753.98 ft^3
e) 132 383.33 mm^3

2. a) 400 in.^{3} **b)** 57 255.53 mm^3

3. a) 8.51 in.

b) $V = \dfrac{4}{3}\pi r^3$

$36\pi = \dfrac{4}{3}\pi r^3$

$(3)(36\pi) = 4\pi r^3$

$108\pi = 4\pi r^3$

$\dfrac{108\pi}{4\pi} = \dfrac{4\pi r^3}{4\pi}$

$27 = r^3$

$3 = r$

The sphere has radius 3 m.

c) 11.88 m   **d)** 2.8 ft

4. a) 18 847.99 cm^3 **b)** 35 116.72 cm^3

5. a) 28 013.33 cm^3 **b)** 21 205.75 cm^3

6. 1 082 696 932 430 km^3 or 1.08×10^{12} km^3

7. a) 94.2 cm^3; This cup meets the standard.
b) 157.1 cm^3; This cup does not meet the standard, as it is too large.

8. a) 5575.3 in.^{3} **b)** 948.1 cm^3
c) 192 666.7 cm^3 **d)** 0.7 m^3

9. a) 225.8 cm^3 **b)** 1 mL = 1 cm^3

10. To determine the volume, you need to know the dimensions of the base. The triangle formed by the height of the pyramid, the slant height of a face, and half the length of the base is a right triangle. Use the Pythagorean relationship. Let x represent half the length of the base of the pyramid:

$x^2 + 24^2 = 25^2$

$x^2 = 25^2 - 24^2$

$x^2 = 49$

$x = 7$

Since 7 cm represents half the base, the base of the pyramid is 14 cm by 14 cm. Substitute into the formula for the volume of a pyramid:

$V = \dfrac{1}{3}lwh$

$V = \dfrac{1}{3}(14)(14)(24)$

$V = 1568$

The volume of the right pyramid is 1568 cm^3.

11. 3.6 cm; This is the minimum radius. If the height of the cylinder decreases, the radius will need to increase.

12. a) 3.7 m **b)** 4.2 cm
c) 30 cm or 0.3 m

13. 21.4 ft

14. a) 196.3 cm^3 **b)** The can is too small.
c) $V = \pi r^2 h$
$250 = \pi (2.5)^2 h$

$\dfrac{250}{6.25\pi} = h$

$12.74 \approx h$
Check by substituting $h = 12.74$ in the formula:
$V = \pi r^2 h$
$V = \pi (2.5)^2 (12.74)$
$V \approx 250.1$

15. a) 4 cm **b)** 4.6 cm
c) 6.2 cm
d) (12.2 cm)(12.2 cm) = 148.84 cm^2

16. 36 077 533.3 ft^3

17. Since the bead is half a sphere, modify the formula for the volume of a sphere:
$V = \frac{1}{2}\left(\frac{4}{3}\pi r^3\right)$
$V = \frac{2}{3}\pi r^3$
$V = \frac{2}{3}\pi \left(\frac{1.85}{2}\right)^3$
$V \approx 1.657\ 615\ 5...$
The volume of the bead is approximately 1.7 cm^3.

18. a) 9.5 cm **b)** 7.5 cm
c) cylinder: 457.1 cm^2; prism 500 cm^2
d) Example: Since both containers meet the requirements for capacity, I recommend the cylinder as it uses less material, and therefore, may be less costly to manufacture.

19. 7743.36 cm^3

20. a) 6 units $\times$ 6 units $\times$ 6 units
b) $r = 3$ units

21. The volume will increase more than the surface area. Many students may incorrectly predict that both the surface area and the volume will double. By creating an example, they should discover that such a prediction is incorrect. Example: A sphere has radius 5 cm. The original volume is about 523.6 cm^3. The

original surface area is about 314.2 cm^2. If the radius is doubled to 10, the new volume is 4188.8 cm^3 and the new surface area is 1256.6 cm^2. In both cases, the volume and surface area more than doubled. In fact, the volume increased by approximately 8 times. The surface area increased by approximately 4 times. Therefore, when the dimensions of an object are doubled, the volume changes more the surface area does.

Chapter 2 Review
2.1 Units of Area and Volume
1. a) 603.22 cm^2 **b)** 3.88 ft^2
2. a) 0.13 m^3 **b)** 1608.8 cm^3
3. 10.49 ft^2
4. 1 yd$^3 \approx$ 0.76 m^3, so 1 yd^3 should cost about $(0.76)(62) = 47.12$. One cubic yard should cost about \$47.12 but the supplier is charging \$50 instead. This means that \$62 per cubic metre is a better price.

2.2 Surface Area
5. a) 170.43 m^2 **b)** 301.59 cm^2
c) 226.98 in.^{2} **d)** 60 ft^2
6. a) $r = 5.98$ in. **b)** $s = 9.43$ cm
c) $s = 1.18$ ft **d)** $h = 5.92$ m
7. Area of floor: $(8)(10) = 80$
Area of walls: $(2)(8)(7) + (2)(10)(7) = 252$
Area of roof: $2\left(\frac{1}{2}(8)(5.4)\right) +$
$2\left(\frac{1}{2}(10)(4.5)\right) = 88.2$
Since the shed does not have a ceiling, it is not necessary to find the area of the base of the pyramid, which is also the top of the prism. The total surface area is 420.2 ft^2.

8. 4750.09 in.^{2} or 32.99 ft^2
9. \$88.77
10. a) Example:

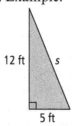
12 ft s 5 ft

b) $r = 5$ ft; $s = 13$ ft **c)** 282.74 ft^2

2.3 Volume

11. a) 7.07 ft^3 or 12 214.51 in.^{3} **b)** 5.33 m^3
   c) 0.52 m^3 **d)** 796.39 cm^3

12. a) 25.98 m   **b)** 4.98 cm
   c) 6 in.   **d)** 6 ft

13. a) 233.33 ft^3
   b) 233.33 ft^3 ≈ 6.61 m^3
$$\frac{233.33}{35} = 6.666\,574\,14...$$
$$\approx 6.67$$
   Mike's estimate is fairly accurate.

14. a) Determine the volume of the bin:
$$V = \pi r^2 h$$
$$V = \pi\left(\frac{1.25}{2}\right)^2(1.1)$$
$$V \approx 1.349\,903...$$
   There is approximately 1.35 m^3 of compost in a full bin.
   b) Determine the area of the garden in square metres:
$$A = lw$$
$$A = \left[\left(\frac{12\text{ ft}}{1}\right)\left(\frac{0.3048\text{ m}}{1\text{ ft}}\right)\right]$$
$$\left[\left(\frac{20\text{ ft}}{1}\right)\left(\frac{0.3048\text{ m}}{1\text{ ft}}\right)\right]$$
$$A = 22.296\,729...$$
   The area of the garden is approximately 22.3 m^2.
   Consider the compost in the garden to occupy a rectangular prism with base 22.3 m^2 and volume 1.35 m^3. Rearrange the formula $V = Bh$ and solve:
$$h = \frac{V}{B}$$
$$h \approx \frac{1.349\,903}{22.296\,729}$$
$$h \approx 0.060\,542\,6$$
   The height of the compost is approximately 0.06 m. This is equivalent to approximately 6 cm.
   Convert this depth to inches:
$$\left(\frac{0.060\,542\,6}{1}\right)\left(\frac{1\text{ in.}}{2.54\text{ cm}}\right) = 2.383\,568...$$
   The compost will be approximately 2.4 in. deep.

15. 502.65 cm^3

16. a) Example: The height will need to double. Example: When the height is 20 cm, the capacity is 1005.31 cm^3, so the prediction was correct.
   b) Example: The diameter will need to double. Example: When the diameter is 16 cm, the radius is 8 cm and the capacity is 2010.62 cm^3, so the prediction was incorrect.

17. a) 169.65 ft^3 **b)** $94.25

Chapters 1–2 Cumulative Review

1. a) 800 000 mm^2 **b)** 97.98 cm^2

2. a) Example: Using an eraser width as a referent for 35 mm, the curve of the O could be about 2 eraser widths.
   b) Using a pen as a referent for 15 cm, the curve of the O could be about 2 pen widths.

3. a) Use a piece of string and lay it along the shape of the letter that you drew, and then measure the string.

4. a) 2.17 m^3 **b)** 399.5 in.^{3}

5. Answers will vary. Students should list the most commonly used conversions.

6. a) 49 mm = 4.9 cm **b)** 9.4 mm = 0.94 cm

7. 53.25 ft^2

8. 1.43 m by 2.85 m

9. a) $\frac{4}{3}\pi(6.2)^3 = 998.3$ cm^3
   b) $\frac{(1.5)(0.7)(2)}{3} = 0.7$ m^3
   c) $\frac{1}{3}\pi(4^2)(7) = 117.3$ mm^3

10. $3\frac{3}{16}$ in.; Example: width of a library card

11. a) 433.5 in.^{2} **b)** 784 cm^2
   c) 78.5 ft^2

12. a) 3 yd   **b)** 5.5 mi
   c) 4550 in.

13. a) $s = 1.58$ ft   **b)** $s = 103.75$ cm
   c) $r = 2.12$ m

14. a) 17 m^2 **b)** 389 tiles

15. 21.06 cm

16. 271.04 km

17. 3.39 cm^3

Chapter 2 Extend It Further

1. A

2. D

   Volume of one scoop of ice cream:
   $$V = \frac{4}{3}\pi r^3$$
   $$= \frac{4}{3}\pi(2)^3$$
   $$= 33.5103...$$
   The volume of one scoop is approximately
   33.5 cm³.
   Since there are two scoops, the total volume
   is twice this amount or approximately
   67 cm³.
   The volume of ice cream remains the same
   when it is placed in the cup.
   Solve the equation:
   $$\pi r^2 h = 67$$
   $$\pi(3)^2 h = 67$$
   $$9\pi h = 67$$
   $$h = \frac{67}{9\pi}$$
   $$h = 2.4$$
   The ice cream raised the height of the juice
   by 2.4 cm to a new height of $10 + 2.4 =$
   12.4 cm.

3. A

   When unfolded, the curve is made up
   of two separate lines. Each line is the
   hypotenuse of a right triangle.

   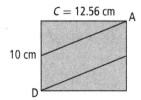

   The circumference is $3.14(4) = 12.56$ cm.

   Each hypotenuse is $\sqrt{(12.56)^2 + 5^2} =$
   13.52 cm.

   The curve is 2(13.52) or 27.04 cm long.

4. B

   From the side view, there are two similar
   triangles.

   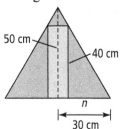

That is, $\frac{50}{40} = \frac{30}{n}$ or $n = 24$ cm.

This gives the radius of the cylinder as
$30 - 24 = 6$ cm.
Determine the lateral surface area of the
cylinder:
$$SA = \pi dh$$
$$SA = \pi(12)(40)$$
$$SA = 480\pi \text{ cm}^2$$

5. Volume of hemisphere:
   $$V = \frac{1}{2}\left(\frac{4}{3}\pi r^3\right)$$
   $$V = \frac{2}{3}\pi r^3$$
   Volume of cylinder:
   $$V = \pi r^2 h$$
   $$V = \frac{2}{3}\pi r^3 + \pi r^2 h$$
   Since the hemisphere has $\frac{1}{6}$ the capacity of
   the test tube:
   $$\frac{2}{3}\pi r^3 = \frac{1}{6}\left(\frac{2}{3}\pi r^3 + \pi r^2 h\right)$$
   $$4\pi r^3 = \frac{2}{3}\pi r^3 + \pi r^2 h$$
   $$12\pi r^3 = 2\pi r^3 + 3\pi r^2 h$$
   $$10\pi r^3 = 3\pi r^2 h$$
   $$10 r^3 = 3 r^2 h$$
   $$10 r = 3 h$$
   $$r = \frac{3}{10} h$$
   $$r:h = 3:10$$

6. Volumes of the cone, cylinder, and
   hemisphere:
   $$V_{cone} = \frac{1}{3}\pi r^2 h$$
   $$V_{cylinder} = \pi r^2 h$$
   $$V_{hemisphere} = \frac{1}{2}\left(\frac{4}{3}\pi r^3\right)$$
   $$= \frac{2}{3}\pi r^3$$
   Equate the volumes of the cylinder and
   hemisphere:
   $$\pi r^2 h_{cylinder} = \frac{2}{3}\pi r^3$$
   $$h_{cylinder} = \frac{2}{3} r$$
   Equate the volumes of the cone and
   hemisphere:
   $$\frac{1}{3}\pi r^2 h_{cone} = \frac{2}{3}\pi r^3$$
   $$\pi r^2 h_{cone} = 2\pi r^3$$
   $$h_{cone} = 2r$$

   Therefore, the ratio of heights $x:y:z$ is
   $2:\frac{2}{3}:1$. To write this ratio using natural
   numbers, multiply each term in the ratio
   by 3 to get $6:2:3$.

Chapter 3 Right Triangle Trigonometry

3.1 The Tangent Ratio

1. **a)** c
   b) a
   c) b

2. **a)** $\tan A = \frac{a}{b}$ **b)** $\tan B = \frac{b}{a}$

3. **a)** 0.83
   b) 1.26
   c) 18

4. 5.31 m

5. **a)** $\tan X = \dfrac{\text{opposite}}{\text{adjacent}}$

   $\tan X = \dfrac{1.85}{1.6}$

   $\tan X = 1.15625$

   Use the inverse function on a calculator to apply the tangent ratio in reverse:

   $\tan X = 1.15625$
   $X = \tan^{-1}(1.15625)$
   $X = 49.1446...°$

   $\angle X$ is 49.1°, to the nearest tenth of a degree.

   b) $\tan Y = \dfrac{\text{opposite}}{\text{adjacent}}$

   $\tan Y = \dfrac{1.6}{1.85}$

   $\tan Y = 0.86486$

   Use the inverse function on a calculator to apply the tangent ratio in reverse:

   $\tan Y = 0.86486$
   $Y = \tan^{-1}(0.86486)$
   $Y = 40.8552...°$

   $\angle Y$ is 40.9°, to the nearest tenth of a degree.

6. $\angle A = 52°$; $\angle B = 38°$; $c = 4.06$ m; Side c, which is opposite the right angle, is the hypotenuse. Because the lengths of the other two sides (a and b) are known, the length of side c can be determined by substituting the values for a and b in the equation $a^2 + b^2 = c^2$ and solving for c.

7. 293 cm

8. **a)** 12.9 m
   b) 14.8°

9. 3.59 m

10. 200 cm, or 2 m

11. Organize the information and sketch a diagram to illustrate the problem.

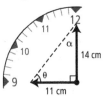

   a) Form the tangent ratio for $\angle\alpha$ from the diagram.

   $\tan \alpha = \dfrac{11}{14}$

   $\alpha = \tan^{-1}\left(\dfrac{11}{14}\right)$

   $\alpha = 38.2°$

   The angle formed between the line and the minute hand is 38.2°.

   b) Form the tangent ratio for $\angle\theta$.

   $\tan \theta = \dfrac{14}{11}$

   $\theta = \tan^{-1}\left(\dfrac{14}{11}\right)$

   $\theta = 51.8°$

   The angle between the line and the hour hand is 51.8°.

12. 359 m

13. The plane travelled 13 186 m.

14. **a)** 6.1 m   **b)** 7.6 m

15. 24.3°

16. **a)** Organize the information and sketch a diagram to illustrate the problem.

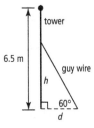

   First, find the value of h, the height in metres up the pole where the wires should be attached.

   $6.5 \text{ m} \times \dfrac{2}{3} = 4.33 \text{ m}$

Next, use a tangent ratio to find the distance, d, in metres, that each wire should extend from the base of the tower.

$$\tan 60° = \frac{4.33}{d}$$
$$d = \frac{4.33}{\tan 60°}$$
$$d = 2.5 \text{ m}$$

Since Ramon needs 2.5 m *on each side* of the tower, the available width of 4.2 m is not enough.

b) Since the available width is 4.2 m, the maximum value of d is $\frac{4.2 \text{ m}}{2}$, or 2.1 m.

To find the corresponding value of h when d equals 2.1 m, use a tangent ratio:

$$\tan 60° = \frac{h}{2.1}$$
$$(2.1) \tan 60° = h$$
$$3.64 \text{ m} = h$$

Since h represents only two thirds of the tower's height, the maximum possible tower height is

$$3.64 \times \frac{3}{2} = 5.46 \text{ m}$$

17. a) $a = 2b$ or $a = \frac{b}{2}$; $b = 2a$ or $b = \frac{a}{2}$

b) $a = \frac{b}{2}$ or $a = 2b$; $b = \frac{a}{2}$ or $b = 2a$

c) The values or ratios in parts a) and b) are the same. This is because the values are simply switched from numerator to denominator, or vice versa.

3.2 The Sine and Cosine Ratios

1. a) $\sin A = \frac{a}{c}$ **b)** $\cos A = \frac{b}{c}$

  c) $\sin B = \frac{b}{c}$ **d)** $\cos B = \frac{a}{c}$

2. a) $\cos A = \frac{12}{17}$ **b)** $\sin A = \frac{10}{15}$

  c) $\sin B = \frac{1.9}{2.4}$ **d)** $\cos B = \frac{2.6}{3.9}$

  e) $a = \frac{75}{6} = \frac{25}{2}$ **f)** $a = \frac{9}{3} = 3$

3. a) $\angle R = 48.4°$ **b)** $\angle S = 41.6°$

4. a) $54.3°$ **b)** $56.7°$
  c) $12.6°$ **d)** $87.2°$

5. a) $x = 1.85$ cm   **b)** $x = 4.39$ m

6. a) $z = 72.48$ mm   **b)** $z = 9.70$ m

7. The angle is 61° and the backing piece must have a height of 155 mm.

8. a) 6.3 ft   **b)** 54.9°

9. 34 m

10. First, label the given diagram.

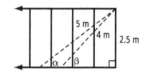

Then, form appropriate ratios:

$$\sin \alpha = \frac{2.5 \text{ m}}{5 \text{ m}} \qquad \sin \beta = \frac{2.5 \text{ m}}{4 \text{ m}}$$

Solve for the angles:

$$\alpha = \sin^{-1}\left(\frac{2.5}{5}\right) \qquad \beta = \sin^{-1}\left(\frac{2.5}{4}\right)$$
$$\alpha = 30° \qquad\qquad \beta = 39°$$

The 5-m rod forms an angle of 30° with the floor. The 4-m rod forms an angle of 39° with the floor.

11. The boat ramp must be 4.8 m in length.

12. First, modify and label the given diagram.

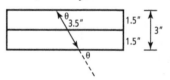

Then, create a simplified diagram.

Select the appropriate trigonometric ratio and solve for θ:

$$\sin \theta = \frac{3}{3.5}$$
$$\theta = \sin^{-1}\left(\frac{3}{3.5}\right)$$
$$\theta = 59°$$

The screws should be driven in at an angle of 59° or less to prevent the points from sticking through.

13. a) The water gun can spray the middle 7.2 m of the opposite side.
  b) 2.8 m (1.4 m at each end)
  c) 7.8 m

14. CD $= 14.7$ cm

15. Consider the teepee as a cone.

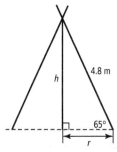

Use a ratio to find the radius of the base.

$\cos 65° = \dfrac{r}{4.8 \text{ m}}$

$(4.8 \text{ m}) \times \cos 65° = r$

$2.03 \text{ m} = r$

Since the radius is one half of the diameter, multiply the value by 2:

diameter $= 2 \times$ radius

diameter $= 2 \times 2.03$ m

diameter $= 4.06$ m, or 4.1 m, to the nearest tenth of a metre

The diameter of the teepee is 4.1 m.

16. a)

θ	tan θ	sin θ	cos θ
15°	0.2679	0.2588	0.9659
30°	0.5774	0.5	0.8660
45°	1	0.7071	0.7071
60°	1.7321	0.8660	0.5
75°	3.7321	0.9659	0.2588

b) As the values of the tangent and sine increase, the value of the cosine decreases.

c) The sine and cosine generate the same values, but in the opposite order.

3.3 Solving Right Triangles

1. a) $\angle B = 23°$; $a = 5.2$; $c = 5.6$

b) $\angle B = 42°$; $b = 12.9$; $c = 19.2$

c) $\angle Z = 49.0°$; $\angle Y = 41.0°$; $x = 2.3$

d) Use the Pythagorean theorem to calculate the length, x, of side YZ:

$(YZ)^2 = (XY)^2 + (XZ)^2$

$x^2 = (1.75)^2 + (1.52)^2$

$x^2 = 3.0625 + 2.3104$

$x^2 = 5.3729$

$x = \sqrt{5.3729}$

$x = 2.317...$, or 2.3 units, to the nearest tenth of a unit

2. a) $\angle A$, $\angle C$

b) $\angle B$, $\angle D$

c) $\angle A = \angle B$, $\angle C = \angle D$

3. a) Both are correct. The name of the angle changes when the point of view changes.

b) The angle of elevation from one point to a second point is equal to the angle of depression from the second point to the first point.

4. a) $\angle C = 48°$; $\angle B = 52°$; $\angle D = 42°$; $b = 18.3$; $c = 23.2$; $x = 20.3$

b) $\angle X = 27°$; $\angle Z = 61°$; $x = 2.6$; $y = 5.4$; $z = 5.3$

5. a) 42.1 cm   **b)** 54.9°

6. Sketch and label a diagram with the given information to illustrate the problem.

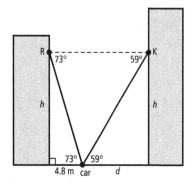

Note that the angles of depression <u>to</u> the car equal the angles of elevation <u>from</u> the car.

Use an appropriate ratio to find h first:

$$\tan 73° = \dfrac{h}{4.8 \text{ m}}$$

$(4.8 \text{ m}) \times \tan 73° = h$

$15.7 \text{ m} = h$

This is the same h as for Kenneth's window. Now we find d:

$$\tan 59° = \dfrac{15.7 \text{ m}}{d}$$

$$d = \dfrac{15.7 \text{ m}}{\tan 59°}$$

$$d = 9.43 \text{ m}.$$

Add the two horizontal distances:

4.8 m + 9.43 m = 14.23 m, or 14.2 m, to the nearest tenth of a metre

The distance between the two windows is 14.2 m.

7. 8.6 m

8. a) 202 m
   b) 714 m
   c) 436 m

9. a) 98 m   **b)** 50°

10. a) No, the diagonal length across the bottom of the box is only 118.5 cm, which is 1.5 cm less than the length of the cane.
   b) Yes, the diagonal distance across opposite corners is 121.8 cm, which is greater than the length of the cane. Therefore, the lid can be closed.

11. Sketch a modified diagram and label it with the given information to illustrate the problem.

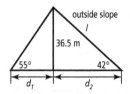

a) Width of dike = $d_1 + d_2$

Find d_1:   Find d_2:

$$\tan 55° = \frac{36.5 \text{ m}}{d_1} \qquad \tan 42° = \frac{36.5 \text{ m}}{d_2}$$

$$d_1 = \frac{36.5 \text{ m}}{\tan 55°} \qquad d_2 = \frac{36.5 \text{ m}}{\tan 42°}$$

$$d_1 = 25.56 \text{ m} \qquad d_2 = 40.54 \text{ m}$$

Width = 25.56 m + 40.54 m = 66.1 m
The width of the dike is 66.1 m.

b) The length of the mesh is the hypotenuse of the outside triangle:

$$\sin 42° = \frac{36.5 \text{ m}}{\ell}$$

$$\ell = \frac{36.5 \text{ m}}{\sin 42°}$$

$$\ell = 54.5 \text{ m}$$

The mesh needs to be 54.5 m long.

c) Let the height be 39 m. Then, solve as in part a):

$$d_1 = \frac{39 \text{ m}}{\tan 55°}$$

$$d_1 = 27.31 \text{ m}$$

$$d_2 = \frac{39 \text{ m}}{\tan 42°}$$

$$d_2 = 43.31 \text{ m}$$

Width = 27.31 m + 43.31 m = 70.6 m
The width at the base must be 70.6 m.

d) Let the height equal 31 m. Then, solve as in part a):

$$d_1 = \frac{31 \text{ m}}{\tan 55°}$$

$$d_1 = 21.71 \text{ m}$$

$$d_2 = \frac{31 \text{ m}}{\tan 42°}$$

$$d_2 = 34.43 \text{ m}$$

Width = 21.71 m + 34.43 m = 56.14 m
The student-engineer is not correct. The base of the dike needs to be 56.1 m wide, not 54.8 m.

12. Sketch a simplified diagram to illustrate the problem, converting all distances to metres.

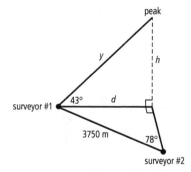

a) Find the distance d, in metres, from surveyor #1 to a point directly under the peak:

$$\sin 78° = \frac{d}{3750 \text{ m}}$$

$$(3750 \text{ m}) \times \sin 78° = d$$

$$3668 \text{ m} = d$$

Now, use this distance in the other triangle to find h:

$$\tan 43° = \frac{h}{3668 \text{ m}}$$

$$(3668 \text{ m}) \times \tan 43° = h$$

$$3420 \text{ m} = h$$

The mountain is 3420 m high.

b) Find the hypotenuse, y, of the second triangle:

$$\cos 43° = \frac{3668 \text{ m}}{y}$$

$$y = \frac{3668 \text{ m}}{\cos 43°}$$

$$y = 5015 \text{ m}$$

The cable needs to be 5015 m long.

c) Use trigonometric ratios as in part a) to determine the distance, in metres, of each of d and h. Then, use the Pythagorean theorem to determine the distance y, in metres:
$$y^2 = d^2 + h^2$$
$$y^2 = (3668)^2 + (3420)^2$$
$$y^2 = 13\,454\,224 + 11\,696\,400$$
$$y^2 = 25\,150\,624$$
$$y = \sqrt{25\,150\,624}$$
$$y = 5015.03\ldots, \text{ or } 5015 \text{ m, to the nearest metre}$$

Chapter 3 Review
3.1 The Tangent Ratio

1. **a)** x
    b) z
    c) y

2. **a)** $\tan Y = \frac{y}{z}$ **b)** $\tan Z = \frac{z}{y}$

3. 30.7 cm

4. $\angle B$ is the smallest angle: 39.75°

5. 2.34 m

6. 30.56 m

3.2 The Sine and Cosine Ratios

7. **a)** $\sin A = \frac{a}{c}$
    b) $\cos A = \frac{b}{c}$
    c) $\sin B = \frac{b}{c}$
    d) $\cos B = \frac{a}{c}$

8. **a)** $b = 4.69$ **b)** $b = 3.59$

9. 2.39 m

10. 5.49 m

11. **a)** 8.5°   **b)** 53.4 ft

3.3 Solving Right Triangles

12. **a)** $\angle B = 73°; a = 3.7$ cm; $b = 12.0$ cm
    b) $\angle Y = 41°; x = 81.1$ m; $z = 107.5$ m
    c) $\angle L = 41.8°; \angle M = 48.2°; m = 5.4$ mm
    d) $\angle D = 57.4°; \angle E = 32.6°; f = 7.6$
    e) $\angle X = 63.3°; \angle Y = 26.7°; x = 22.8$

13. **a)** 87 cm   **b)** 34°

13. 701 m

14. One goalie is at a distance of 22 m. The second goalie is at a distance of 78 m.

16. **a)** 233.2 m
    b) 223.6 m
    c) 63.4°

Chapters 1–3 Cumulative Review

1. **a)** Example: 12 cm
    b) 11.4 cm
    c) 3.82 cm²

2. 448 ft²

3. **a)**

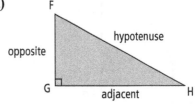

b) $\tan H = \frac{FG}{GH}; \sin H = \frac{FG}{FH}; \cos H = \frac{GH}{FH}$

4. **a)** slant height = 1.11 m
    b) slant height = 37.00 cm
    c) radius = 6.15 mm

5. **a)** 76°
    b) 62°
    c) 53°

6. **a)** $1\frac{5}{16}$ in.; 3.33 cm
    b) 2.64 cm; 1.04 in.

7. 1152.3 cm²

8. **a)** 9650.97 ft³   **b)** 279.8 cm³
    c) 192 ft³   **d)** 998.31 cm³
    e) 169.65 in.³   **f)** 60 m³

9. **a)** radius = 0.89 m
    b) height = 7.41 cm
    c) side length = 4.03 m
    d) radius = 9.39 cm
    e) radius = 0.62 in.
    f) height = 3.00 ft

10. **a)** $\angle A = 25.8°; \angle C = 64.2°; a = 1.3$ m
    b) $\angle A = 48.0°; a = 74.4$ cm; $c = 100.1$ cm

11. **a)** 2041.92 m   **b)** 820.26 m

12. **a)** 66.6 m³; 333 000 m³
    b) 0.59 truckloads; 2950 truckloads
    c) 621 125 m²

13. **a)** 1 : 12 500 000
    b) 317.5 km
    c) Example: approximately 179 mi
    d) approximately 62 mi

Chapter 3 Extend It Further

1. A

2. C; Sketch and label a diagram with the given information to illustrate the problem.

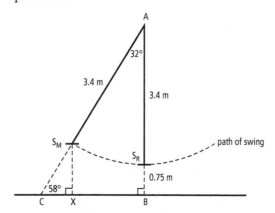

In the diagram, S_R represents the position of the swing at rest. S_M represents the position of the swing at its highest point. At this point, as the diagram illustrates, the swing reaches a maximum angle of 32° with the vertical. The line $S_M X$ represents the maximum height of the swing above the ground.
To calculate the length of $S_M X$, first determine the length of the line segment $S_M C$. The length of that segment is equal to the length of the line AC (the hypotenuse of right $\triangle ABC$) minus the length of the swing. Use the cosine ratio to determine the length of AC:

$$\cos 32° = \frac{\text{adjacent}}{\text{hypotenuse}}$$

$$\cos 32° = \frac{4.15 \text{ m}}{AC}$$

$$0.84804 = \frac{4.15 \text{ m}}{AC}$$

$$AC = 4.8936 \text{ m}$$

The length of line segment
$S_M C = 4.8936 \text{ m} - 3.4 \text{ m} = 1.4936 \text{ m}$

In $\triangle S_M XC$, $\angle C = 58°$. Use the sine ratio to determine the length of $S_M X$:

$$\sin 58° = \frac{\text{opposite}}{\text{hypotenuse}}$$

$$\sin 58° = \frac{S_M X}{1.4936 \text{ m}}$$

$$0.84804 = \frac{S_M X}{1.4936 \text{ m}}$$

$$S_M X = 1.2666 \text{ m}$$

The maximum height of the swing above the ground is 1.2666 m. Therefore, the best answer is C: 1.27 m.

3. B

4. vertically = 0.28 m; horizontally = 0.48 m. The two distances are different as the two ends of the ladder are travelling at different speeds.

5. AC = 15.3 cm; BD = 12.9 cm

6. a) 108°   **b)** 80.9 cm

7. 76 507 cm³

Unit 1 Review

1. C
2. B
3. B
4. A
5. B
6. C
7. B
8. D
9. B
10. C
11. B
12. B
13. B
14. C
15. B
16. C
17. $3\frac{1}{4}''$
18. 30.5 mm
19. 90 in.
20. 166.4 cm²
21. 26 m
22. 11 ft
23. 25.7 yd³
24. 128.9°
25. **a)** $r = 12.7$ cm, $h = 30.5$ cm
    b) 1316.0 cm²
    c) 5148.9 cm³

26. **a)**

    b) tangent ratio
    c) 4.8 m

27. **a)**

    b) 26.6°

28. **a)** 6.7 ft
    b) 449.0 ft3
    c) 17.9 ft

29. **a)** $1\frac{5}{8}$ in.
    b) 4.6 in.²
    c) 0.5 in.³

30. **a)** Answers may vary.
    b) outer radius = 6.35 cm,
    inner radius = 1.91 cm
    c) 1170 cm³

31. **a)** Use the Pythagorean theorem to determine the length of side BC. Triangle ABC is a right triangle (the sum of the angles is 180°). Use the tangent ratio to find the length of side AB.
    b) 1.7 m

Chapter 4 Exponents and Radicals

4.1 Square Roots and Cube Roots

1. **a)** 81   **b)** 225

     c) −625   **d)** $\frac{4}{9}$

     e) $\frac{-25}{8}$ **f)** $\left(\frac{36}{49}\right)$

2. **a)** 729   **b)** −27

     c) −216   **d)** 8

     e) $\frac{-1}{3}$ **f)** $\frac{125}{343}$

3. **a)** 5   **b)** 14

     c) 28   **d)** 2

     e) $\frac{2}{3}$ **f)** $\frac{4}{7}$

     g) $\frac{1}{3}$ **h)** $6x$

     i) $\frac{7a}{13b}$

4. **a)** 2   **b)** 3

     c) 12   **d)** 20

     e) 3   **f)** $\frac{3}{5}$

     g) $\frac{2}{7}$ **h)** $5y$

     i) $9a$

5. **a)** perfect cube

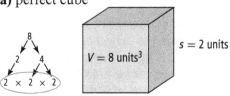

     b) perfect cube

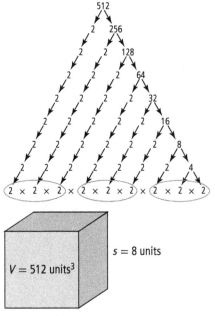

c) both

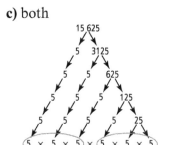

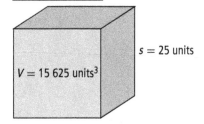

d) perfect square

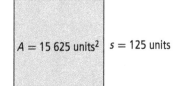

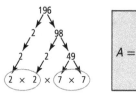

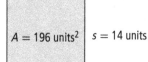

e) both

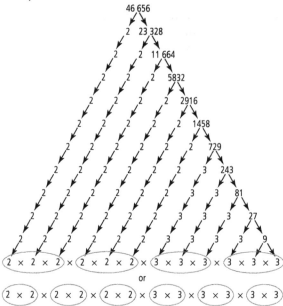

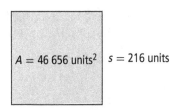

$A = 46\,656$ units^2 | $s = 216$ units

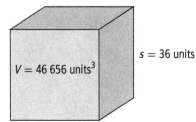

$s = 36$ units

$V = 46\,656$ units^3

f) both

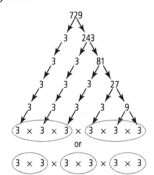

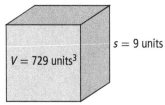

$A = 729$ units^2 | $s = 27$ units

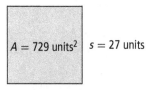

$s = 9$ units

$V = 729$ units^3

6. a) perfect square **b)** perfect square
   c) both **d)** perfect square
   e) both **f)** neither

7. a) perfect square **b)** perfect cube
   c) perfect cube **d)** perfect square
   e) perfect square **f)** neither

8. a) 17 **b)** 23
   c) 14 **d)** 22
   e) 31 **f)** 27

9. The storage container will measure 1.4 m by 1.4 m by 1.4 m (or 140 cm by 140 cm by 140 cm).

10. The side length of the patio is 23 ft.

11.
$$V = s^3$$
$$2146.2 = s^3$$
$$\sqrt[3]{2146.2} = s$$
$$12.899\,02\ldots = s$$

The edge length of the cube would be approximately 12.9 cm.

12. 24 ft

13. 12.5 ft

14. 6 m $\times$ 6 m $\times$ 6 m

15. 1331 mm^3

16. approximately 6.2 m

17. 9 m by 9 m by 9 m

18. 16 cm

19. a) $y = 60$ **b)** $y = 192$

20. a) $x = 6$ **b)** $x = 23$

21. Volume of the tank in cubic inches:
$$1\text{ ft}^3 = (12\text{ in.})(12\text{ in.})(12\text{ in.})$$
$$= 1728\text{ in.}^3$$
$$54\text{ ft}^3 = (54)(1728)$$
$$= 93\,312$$

The volume of the tank is equal to 93 312 in.^{3}
Volume of one balloon:
$$V = \frac{4}{3}\pi r^3$$
$$V = \frac{4}{3}\pi(6)^3$$
$$V = 288\pi$$
$$V = 904.778\,761\ldots$$

The volume of one balloon is approximately 904.78 in.^{3}
Number of balloons inflated per full tank:
$$\frac{\text{volume of tank}}{\text{volume of balloon}} = \frac{93\,312}{904.778\,761\ldots}$$
$$V = 103.13\ldots$$

A full tank will inflate approximately 103 balloons.

22. 575 cm^2

23. a)

$\sqrt{25}$	5
$\sqrt{2.5}$	1.581...
$\sqrt{0.25}$	0.5
$\sqrt{0.025}$	0.158...
$\sqrt{0.0025}$	0.05
$\sqrt{0.00025}$	0.015...

b)

$\sqrt{81}$	9
$\sqrt{8.1}$	2.846...
$\sqrt{0.81}$	0.9
$\sqrt{0.081}$	0.284...
$\sqrt{0.0081}$	0.09
$\sqrt{0.00081}$	0.028...

c) Answers may vary. Look for the idea that a perfect decimal square exists if it has an even number of zeros before the perfect square number.

24. The expression $\sqrt{-25}$ is not a perfect square because when you multiply two positive or two negative numbers the answer is always positive. The expression $\sqrt[3]{-27}$ is a perfect cube because when you multiply three negative numbers, such as $(-3)(-3)(-3)$, the answer is negative. Therefore, it is possible to have a negative perfect cube.

25. a) When you double the side lengths of a square, the area increases by a factor of 2^2 or 4. Example:
$A = s^2$
$\quad = (2s)^2$
$\quad = 4s^2$
When you triple the side lengths, the area increases by a factor of 3^2 or 9. Example:
$A = s^2$
$\quad = (3s)^2$
$\quad = 9s^2$

b) When you double the edge lengths of a cube, the volume increases by a factor of 2^3 or 8. Example:
$V = s^3$
$\quad = (2s)^3$
$\quad = 8s^3$

When you triple the edge lengths, the volume increases by a factor of 3^3 or 27. Example:
$V = s^3$
$\quad = (3s)^3$
$\quad = 27s^3$

4.2 Integral Exponents

1. a) $\frac{1}{4^2}$ **b)** $\frac{3}{x^3}$

c) $\frac{1}{(5x)^2}$ or $\frac{1}{25x^2}$ **d)** $\frac{6}{a^3b^2}$

e) $\frac{-5}{a^4}$ **f)** $\frac{-4a^4}{b^5}$

g) $\left(\frac{3}{2}\right)^3$ **h)** $-3x^2y^4$

i) $\frac{6}{a^3b^4}$

2. No. Shelby's answer is incorrect. The correct answer is $\frac{16x^{10}}{y^6}$.

3. a) 0.3644 **b)** -0.125
c) 0.0625 **d)** -1
e) 4096 **f)** 2.8477

4. a) $\frac{a^4}{b^5}$ **b)** $\frac{-2b^2}{a^3}$

c) p^{12} **d)** $3s^{10}$

e) $\frac{x^8}{6^2}$ **f)** t^{16}

g) $\frac{1}{n^4}$ **h)** $\frac{y^6}{x^2}$

5. a) $(6)^{-3}(6) = 6^{-3+1}$
$\qquad\qquad\ = 6^{-2}$
$\qquad\qquad\ = \frac{1}{6^2}$

b) $\frac{(-2)^{-6}}{(-2)^{-3}} = (-2)^{-6-(-3)}$
$\qquad\qquad\ = (-2)^{-3}$
$\qquad\qquad\ = \frac{1}{(-2)^3}$

c) $\frac{3^3}{3^{-2}} = 3^{3-(-2)}$
$\qquad\ = 3^5$

d) $\left(\frac{4^0}{4^{-2}}\right)^2 = \left(4^{0-(-2)}\right)^2$
$\qquad\qquad = \left(4^2\right)^2$
$\qquad\qquad = 4^4$

e) $\left(6^{-4}\right)^2 = 6^{(-4)(2)}$
$\qquad\qquad = 6^{-8}$
$\qquad\qquad = \frac{1}{6^8}$

f) $-(3^4)^{-3} = -(3)^{(4)(-3)}$

$\qquad = -(3)^{-12}$

$\qquad = \dfrac{-1}{(3)^{12}}$

g) $[(2^4)(2^{-7})]^{-3} = [(2)^{4+(-7)}]^{-3}$

$\qquad = [(2)^{-3}]^{-3}$

$\qquad = 2^{(-3)(-3)}$

$\qquad = 2^9$

h) $\left(\dfrac{3^3}{4^3}\right)^{-2} = \dfrac{(3)^{(3)(-2)}}{(4)^{(3)(-2)}}$

$\qquad = \dfrac{3^{-6}}{4^{-6}}$

$\qquad = \dfrac{4^6}{3^6}$

i) $(4a^{-3})^{-2} = (4)^{-2}\,a^{(-3)(-2)}$

$\qquad = (4)^{-2}\,a^6$

$\qquad = \dfrac{a^6}{4^2}$

j) $-3[(2^4)(2^{-3})]^{-2} = -3[(2)^{4+(-3)}]^{-2}$

$\qquad = -3[(2)^1]^{-2}$

$\qquad = -3(2)^{-2}$

$\qquad = \dfrac{-3}{2^2}$

6. a) 27 200 cm^2 **b)** 7 130 316 800 cm^2

7. approximately 1638 caribou

8. a) 3200 bacteria **b)** 6 710 886 400 bacteria
  c) 50 bacteria

9. $\left[\left((2^{-1})^2\right)^3\right]^{-1} = \left[\left(\left(\tfrac{1}{2}\right)^2\right)^3\right]^{-1}$

$\qquad = \left[\left(\tfrac{1}{4}\right)^3\right]^{-1}$

$\qquad = \left[\tfrac{1}{64}\right]^{-1}$

$\qquad = 64$

Or, some students may evaluate as $2^6 = 64$.

10. No. Kevin is incorrect. Example: Since the bases are not the same, you cannot add the exponents. When simplified, the expression $(2^3)(3^2) = (8)(9) = 72$. The power $6^5 = 7776$.

11. a) 25 g **b)** 800 g

12. a) $d = \tfrac{1}{2}gt^2$

$\qquad = \tfrac{1}{2}(9.8)(12.4^2)$

$\qquad = (4.9)(153.76)$

$\qquad = 753.424$

The penny falls from a height of approximately 753.4 m.

b) $\qquad d = \tfrac{1}{2}gt^2$

$28.5 = \tfrac{1}{2}(9.8)t^2$

$28.5 = (4.9)t^2$

$\dfrac{28.5}{4.9} = t^2$

$\qquad t^2 = 5.816\,326\,5...$

$\qquad t = \sqrt{5.816\,326\,5}$

$\qquad t = 2.411\,706\,1...$

It takes approximately 2.4 s for the penny to fall.

c) $\qquad d = \tfrac{1}{2}gt^2$

$248 = \tfrac{1}{2}(9.8)t^2$

$248 = (4.9)t^2$

$\dfrac{248}{4.9} = t^2$

$\qquad t^2 = 50.612\,244...$

$\qquad t = \sqrt{50.612\,244...}$

$\qquad t = 7.114\,228\,2...$

It takes approximately 7.1 s for the penny to fall.

13. a) approximately 7.6×10^9 or 7.6 billion people
  b) approximately 8.3×10^9 or 8.3 billion people

14. a) approximately 3.65×10^7 or 36.5 million people
  b) approximately 3.75×10^7 or 37.5 million people

15. a) $A = 0.01(2)^3 = 0.08$ After 3 years, the payment will be $0.08.
$A = 0.01(2)^{10} = 10.24$ After 10 years, the payment will be $10.24.
$A = 0.01(2)^{25} = 335\,544.32$. After 25 years, the payment will be $335 544.32.

b) Accept any reasonable justification. Examples:
- I would accept the double the money offer because it is worth more over time.
- I would accept the cash prize because it is immediate and I have few financial resources at the present time.

c) Years 0–10 total = \$20.47; years 11–20 total = \$20 951.04; years 21–25 total = \$650 117.12. The total value over 25 years is \$671 088.63.

16. a) 21.5 g   **b)** approximately 1.34 g
c) approximately 0.34 g

17. a) $x = -4$ **b)** $x = 6$
c) $x = \frac{2}{3}$ **d)** $x = 3$

18. a) approximately 1.05 g
b) approximately 0.22 g

19. Yes. Example: When you multiply the exponents within each expression, both are equal to 2^{24}.

20. $2^x + 2^x + 2^x + 2^x = 256$

$$2^x(1 + 1 + 1 + 1) = 256$$
$$2^x = \frac{256}{4}$$
$$2^x = 64$$
$$2^x = 2^6$$
$$x = 6$$

or

$$2^x + 2^x + 2^x + 2^x = 256$$
$$2^x(4) = 256$$
$$2^x(2^2) = 256$$
$$2^{x+2} = 2^8$$
$$x + 2 = 8$$
$$x = 6$$

21. For $2^2 + 2^3 + 2^4$, use the order of operations to evaluate each power and then add the resulting values: $4 + 8 + 16 = 28$. For $(2^2)(2^3)(2^4)$, since the powers have a common base, you can multiply by adding the exponents: $2^9 = 512$.

22. Example: calculating student enrollment at schools in the community.

a) You would use a positive exponent to predict enrollment in future years beyond the current year.

b) You would use a negative exponent to calculate student enrollment in years before the current year.

4.3 Rational Exponents

1. a) $a^{\frac{15}{2}}$ **b)** $y^{\frac{5}{6}}$
c) $x^{0.9}$ or $x^{\frac{9}{10}}$ **d)** $a^{0.6}$
e) x^{-4} or $\frac{1}{x^4}$ **f)** 9
g) $\frac{-4x^{\frac{1}{12}}}{3}$ **h)** $-10a^{\frac{11}{10}}$
i) $4a^{1.5}$ or $4a^{\frac{3}{2}}$

2. a) $\frac{1}{a^{\frac{5}{4}}}$ **b)** $\frac{1}{4}$
c) $y^{\frac{2}{3}}$ **d)** $\frac{1}{a^{\frac{7}{8}}}$
e) $a^{1.5}b^3$ or $a^{\frac{3}{2}}b^3$ **f)** $\frac{64x^{\frac{9}{4}}}{125}$
g) $\frac{3y^{\frac{2}{3}}}{2x^{\frac{3}{2}}}$ **h)** $\frac{3x^{\frac{1}{6}}}{5y^{\frac{3}{20}}}$

3. a) $\left(x^{\frac{2}{3}}\right)^q = x^{\frac{4}{3}}$

$$x^{\frac{2q}{3}} = x^{\frac{4}{3}}$$
$$\frac{2q}{3} = \frac{4}{3}$$
$$2q = 4$$
$$q = 2$$
$$\left(x^{\frac{2}{3}}\right)^2 = x^{\frac{4}{3}}$$

b) $\left(x^{\frac{-2}{3}}\right)(x^q) = x^{\frac{-1}{6}}$

$$x^{\frac{-2}{3}+q} = x^{\frac{-1}{6}}$$
$$\frac{-2}{3} + q = \frac{-1}{6}$$
$$q = \frac{-1}{6} + \frac{2}{3}$$
$$q = \frac{-1}{6} + \frac{4}{6}$$
$$q = \frac{3}{6} = \frac{1}{2}$$
$$\left(x^{\frac{-2}{3}}\right)\left(x^{\frac{1}{2}}\right) = x^{\frac{-1}{6}}$$

c) $\dfrac{y^{\frac{2}{3}}}{y^q} = y^{\frac{11}{12}}$

$y^{\frac{2}{3} - q} = y^{\frac{11}{12}}$

$\dfrac{2}{3} - q = \dfrac{11}{12}$

$-q = \dfrac{11}{12} - \dfrac{2}{3}$

$-q = \dfrac{11}{12} - \dfrac{8}{12}$

$-q = \dfrac{3}{12}$

$q = \dfrac{-3}{12}$

$q = \dfrac{-1}{4}$

$\dfrac{y^{\frac{2}{3}}}{y^{\frac{-1}{4}}} = y^{\frac{11}{12}}$

d) $(27x^2)^{\frac{1}{3}} (qx^2)^{\frac{-1}{2}} = \dfrac{3}{2x^{\frac{1}{3}}}$

$\left(3x^{\frac{2}{3}}\right)\left(\dfrac{x^{-1}}{q^{\frac{1}{2}}}\right) = \dfrac{3}{2x^{\frac{1}{3}}}$

$\dfrac{3x^{\frac{2}{3} + (-1)}}{q^{\frac{1}{2}}} = \dfrac{3}{2x^{\frac{1}{3}}}$

$\dfrac{3x^{\frac{2}{3} + \left(\frac{-3}{3}\right)}}{q^{\frac{1}{2}}} = \dfrac{3}{2x^{\frac{1}{3}}}$

$\dfrac{3x^{\frac{-1}{3}}}{q^{\frac{1}{2}}} = \dfrac{3}{2x^{\frac{1}{3}}}$

$\dfrac{3}{q^{\frac{1}{2}} x^{\frac{1}{3}}} = \dfrac{3}{2x^{\frac{1}{3}}}$

$q^{\frac{1}{2}} = 2$

$\sqrt{q} = 2$

$q = 4$

$(27x^2)^{\frac{1}{3}} (4x^2)^{\frac{-1}{2}} = \dfrac{3}{2x^{\frac{1}{3}}}$

e) $(5^q)(-3^{-q}) = \dfrac{-125}{27}$

$\left(\dfrac{5^q}{-3^q}\right) = \dfrac{-125}{27}$

$\left(\dfrac{5}{-3}\right)^q = \dfrac{-125}{27}$

$\left(\dfrac{5}{-3}\right)^q = \left(\dfrac{-5^3}{3^3}\right)$

$\left(\dfrac{5}{-3}\right)^q = \left(\dfrac{-5}{3}\right)^3$

$q = 3$

$(5^3)(-3^{-3}) = \dfrac{-125}{27}$

4. a) 8   **b)** 9

c) $\dfrac{1}{32}$ **d)** $\dfrac{343}{27}$

e) $\dfrac{25x^{\frac{4}{3}}}{4y^2}$ **f)** 5

5. a) 0.037   **b)** 512

c) 52.1959   **d)** 11.0553

e) 0.037   **f)** 6.3227

6. a) 863 trout   **b)** 1409 trout

c) 911 trout   **d)** 1264 trout

7. a) Error: A common denominator is needed to subtract exponents.

$\dfrac{a^{\frac{2}{3}}}{a^{\frac{1}{4}}} = a^{\frac{2}{3} - \frac{1}{4}}$

$\qquad = a^{\frac{8}{12} - \frac{3}{12}}$

$\qquad = a^{\frac{5}{12}}$

b) Errors: The negative exponent needs to be converted to a positive exponent. The expression $16^{0.5}$ is equal to 4, not 8.

$\left(16y^{-6}\right)^{-0.5} = (16)^{-0.5} \left(y^{-6}\right)^{-0.5}$

$\qquad = \dfrac{1}{16^{0.5}} y^{(-6)(-0.5)}$

$\qquad = \dfrac{1}{4} y^3$

8. a) $1651.05   **b)** $1624.86

9. a) 1.5 represents the growth rate; 1000 represents the starting population
b) approximately 2646 bacteria
c) approximately 614 bacteria

10. a) 35.600 million people
b) 33.155 million people

11. a) $A = 28(0.5)^{\frac{t}{20}}$

$\qquad = 28(0.5)^{\frac{45}{20}}$

$\qquad = 5.886\,274\ldots$

After 45 min, approximately 5.89 g remain.

b) $A = 28(0.5)^{\frac{t}{20}}$

$\qquad = 28(0.5)^6$

$\qquad = 0.4375$

After 2 h, approximately 0.44 g remain.

c) $A = 28(0.5)^{\frac{t}{20}}$

$\qquad = 28(0.5)^{\frac{195}{20}}$

$\qquad = 0.032\,58$

After $3\frac{1}{4}$ h, approximately 0.03 g remain.

12. a)

Time (t)	0	3	6	9	12
Concentration (C)	50	25	12.5	6.25	3.125

b)

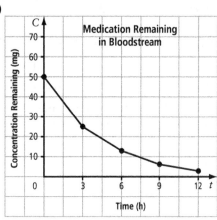

c) $t = 24$ h   **d)** $A = 0.00305$ mg

13. 81.92 g

14. a) \$3432.14   **b)** \$759.57

15. $4^{\frac{1}{2}} + 4^{\frac{1}{2}} + 4^{\frac{1}{2}} + 4^{\frac{1}{2}} = 4^x$

$$4^{\frac{1}{2}}(1 + 1 + 1 + 1) = 4^x$$
$$4^{\frac{1}{2}}(4) = 4^x$$
$$4^{\frac{1}{2}+1} = 4^x$$
$$4^{\frac{1}{2}+\frac{2}{2}} = 4^x$$
$$4^{\frac{3}{2}} = 4^x$$
$$x = \frac{3}{2}$$

4.4 Irrational Numbers

1. a) $\left(\sqrt[3]{5}\right)^2$ **b)** $\left(\sqrt[4]{8}\right)^3$
   c) $\left(\sqrt[5]{6}\right)^3$ **d)** $\sqrt{81}$

   e) $\dfrac{1}{9^{\frac{5}{3}}} = \left[\left(\frac{1}{9}\right)^{\frac{1}{3}}\right]^5 = \left(\sqrt[3]{\frac{1}{9}}\right)^5$

   f) $\sqrt[4]{x^3}$ **g)** $\left(\sqrt[3]{a}\right)^2$

   h) $\left(\sqrt[3]{\frac{x}{y}}\right)^2$

2. a) $3^{\frac{3}{4}}$ **b)** $(5t)^{\frac{4}{3}}$
   c) $x^{\frac{2}{3}}$ **d)** $\left(\dfrac{a^2}{b^3}\right)^{\frac{1}{5}}$ or $\dfrac{a^{\frac{2}{5}}}{b^{\frac{3}{5}}}$
   e) $y^{\frac{5}{6}}$ **f)** $2^{\frac{3}{a}}$

3. a) 0.5   **b)** 4
   c) 10.3923   **d)** 1.25
   e) 4.5861   **f)** 0.7274

4. a) $4\sqrt{5} = \sqrt{(4^2)}\sqrt{5}$ **b)** $\sqrt{36}$
          $= \sqrt{(16)(5)}$
          $= \sqrt{80}$
   c) $\sqrt{325}$ **d)** $\sqrt{384.4}$
   e) $\sqrt{174.24}$ **f)** $\sqrt{\dfrac{10}{25}}$ or $\sqrt{\dfrac{2}{5}}$

5. a) $\sqrt[3]{135}$ **b)** $\sqrt[3]{1029}$
   c) $\sqrt[3]{750}$ **d)** $\sqrt[4]{112}$
   e) $\sqrt[3]{\dfrac{5}{8}}$ **f)** $\sqrt[4]{50.625}$

6. a) $4\sqrt{2}$ **b)** $2\sqrt{11}$
   c) $3\sqrt{10}$ **d)** $4\sqrt{5}$
   e) $6\sqrt{10}$ **f)** $5\sqrt{19}$

7. a) $2\sqrt[3]{6}$ **b)** $2\sqrt[3]{15}$
   c) $3\sqrt[4]{12}$ **d)** $2\sqrt[3]{3}$
   e) $3\sqrt[4]{5}$ **f)** $2\sqrt[4]{13}$

8. a) $0.\overline{7}, \frac{3}{4}, 0.5\sqrt{2}, \sqrt{0.49}$; $0.5\sqrt{2}$ is an irrational number.
   b) $\sqrt[3]{0.343}, \frac{2}{3}, 0.62, \sqrt{0.38}$; $\sqrt{0.38}$ is an irrational number.

9. a)

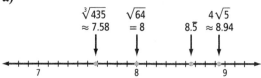

$\sqrt[3]{435}$ and $4\sqrt{5}$ are irrational numbers.

b)

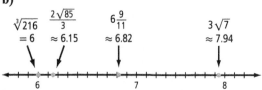

$\dfrac{2\sqrt{85}}{3}$ and $3\sqrt{7}$ are irrational numbers.

10. approximately 10.093 cm

11. approximately 16.54 cm

12. $V = s^3$
          $(1.3)(10^9) = s^3$
          $\sqrt[3]{(1.3)(10^9)} = s$
          $1091 = s$

The edge length of a cube that contained Earth's estimated total volume of water would be approximately 1091 km.

13. a) approximately 3.16 cm
  b) approximately 7.68 cm

14. 2.72 s

15. approximately 86 cm

16. a) solution B: 0.15 M
  b) solution A: 0.73 M

17. a) approximately 110 m
  b) approximately 38 013.3 m²

18. $SA = 2\pi\left[h\left(\sqrt{\dfrac{V}{\pi h}}\right) + \left(\dfrac{V}{\pi h}\right)\right]$

$\quad = 2\pi\left[26\left(\sqrt{\dfrac{26\,465}{26\pi}}\right) + \left(\dfrac{26\,465}{26\pi}\right)\right]$

$\quad = 2\pi[26(18.000\,076) + (324.002\,736)]$

$\quad = 2\pi[468.001\,976 + 324.002\,736]$

$\quad = 2\pi[792.004\,712]$

$\quad = 4976.312\,37$

The surface area of the cylinder is 4976 m².

19. a) 2   **b)** 5

c) $\sqrt{4 + \sqrt{19 + \sqrt{36}}} = \sqrt{4 + \sqrt{19 + 6}}$

$\qquad\qquad = \sqrt{4 + \sqrt{25}}$

$\qquad\qquad = \sqrt{4 + 5}$

$\qquad\qquad = \sqrt{9}$

$\qquad\qquad = 3$

d) $\sqrt[4]{13 + \sqrt[3]{22 + \sqrt[3]{125}}} = \sqrt[4]{13 + \sqrt[3]{22 + 5}}$

$\qquad\qquad = \sqrt[4]{13 + \sqrt[3]{27}}$

$\qquad\qquad = \sqrt[4]{13 + 3}$

$\qquad\qquad = \sqrt[4]{16}$

$\qquad\qquad = 2$

20. a) $\sqrt[3]{\sqrt{7}} = \left(\sqrt{7}\right)^{\frac{1}{3}}$

$\qquad = \left(7^{\frac{1}{2}}\right)^{\frac{1}{3}}$

$\qquad = 7^{\frac{1}{6}}$

b) $\sqrt[4]{\sqrt[3]{5^2}} = \left(\sqrt[3]{5^2}\right)^{\frac{1}{4}}$

$\qquad = \left[(5^2)^{\frac{1}{3}}\right]^{\frac{1}{4}}$

$\qquad = 5^{(2)\left(\frac{1}{3}\right)\left(\frac{1}{4}\right)}$

$\qquad = 5^{\frac{1}{6}}$

c) $\left(\dfrac{1}{8}\right)^{\frac{1}{10}}$ **d)** $\left(\dfrac{2}{5}\right)^{\frac{1}{2}}$

21. The expression $\sqrt[4]{x^3}$ does not have a solution when x is negative. It is not possible to determine the even root of a negative number. Example: The expression $\sqrt[4]{x^3} = \sqrt[4]{(-3)^3} = \sqrt[4]{-27}$ has no solution.

22. The expression $\sqrt[3]{x^4}$ always has a solution because when you raise a negative number to an even exponent, the result is always a positive number and then it is possible to take the cube root of the positive number.

23. a) Example: For all non-perfect squares, the calculator screen shows 9 decimals.
  b) Yes. Example: The square root of each non-perfect square is an irrational number since it cannot be expressed as a terminating or a repeating decimal.

Chapter 4 Review
4.1 Square Roots and Cube Roots

1. a) perfect square   **b)** perfect cube
  c) perfect square   **d)** perfect cube
  e) perfect square   **f)** both

2. a)

There is one group of 2 and one group of 7.
Therefore, the square root of 196 is (2)(7) = 14.

b)

512
2 256
2 2 128
2 2 2 64
2 2 2 2 32
2 2 2 2 2 16
2 2 2 2 2 2 8
2 2 2 2 2 2 2 4
(2 × 2 × 2) × (2 × 2 × 2) × (2 × 2 × 2)
  8   8   8
There are three equal groups of 2s.
Therefore, the cube root of 512 is (2)(2)(2) = 8.

3. a) 16 **b)** 13
c) 30

4. 19 cm by 19 cm

5. a) Area of floor $= 81$ ft^2
Area of one tile: Convert from inches to feet: 6 in. $= 0.5$ ft
Area of tile in feet: $(0.5)^2 = 0.25$ ft^2
Divide the area of the floor by the area of the tile to determine the number of tiles needed:
$$\frac{\text{area of floor}}{\text{area of tile}} = \frac{81}{0.25} = 324$$
She will need 324 tiles.

b) $324 \times 1.38 = 447.12$ The tiles will cost $447.12.

4.2 Integral Exponents

6. a) $\dfrac{1}{a^6}$ **b)** $(3.5)^7$

c) $\left(\dfrac{b^2}{b^{-5}}\right)^2 = \dfrac{b^{(2)(2)}}{b^{(-5)(2)}}$
$= \dfrac{b^4}{b^{-10}}$
$= b^{4-(-10)}$
$= b^{4+10}$
$= b^{14}$

7. a) $\dfrac{1}{81}$ or 0.012 **b)** 2.097
c) 3933.798

8. a) approximately 11.56 g
b) approximately 0.045 g
c) approximately 11 840 g

9. a) 146 475 moose
b) 158 925 moose
c) 202 993 moose

10. a) approximately 331 177 moose
b) approximately 64 783 moose

4.3 Rational Exponents

11. a) As a fraction:
$(5^{-0.5})^{\frac{3}{4}} = \left(5^{\frac{-1}{2}}\right)^{\frac{3}{4}}$
$= 5^{\left(\frac{-1}{2}\right)\left(\frac{3}{4}\right)}$
$= 5^{\frac{-3}{8}}$
$= \dfrac{1}{5^{\frac{3}{8}}}$

As a decimal:
$(5^{-0.5})^{\frac{3}{4}} = (5^{-0.5})^{0.75}$
$= 5^{(-0.5)(0.75)}$
$= 5^{-0.375}$
$= \dfrac{1}{5^{0.375}}$

b) As a fraction:
$\dfrac{2.8^{0.4}}{2.8^{\frac{-1}{2}}} = \dfrac{2.8^{\frac{4}{10}}}{2.8^{\frac{-1}{2}}}$
$= 2.8^{\frac{4}{10} - \frac{-1}{2}}$
$= 2.8^{\frac{4}{10} + \frac{5}{10}}$
$= 2.8^{\frac{9}{10}}$

As a decimal:
$\dfrac{2.8^{0.4}}{2.8^{\frac{-1}{2}}} = \dfrac{2.8^{0.4}}{2.8^{-0.5}}$
$= 2.8^{0.4-(-0.5)}$
$= 2.8^{0.4 + 0.5}$
$= 2.8^{0.9}$

c) $(27x^{-2})^{\frac{-2}{3}} = (27)^{\frac{-2}{3}}(x^{-2})^{\frac{-2}{3}}$
$= \left(\dfrac{1}{27^{\frac{2}{3}}}\right)\left(x^{(-2)\left(\frac{-2}{3}\right)}\right)$
$= \left(\dfrac{1}{\sqrt[3]{27^2}}\right)\left(x^{\frac{4}{3}}\right)$
$= \left(\dfrac{1}{3^2}\right)\left(x^{\frac{4}{3}}\right)$
$= \dfrac{x^{\frac{4}{3}}}{9}$

12. $(27x)^{\frac{-1}{3}}(9x)^{\frac{1}{2}} = \dfrac{3x^{\frac{1}{2}}}{3x^{\frac{1}{3}}}$, not $243x^{\left(\frac{-1}{3} + \frac{1}{2}\right)}$.
The correct answer is $x^{\frac{1}{6}}$.

13. a) $\dfrac{8^{\frac{5}{3}}}{4^2} = \dfrac{(2^3)^{\frac{5}{3}}}{(2^2)^2}$
$= \dfrac{2^{(3)\left(\frac{5}{3}\right)}}{2^{(2)(2)}}$
$= \dfrac{2^5}{2^4}$
$= 2^{5-4}$
$= 2$

b) $\dfrac{125^{\frac{2}{3}}}{5^{-1}} = \dfrac{(5^3)^{\frac{2}{3}}}{5^{-1}}$

$= \dfrac{5^{(3)\left(\frac{2}{3}\right)}}{5^{-1}}$

$= 5^{2-(-1)}$

$= 5^3$

$= 125$

c) $\dfrac{9^{\frac{3}{2}}}{27^{\frac{1}{3}}} = \dfrac{(3^2)^{\frac{3}{2}}}{(3^3)^{\frac{1}{3}}}$

$= \dfrac{3^3}{3}$

$= 3^{3-1}$

$= 3^2$

$= 9$

d) $\dfrac{8^{\frac{2}{3}}}{32^{\frac{4}{5}}} = \dfrac{(2^3)^{\frac{2}{3}}}{(2^5)^{\frac{4}{5}}}$

$= \dfrac{2^{(3)\left(\frac{2}{3}\right)}}{2^{(5)\left(\frac{4}{5}\right)}}$

$= \dfrac{2^2}{2^4}$

$= 2^{2-4}$

$= 2^{-2}$

$= \dfrac{1}{2^2}$

$= \dfrac{1}{4}$

14. a) 15.5816 **b)** 0.0917
c) 9.8821 **d)** 19.5313

15. $1651.05

16. approximately $525.28

17. 0.706 mg

4.4 Irrational Numbers

18. a) $\sqrt[5]{x^2}$ **b)** $\left(\sqrt[5]{16s^3}\right)^3$

c) $\left(\sqrt[4]{\dfrac{a^5}{7}}\right)^3$ **d)** $\sqrt[3]{\dfrac{1}{5a^4}}$

19. a) $x^{\frac{5}{2}}$ **b)** $5^{\frac{1}{2}}$

c) $4x^{\frac{3}{5}}$ **d)** $(4y)^{\frac{4}{3}}$

20. a) $\sqrt{112}$ **b)** $\sqrt{180}$
c) $3\sqrt[3]{2} = \sqrt[3]{(3^3)}\sqrt[3]{2}$ **d)** $\sqrt[3]{-375}$

$= \sqrt[3]{(3^3)(2)}$

$= \sqrt[3]{(27)(2)}$

$= \sqrt[3]{54}$

21. a) $6\sqrt{7}$ **b)** $4\sqrt[3]{6}$
c) $2\sqrt[4]{3}$ **d)** $3\sqrt[3]{15}$

22. a) Irrational numbers: $\dfrac{4\sqrt{5}}{2}$; Order: $\sqrt[3]{216}$, $\dfrac{4\sqrt{5}}{2}$, $\sqrt{0.25}$, $0.2\overline{3}$

b) Irrational numbers: $\sqrt[3]{32}$; Order: $\dfrac{3\sqrt{25}}{4}$, $\sqrt[3]{32}$, $\sqrt{0.81}$, $0.\overline{49}$

23. a) approximately 68 641.97 cm³
b) approximately 4.5 cm

Chapters 1–4 Cumulative Review

1. 10 cm

2. a) 92 500 mm² **b)** 0.0097 m²
c) 74 322.432 cm²

3. a) perfect cube **b)** both
c) perfect cube **d)** perfect square
e) neither

4. a) hypotenuse : ZX; adjacent side: ZY; opposite side: XY
b) hypotenuse: ST; adjacent side: SR; opposite side: RT
c) hypotenuse: ML; adjacent side: MN; opposite side: LN

5. a) $2\dfrac{13}{16}$ in.; 7.1 cm **b)** 3.52 cm; 1.4 in.

6. 17.76 lb; 6 bags

7. a)

b)

c)

d)

8. $13 \text{ cm} \times 13 \text{ cm} \times 13 \text{ cm}$

9. a) 3845.31 mm^2 **b)** 4300.84 cm^2
   c) 421 ft^2

10. a) 107.11 m
   b) He is closer to the building. He is now 89.38 m from the building instead of 107.11 m.

11. a) 0.0000 **b)** 0.3875
   c) 0.3090 **d)** 0.5317

12. a) $\dfrac{1}{x^{15}}$ **b)** b^8
   c) $\dfrac{1}{(-5.6)^5}$

13. a) $1:3$ **b)** 53.1 rotations
   c) 560.2 rotations

14. a) 0.99 kg **b)** 0.42 kg

15. a) $x \approx 9.1$ units; $y \approx 4.2$ units
   b) $x \approx 8.3$ units; $y \approx 10.9$ units
   c) $\angle B = 25°$; $\angle C = 65°$; $CB \approx 16.6$ units

16. a) 10.13 cm **b)** 9.2 in.
   c) 1.02 yd

17. a) 13.9666 **b)** -0.5946
   c) 0.0001 **d)** 3.6742

18. a) $511\,185\,932.5 \text{ km}^2$
   b) $37\,936\,694.79 \text{ km}^2$
   c) 1347.47%

19. a) $14\frac{3}{4} \text{ in.}$ **b)** $2\frac{3}{4} \text{ yd}$
   c) 28.4 mi **d)** $42\,240 \text{ ft}$

20. $8 \text{ cm} \times 8 \text{ cm} \times 8 \text{ cm}$

21. $20.8°$

22. a) $3\sqrt{6}$ **b)** $16\sqrt{2}$
   c) $3\sqrt[3]{5}$ **d)** $2\sqrt[4]{9}$

23. a) $\sqrt[7]{x^2}$ **b)** $\sqrt[5]{13t^4}$
   c) $\sqrt{\dfrac{h^2}{12}}$

Chapter 4 Extend It Further

1. B

2. C

3. D

4. D

5. C

6. C

7. $(\sqrt{5})(\sqrt[3]{7}) = \left(5^{\frac{1}{2}}\right)\left(7^{\frac{1}{3}}\right)$
$= \left(5^{\frac{3}{6}}\right)\left(7^{\frac{2}{6}}\right)$
$= \left[(5^3)(7^2)\right]^{\frac{1}{6}}$
$= 6125^{\frac{1}{6}}$

8. No. Let $a = \sqrt{3}$ and $b = \sqrt{2}$. It follows that $a^b = (\sqrt{3})^{\sqrt{2}}$, which could be irrational. Then, consider $\left[(\sqrt{3})^{\sqrt{2}}\right]^{\sqrt{2}} = (\sqrt{3})^2 = 3$, which is rational.

9. $\dfrac{3^{n+2} - 3^{n+1}}{3^{n+3}} = \dfrac{9(3^n) - 3(3^n)}{27(3^n)}$
$= \dfrac{6}{27}$
$= \dfrac{2}{9}$

10. $\sqrt[3]{2} = 1.2599$ or 26%

11. a) 64 **b)** -64
   c) $n > 0$ **d)** 64
   e) -64

12. n must be a perfect square. Only perfect squares have square roots.

13. $t = \dfrac{-3}{4}$

14. $\dfrac{1}{2009}$

15. 6: The factors of 32 are 1, 2, 4, 8, 16, and 32. Each gives a different solution. They are $(2^1)^{32} = (2^{32})^1 = (2^2)^{16} = (2^{16})^2 = (2^4)^8 = (2^8)^4$.

16.
$$A = P(1 + i)^n$$
$$(12\,500.00 + 878.29) = 12\,500.00\,(1 + i)^{\frac{33}{12}}$$
$$13\,378.29 = 12\,500.00(1 + i)^{2.75}$$
$$\frac{13\,378.29}{12\,500.00} = \frac{12\,500.00(1 + i)^{2.75}}{12\,500.00}$$
$$1.070\,263\,2 = (1 + i)^{2.75}$$
$$\sqrt[2.75]{1.070\,263\,2} = (1 + i)$$
$$1.024\,999\,968 = (1 + i)$$
$$1.024\,999\,968 - 1 = i$$
$$0.024\,999\,968 = i$$
$$i = 2.5\%$$

Chapter 5 Polynomials

5.1 Multiplying Polynomials

1. **a)** $3x^2 - 5x + 2$; $(3x - 2)(x - 1)$
   b) $2x^2 + x - 6$; $(2x - 3)(x + 2)$

2. **a)**

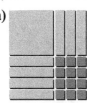

   b)

   c)

   d)

   e)

   f)

3. **a)** $2x^2 - 4x - 16$
   b) $t^2 + 9t + 20$
   c) $6w^2 - 23w - 18$
   d) $z^2 - 4$
   e) $a^2 + 2ab + b^2$
   f) $30e^2 + 25e - 5$

4. **a)** E   **b)** H
   c) A   **d)** G
   e) B   **f)** C
   g) D   **h)** F

5. **a)** A   **b)** D
   c) C   **d)** B
   e) B   **f)** A

6. **a)** $2d^3 + 11d^2 + 13d - 6$
   b) $4s^3 - 41s^2 + 41s + 5$
   c) $5k^3 - k^2 + 7k$
   d) $3c^3 + 18c^2 + 45c + 42$
   e) $10y^4 + 8y^3 - 32y^2 + 6y$
   f) $(r^2 - 5r - 3)(3r^2 - 4r - 5)$
   $= r^2(3r^2 - 4r - 5) - 5r(3r^2 - 4r - 5)$
   $\quad -3(3r^2 - 4r - 5)$
   $= 3r^4 - 4r^3 - 5r^2 - 15r^3 + 20r^2 + 25r$
   $\quad - 9r^2 + 12r + 15$
   $= 3r^4 - 4r^3 - 15r^3 - 5r^2 - 9r^2 + 20r^2$
   $\quad + 25r + 12r + 15$
   $= 3r^4 - 19r^3 + 6r^2 + 37r + 15$

7. **a)** $120y^3 - 68y^2 - 144y - 36$
   b) $8a^2 - 25a + 47$
   c) $12d^2 - 32de - 15e^2$
   d) $9n^2 - 4n + 58$
   e) $6w^4 - 13w^3 - 15w^2 - 26w - 24$
   f) $2(4t + 5s)(2t - 3s) - (5t - s)$
   $= 2[4t(2t - 3s) + 5s(2t - 3s)] - 5t + s$
   $= 2[8t^2 - 12st + 10st - 15s^2] - 5t + s$
   $= 2[8t^2 - 2st - 15s^2] - 5t + s$
   $= 16t^2 - 4st - 30s^2 - 5t + s$
   $= 16t^2 - 5t - 4st + s - 30s^2$

8. **a)** $8a^2 + 5a + 1$
   b) $4b^2 + 6b + 21$
   c) $5x^2 - 5xy + 5y^2$
   d) $23a^2 - 68ac - 28c^2$
   e) $2x^4 - x^3 - 4x^2 + 17x - 12$
   f) $12b^2 - 18bd - 5d^2$

9. **a)** Step 2;
   $28t^2 - 33t - 7$
   b) Step 3;
   $2xy^2 + x^2y + xy - 3x$

10. a) The dimensions of the deck and the pool are $(x + 4)$ by $(x + 4)$.
The area of the deck and pool is
$(x + 4) \times (x + 4) = (x + 4)^2$.
$(x + 4)^2 = x(x + 4) + 4(x + 4)$
$= x^2 + 4x + 4x + 16$
$= x^2 + 8x + 16$.
b) The area of the pool is 49 m². If $x^2 = 49$, then $x = \sqrt{49} = 7$.
The area of pool and deck is $x^2 + 8x + 16$.
Using the value for x, the total area is $(7)^2 + 8(7) + 16 = 49 + 56 + 16 = 121$.
Thus, the area of the deck and the pool is 121 m².

11. a) $A(5x + 6)(2x + 4) = 10x^2 + 32x + 24$
b) 920 in.²

12. a) $A = x^2 + 8x + 12$
b) The area of the diamond is one half the area of the rectangle.

13. a) $(5x - 2)(2x + 1)$
b) $(x - 1)(x + 3)$
c) $(5x - 2)(2x + 1) - (x - 1)(x + 3)$, $9x^2 - x + 1$

14. a) length: $30 - 2x$; width: $20 - 2x$; height: x
b) $x(30 - 2x)(20 - 2x)$
c) $600x - 100x^2 + 4x^3$

15. a) $4 \text{ cm} \times 5 \text{ cm} \times 6 \text{ cm} = 120 \text{ cm}^3$
b) $V = n(n + 1)(n + 2)$
c) One way:
$10 \text{ cm} \times 11 \text{ cm} \times 12 \text{ cm} = 1320 \text{ cm}^3$
Another way:
$V = n(n + 1)(n + 2)$
$V = n^3 + 3n^2 + 2n$
$V = (10)^3 + 3(10)^2 + 2(10)$
$V = 1000 + 300 + 20$
$V = 1320 \text{ cm}^3$

16. a) The square of the middle number is 4 greater than the product of the first and third numbers.
b) $(x - 2)$ and $(x + 2)$
c) $(x - 2)(x + 2) = x(x + 2) - 2(x + 2)$
$(x - 2)(x + 2) = x^2 + 2x - 2x - 4$
$(x - 2)(x + 2) = x^2 - 4$
$x^2 = (x - 2)(x + 2) + 4$

17. a)

Table A	
Numbers	Total
6, 7	42
7, 8	56
8, 9	72
9, 10	90
10, 11	110

Table B				
Numbers				Total
5	25	15	2	42
6	36	18	2	56
7	49	21	2	72
8	64	24	2	90
9	81	27	2	110

b) $(n + 1)(n + 2) = n^2 + 3n + 2$

18. a) $(n + 3)(n + 2) - n(n + 1)$
b) $4n + 6$
c) $12 - 2 = 10, 4(1) + 6 = 10; 20 - 6 = 14$, $4(2) + 6 = 14; 30 - 12 = 18, 4(3) + 6 = 18$; $42 - 20 = 22; 4(4) + 6 = 22$

5.2 Common Factors

1. a) 10: 1, 2, 5, 10; 15: 1, 3, 5, 15; GCF: 5
b) 24: 1, 2, 3, 4, 6, 8, 12, 24; 36: 1, 2, 3, 4, 6, 9, 12, 18, 36; GCF: 12
c) 16: 1, 2, 4, 8, 16; 48: 1, 2, 3, 4, 6, 8, 12, 16, 24, 48; GCF: 16
d) 40: 1, 2, 4, 5, 8, 10, 20, 40; 60: 1, 2, 3, 4, 5, 6, 10, 12, 15, 20, 30, 60; GCF: 20
e) 18: 1, 2, 3, 6, 9, 18; 45: 1, 3, 5, 9, 15, 45; GCF: 9
f) 14: 1, 2, 7, 14; 24: 1, 2, 3, 4, 6, 8, 12, 24; GCF: 2

2. a) $6x^2 = (2)(3)(x)(x)$; $12x = (2)(2)(3)(x)$
b) $20c^2d^3 = (2)(2)(5)(c)(c)(d)(d)(d)$; $30cd^2 = (2)(3)(5)(c)(d)(d)$
c) $4b^2c^3 = (2)(2)(b)(b)(c)(c)(c)$; $6bc^2 = (2)(3)(b)(c)(c)$
d) $18xy^2z = (2)(3)(3)(x)(y)(y)(z)$; $24x^2y^3z^2 = (2)(2)(2)(3)(x)(x)(y)(y)(y)(z)(z)$
e) $5m^3n = (5)(m)(m)(m)(n)$; $20mn^2 = (2)(2)(5)(m)(n)(n)$

3. a) 2, 3, x; GCF: $(2)(3)(x) = 6x$
   b) 2, 5, c, d; GCF: $(2)(5)(c)(d)(d) = 10cd^2$
   c) 2, b, c; GCF: $(2)(b)(c)(c) = 2bc^2$
   d) 2, 3, x, y, z;
       GCF: $(2)(3)(x)(y)(y)(z) = 6xy^2z$
   e) 5, m, n; GCF: $(5)(m)(n) = 5mn$

4. a) 7   **b)** $-5n$
   c) 1   **d)** $4fg^2$
   e) $-15de$ **f)** $9j^2k$

5. a) 80   **b)** 120
   c) $18x$ **d)** $12t^3$
   e) $2ab$ **f)** $504c^3d^2e^3$

6. a) $6(s + 5)$ **b)** $4(t + 7)$
   c) $5(a - 1)$ **d)** $4r(4r - 3)$
   e) $7x(y + 2y - 7z)$ **f)** $3(c^3 - 3c^2 - 9d^2)$

7. a) $3w - 1$ **b)** $2a^2$
   c) $x^2y - 5x$ **d)** $g + 2$
   e) $5xy$ **f)** $2r$

8. a) $(x - 6)$ **b)** $(a + 3)$
   c) $(d - 9)$ **d)** $ab(b + 2)$
   e) $x(x + 2)$ **f)** $2m(n - 1)$

9. a) $(s + 5)(s - 2)$ **b)** $(r - 7)(r - 4)$
   c) $(g + 6)(g + 9)$ **d)** $(p + 3)(p + 4)$
   e) $(b - 3)(b - 7)$ **f)** $(r - 3)(r + 2s)$

10. a) To find the largest number of centrepieces, identify the GCF of 36, 48, and 60.
   The factors of 36 are 1, 2, 3, 4, 6, 9, 12, 18, and 36.
   The factors of 48 are 1, 2, 3, 4, 6, 8, 12, 16, 24, and 48.
   The factors of 60 are 1, 2, 3, 4, 5, 6, 10, 12, 15, 20, 30, and 60.
   The GCF is 12, so that factor represents the largest number of centrepieces.
   To determine how many of each type of flower per centrepiece, divide the number of each flower by 12:
   $\frac{36}{12} = 3, \frac{48}{12} = 4, \frac{60}{12} = 5$
   Each centrepiece will contain three roses, four daffodils, and five tulips.
   b) The cost of each centrepiece will be the unit cost of each flower multiplied by the number of each flower added together:
   $3 \times \$2.50 + 4 \times \$1.70 + 5 \times \$1.50 = \$21.80$
   Therefore, the cost of each centrepiece is $21.80.

11. a) no; $6(2x - 1)$ **b)** no; $-10w(w + 1)$
   c) yes   **d)** no; $(x + 3)(x + 2y)$
   e) yes   **f)** yes

12. Examples:
   a) $4x^2 + 8x$
   b) $6r^2s^2 + 9rs$
   c) $10m^2n^2 + 15m^3n^3$
   d) $a^3b^3 + 2a^2b^2 + 3ab$
   e) $4c^4d^4 + 6c^3d^3 + 8c^2d^2$
   f) $2e^4 + 6e^3 + 8e^2 + 4e$
   g) $ac + 4a - bc - 4b$

13. a) 4 by $(x - 1)$; $4(x - 1) = 4x - 4$
   b) $(x - 2)$ by $(x + 3)$;
       $(x - 2)(x + 3) = x^2 + 3x - 2x - 6$
       $= x^2 + x - 6$
   c) $(2x - 3)$ by $(x + 2)$;
       $(2x - 3)(x + 2) = 2x^2 + 4x - 3x - 6$
       $= 4x^2 + x - 6$

14. a) The length is $t - 3 - 3 = t - 6$ and the width is $s - 3 - 3 = s - 6$.
   b) Substituting 10 cm for t, and 8 cm for s, the dimensions are $(10 - 6)$ by $(8 - 6)$ or 4 by 2. So, the area is 4 cm $\times$ 2 cm $= 8$ cm^2. Multiplying the binomials to find the area first, and then substituting, is another way to find the area:
   $(t - 6)(s - 6) = ts - 6t - 6s + 36$
       $= (10)(8) - (6)(10) -$
       $(6)(8) + 36$
       $= 80 - 60 - 48 + 36$
       $= 8$ cm^2

15. a) 6" by 3"
   b) 3" by 3" (22 servings)

16. 30 and 90, 45 and 60. The only other number with a GCF of 15 less than 30 is 15. The other number has to be greater than 100, because 90 is already close to 100.

17. 5

18. a) $A = \pi r^2 + \pi(r + 3)^2 + \pi(r + 6)^2$;
   Other algebraic expressions are possible, depending on which radius is assigned the value of r; examples:
   $A = \pi r^2 + \pi(r - 3)^2 + \pi(r + 3)^2$ or
   $A = \pi r^2 + \pi(r - 3)^2 + \pi(r - 6)^2$
   b) $A = 3\pi(r^2 + 6r + 15)$

19. $8x^5 - 16x^3 + 24x$

20. 1948 and 2922

21. a)

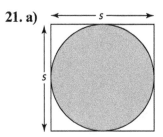

b) $A = \pi\left(\frac{s}{2}\right)^2 = \frac{\pi s^2}{4}$

c) $A = s^2 - \frac{\pi s^2}{4}$;

$A = s^2\left(1 - \frac{\pi}{4}\right)$

22. a) $3\,s$

b) $15t - 5t^2 = 5t(3 - t)$. The product equals 0 when $t = 0$ or when $t = 3$. Because the ball is at its initial height when the product is 0, it can be seen that the ball will be at the same height when $t = 3$. Thus, factoring simplifies the process used to calculate the answer in part a).

23. a) $5x$

b) The width is 10 cm, the length is 15 cm and the volume is 900 cm³.

5.3 Factoring Trinomials

1. a) $x^2 + 5x + 6$; $x + 2$ by $x + 3$
  b) $x^2 - 9$; $x - 3$ by $x + 3$
  c) $x^2 - 3x - 4$; $x - 4$ by $x + 1$
  d) $x^2 - x - 6$; $x - 3$ by $x + 2$

2. a) $(2x + 1)(x + 1)$

  b) $(3x - 1)(x + 2)$

c) $(3x - 2)(2x - 3)$

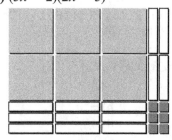

d) $(2x - 3)(x + 4)$

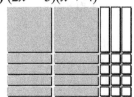

e) $(4x + 2)(x - 5)$

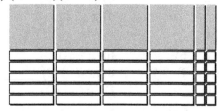

f) $(3x - 4)(x + 7)$

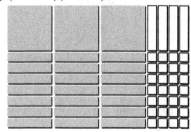

3. a) 2, 6   **b)** not possible
  c) -4, 1   **d)** -8, -3
  e) -2, 21   **f)** not possible

4. a) $(y + 6)(y + 2)$ **b)** $(x + 3)(x + 7)$
  c) $(a - 10)(a - 9)$ **d)** not possible
  e) $(m - 7n)(m + 6n)$ **f)** $(b + 2)(b + 17)$

5. a) $(g - 4)(g - 6)$ **b)** $(n - 2)(n - 13)$
  c) $(c - 8)(c - 7)$ **d)** $(s - 2t)(s - 5t)$
  e) not possible   **f)** $(3v - 2)(v + 1)$

6. a) $(2r + 7)(r + 2)$ **b)** $(2l + 3)(l + 4)$
  c) $(3w + 6)(w + 1)$ **d)** not possible
  e) $(y + 3z)(y + 2z)$ **f)** $(3a + 4)(4a + 1)$

7. a) $(2f - 3)(f + 5)$ **b)** $(r - 10)(r + 11)$
  c) not possible   **d)** $(5m - n)(2m - 3n)$
  e) not possible   **f)** $(3g - 2f)(3g - f)$
  g) $2(l + 3)(3l + 7)$ **h)** $(5a - 7)(a - 9)$

8. Examples:
  a) 5, 7, −5, −7
  b) 2, 14, −2, −14
  c) 9, 11, 19, −9, −11, −19
  d) 5, 13, −5, −13

9. Examples:
  a) −5, 5, −1, 1
  b) −9, 9, −6, 6
  c) −57, 57, −30, 30, −18, 18, −15, 15
  d) −19, 19, −1, 1, −8, 8

10. Examples:
  a) There are four sets of two integers with the product of −10: −1 and 10, 1 and −10, −2 and 5, and 2 and −5. Possible values of p are the sums of each set: −1 + 10, 1 + −10, −2 + 5, and 2 + −5. So, the possible values of p are 9, −9, 3, and −3.
  b) −4, 4
  c) 9, 15
  d) 12, 36

11. a) 12   **b)** 28
  c) 7   **d)** −12
  e) 21   **f)** 6

12. a) width $= 2x − 6$; length $= 3x + 8$
  b) 18 yards by 44 yards

13. a) $A = x^2 + 11x + 24 = (x + 8)(x + 3)$; width: $x + 3 = (12) + 3 = 15$ cm; length: $x + 8 = (12) + 8 = 20$ cm
  b) $A = 8x^2 + 6x − 2 =)(2x + 2)(4x − 1)$; width: $2x + 2 = 2(12) + 2 = 26$ cm; length: $4x − 1 = 4(12) − 1$
                      $= 48 − 1$
                      $= 47$ cm
  c) $A = x^2 + 3x − 10 = (x − 2)(x + 5)$; width: $x − 2 = (12) − 2 = 10$ cm; length: $x + 5 = (12) + 5 = 17$ cm

14. a) $(−6t − 3)(t − 5)$
  b) 27 ft

15. a) $h = (x + 6)$, $b = (x + 7)$; $h = 24$ cm, $b = 25$ cm
  b) $h = (2x + 3)$, $b = (3x − 1)$; $h = 39$ cm, $b = 53$ cm

16. 7 by 1 and 6 by 4

17. 14

18. a) square
  b) 16 and 36 are squares.
  c) $(4s − 6)(4s − 6) = (4s − 6)^2$

19. a) square
  b) $(x + 3)(x + 3)$
  c) The area of the second figure is four times the area of the original square, meaning that the side dimension is doubled: $2(x + 3) = 2x + 6$.

20. Example: In trinomials such as $n^2 − 20n − 44$, one needs to find two numbers whose sum is −20 and whose product is −44. The important thing to notice to make a connection between the two types of trinomials is that the product −44 comes from multiplying the coefficient for n, which is 1, by the final term in the trinomial. For trinomials such as $6n^2 + 13n − 5$, one must ask what two numbers have a product of −30 (because $6 \times −5 = −30$) and a sum of 13. These two numbers are used to break up the middle term. Then, factoring by grouping completes the process.

21. a) 5, 6
  b) $(x + m)(x + n)$
       $= x^2 + nx + mx + mn$
       $= x^2 + (n + m)x + mn$
  c) 30, 13
  d) $(ax + m)(x + n)$
       $= ax^2 + anx + mx + mn$
       $= ax^2 + (an + m)x + mn$

22. a) x by $2x − 5$ by $3x + 1$
  b) dimensions: 5 cm by 5 cm by 16 cm; volume: 400 cm^3

5.4 Factoring Special Trinomials

1. **a)** $(x − 2)^2$ **b)** $(x + 3)^2$
   c) $(x + 2)(x − 2)$ **d)** $(3x − 2)^2$

2. **a)** $x^2 − 25$ **b)** $9r^2 − 16$
   c) $5w^2 − 180$ **d)** $4b^2 − 49c^2$
   e) $16x^2 − 36y^2$ **f)** $2x^2y − 18y$

3. **a)** $y^2 + 10y + 25$
   b) $9d^2 + 12d + 4$
   c) $16m^2 − 40mp + 25p^2$
   d) $2e^2 − 24ef + 72f^2$
   e) $12z^2 − 48z + 48$
   f) $4x^2 − 12xy + 9y^2$

4. a) $n^2 - 10n + 25 = (n - 5)^2$
b) $r^2 - s^2 = (r + s)(r - s)$
c) $9c^2 - 16d^2 = (3c - 4d)(3c + 4d)$
d) $4s^2 + 24s + 36 = (2s + 6)^2$
e) $4x^2 + 8x + 4 = (2x + 2)^2$
f) $(4x - 2)^2 = 16x^2 - 16x + 4$

5. a) $(a + 10)(a - 10)$
b) $(t + 7)(t - 7)$
c) not possible
d) $(8 + h)(8 - h)$
e) $2(5g + 6h)(5g - 6h)$
f) $3(3p^2 - 5r^2)$
g) not possible
h) $2(6g + 4h)(6g - 4h)$

6. a) $(y + 6)^2$
b) $(x - 3)^2$
c) $2(z + 3)^2$
d) not possible
e) $-4(b^2 + 12b - 36)$
f) $(3s + 8)^2$
g) $(5n - 11)^2$
h) not possible

7. a) $16(d + 2e)(d - 2e)$
b) $3(3m + 4)(3m - 4)$
c) $-2(k + 6)^2$
d) $3c(c^2 + 17c + 49)$
e) $25(2a + b)(2a - b)$
f) $st(s - 9)^2$
g) $(9g^2 + 4)(3g + 2)(3g - 2)$
h) $3l(2m + n)^2$

8. a) $(2a - b)(2a + b)$
b) $(3x + 1)^2$
c) $9(24 - y^2)$
d) $d^2 - 4e^2 = (d + 2e)(d - 2e)$
e) $(7 - h)^2$

9. a) $-2, 2$ **b)** $-24, 24$
c) $-60, 60$ **d)** $-48, 48$

10. a) $3x^2 + 24x + 48 = 3(x^2 + 8x + 16)$
$= 3(x + 4)^2$
b) $3(x + 4) = 3x + 12$; The dimensions are $x + 4$ by $3x + 12$.
c) Since $x = 5$, the width is $(5) + 4 = 9$ cm and the length is $3(5) + 12 = 27$ cm.
d) Area $= 9 \times 27 = 243$ cm^2; check: $3(5)^2 + 24(5) + 48 = 3(25) + 120 + 48 = 243$

11. a) $16^2 - 4^2 = (16 + 4)(16 - 4) = (20)(12)$
$= 240$
b) $7^2 - 27^2 = (7 + 27)(7 - 27)$
$= (34)(-20) = -680$
c) $45^2 - 15^2 = (45 + 15)(45 - 15)$
$= (60)(30) = 1800$
d) $113^2 - 13^2 = (113 + 13)(113 - 13)$
$= (126)(100) = 12\,600$

12. a) Area $= \pi(r + 5)^2 - \pi(r + 3)^2 + \pi r^2$
b) Area $= \pi(r^2 + 4r + 16)$
c) Area $= 28\pi = 28(3.14) = 87.9$ cm^2

13. $2r(r - 1)^2(r + 1)^2$; solution:
$$2r^5 - 4r^3 + 2r = 2r(r^4 - 2r^2 + 1)$$
$$= 2r(r^2 - 1)^2$$
$$= 2r(r^2 - 1)(r^2 - 1)$$
$$= 2r(r + 1)(r - 1)(r + 1)$$
$$(r - 1)$$
$$= 2r(r - 1)^2(r + 1)^2$$

14. $(x + 2y)$, $(x - 2y)$, and $(xy - 4)$

15. a) $391, 775$
b) $(x - 3)(x + 3) = x(x - 3) + 3(x - 3)$
$(x - 3)(x + 3) = x^2 - 3x + 3x - 9$
$(x - 3)(x + 3) = x^2 - 9$
$x^2 = (x - 3)(x + 3) + 9$

16. $9b^2 - 12b$

17. a) $A = \pi r^2$
b) $A = \pi(r + 3)^2 = \pi(r^2 + 6r + 9)$
$= \pi r^2 + 6\pi r + 9\pi$
c) Area of walkway = (area of walkway + area of garden) − area of garden
Area of walkway $= (\pi r^2 + 6\pi r + 9\pi)$
$- \pi r^2 = 6\pi r + 9\pi = 3\pi(2r + 3)$
d) $3\pi[2(8) + 3] = 3\pi(19) = 179.1$ m

18. a) $144, 143, 169, 168, 196, 195, 15^2 = 225$,
$14 \times 16 = 224$
b) The product of the factors that are 1 less and 1 more than the squared number is 1 less than the product of the squared number, the difference of squares equation.
c) $(n - 1)(n + 1) = n^2 - 1$

19. a) 600 cm^2
b) The difference between $a^2 + b^2$ and $(a + b)^2$ is $2ab$. So, the difference between $15^2 + 20^2$ and $(15 + 20)^2$ is $2(15 \times 20)$ which equals 600.

Chapter 5 Review

1. a)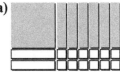

b)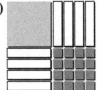

2. a) $a^2 + 12a + 35$
 b) $y^2 - 64$
 c) $10v^2 + 32vw + 24w^2$
 d) $4c^2 - 1$
 e) $-2r^2 + 18s^2$
 f) $-g^2 - 8gh - 16h^2$

3. a) $r^3 - 3r^2 - 36r - 32$
 b) $-48p^3 + 121p^2 + 185p$; solution:
   $3p(4p - 5)(p - 7) - 5p(6p + 2)(2p - 8)$
   $= 3p[4p(p - 7) - 5(p - 7)] -$
    $5p[6p(2p - 8) + 2(2p - 8)]$
   $= 3p(4p^2 - 28p - 5p + 35) - 5p(12p^2 -$
    $48p + 4p - 16)$
   $= 12p^3 - 84p^2 - 15p^2 + 105p - 60p^3 +$
    $240p^2 - 20p^2 + 80p$
   $= (12 - 60)p^3 + (-84 - 15 + 240)p^2 +$
    $(105 + 80)p$
   $= -48p^3 + 121p^2 + 185p$

4. $2a^2 + 5ab + 2a - 2b + 2b^2$; solution:
 From the diagram it can be seen that the
 area of the figure is equal to the area of
 the original square less the area of the
 rectangular shape that is removed.
 Area of square $= (2a + b)^2$
  $= 2a(2a + b) + b(2a + b)$
  $= 4a^2 + 2ab + 2ab + b^2$
  $= 4a^2 + 4ab + b^2$
 Area of rectangular shape
 $= (a - b)(2a + b - 2)$
 $= a(2a + b - 2) - b(2a + b - 2)$
 $= 2a^2 + ab - 2a - 2ab - b^2 + 2b$
 $= 2a^2 - ab - 2a + 2b - b^2$
 Area of figure $= (4a^2 + 4ab + b^2) - (2a^2$
   $- ab - 2a + 2b - b^2)$
  $= 4a^2 + 4ab + b^2 - 2a^2 +$
   $ab + 2a - 2b + b^2$
  $= 2a^2 + 5ab + 2a - 2b + 2b^2$

5. $2x^2 - 30x + 100$

6. a) 15   **b)** 28
 c) 18   **d)** $2d$
 e) $17ab$ **f)** $5rst$

7. a) 75   **b)** 128

8. a) 9   **b)** 13
 c) $4ab$ **d)** $12xy^2z$
 e) m^3n^5

9. a) $2x(x + 2)$

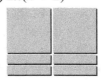

b) $x(x + 3)$

10. $a^2 + 2ab + 3a + 2b - 2$

11. a)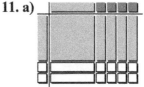

b)

c)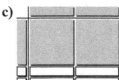

d)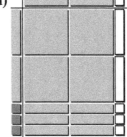

12. a) $(x - 4)(x - 2)$
   b) $(x - 5)(x + 4)$
   c) $(3x + 1)(3x - 5)$
   d) not possible
   e) $-3(x - 3)(2x - 9)$
   f) $-2x(2x + 1)(3x - 2)$

13. $x, x + 1, x - 3$; 5 cm by 6 cm by 2 cm

14. a) $9x^2 - 42x + 49 = (3x - 7)^2$, so the side length of the field is $3x - 7$ and the perimeter is $4(3x - 7) = 12x - 28$.
   b) The length of the fence that borders the field is $12(20) - 28 = 212$ m. The length of each side is $3(20) - 7 = 53$ m. So the length of the diagonal section is $\sqrt{53^2 + 53^2} \doteq 75$ m. The total length of the fence is $212 + 75 = 287$ m.

15. a) $(s + 8)(s - 8)$ **b)** $(d + 11)(d - 11)$
   c) $(2h + 5)(2h - 5)$ **d)** $9(n + 3)(n - 3)$
   e) $4(6 - b)(6 + b)$ **f)** $2c(7 - 3d)(7 + 3d)$

16. a) $(b + 7)^2$ **b)** $(12 + w)^2$
   c) $(4 - 3g)^2$ **d)** $(8s - 13t)^2$

17. a) $(9 - x)(9 + x)$
   b) $10y(x^2 + 1)(x - 1)(x +1)$
   c) $(3x +5)(3x + 5)$
   d) $4(2x + 5y)(2x - 5y)$
   e) $(x^2 - 8)(x^2 - 8)$
   f) $-2y(2x + 3)(2x + 3)$

18. a) -36 should be 36.
   b) There needs to be a *difference* of squares.
   c) $3y^2$ needs to be $9y^2$.
   d) 40 is not a square. The value should be 49.

Chapters 1−5 Cumulative Review

1. $C = 1\frac{5}{16}$; $D = 3\frac{1}{8}$; $CD = 1\frac{13}{16}$
2. a) 18 000 mm^2 **b)** 30.94 m^2
   c) 522.58 cm^2
3. $RS = 9$; $XY = \frac{9}{4}$; $ZX = \frac{15}{4}$
4. a) 13   **b)** 12
   c) $\frac{8}{3}$ **d)** $14x$
5. a) $x^2 + 6x + 8$
   b) $b^2 - 9$
   c) $y^2 - 64$
   d) $8a^2 + 2ab - 21b^2$
   e) $-100x^2 - 120xy - 36y^2$
   f) $-x^2 + y^2$

6. 0.486; Example: diameter of a pen
7. The new shed has the larger floor area. It is 23.5% larger.
8. a)

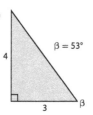

9. a) $\frac{-216}{x^{18}}$ **b)** $\frac{1}{400b^4}$
   c) $\frac{1}{25}$ **d)** 6480

10. 125.66 cm; 543.36 cm^2

11. a) 2258.57 m^3 **b)** 41 547.56 in^3
   c) 15 828.08 mm^3 **d)** 26 521.85 cm^3

12. a) 0.8660   **b)** 0.6613
   c) 1   **d)** 0.7071
   e) 3.0777

13. a) -4 **b)** $-\frac{17}{5}$
   c) $\frac{1}{2}$

14. a) $2(x + 5)$ **b)** $z(7 + 8z)$
   c) $a^3(q + r + s)$ **d)** $4mn(m^4 - 3n^2)$

15. a) 352.5 ft^2 **b)** 3 cans
   c) $107.85

16. 17.6 m

17. a) the population, in millions, of BC in 2001
   b) 5 158 947
   c) 3 667 300

18. a) $(x + 9)(x - 3)$ **b)** $-2(x + 6)(x - 3)$
   c) $-2(2x - 1)(x - 7)$ **d)** not possible
   e) $x(x - 7)(x + 1)$

19. a) 9.12 cm   **b)** 9.17 in.

20. a) $\angle C = 38°$; AB = 4.14 km; AC = 6.73 km
  b) DF = 20; $\angle D = 53.13°$; $\angle F = 36.87°$

21. a) $4^{\frac{5}{3}}$ **b)** $(xt)^{\frac{3}{2}}$
  c) $-2a^{\frac{-5}{6}}$

22. a) 366.6 km **b)** 22.86 m

23. 6.44 cm

24. 128.67 m

25. a) $10\sqrt{2}$ **b)** $15\sqrt{7}$
  c) $4\sqrt[3]{2}$ **d)** $2\sqrt[4]{5}$

26. a) 12 or -12; $(x + 6)^2$ or $(x - 6)^2$
  b) 36 or -36; $(2x + 9)^2$ or $(2x - 9)^2$

Extend It Further

1. B

2. B

3. A

4. C

5. A

6. $-17, 2x - 3$

7. $(2m)^2 = 4m^2$
$(m^2 - 1)^2 = m^4 - 2m^2 + 1$
$(m^2 + 1)^2 = (m^2 - 1)^2 + (2m)^2$

8. $\dfrac{2^{20} - 2^{16} + 15}{2^{16} + 1} = \dfrac{2^{16}(2^4 - 1) + 15}{2^{16} + 1}$
$= \dfrac{15(\cancel{2^{16} + 1})}{\cancel{2^{16} + 1}}$
$= 15$

9. $\dfrac{x^2 - y^2}{(x + y)^2} = \dfrac{(x + y)(x - y)}{(x + y)(x + y)} = \dfrac{(x - y)}{(x + y)}$

10. $a^2 - 6a + 9 = (a - 3)^2$ and $9 - a^2$
$= -(a^2 - 9) = -(a - 3)(a + 3)$;
GCF $= (a - 3)$ and LCM $= (a + 3)$
$(a - 3)^2$.

11. $\dfrac{a^2}{a - 1}$;
solution:
$\dfrac{1 + a}{1 - \frac{1}{a^2}} = \dfrac{1 + a}{\frac{a^2 - 1}{a^2}}$

$= (1 + a)\left(\dfrac{a^2}{a^2 - 1}\right)$

$= (\cancel{1 + a})\left(\dfrac{a^2}{(\cancel{a + 1})\,(a - 1)}\right)$

$= \dfrac{a^2}{a - 1}$

12. $\sqrt{14} + \sqrt{12}$; solution:
$(\sqrt{14} + \sqrt{12})^2 = 14 + 2\sqrt{168} + 12$
$(\sqrt{15} + \sqrt{11})^2 = 15 + 2\sqrt{165} + 11$

13. A $= -4$, B $= 25$

14. -2010, $(4321)(4319) - (4320)^2$ is of the
  form $(x + 1)(x - 1) - x^2 = -1$

15. 4

16. 600

17. $-1, 1, 2009$

Unit 2 Review

1. C

2. B

3. B

4. B

5. C

6. D

7. A

8. B

9. D

10. B

11. B

12. C

13. C

14. B

15. B

16. A

17. 3

18. $\sqrt[5]{4}, \sqrt[4]{5}, \sqrt[3]{12}, \sqrt{12}$

19. 16

20. 14 896 cm^2

21. 16

22. 4

23. 8

24. -1

25. 22

26. 0.5 or $\frac{1}{2}$

27. **a)** $-6, 6; (x + 3)^2; (x - 3)^2$
    b) $-24, 24; (x + 12)^2; (x - 12)^2$
    c) $-64, 64; (4d + 8)^2; (4d - 8)^2$
    d) $-140, 140; (7r + 10)^2; (7r - 10)^2$

28. Examples: 19, 23, 47, 33, 91

29. 14

30. $12k$, where $k = 1, 2, 3, 4 \ldots$

31. $2x - 1$

32. **a)** 508 212
    b) 13 569 264
    c) No; Example: At the rate of growth that the equation models, the number of subscribers would exceed the total population of the world (approximately 7 billion) within 7 months.

33. **a)** $5a$ and -3 were not distributed properly into binomials.
    b) $20a^2 + 23a - 21$
    c) Each side of the equation should equal 105.

34. **a)** $(x + 4)^2$ **b)** $(x + 3)(x + 5)$
    c) $3(y + 2)(y - 4)$ **d)** $(b - 7)(2a - 5)$
    e) $(x - 11)(x + 11)$ **f)** $4(4x - 7y)(4x + 7y)$

35. **a)** $(x + 3)$ and $(x + 2)$
    b)
    c) $x^2 + 5x + 6$

36. **a)** $8k^3 - 12k^2 + 6k - 1$
    b) $7k^3 - 15k^2 + 3k - 2$

37. $5x^2 + 15x + 11$

38. **a)** No
    b) $-1, 0, 1$ or $-2, -1, 0$

39. $2r(r - 1)^2(r + 1)^2$

40. **a)** $(20x + 3)(x - 5)$
    b) length = 803 m; width = 35 m

41. **a)** Find the greatest common factor. In this case, GCF = $6a$.
    b) $6a(2b - c)(7b - c)$

42. **a)** Yes
    b) No. They are factored, but not factored in the simplest form.
    c) $9x^2 - 9$
    $= 9(x^2 - 1)$
    $= 9(x + 1)(x - 1)$
    $16m^2 - 64$
    $= 16(m^2 - 4)$
    $= 16(m - 2)(m + 2)$
    $36d^2 - 100$
    $= 4(9d^2 - 25)$
    $= 4(3d + 5)(3d - 5)$
    d) If it is possible to remove a common factor with a result that a difference of squares still exists, then that needs to be done first, before continuing with the factoring process.

43. **a)** Example: $3y^2 + 6y - 12$
    b) c must be a multiple of 3

Chapter 6 Linear Relations and Functions

6.1 Graphs of Relations

1. Examples:
   a) a straight line starting at the origin and rising gently to the right
   b) a straight line starting at a point on the distance axis (y-axis) above the origin and descending rapidly to the right to the time axis (x-axis)
   c) a curved line starting at the origin and rising to the right quickly at first and then becoming less and less steep, but always moving further from the time axis
   d) a straight horizontal line quite high above the time axis
   e) an inverted V, starting at the origin, with the first segment steeper than the second
   f) a straight line starting at the origin and rising to the right, and then becoming a horizontal line leading to the right side of the graph

2. Examples:
   a) Graph A: the lines are straight (suggesting constant rate of change), have the same steepness, and are increasing; Graph B: the lines are straight and have the same steepness; Graph C: the lines are straight, start at the same point on the vertical axis, and are increasing; Graph D: the lines start at the same point on the vertical axis and are increasing
   b) Graph A: each line starts at a different point on the vertical axis; Graph B: each line starts at a different point on the vertical axis and one line is increasing, while the other is decreasing; Graph C: the lines have different steepness; Graph D: one line is straight (suggesting constant rate of change) while the other is curved (suggesting a decreasing rate of change)

   c) Graph A: The cost to rent DVDs versus the number of DVDs rented. The upper line includes a membership fee and the lower one has no extra fee. The costs of individual DVD rentals are the same for both lines.; Graph B: The increasing line could represent the number of pages read in a book versus time. The decreasing line, then, is the number of pages left to read.; Graph C: The steeper line could represent the cost of removing computer viruses versus the time taken to do the job. The less steep line could represent the same scenario, but at a lower hourly rate.; Graph D: The straight line could represent the height of a jet after takeoff versus time. The curved line could be the height of a smaller, less powerful, private plane.

3. Examples:
   a)

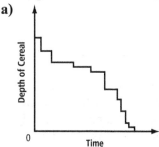

The height of each "step" on the graph illustrates the amount that the cereal goes down with each spoonful. The width of each step is the time between mouthfuls. This graph suggests that the eater starts of at a leisurely pace, perhaps while reading the paper. However, the size of spoonful increases and the time between mouthfuls decreases as if the eater has suddenly realized that the school bus is coming. The point at the x-axis is where the cereal is gone.

b)

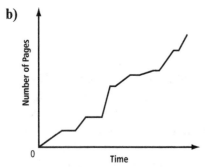

The number of pages read over time changes with the pace of reading. The steeper the slope, the faster the person is reading. At one point, where the slope is very steep the person may even be skimming the text. Where the slope is almost flat, the person is reading very slowly and carefully. The horizontal lines are places are periods where the reader may not even be reading.

c)

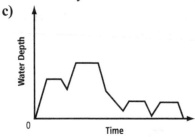

This graph shows that the water rises when the washing machine is turned on. The water reaches a particular height, where the clothes soak. The level of the water level dips as the more of the clothes slide into the water, absorbing some of it. At the end of the soaking cycle, more water is added to the tub and the water begins to agitate for a period of time. Then, all the water is drained and fresh water is added to rinse the clothes. This rinse cycle is repeated and then the water drains out to complete the wash cycle.

d)

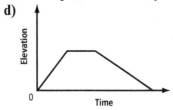

This graph shows a quick elevation change as the airplane takes off. The plane then levels out. Notice that this is a short flight, so the plane is at cruising altitude for not much longer than it took to get to that elevation. The plane then begins a slower descent to its destination.

4. Examples:
Using line segments: (constant change theme)
- graphing water used each time a toilet is flushed
- buying grapes at a fixed price per kilogram

Using curves: (changing rate occurring)
- driving in traffic that is speeding up and slowing down
- elevation of a road through a mountain park

5. **a)** line segments and curves follow a similar path
b) The person graphing may have realized that the relation had more constant increases and decreases, which are best represented by line segments.

6.

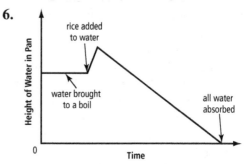

The height of the water rises sharply as the rice is added. This rise is not exactly vertical because it takes some time, even though it very little, to add the rice. As the rice absorbs the water and some evaporates, the water level decreases steadily. When the line reaches the x-axis, all the water has been absorbed and there is none left in the pan.

7.

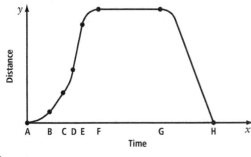

Example: The symmetry occurs because the skater moves away from and then returns to the finish line repeatedly and keeps the same pace. If the skater's pace varied, the distance between the points where the graph meets the x-axis would change.

8. a) Example: Section B to C should not be horizontal; it should be increasing, but not as steeply as in D to E. Section F to G should not be decreasing; it should be horizontal. Section G to H should not be decreasing to the left. If this were the case, the car would be in two different places at the same time between times A and G. Rather, it should decrease to the right with steepness between that in B to C and D to E.

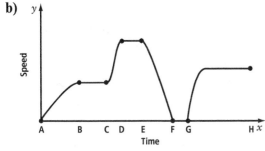

b)

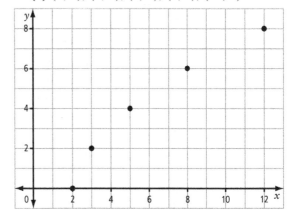

9. a) Example: The darker line is the revenue and the lighter line is cost. We know this because there are 0 revenues when 0 belts have been made and sold. Also, the dark line exceeds the lighter line after 500 belts. The distance between the lines is the profit. If the darker line represented cost, the company would lose money as it sold more belts, which does not make sense.
b) $4000.00
c) 500
d) $9000.00
e) $4000.00
f) $4000.00
g) $18.00

10. Example: $-40\ °C = -40\ °F$; one degree F is smaller than one degree C; $0\ °C = 32\ °F$ (water freezes); $100\ °C = 212\ °F$ (water boils); as the temperature in C rises, so does the temperature in F; the F scale is positive from about $-18°$ C to $0°$ C and beyond; doubling the temperature in C is less than doubling the corresponding temperatures in F.

11. Example: Consumer income, competition between stores, scarceness of resource, input or cost of production prices.

6.2 Linear Relations
1. (a) (2, 0), (3, 2), (5, 4), (8, 6), (12, 8)

(b) (10, 2), (8, 4), (6, 6), (4, 8), (2, 10)

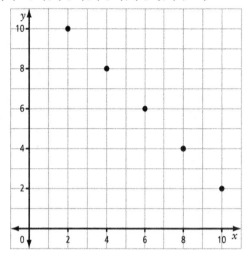

2. a) $C = 23p$

p	C
1	23
2	46
3	69
4	92

This relation is discrete because you cannot buy a part of a ticket.

b) $ab = 24$

a	b
2	12
2.5	9.6
3	8
3.5	6.857142857

This relation is continuous because you can choose any positive a-value and divide this number into 24 to find a b-value. If you only considered whole numbers, this relation would be discrete.

3. a) Non-linear; The number is always multiplied by one more than itself. $y = (x)(x + 1)$
b) Linear; The number is doubled, then increased by one. $y = 2x + 1$
c) Linear; The number is always subtracted from 3. $y = (3 - x)$
d) Linear; The number is always multiplied by negative one: $y = -x$.

4. a)

r	A
1	3.14
2	12.57
3	28.27
4	50.27

This is non-linear as there is no constant change in the values of A. The radius is independent; the area is dependent.

b)

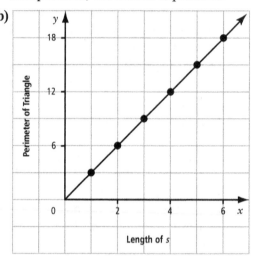

This is linear as the perimeter is constantly three times the length of the side. The side length is independent, and perimeter is dependent.

c)

Polygon with n Sides	3	4	5	6
Number of Diagonals	0	2	5	9

This is non-linear as there is no constant change in the values of the numbers of diagonals. The number of sides in a polygon is the independent variable; the number of diagonals is the dependent variable.

5. a) linear   **b)** linear
c) non-linear   **d)** non-linear

6. a) independent variable: number of movies; dependent variable: cost
b) The cost for renting one new release movie is $4.50. The cost for renting two is $9.00. The cost for renting three is $13.50. The cost of renting four is $18.00. The cost for renting five is $22.50.

c) $C = \$4.50(m)$

d) (1, 4.50), (2, 9.00), (3, 13.50), (4, 18.00), (5, 22.50)

e)

Movies Rented	1	2	3	4	5
Cost ($)	4.50	9.00	13.50	18.00	22.50

f)

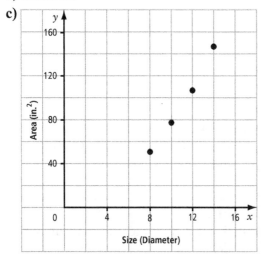

Number of Movies

Plotting for zero does not make sense because people know that if they do not rent anything, the cost is $0.00.

g) Example: The table of values would be easiest for customers to understand.

7. a)

Size (Diameter)	Area of Pizza
8 in.	50.27 in.^{2}
10 in.	78.54 in.^{2}
12 in.	113.1 in.^{2}
14 in.	153.94 in.^{2}

b) diameter

c)

Area (in.^{2})

Size (Diameter)

d) non-linear
e) discrete

8. a) 4 in., 5 in., 6 in., 7 in.
  b) 50 in.^{2}, 79 in.^{2}, 113 in.^{2}, 154 in.^{2}
  c) $0.20
  d) $15.80, $22.60, $30.80
  e) Example: No. The price for the large pizzas is too high and may not compete well with the competition. Yes. He is charging the same rate for all the pizzas.
  f) linear; discrete
  g) non-linear

9. a) This would be a linear relation given a fixed or constant speed.
  b)

Time (h)	1	2	3	4	5
Distance (km)	10	20	30	40	50

Distance (km)	Time (min)
1	6
2	12
3	18
4	24
5	30
6	36
7	42
8	48

The second table gives more realistic and detailed information to a reader. Distances of 40 or 50 km are unlikely for most joggers.

c) The independent variable would be time.

d)

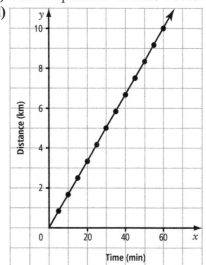

Time (min)

e) The graph would be continuous because at any distance there would be a specific time.

10. a)

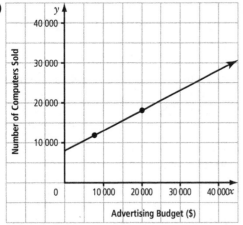

b) 28000

c) $26000

d) 8000

11. a) Answers will vary.

b) Answers will vary.

c) Either variable can be independent or dependent because you are measuring in centimetres for both.

d) linear

e) discrete, but in a population it would be continuous from the shortest arm/foot length to the longest

12. a) bags of flour, jugs of milk, single cans of soup, loaves of bread, packages of cookies

b) independent: number of items; dependent: cost

c) discrete.

d) Example: discrete; jars of pickles (even if bought by the case); continuous: roasts, which are priced per pound or kilogram

e) Items for which the price drops by a fraction if bought in multiples, such as 2 for a price, or 3 for a price.

13. $y = 3x(x - 2)$:

x	0	1	2	3	4	5
y	0	−3	0	9	24	45

This equation is non-linear because the y-value does not change consistently with consistent change in the x-value.

The points on the graph are in the shape of a parabola so this is a non-linear function.

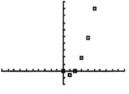

$y = 5(x - 2)$:

x	0	1	2	3	4	5
y	−10	−5	0	5	10	15

Each increase of 1 in the x-value results in an increase of 5 in the y-value. Since the y-value changes consistently with a consistent change in the x-value, this is a linear equation.

The points on the graph form a straight line, so the function is linear.

$y = \dfrac{(x - 2)}{2}$:

x	0	1	2	3	4	5
y	−1	−0.5	0	0.5	1	1.5

This equation is linear because the y-value changes consistently by 0.5 whenever the x-value increases by one.

The points on the graph form a straight line, so the function is linear.

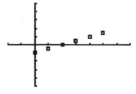

14. a) linear if the independent variable is of degree 1 and multiplied by a constant number

b) linear if both the independent and dependent values change at a constant rate

c) linear if both the independent and dependent values change at a constant rate

d) linear if all the points, whether discrete or continuous, form a line

e) Find at least 3 pairs of answers and see if there are regular changes between them. If so, it is linear.

15. Example:
Look back at whether you had freedom to pick any numbers or values you wanted to for the independent variable. If you did, and you could choose numbers like fractions and decimals that work, it is continuous. If you are only allowed certain numbers, or only integers, then a discrete graph is best.

6.3 Domain and Range

1. a)
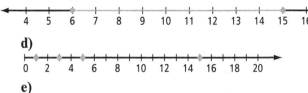

b)

c) Example:

d)

e)

f)

2. a) D = {0, 1, 2, 3, 4};
R = {$0.00, $0.38, $0.76, $1.14, $1.52}
b) D = {penny, nickel, dime, quarter, loonie, twoonie}
R = {$0.01, $0.05, $0.10, $0.25, $1.00, $2.00}
c) D = {1, 2, 3, 4, 5, 6, 7, 8, 9, 10};
R = {1, 4, 9, 16, 25, 36, 49, 64, 81, 100}
d) D = {1, 2, 3, 4, 5, 6}
R = {$35.00, $70.00, $105.00, $140.00, $175.00, $210.00}
e) D = {0, 1, 2, 3, 4, 5, 6}
R = {$0.00, $1.50, $3.00, $4.50, $6.00, $7.50, 9.00}

3. a) D = {$x \mid -4 < x \le 5$} or (–4, 5]
R = {$y \mid -2 \le y < 2$} or [–2, 2)
b) D = {$x \mid 0 \le x \le 4$} or [0, 4]
R = {$y \mid 0 \le y \le 4$} or [0, 4]

c) D = {$x \mid -3 \le x \le 6$} or [–3, 6]
R = {$y \mid -4 \le y \le 5$} or [–4, 5]
d) D = {$x \mid -6 \le x \le 0$} or [–6, 0]
R = {$y \mid -8 \le y \le 0$} or [–8, 0]
e) D = {$x \mid -3 \le x \le 5$} or [–3, 5]
R = {$y \mid -3 \le y \le 7$} or [–3, 7]
f) D = {$x \mid -6 \le x \le 1$} or [–6, 1]
R = {$y \mid -4 \le y \le 7$} or [–4, 7]

4. a) The domain is the number of litres of fuel that might be purchased. Since the capacity of the fuel tank is 40 L, the domain is 0, if no fuel is purchased, to 40 L, if the tank is empty and then filled to capacity. In set notation,
D = {$x \mid 0 \le x \le 40$}
b) The range is the possible cost incurred by purchasing gas and getting a car wash. The assumption is that the car wash will be purchased, regardless if any gasoline is purchased. So the lowest end of the range is $8.00. If the tank is empty and is filled with 40 L of gas, C = 0.92(40) + 8.00, or 44.80. So, the range is $8.00 to $44.80, or
R = {$y \mid 8 \le y \le 44.80$}
c) The cost is dependent on the number of litres of gasoline that is purchased, so n is the independent and C is the dependent variable.

5. a) The lowest internal temperature in the table is for medium-rare beef, veal, and lamb at 63° C. The highest internal temperature is for whole poultry at 85° C. So, the range is from 63 to 85, or R = {$T \mid 63 \le T \le 85$}
b) It would be better to make a list of each temperature expectation. It would make a chef check carefully which temperature should be chosen.
c) Each temperature depends on the type of food you are cooking. Some are very specific and a range of values will not work. This is especially true for poultry, which must have the highest temperature value of 85.

6. Example:

a)

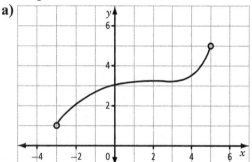

b)

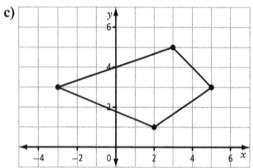

c)

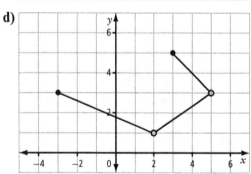

d)

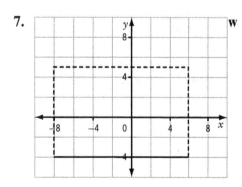

7.

8. a ray

9. a) Example:

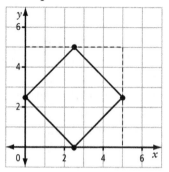

b) Example:

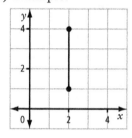

c) Example:

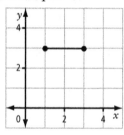

10. Example: A domain must be present for a relation to exist. It must have a minimum of one domain element matched with one range element

11. Example: A balloon being blown up: when empty it has no air in it, but it can get bigger and bigger and then pop when it gets to 20 cm

12. Example: Domains: player names, position on the team, team jersey number. Ranges: salary, game minutes, points scored

6.4 Functions

1. **a)** This is not a function because there are two ordered pairs with an x-value of 2, but with different y-values: 4 and 1. If you drew the vertical line, $x = 2$, the line would pass through two y-values proving that this is not a function.
   b) This is a function because each of the x-values is different and has only one corresponding y-value. You could draw a vertical line through each x-value, and it would intersect with only one y-value.
   c) This is not a function because each of the x-values, 1, 4, and 9, has two corresponding y-values. A vertical line drawn through any of these x-values would intersect two y-values.
   d) This is a function because each person has only one shoe size. If you were to plot these points on a graph, a vertical line could be drawn from any of the names and there would only be one corresponding shoe size (y-value).
   e) This is not a function because Anika has 3 different siblings.
   f) This is function because each of the x-values has one and only one corresponding y-value. In other words, you can draw a vertical line through any point on the graph, and it will not pass through any other point.
   g) This is not a function because if you draw a vertical line through any of these points, the line will pass through at least one other point.

2. $A(n) = 500(1 + 0.08)^n$

3. $W = 26p + 1200$

4. **a)** $z(-3) = 16$ **b)** $z(2) = 1$
   c) $a = 0$

5. **a)** $t(1) = 5$ **b)** $t(20) = 81$
   c) $n = 10$

6. **a)** The price, P, is dependent on the number of months you are a member, m. So, m is independent variable and it represents the number of months you are a member of the club.
   b) The cost of being a member for a year is equal to 12 months of monthly dues plus the \$55 initiation fee: $P(12) = 35(12) + 55$, or \$475.00.
   c) To find after how many months you will have spent \$1000, set P equal to 1000 and then solve for m:
$$1000 = 35m + 55$$
$$1000 - 55 = 35m + 55 - 55$$
$$945 = 35m$$
$$\frac{945}{35} = \frac{35m}{35}$$
$$27 = m$$
   d) The competitor sells its membership by the week, so you must solve the equation for 52 weeks, which is equal to one year: $P(52) = 10(52) + 100$, or \$620.00. This option is more expensive than belonging to FITFIT.

7. **a)** $f(5) = 9$ **b)** $f(5) = 1$
   c) $f(5) = 5$ **d)** $f(5) = -\frac{1}{2}$

8. **a)** $x = -3$ **b)** $x = 13$
   c) $x = -35$ **d)** $x = 63$

9. **a)** $x = 4$

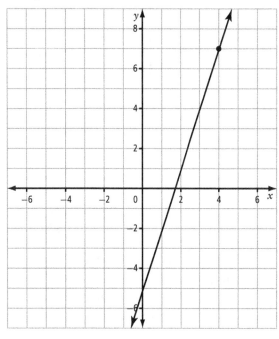

b) $x = 0$

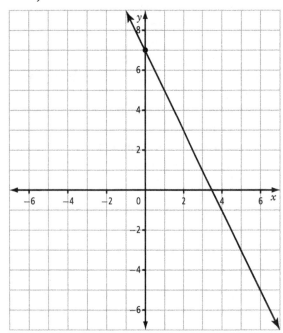

c) $x = 5$

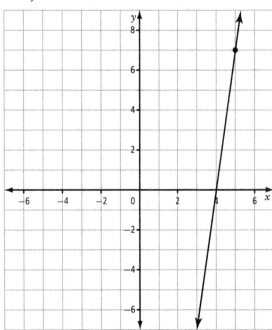

10. a) $x = 6$ produces the prime number 7
b) $x = 9$ produces the multiple of 8 that is 16
c) $x = 38$ produces the number 103, which is larger than 100
d) $x = 3$ produces -2, the largest negative number in the function

11. $T(m) = (A)m + (B)$ would be $T(m) = (-4)m + (90)$, where $A = -4$ and $B = 90$

12. a) V0B 2P0 is the postal code for all of Yahk, BC. T0H 2P0 is the postal code for all of Meander River, AB. These are not functions. R2J 0A1 refers to only one address: 520 Lagimodiere Blvd, Winnipeg, MB (the Royal Canadian Mint). This postal code is a function. (Notice that this postal code returns two results when you search Canada Post's online database: one response in English and one in French. Therefore, you might also answer that this postal code is not a function within the context of the database because there are two records associated with it.)
b) Postal codes are usually specific to one street name and either even or odd street numbers. If you live in a rural setting or are the ONLY even or odd numbered house on a street, you may be unique. If your postal code is used only for you, then it is a function. If you share your postal code with other addresses, it is not a function.

6.5 Slope

1.

Positive Slope	Negative Slope	Zero Slope
AH GH FE BE	AB HE GF ED BC	HB DC

2. Slopes are: $AB = -\frac{1}{3}$; $BC = -\frac{2}{1}$; $CD = 0$; $DE = \frac{2}{1}$; $EF = -\frac{1}{3}$; $FG = 2$; $GA = -\frac{7}{2}$;

3. a) $m = +\frac{1}{2}$, less steep than a 45° line
b) $m = +\frac{8}{5}$, steeper than a 45° line
c) $m = -\frac{9}{4}$, steeper than a 45° line
d) $m = -\frac{1}{3}$, less steep than a 45° line

4. a) $m = -\frac{1}{2}$ **b)** $m = 0$
c) $m = \frac{3}{7}$ **d)** $m = \frac{5}{2}$

5.

Given Point A(x, y)	Slope	Next Point to the Right of A
(3, 5)	$-\dfrac{1}{2}$	(5, 4)
(3, 5)	$\dfrac{2}{3}$	(6, 7)
(−3, 7)	$\dfrac{3}{7}$	(4, 10)
(2, −5)	$-\dfrac{4}{1}$	(3, −9)
(0, −4)	$\dfrac{5}{4}$	(4, 1)

6. 10.08 m or approximately 10 m

7. $7.50: the amount of money she gives her mother each week

8. a) The slope is equal to $\dfrac{\text{vertical change}}{\text{horizontal change}}$, or $\dfrac{\text{rise}}{\text{run}}$. The slope on this road is 32% grade. So, $0.32 = \dfrac{130}{d}$, where d is the horizontal distance. Solving for d,
$$0.32 = \frac{130}{d}$$
$$d(0.32) = d\left(\frac{130}{d}\right)$$
$$d(0.32) = 130$$
$$\frac{d(0.32)}{(0.32)} = \frac{130}{0.32}$$
$$d = 406.25$$
The horizontal distance is approximately 406 m.

b) Expressed as rise over run, the slope of this road is $\dfrac{130}{406}$.

c) The actual road surface is approximately 426 m long.

9. 1.25 cm of hair growth per month

10. 3 cm

11. increase of 1925 people per year; in 2021, an increase of 28 878, or a population to 231 218

12. a) For both trips, the employee paid for 3 days of use. The only variable that changes to account for the change in cost is the number of kilometres driven. On the second trip, the cost of the car was $63.75 more and the number of additional kilometres driven was 255 more km. So, $255(d) = 63.75$, where d is the charge per kilometre:
$$255(d) = 63.75$$
$$\frac{255(d)}{255} = \frac{63.75}{255}$$
$$d = 0.25$$
The company charges $0.25/km.

b) The daily cost vehicle, C, is the number of kilometres × 0.25 plus the daily charge. In this case, the employee paid for 3 days for both trips. Since the daily charge does not change for each trip, so we can solve the equation $C = 0.25(d) + 3(r)$, where d is the number of kilometres driven and r is the daily rate. Solving for Trip A:
$$301.25 = 0.25(425) + 3(r)$$
$$301.25 = 106.25 + 3r$$
$$301.25 - 106.25 = 106.25 - 106.25 + 3(r)$$
$$195 = 3(r)$$
$$\frac{195}{3} = \frac{3(r)}{3}$$
$$65 = r$$
The daily fee for the car is $65.00.

c) If the company simply paid employees $0.50/km to use their own car, Trip A would have cost $212.50, while Trip B would cost $340.00. This means that paying the employee for the use of their car would be cheaper.

d) The cost for renting a car is the same as for using the employees car when the kilometres travelled is 780 km. The cost in both scenarios is $390.00. However, since the rental company charges less per kilometre, if the trip is more than 780 km long in a 3-day period, it becomes cheaper to rent.

13. Example: If the slope definition were run over rise, when the line segments got steeper, the ratios would be getting smaller and smaller, rather than larger. Having the slope formula as rise over run makes these ratios increase in value as the actual line segments get steeper.

14. Example: The denominator is increasing quicker than the numerator, so the slope is getting increasingly smaller. However, since the numerator will never equal 0, no matter how small the slope gets, it will never be 0.

Chapter 6 Review
6.1 Graphs of Relations
1. a) items: **i)** bananas, **ii)** deli ham, **iii)** granola, **iv)** milk, **v)** bread

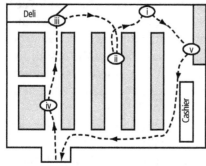

b) For speed, use either metres per minute or feet per minute. Time would best be measured in minutes.

c)

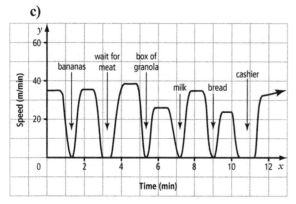

2. a) Example: mile 0 to approximately mile 3, the cyclist would face a long, steep climb and then would go downhill steeply for almost 2 miles; mile 15 to mile 20 might be a rolling portion of the ride, with short climbs and descents

b) Example: easiest portion: mile 23 to mile 28, where the riding is flat, with no elevation gain; most difficult: mile 0 to mile 8, where there are a series of steep climbs and descents

6.2 Linear Relations
3. a) Discrete. The number will always be a whole number. The numbers between have no meaning.

b) Continuous. Time increases constantly. The player could have any number of minutes and seconds.

c) Discrete. The number is always countable. Again, numbers between have no meaning.

4. a) fee charged $= f$ (fee)
insured amount $= v$ (value)
The insured amount would be the independent variable, as the fee depends on the value shipped.

b) Non-linear. The fees do not rise in a pattern. Some sections are linear, going up by $1.00 for each $100 increase in value; others don't change by that same amount.

c)

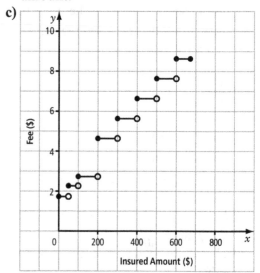

6.3 Domain and Range
5. a) D $= \{0, 3, 5\}$; R $= \{-7, -4, 0, 5, 11\}$

b) Factors of 10 are D $= \{1, 2, 5, 10\}$; Answers are R $= \{10, 5, 2, 1\}$

6.

Set Notation	Interval Notation
$\{x \mid 3 < x < 7\}$	$(3, 7)$
$\{x \mid -5 \leq x \leq 0\}$	$[-5, 0]$
$\{x \mid -13 \leq x < 27\}$	$[-13, 27)$
$\{x \mid x \leq 5\}$	$(-\infty, 5]$

7. **a)** D = {$x\,|\,-5 \le x \le 1$};
R = {$y\,|\,-4 \le y \le 1$}
b) D = {$x\,|\,1 \le x < 6$};
R = {$y\,|\,-5 < y < 1$}

6.4 Functions

8. **a)** $f(0) = 1$
b) $f(-1) = 5$
c) $f(3) = 13$
d) Different domain values giving the same range value still defines a function. It is when the same input value produces 2 different outcomes that a relation is then not a function.
e)

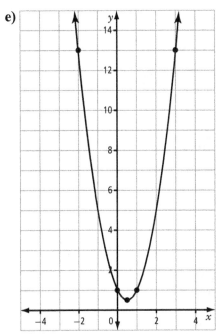

It passes the vertical line text because a vertical line passes through only one point on the graph.

9. **a)** $V(s) = s^3$; $V(r) = (4/3)\pi r^3$.
b)

Side Length of Cube	Volume of Cube	Volume of Sphere Inside
10 cm	1000 cm³	523.6 cm³
20 cm	8000 cm³	4188.8 cm³
30 cm	27 000 cm³	14 137 cm³
40 cm	64 000 cm³	33 510 cm³

6.5 Slope

10. **a)** $-\frac{5}{9}$; negative   **b)** $\frac{4}{3}$; positive

c) $-\frac{12}{1}$; negative

11. **a)**

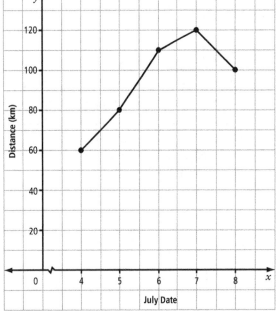

b) The four slopes are $+\frac{20}{1}$, $+\frac{30}{1}$, $+\frac{10}{1}$, and $-\frac{20}{1}$.

c) These slope values show the rate of increase in daily distance from one day to the next.

d) A negative slope means that he didn't increase his daily distance, but decreased it instead.

Chapters 1–6 Cumulative Review

1. D = $3\frac{5}{8}$ in.; CD = $2\frac{15}{16}$ in.; $3\frac{5}{8} - \frac{11}{16} = 2\frac{15}{16}$ in. or you could count the ticks on the ruler

2. 26 cm

3. **a)** $a^3 + 5a^2 - 10a - 8$ **b)** $10b^2 - 10b$

4. 0.82 cm; example: an ant

5. **a)** linear; each new person will add the same amount to the cost: $10
b) p = people (independent variable) and C = cost (dependent variable)

c)

p	C (\$)
0	200
10	300
20	400
30	500
40	600
50	700
100	1200

d) The data is discrete because numbers of people can only be whole numbers.

e) Yes, this relation is a function because there is only one value of C for each value of p. Linear relationships are always functions.

f)

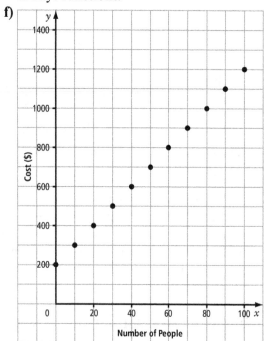

Number of People

6. CE = 10 cm

7. a) \$1795.02   **b)** \$295.02
c) \$2148.07

8. a)

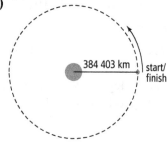

384 403 km   start/finish

b) 89 870.42 km
c) 3744.60 km/h

9. a) $V = 1321.01$ m³; $SA = 738.68$ m²
b) $V = 7938.80$ in.³; $SA = 3103.89$ in.²
c) $V = 17.65$ mm³; $SA = 44.42$ mm²
d) $V = 197.17$ ft³; $SA = 226.4$ ft²
e) $V = 36\ 086.95$ cm³; $SA = 5281.02$ cm²

10. a)

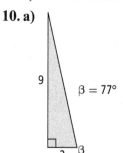

9   $\beta = 77°$ 2 β

b)

$\theta = 9°$ 1   6 θ

c)

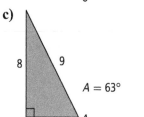

8   9 $A = 63°$ A

d)

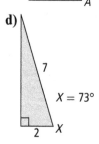

7   $X = 73°$ 2 X

11. a) $\dfrac{1}{x^3}$ **b)** $\dfrac{1}{32}$

c) $k^{\frac{31}{12}}$ **d)** $\dfrac{1}{2p^{\frac{7}{3}}}$

12. a) $(3x + 9)(x - 5)$
b) $(2z - 1)(2y + 5)$
c) $7ab(2ab - 3)$
d) $3xy(4x^2 - 3x + 1)$

13. a) $(x + 7)(x - 8)$
b) $-4(x^2 - 4x + 12)$
c) $(3m + 2n)(2m + 1n)$
d) $(5s + 2)(7s + 9)$

14. a) $(c - 11)(c + 11)$
  b) $(1 + 9y^2)(1 + 3y)(1 - 3y)$
  c) $3(3h - 7)(3h + 7)$
  d) $(y + 2)^2$
  e) $(5x - 11)^2$

15. $\frac{4}{6} = \frac{2}{3}$ and $\frac{1.5}{2.5} = \frac{3}{5}$; $\frac{2}{3} \neq \frac{3}{5}$, so, no, it cannot be enlarged without cropping.

16. $39°$

17. a) $\sqrt[3]{c^4}$ **b)** $\sqrt[5]{324t^6}$

  c) $\sqrt[4]{\dfrac{m^2}{12}}$

18. 4.36 km

19. a) Domain:

  Words: all real numbers between but not including -6 and positive infinity

  Interval Notation: $(-6, \infty)$

  Set Notation: $\{x \,|\, -6 < x < \infty, x \in R\}$

  Range:

  Words: all real numbers between but not including -1 and negative infinity

  Interval Notation: $(-1, -\infty)$

  Set Notation: $\{y \,|\, -1 < y < -\infty, y \in R\}$

  b) Domain:

  Words: all real numbers between -7 and 0, inclusive

  Interval Notation: $[-7, 0]$

  Set Notation: $\{x \,|\, -7 \leq x \leq 0, x \in R\}$

  Range:

  Words: all real numbers between -5 and 2, inclusive

  Interval Notation: $[-5, 2]$

  Set Notation: $\{y \,|\, -5 \leq y \leq 2, y \in R\}$

20. a) $AC = 19.49$ km; $BC = 15.36$ km; $\angle C = 38°$,
  b) $DE = 14.25$ m; $\angle D = 37.67°$; $\angle F = 52.33°$

21. a) $\dfrac{6}{7}$ **b)** -2

Extend It Further

1. C

2. C

3. A

4. D

5. D

6. domain $= \{x \,|\, 7 < x < 31, x \in N\}$
  range $= \{f(x) \,|\, 39 \leq f(x) \leq 61, f(x) \in N\}$

7. The slope of the line joining $(-3, 0)$ and $(0, 6)$ is 2. The slope of the line joining $(-3, 0)$ and $(0, -1.5)$ is $\frac{-1}{2}$. The product of the two slopes is -1, which means that the lines are perpendicular to each other. An alternative solution is to use the Pythagorean relationship; the sides have lengths $\sqrt{45}$, $\sqrt{11.25}$, and $\sqrt{56.25}$. Since $(\sqrt{45})^2 + (\sqrt{11.25})^2 = (\sqrt{56.25})^2$, the triangle is a right triangle.

8. domain $= \{x \,|\, x \geq -200.9, x \in R\}$

9. $f(12) = f(3) + f(4) = x + y$
  $f(144) = f(12) + f(12) = (x + y) + (x + y)$
  $= 2(x + y)$

10. $(2, 0)$

11. 6 units^2

12. **a)** $24°$; $\frac{5}{11}$ **b)** -1

13. **a)** $23°$; $\frac{5}{12}$
  b) $\angle n = \angle m$ because they are corresponding angles.

14. **b)** $y = 4, -4$
  c) $3, -3$
  d) a relation

Chapter 7 Linear Equations and Graphs

7.1 Slope-Intercept Form

1. **a)** $m = \frac{1}{2}$, y-intercept: -2
   b) $m = -4$, y-intercept: 3
   c) $m = 1$, y-intercept: 0
   d) $m = 0.75$, y-intercept: 3.5

2. **a)** $x - x + y = 7 - x$
   $$y = -x + 7$$
   $m = -1$, y-intercept: 7
   b) $y - 4x + 4x = 12 + 4x$
   $$y = 4x + 12$$
   $m = 4$, y-intercept: 12
   c) $5x - 5x + 2y = -5x + 10$
   $$2y = -5x + 10$$
   $$\frac{2y}{2} = \frac{-5x + 10}{2}$$
   $$y = \frac{-5}{2}x + 5$$
   $m = \frac{-5}{2}$, y-intercept: 5
   d) $x - 3y + 3y - 12 = 0 + 3y$
   $$x - 12 = 3y$$
   $$\frac{x - 12}{3} = \frac{3y}{3}$$
   $$\frac{1}{3}x - 4 = y$$
   $$y = \frac{1}{3}x - 4$$
   $m = \frac{1}{3}$, y-intercept: -4

3. **a)** $y = 4x - 1$ **b)** $y = \frac{-1}{2}x + 7$
   c) $y = \frac{2}{3}x - 2$ **d)** $y = 0.5x$
   e) $y = -5x + 1$ **f)** $y = x + \frac{4}{5}$

4. **a)**
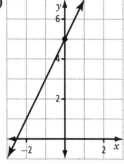

b)
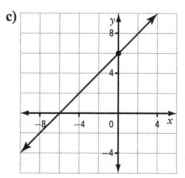

c)
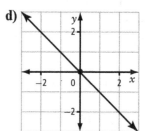

d)
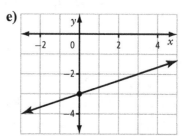

e)
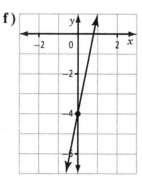

f)

5. a) $m = 1, b = 1, y = x + 1$

b) $m = -1, b = 4, y = -x + 4$

c) $m = \frac{2}{3}, b = 0, y = \frac{2}{3}x$

d) $m = -4, b = 2, y = -4x + 2$

e) $m = 0.6, b = -2, y = 0.6x - 2$

f) $m = \frac{-6}{5}, b = 6, y = \frac{-6}{5}x + 6$

6. a) Replace x with 12 and y with 8 in the equation $y = \frac{1}{2}x + b$.

$$y = \frac{1}{2}x + b$$
$$8 = \frac{1}{2}(12) + b$$

Solve for b.

$$8 = 6 + b$$
$$8 - 6 = 6 - 6 + b$$
$$2 = b$$

b) Replace x with -3 and y with $\frac{1}{2}$ in the equation $y = \frac{1}{2}x + b$.

$$y = \frac{1}{2}x + b$$
$$\frac{1}{2} = \frac{1}{2}(-3) + b$$

Solve for b.

$$\frac{1}{2} = \frac{-3}{2} + b$$
$$\frac{1}{2} + \frac{3}{2} = \frac{-3}{2} + \frac{3}{2} + b$$
$$\frac{4}{2} = b$$
$$2 = b$$

7. a) $m = 2$ **b)** $m = -4$

8. a) $y = 2x - 250$

b) $m = 2$; the price per raffle ticket

c) $b = -250$; the cost of the pair of hockey tickets

d) 275 tickets

9. a) $y = 75x - 600$

b) $255 loss; $525 profit; $1275 profit

c) 8 competitors

10. a) $25

b) $y = 15x + 25$

c) $b = 25$, which represents the fixed charge

d) discrete because rental is charged per whole hour

11. a)

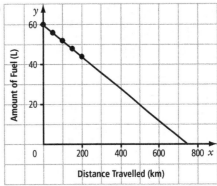

b) Substitute two points on the line, for example, $(0, 60)$ and $(50, 56)$, into the slope formula:

$$m = \frac{y_2 - y_1}{x_2 - x_1}$$
$$m = \frac{56 - 60}{50 - 0}$$
$$m = \frac{-4}{50}$$
$$m = \frac{-2}{25}$$

The line intersects the y-axis at 60, so $b = 60$.

c) Replace m with $\frac{-2}{25}$ and b with 60 in the slope-intercept form: $y = \frac{-2}{25}x + 60$.

d) The amount of fuel in the car's tank before driving any distance.

e) The tank is empty when $y = 0$. Replace y with 0 and solve for x:

$$y = \frac{-2}{25}x + 60$$
$$0 = \frac{-2}{25}x + 60$$
$$0 - 60 = \frac{-2}{25}x + 60 - 60$$
$$-60 = \frac{-2}{25}x$$
$$\left(\frac{-25}{2}\right)(-60) = \left(\frac{-25}{2}\right)\left(\frac{-2}{25}x\right)$$
$$750 = x$$

The tank will be empty after 750 km.

12. a)

Number of Programs	Cost of Printing ($)
0	200.00
50	212.50
100	225.00
150	237.50
200	250.00
250	262.50

b)

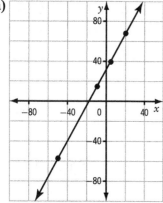

c) $m = \frac{1}{4}$; the cost of printing each program

d) $b = 200$; the fixed cost

e) $y = \frac{1}{4}x + 200$

f) 600 programs

13. a)

b) Use two points from the table to find the slope: $(20, 68)$ and $(-10, 14)$.

$$m = \frac{y_2 - y_1}{x_2 - x_1}$$
$$m = \frac{14 - 68}{-10 - 20}$$
$$m = \frac{-54}{-30}$$
$$m = \frac{9}{5}$$

c) $b = 32$, which represents the temperature in Fahrenheit when the temperature is 0 °C.

d) Replace m with $\frac{9}{5}$ and b with 32 in the slope-intercept form: $y = \frac{9}{5}x + 32$.

e) In the equation $y = \frac{9}{5}x + 32$, replace y with x and x with y. Then, solve for y.

$$x = \frac{9}{5}y + 32$$
$$x - 32 = \frac{9}{5}y + 32 - 32$$
$$x - 32 = \frac{9}{5}y$$
$$\frac{5}{9}(x - 32) = \left(\frac{5}{9}\right)\left(\frac{9}{5}y\right)$$
$$\frac{5}{9}x - \frac{160}{9} = y$$

f) Use the $y = \frac{9}{5}x + 32$ form of the equation, replacing x with -40.

$$y = \frac{9}{5}x + 32$$
$$y = \frac{9}{5}(-40) + 32$$
$$y = -72 + 32$$
$$y = -40$$
$$-40 \,°C = -40 \,°F$$

Use the $y = \frac{5}{9}x - \frac{160}{9}$ form of the equation, replacing x with 100.

$$y = \frac{5}{9}(100) - \frac{160}{9}$$
$$y = 37.8$$
$$100 \,°F = 37.8 \,°C$$

Use the $y = \frac{9}{5}x + 32$ form of the equation, replacing x with 0.

$$y = \frac{9}{5}x + 32$$
$$y = \frac{9}{5}(0) + 32$$
$$y = 32$$
$$0 \,°C = 32 \,°F$$

14. 80 people

15. a) Example:

x	y
0	12
-3	0
-2	4
-1	8

b) The slope is 4 and the y-intercept is (0, 12).

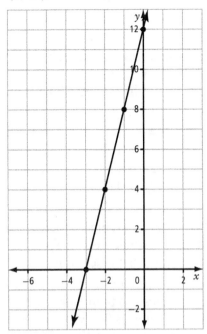

c) Example: I prefer using the slope and y-intercept. There is less computation involved when writing the equation in slope-intercept form. It is simple to graph the line using the slope and the y-intercept.

7.2 General Form

1. a) $x - 3y + 15 = 0$ **b)** $2x + 7y = 0$
   c) $8y - 1 = 0$ **d)** $2x + 10y - 12 = 0$

2. a) (4, 0), (0, −8)

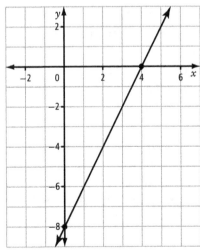

b) (0, 0)

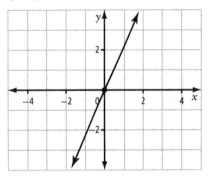

c) (4, 0), no y-intercept

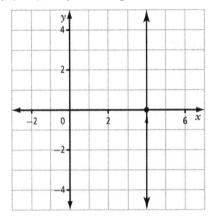

d) no x-intercept, $(0, \frac{-1}{2})$

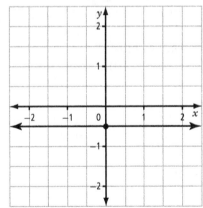

3. a) domain: $x \in R$; range: $y \in R$

To find the slope, use the points $(0, 4)$ and $(3, 0)$.

$$m = \frac{y_2 - y_1}{x_2 - x_1}$$
$$m = \frac{4 - 0}{0 - 3}$$
$$m = \frac{-4}{3}$$

The x-intercept is $(3, 0)$ and the y-intercept is $(0, 4)$.

In the slope-intercept form, replace m with $\frac{-4}{3}$ and b with 4:

$$y = \frac{-4}{3}x + 4.$$

Multiply both sides of the equation by 3:

$$3y = 3\left(\frac{-4}{3}x + 4\right)$$
$$3y = -4x + 12$$

Bring all terms to one side of the equation:

$$3y = -4x + 12$$
$$3y + 4x = -4x + 4x + 12$$
$$4x + 3y = 12$$
$$4x + 3y - 12 = 12 - 12$$
$$4x + 3y - 12 = 0$$

b) domain: $x \in R$; range: $y = -3$

Since this is a horizontal line, the slope is 0.

The y-intercept is $(0, -3)$.

The equation of the line in general form is $y + 3 = 0$.

4. Examples:

a) $y + 5 = 0$ **b)** $x + 0 = 0$

c) $x - 8 = 0$ **d)** $3x - 7y = 0$

e) $x + y - 3 = 0$

5. a) $B = -1$ **b)** $A = 4$

c) $C = 0$

6. a) Let $14x$ represent the number of calories burned swimming for x minutes. Let $12y$ represent the number of calories burned biking for y minutes. The equation to represent the total number of calories burned is $14x + 12y = 4200$.

b) To find the x-intercept, replace y with 0.

$$14x + 12y = 4200$$
$$14x + 12(0) = 4200$$
$$14x = 4200$$
$$x = 300$$

The x-intercept represents how many minutes he would need to spend swimming if he burned 4200 calories by only swimming.

To find the y-intercept, replace x with 0.

$$14x + 12y = 4200$$
$$14(0) + 12y = 4200$$
$$12y = 4200$$
$$y = 350$$

The y-intercept represents how many minutes he would need to spend biking if he did not spend any time swimming.

c) The domain is $0 \le x \le 300$. There can be no values less than 0 or greater than 300. The range is $0 \le y \le 350$. There can be no values less than 0 or greater than 350.

d) Replace y with 120 and solve for x.

$$14x + 12y = 4200$$
$$14x + 12(120) = 4200$$
$$14x + 1440 = 4200$$
$$14x + 1440 - 1440 = 4200 - 1440$$
$$14x = 2760$$
$$x = 197$$

He would need to swim 197 minutes, or 3 hours and 17 minutes.

7. a) $5x + 2y - 2250 = 0$

b) $m = \frac{-5}{2}$; $(450, 0)$ and $(0, 1125)$; domain: $0 \le x \le 450$, range: $0 \le y \le 1125$

c) 400 minutes, or 6 hours and 40 minutes

8. 108 square units

9. Examples:

a) $(-4, 1)$ and $(6, 4)$, $3x - 10y + 22 = 0$

b) $(2, 8)$ and $(7, 8)$, $y - 8 = 0$

c) $(-2, -1)$ and $(6, -4)$, $3x + 8y + 14 = 0$

d) $(-3.5, 6)$ and $(-3.5, -2)$, $2x + 7 = 0$

7.3 Slope-Point Form

1. a) $m = 4$, $(3, -7)$

   b) $m = \frac{1}{3}$, $(-5, 5)$

   c) $m = -2$, $(6, 0)$

   d) $m = 1$, $(3, -1)$

2. a) $y = \frac{2}{3}x + \frac{11}{3}$; $2x - 3y + 11 = 0$

   b) $y = -2x - 2$; $2x + y + 2 = 0$

   c) $y = \frac{3}{4}x - 3$; $3x - 4y - 12 = 0$

   d) $y = 3x + 19$; $3x - y + 19 = 0$

3. a) For slope-point form, replace m with $\frac{4}{3}$ and (x_1, y_1) with $(-1, -5)$:

$$y - y_1 = m(x - x_1)$$
$$(y + 5) = \frac{4}{3}(x + 1)$$

For slope-intercept form, rewrite $(y + 5) = \frac{4}{3}(x + 1)$ in the form $y = mx + b$:

$$(y + 5) = \frac{4}{3}(x + 1)$$
$$y + 5 = \frac{4}{3}x + \frac{4}{3}$$
$$y + 5 - 5 = \frac{4}{3}x + \frac{4}{3} - 5$$
$$y = \frac{4}{3}x - \frac{11}{3}$$

For general form, rewrite $y = \frac{4}{3}x - \frac{11}{3}$ in the form $Ax + By + C = 0$:

$$3y = 3\left(\frac{4}{3}x - \frac{11}{3}\right)$$
$$3y = 4x - 11$$
$$3y - 3y = 4x - 3y - 11$$
$$0 = 4x - 3y - 11$$

   b) Slope-point form: $(y + 3) = 1\left(x + \frac{1}{2}\right)$

Slope-intercept form: $y = x - \frac{5}{2}$

General form: $0 = 2x - 2y - 5$

   c) Slope-point form: $(y - 4) = -1.5(x - 1)$

Slope-intercept form: $y = -1.5x + 5.5$

General form: $0 = 15x + 10y - 55$

   d) Slope-point form:

First find the slope of the line through the points $(-5, -8)$ and $(-7, -9)$.

$$m = \frac{y_2 - y_1}{x_2 - x_1}$$
$$m = \frac{-9 - (-8)}{-7 - (-5)}$$
$$m = \frac{1}{2}$$

Then, replace m with $\frac{1}{2}$ and (x_1, y_1) with $(-5, -8)$ in the slope-point form.

$$y - y_1 = m(x - x_1)$$
$$(y + 8) = \frac{1}{2}(x + 5)$$

Slope-intercept form:

$$y = \frac{1}{2}x - \frac{11}{2}$$

General form:

$$y = \frac{1}{2}x - \frac{11}{2}$$
$$2y = 2\left(\frac{1}{2}x - \frac{11}{2}\right)$$
$$2y = x - 11$$
$$2y - 2y = x - 2y - 11$$
$$0 = x - 2y - 11$$

   e) Slope-point form: $(y + 2) = \frac{1}{2}(x + 1)$

Slope-intercept form: $y = \frac{1}{2}x - \frac{3}{2}$

General form: $0 = x - 2y - 3$

4. Examples:

   a) $y - 2 = \frac{1}{2}(x - 6)$

   b) $y - 2 = -1(x - 2)$

   c) $y + 5 = \frac{-4}{3}(x - 2)$

5. a) $y - 1 = 0(x + 3)$; $y - 1 = 0$

   b) $y - 8 = 2(x + 1)$; $2x - y + 10 = 0$

   c) The slope of the line $5x + 2y - 10$ is $-\frac{5}{2}$. So, the second line must have this same slope. Since it passes through the point $(-1, 4)$, the equation of the second line in slope-point form is $y - 4 = \frac{-5}{2}(x + 1)$. To convert this to general form, move all terms to the left side of the equation:

$$y - 4 = \frac{-5}{2}(x + 1)$$
$$y - 4 = \frac{-5}{2}x - \frac{5}{2}$$
$$(2)(y - 4) = (2)\left(\frac{-5}{2}x - \frac{5}{2}\right)$$
$$2y - 8 = -5x - 5$$
$$2y - 8 + 5 = -5x - 5 + 5$$
$$2y - 3 = -5x$$
$$5x + 2y - 3 = -5x + 5x$$
$$5x + 2y - 3 = 0$$

   d) $y + 6 = \frac{-5}{2}(x - 2)$; $5x + 2y + 2 = 0$

   e) $y - 3 = \frac{3}{5}(x - 0)$; $3x - 5y + 15 = 0$

   f) $y - 0 = \frac{-3}{2}(x - 0)$; $3x + 2y = 0$

6. Write the equation of the line with x-intercept (10, 0) and y-intercept (0, −5). Find the slope.

$$m = \frac{y_2 - y_1}{x_2 - x_1}$$

$$m = \frac{-5 - 0}{0 - 10}$$

$$m = \frac{-5}{-10}$$

$$m = \frac{1}{2}$$

Substitute $m = \frac{1}{2}$ and $b = -5$ into the slope-intercept form: $y = \frac{1}{2}x - 5$.

Replace x with −2 and y with −6.

$$y = \frac{1}{2}x - 5$$

$$-6 = \frac{1}{2}(-2) - 5$$

$$-6 = -1 - 5$$

$$-6 = -6$$

Since replacing x with −2 and y with −6 in the equation of the line results in a true statement, the point (−2, −6) is on the line.

7.

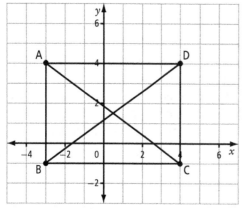

AC: $5x + 7y - 13 = 0$
BD: $5x - 7y + 8 = 0$

8. The x-intercept is (−6, 0) and the y-intercept is (0, 4).

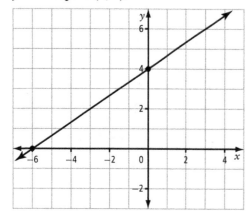

9. $k = 1$

10. a) Lines 3 and 4   **b)** Line 5
    c) Lines 1 and 2

11. a)

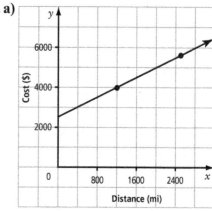

b) $m = \frac{5}{4}$, which represents the cost of operating a snowmobile per mile
c) $b = 2500$; the fixed cost of operating a snowmobile
d) $5x - 4y + 10\,000 = 0$
e) \$3625

12. a) $5x - 2y - 52 = 0$
    b) 2.5 cm/h; at 1400 hours it was 21 cm tall
    c) rate of burn per hour
    d) the height at 1400 hours

13. Rewrite each equation in slope-intercept form. Enter the equations into a graphing calculator or graphing program and read the intersection points, which are the vertices.

Line 1:

$$2x + 3y - 18 = 0$$
$$2x - 2x + 3y - 18 = 0 - 2x$$
$$3y - 18 = -2x$$
$$3y - 18 + 18 = -2x + 18$$
$$3y = -2x + 18$$
$$\frac{3y}{3} = \frac{-2x}{3} + \frac{18}{3}$$
$$y = \frac{-2x}{3} + 6$$

Line 2:

$$5x + y + 7 = 0$$
$$5x - 5x + y + 7 = 0 - 5x$$
$$y + 7 = -5x$$
$$y + 7 - 7 = -5x - 7$$
$$y = -5x - 7$$

Line 3:
$$3x - 2y - 14 = 0$$
$$3x - 3x - 2y - 14 = 0 - 3x$$
$$-2y - 14 = -3x$$
$$-2y - 14 + 14 = -3x + 14$$
$$-2y = -3x + 14$$
$$\frac{-2y}{-2} = \frac{-3x}{-2} + \frac{14}{-2}$$
$$y = \frac{3x}{2} - 7$$

Enter the equations into a graphing calculator or graphing program.

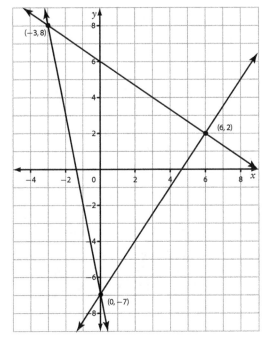

The vertices of the triangle are $(-3, 8)$, $(0, -7)$, and $(6, 2)$.

14. a) $3x - 4y + 24 = 0$

b) The x-intercept is $(-8, 0)$ and the y-intercept is $(0, 6)$. The denominator of the x-term in the original equation is the x-intercept. The denominator of the y-term in the original equation is the y-intercept.

c) Example: Predict that the x-intercept is $(3, 0)$ and the y-intercept is $(0, -5)$. Verify by replacing y with 0 and solving for x to find the x-intercept.
$$\frac{x}{3} - \frac{y}{5} = 1$$
$$\frac{x}{3} - \frac{0}{5} = 1$$
$$\frac{x}{3} = 1$$
$$x = 3$$

Therefore, the x-intercept is $(3, 0)$.
Verify by replacing x with 0 and solving for y to find the y-intercept.
$$\frac{x}{3} - \frac{y}{5} = 1$$
$$\frac{0}{3} - \frac{y}{5} = 1$$
$$0 - \frac{y}{5} = 1$$
$$\frac{-y}{5} = 1$$
$$y = -5$$

Therefore, the y-intercept is $(0, -5)$.
The above shows that the prediction was correct.

15. a) Example: $y - 1.4 = -\frac{31}{90}(x - 2010)$
b) in the year 2014

7.4 Parallel and Perpendicular Lines

1. a) perpendicular   **b)** parallel
   c) perpendicular   **d)** perpendicular
   e) perpendicular   **f)** parallel

2. a) parallel: -3; perpendicular: $\frac{1}{3}$
   b) parallel: 1; perpendicular: -1
   c) parallel: -4; perpendicular: $\frac{1}{4}$
   d) parallel: 0; perpendicular: undefined
   e) parallel: $\frac{5}{2}$; perpendicular: $\frac{-2}{5}$

3. a) $n = 4$ **b)** $n = -2$
   c) $n = 2.5$ **d)** $n = \frac{3}{2}$

4. a) $r = -2$ **b)** $r = 15$
   c) $r = -18$ **d)** $r = 8$

5. a) $5x + y - 7 = 0$ **b)** $x + 3y + 4 = 0$
   c) $x + y - 4 = 0$

6. a) $2x + y - 5 = 0$ **b)** $4x + 7y = 0$
   c) $2x - y - 12 = 0$

7. a) $\frac{1}{2}, \frac{1}{2}$
   b) no, the equations represent the same line

8. a) $x - 5y - 31 = 0$ **b)** $3x - y + 10 = 0$

9. $y - 15 = 0$

10. a) The slope of side MN is $-\frac{4}{3}$, the slope of side NC is $\frac{-7}{5}$, and the slope of side MC is $\frac{-3}{2}$. Since no two slopes have a product of -1, these points do not represent the vertices of a right triangle.

b) The slope of DF is $\frac{1}{2}$, the slope of FG is $\frac{-4}{7}$, and the slope of DG is -2. Since the product of the slopes of sides DF and DG is -1, the points represent the vertices of a right triangle.

11. Examples:

a) Find the slope of $4x + y - 11 = 0$ by writing the equation in slope-intercept form, $y = mx + b$:
$$4x + y - 11 = 0$$
$$4x - 4x + y - 11 = 0 - 4x$$
$$y - 11 = -4x$$
$$y - 11 + 11 = -4x + 11$$
$$y = -4x + 11$$
The slope is -4.

Any line with the same slope but a different y-intercept will be parallel to the given line. Example, $y = -4x + 16$. An infinite number of equations can be written in the form $y = mx + b$, where $m = -4$ and $b \ne 11$.

b) A line perpendicular to $4x + y - 11 = 0$ has a slope that is the negative reciprocal of -4, or $\frac{1}{4}$. Example, $y = \frac{1}{4}x - 6$.

Any line with a slope of $\frac{1}{4}$ will be perpendicular to the given line, regardless of the y-intercept. There is an infinite number of these lines.

12. $12x + y - 3 = 0$

13. The line must have a slope of $\frac{-1}{2}$ and a y-intercept of 0.

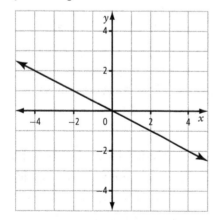

14. $k = -4$

15. $k = -4$

16. $k = \frac{7}{6}$

17. **a)** Write the equation in slope-intercept form:
$$kx - 2y - 1 = 0$$
$$kx - kx - 2y - 1 = 0 - kx$$
$$-2y - 1 = -kx$$
$$-2y - 1 + 1 = -kx + 1$$
$$-2y = -kx + 1$$
$$\frac{-2y}{-2} = \frac{-kx}{-2} + \frac{1}{-2}$$
$$y = \frac{kx}{2} - \frac{1}{2}$$
Therefore, the slope of the first line is $\frac{k}{2}$.
$$8x - ky + 3 = 0$$
$$8x - 8x - ky + 3 = 0 - 8x$$
$$-ky + 3 = -8x$$
$$-ky + 3 - 3 = -8x - 3$$
$$-ky = -8x - 3$$
$$\frac{-ky}{-k} = \frac{-8x}{-k} - \frac{3}{-k}$$
$$y = \frac{8x}{k} + \frac{3}{k}$$

The slope of the second line is $\frac{8}{k}$.

Since the lines are parallel, the slopes must be equal. Set the two slopes equal to each other and solve for k.
$$\frac{k}{2} = \frac{8}{k}$$
$$k^2 = 16$$
$$k = \sqrt{16}$$
$$k = \pm 4$$

The values of k are 4 and -4.

b) Since the lines are perpendicular, the slope must have a product of -1.
$$\left(\frac{k}{2}\right)\left(\frac{8}{k}\right) = -1$$
$$\frac{8k}{2k} = -1$$
$$4 \ne 1$$

Therefore, there are no values of k that will work.

18. **a)** $y - 1 = 0$
b) $x + 2y - 4 = 0$

19. Example:

$7x + 9y - 82 = 0, 7x + 9y + 48 = 0,$
$9x - 7y + 6 = 0, 9x - 7y + 136 = 0$

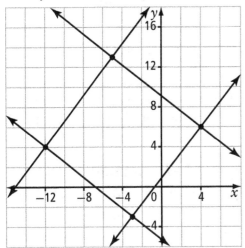

Chapter 7 Review

7.1 Slope-Intercept Form

1. **a)** $m = \frac{3}{2}; b = -2; y = \frac{3}{2}x - 2$

b) $m = -1; b = 5; y = -x + 5$

c) $m = \frac{-1}{6}; b = 1; y = \frac{-1}{6}x + 1$

d) $m = 3; b = -4; y = 3x - 4$

2. $b = 8$

3. If the line $y = mx - 8$ passes through the point $(-2, 6)$, replace x with -2 and y with 6. Solve for m.

$$y = mx - 8$$
$$6 = m(-2) - 8$$
$$6 = -2m - 8$$
$$6 + 8 = -2m - 8 + 8$$
$$14 = -2m$$
$$\frac{14}{-2} = \frac{-2m}{-2}$$
$$-7 = m$$

4. **a)** $y = 0.25x + 500$

b)

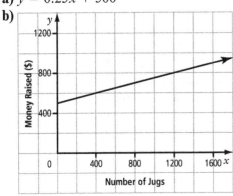

c) $m = 0.25; b = 500$; the slope represents the redemption value per jug; the y-intercept represents the amount of money already raised

d) 1400 jugs

7.2 General Form

5. **a)** $x + 2y + 18 = 0$ **b)** $2x - 3y + 6 = 0$

c) $x + y + 3 = 0$

6. **a)** y-intercept is $(0, 4)$; x-intercept is $(2, 0)$

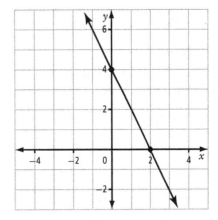

b) y-intercept is $(0, 5)$; x-intercept is $(-4, 0)$

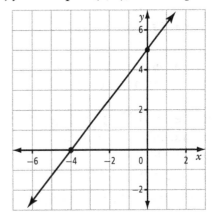

7. **a)** $60x + 10y - 4200 = 0$

b) x-intercept is $(70, 0)$, y-intercept is $(0, 420)$; The x-intercept represents the number of days of growth under ideal conditions to reach a height of 42 m. The y-intercept represents the number of days of growth under less than ideal condition to reach a height of 42 m.

c) $0 \le x \le 70, 0 \le y \le 420$

d) 90 days

7.3 Slope-Point Form

8. $y + 5 = 2(x + 6)$; $2x - y + 7 = 0$

9. $y - 4 = 8(x - 0)$; $8x - y + 4 = 0$

10. a) Example:
Use the points $(8570, 3)$ and $(5570, 12)$ to find the slope:

$$m = \frac{y_2 - y_1}{x_2 - x_1}$$

$$m = \frac{12 - 3}{5570 - 8570}$$

$$m = \frac{9}{-3000}$$

$$m = \frac{-3}{1000}$$

Choose the point $(8570, 3)$. Write the equation in slope-point form:

$$y - 3 = \frac{-3}{1000}(x - 8570)$$

b) Replace x with 6500, and solve for y:

$$y - 3 = \frac{-3}{1000}(x - 8570)$$

$$y - 3 = \frac{-3}{1000}(6500 - 8570)$$

$$y - 3 = \frac{-3}{1000}(-2070)$$

$$y - 3 = 6.21$$

$$y - 3 + 3 = 6.21 + 3$$

$$y = 9.21$$

The temperature at the base of Eagle Chair is approximately 9 °F.

7.4 Parallel and Perpendicular Lines

11. a) perpendicular   **b)** parallel
c) perpendicular

12. $x + 2y - 12 = 0$

13. Find the slope of the line through the points $(-1, 3)$ and $(2, 1)$.

$$m = \frac{y_2 - y_1}{x_2 - x_1}$$

$$m = \frac{1 - 3}{2 - (-1)}$$

$$m = \frac{-2}{3}$$

The negative reciprocal of $\frac{-2}{3}$ is $\frac{3}{2}$. The x-intercept is $(-4, 0)$. Place these values in the slope-point form of the equation of a line:

$$y - 0 = \frac{3}{2}(x - (-4))$$

$$y = \frac{3}{2}x + 6$$

Multiply the equation by 2:

$$2y = 2\left(\frac{3}{2}x + 6\right)$$

$$2y = 3x + 12$$

Write in general form.

$$2y - 2y = 3x - 2y + 12$$

$$0 = 3x - 2y + 12$$

14. All of the lines have a slope of $\frac{-2}{3}$ and all of the lines have different intercepts, therefore, the equations represent parallel lines.

Chapters 1–7 Cumulative Review

1. a) $m = -7$; $b = 10$ **b)** $m = \frac{-9}{2}$; $b = \frac{15}{2}$

2. a) 1277.4 cm^2 **b)** 57.6 m^2

3.

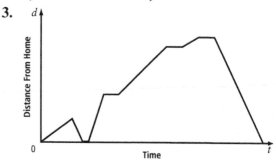

4. a) 8   **b)** 9
c) 30

5. a) $(x + 12)(x + 1)$
b) $3(2m - n)(m - n)$
c) $(3x + y)(5x - y)$
d) $2t(s - 3)(s + 2)$
e) $(c - 9)(c + 9)$
f) $(x - 4)(x + 4)(x - 3)(x + 3)$
g) $(1 - 2y)(1 + 2y)(1 + 4y)^2$
h) $7(2h - 11f)(2h + 11f)$

6. a) $31n^2 - 13n - 50$
b) $-8s^4 + 16s^3 + 20s^2 - 13s - 3$

7. 17.5 cm

8. a) Example: amount of gasoline (L) = g, dependent variable; distance (km) = d, independent variable
b) Example: $(0, 0)$, $(50, 6.9)$, $(100, 13.8)$, $(150, 20.7)$, $(200, 27.6)$, $(250, 34.5)$
c) The relation is continuous because vehicles can travel for a fraction of a kilometre.

d)

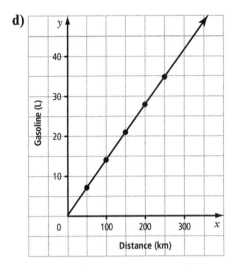

Distance (km)

e) The relation is linear because the amount of gas used is constant with the number of kilometres driven.

9. a) x-intercept $(-7, 0)$; y-intercept does not exist

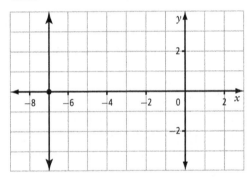

b) x-intercept $(0.5, 0)$; y-intercept $(0, -2)$

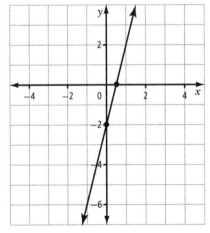

10. a) 878.9 mg   **b)** 3686.4 kg

11. a) $2ac$ **b)** $1 - 4s$
  c) $3z^2 - 2x$

12. a) $\angle C = 63°$; AB $= 16.49$ km; BC $= 18.50$ km
  b) DE $= 10.96$ m; $\angle D = 56.14°$; $\angle F = 33.84°$

13. a) $y - 4 = -3(x + 5)$; $y = -3x - 11$; $y + 3x + 11 = 0$
  b) $y - 2 = \frac{1}{2}(x + 3)$; $y = \frac{1}{2}x + \frac{1}{2}$; $x + 2y - 1 = 0$

14. AC $= 37.5$ cm

15. a) $\dfrac{1}{x^{\frac{2}{15}}}$ **b)** $\dfrac{1}{27h^6}$

  c) $8^{\frac{23}{20}}$ **d)** $64x^9$

16. 2787 m; 1.6 km; 2865 m

17. a) 1006.72 cm^2 **b)** 7585 cm^2
  c) 78.54 cm^2 **d)** 431.97 cm^2
  e) 38.62 cm^2

18. 44.2 mi

19. a) $\sqrt[3]{3^2}$ **b)** $\sqrt{16}$

  c) $\sqrt{\left(\dfrac{y^3}{x^5}\right)^3}$

20. a) Domain
    Words: all real numbers between -4 and 4, not inclusive
    Interval Notation: $(-4, 4)$
    Set Notation: $\{x \mid -4 < x < 4, x \in R\}$
    Range
    Words: all real numbers between 4 and 8, not inclusive
    Interval Notation: $(4, 8)$
    Set Notation: $\{y \mid 4 < y < 8, y \in R\}$
  b) Domain
    Words: all real numbers
    Interval Notation: $(-\infty, \infty)$
    Set Notation: $\{x \mid -\infty < x < \infty\ x \in R\}$
    Range
    Words: all real numbers
    Interval Notation: $(-\infty, \infty)$
    Set Notation: $\{y \mid -\infty < y < \infty, y \in R\}$

21. 118.3 m

22. 0.5 m^3

23. a) $-\dfrac{2}{3}$
  b) 3

24. 25%

25. $y = 2x + 16$

Chapter 7 Extend It Further

1. D

The shortest distance between a point and a line is the length of the line segment that passes through the point and runs perpendicular to the original line. The given line in this question is $2x + 5y = 10$, or $y = \frac{-2}{5}x + 2$ in slope-intercept form. The line has a slope of $\frac{-2}{5}$. The perpendicular line has a slope of $\frac{5}{2}$ and, since it passes through the origin, its equation is $y = \frac{5}{2}x$. The point where the two lines intersect is the point on the original line that is closest to the origin.

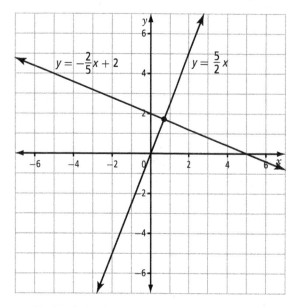

To find the intersection point, first find a value of x that lies on both lines:

$$\frac{-2}{5}x + 2 = \frac{5}{2}x$$
$$(5)\left(\frac{-2}{5}x + 2\right) = (5)\frac{5}{2}x$$
$$-2x + 10 = \frac{25}{2}x$$
$$(2)(-2x + 10) = (2)\frac{25}{2}x$$
$$-4x + 20 = 25x$$
$$-4x + 4x + 20 = 25x + 4x$$
$$20 = 29\,x$$
$$\frac{20}{29} = x$$

Substitute this value into the equation for either of the lines to find the y-coordinate:

$$y = \frac{5}{2}\left(\frac{20}{29}\right)$$
$$y = \frac{100}{58}$$
$$y = \frac{50}{29}$$

So, the point on the line that is closest to the origin is $\left(\frac{20}{29}, \frac{50}{29}\right)$.

2. B

3. D

4. Let $A(a, 0)$, $B(0, b)$, and $C(0, 0)$ be the three vertices. It follows that the midpoint M has coordinates $\left(\frac{a}{2}, \frac{b}{2}\right)$. Using the Pythagorean relation or the midpoint formula,

$$MA = \sqrt{\left(\frac{a}{2} - a\right)^2 + \left(\frac{b}{2} - 0\right)^2} = \sqrt{\frac{a^2}{4} + \frac{b^2}{4}}$$

$$MB = \sqrt{\left(\frac{a}{2} - 0\right)^2 + \left(\frac{b}{2} - b\right)^2} = \sqrt{\frac{a^2}{4} + \frac{b^2}{4}}$$

$$MC = \sqrt{\left(\frac{a}{2} - 0\right)^2 + \left(\frac{b}{2} - 0\right)^2} = \sqrt{\frac{a^2}{4} + \frac{b^2}{4}}$$

5. a) $A = 3$ and $B = 4$
   b) $s = -1505$

6. a) the slope of the line becomes more steep
   b) the slope of the line becomes less steep
   c) the line shifts upward, parallel to the first line
   d) the line shifts downward, parallel to the first line

7. a) $F - 32 = \frac{9}{5}C$
   b) $-40\ ^\circ\text{F}$

8. a) $y = \frac{3}{4}x + \frac{9}{4}$
   b) The y-intercept represents the base fare when you enter the taxi.

9. a) $<, >$ **b)** $>, >$
10. a) $<, <$ **b)** $<, >$

Unit 3 Review

1. A
2. C
3. D
4. C
5. B
6. B
7. B
8. D
9. C
10. B
11. A
12. A
13. $20.00 per ticket
14. 3
15. 2
16. 20
17. 21
18. 8
19. $8x + 5y - 1 = 0$

20. a) $y = 2.5x - 150$
    b) slope is 2.5; price of a single bar
    c) y-intercept is -150; initial expenses
    d) 60 bars

21. a) $y = -\frac{3}{2}x - 2$
    b) $3x + 2y + 4 = 0$
    c) use the x-intercept and y-intercept to graph; use a table of values

22. a)

Number of Songs	Cost ($)
1	0.49
2	0.98
3	1.47
4	1.96
5	2.45

   b) function; each number of songs downloaded results in a unique cost
   c) $C = 0.49s$
   d) discrete; the domain must be natural numbers

Chapter 8 Solving Systems of Linear Equations Graphically

8.1 Systems of Linear Equations and Graphs

1. a) $y = -x + 6$

$y = \frac{2}{3}x - \frac{2}{3}$

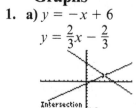

The point of intersection is (4, 2).

b) $y = \frac{1}{4}x + \frac{1}{2}$

$y = -x - 5$

The point of intersection is $\left(-\frac{22}{5}, -\frac{3}{5}\right)$.

c) $y = -\frac{3}{4}x$

$y = x + 7$

The point of intersection is $(-4, 3)$.

2. a) yes   **b)** no

3. a) $y = -2x + 5$

$y = -\frac{1}{2}x + 2$

The point of intersection is (2, 1).

b) $d = 3.5t$

$d = 1.5t + 10$

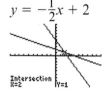

The point of intersection is (5, 17.5).

4. a) table of values for $y = 8x - 3$

x	−1	0	1	2
y	−11	−3	5	13

table of values for $y = 2x + 3$

x	−2	−1	0	1
y	−1	1	3	5

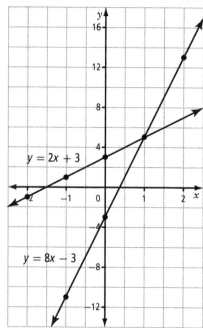

solution is (1, 5)
The solution (1, 5) can be verified by substitution.

$y = 8x - 3$

Left Side	Right Side
y	$8x - 3$
$= 5$	$= 8(1) - 3$
	$= 5$

Left Side = Right Side

$y = 2x + 3$

Left Side	Right Side
y	$2x + 3$
$= 5$	$= 2(1) + 3$
	$= 5$

Left Side = Right Side

b) table of values for $x - y = -2$

x	−1	0	1	3
y	1	2	3	5

table of values for $4x + y = 12$

x	0	1	2	3
y	12	8	4	0

c) table of values for $y = \frac{1}{2}x - 6$

x	−4	2	4	12
y	−8	−5	−4	0

table of values for $3x - y = -4$

x	−2	−1	0	2
y	−2	1	4	10

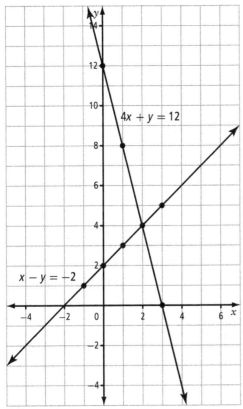

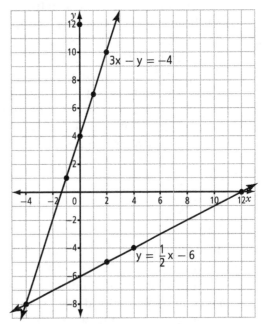

solution is $(2, 4)$
The solution $(2, 4)$ can be verified by substitution.
$x - y = -2$

Left Side	Right Side
$x - y$	-2
$= 2 - 4$	$= -2$
$= -2$	

   Left Side = Right Side
$4x + y = 12$

Left Side	Right Side
$4x + y$	12
$= 4(2) + 4$	$= 12$
$= 8 + 4$	
$= 12$	

   Left Side = Right Side

solution is $(-4, -8)$
The solution $(-4, -8)$ can be verified by substitution.
$y = \frac{1}{2}x - 6$

Left Side	Right Side
y	$\frac{1}{2}x - 6$
$= -8$	$= \frac{1}{2}(-4) - 6$
	$= -2 - 6$
	$= -8$

   Left Side = Right Side
$3x - y = -4$

Left Side	Right Side
$3x - y$	-4
$= 3(-4) - (-8)$	$= -4$
$= -12 + 8$	
$= -4$	

   Left Side = Right Side

5. a) $M = 10 + 0.5d$
$M = 5 + d$
b) Amounts of money are equal on day 10, when both have $15.

6. a) The initial volume of oil in the first tank is 125 m³. If the tank is being drained at the rate of 2.5 m³ per minute, the amount of oil remaining at any time is the initial amount less 2.5 times the number of minutes for which the tank has been emptied. Therefore, the amount of oil remaining in the first tank may be modelled by the equation $A = 125 - 2.5t$. Applying the same analysis in the case of the second tank yields the equation $A = 80 - t$ to model the amount of oil remaining in that tank. Thus, the system of linear equations to model this situation is $A = 125 - 2.5t$ and $A = 80 - t$.

b)

Intersection
X=30   Y=50

The point of intersection is (30, 50).

c) The point of intersection represents the time when the amounts of oil in the two tanks are equal and describes that amount. At the point (30, 50), both tanks have 50 m³ of oil in them. This occurs after 30 min of draining.

d) The tank containing 125 m³ of oil will drain first. From the graph you can see that the line of its equation intersects the x-axis first. At this point, $A = 0$, which means that the tank is empty.

Zero
X=50   Y=0

7. a) $a + c = 69$
$15a + 10c = 900$
b) $c = -a + 69$
$c = -1.5a + 90$
c) The point of intersection is (42, 27).
d) The point of intersection describes the numbers of both types of tickets sold: 42 adults' tickets and 27 children's tickets.

8. a) $V = 200 - 8t$
$V = 0 + 8t$
b) The point of intersection is (12.5, 100).
c) The volumes in both tanks are equal at 100 L in each.
d) 25 min
e) no

9. a) x-intercept = 8; x-intercept = −1
b) y-intercept = 4; y-intercept = 1
c) slope is 1; slope is $-\frac{1}{2}$
d) (2, 3)
e) $y = x + 1$; $y = -\frac{1}{2}x + 4$

10. a) $x + y = 62$
$\frac{1}{2}x = 1 + y$
b) Mr. Darwal is 42 years old. His daughter is 20 years old.

11. a) $d = 210t$
$d = 150t$
b) (0, 0)
c) 240 km farther

12. Since two points are given for each line, you can use the slope formula to calculate the slopes of the lines. Slope of the first line passing through points (1, 1) and (4, 7):
$$m = \frac{y_2 - y_1}{x_2 - x_1}$$
$$m = \frac{7 - 1}{4 - 1}$$
$$m = \frac{6}{3}$$
$$m = 2$$
Slope of the second line passing through the points (1, 6) and (3, 0):
$$m = \frac{y_2 - y_1}{x_2 - x_1}$$
$$m = \frac{0 - 6}{3 - 1}$$
$$m = -\frac{6}{2}$$
$$m = -3$$
Using slope-point form, write the equation of each line.
First line: Use the point (1, 1) and slope 2.
$$y - y_1 = m(x - x_1)$$
$$y - 1 = 2(x - 1)$$
$$y - 1 = 2x - 2$$
Isolate y to express the equation in slope-intercept form.

$$y - 1 = 2x - 2$$
$$y - 1 + 1 = 2x - 2 + 1$$
$$y = 2x - 1$$

The equation of the first line is $y = 2x - 1$.
Second line: Use the point $(3, 0)$ and slope -3.

$$y - y_1 = m(x - x_1)$$
$$y - 0 = -3 (x - 3)$$
$$y = -3x + 9$$

The equation of the second line is $y = -3x + 9$.
Graphing these lines produces a point of intersection at $(2, 3)$.

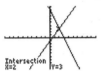

13. $-40°C = -40°F$

14. a) $d = 10t$
    $d = 40(1 - t)$
    or
    $d = 40t$
    $d = 10(1 - t)$

   b) The x-coordinate represents the time required to travel between Ferdinand's home and the school in one of the directions. The y-coordinate represents distance travelled.

   c) 0.2 h or 12 min; 0.8 h or 48 min

   d) 8 km

15. Yes, if lines are parallel they will have no point of intersection.

16. 8

17. In a parallelogram, opposite angles are equal and alternate interior angles are equal. Therefore, from the diagram you can see that $x + y = 35$ and $2x - y = 130$. Express the equations in slope-intercept form:

$x + y = 35$	$2x - y = 130$
$x + y - x = 35 - x$	$2x - y - 2x = 130 - 2x$
$y = 35 - x$	$-y = 130 - 2x$
$y = -x + 35$	$y = 2x - 130$

Graphing these produces two lines that intersect at $(55, -20)$.

Therefore, the value of x is 55 and the value of y is -20.

8.2 Modelling and Solving Linear Systems

1. a) $s = 3c$ and $s + 4 = 2(c + 4)$
   b) $V = 5 + 0.9t$ and $V = 3 + 1.2t$

2. a)

x	y	$x - y$
30	138	-108
50	118	-68
70	98	-28
80	88	-8
90	78	12
100	68	32

It can be inferred that $90 < x < 100$ and $68 < y < 78$.

   b) $x + y = 168$
        $x - y = 18$

   c)
$x + y = 168$	$x - y = 18$
$x + y - x = 168 - x$	$x - y - x = 18 - x$
$y = -x + 168$	$-y = 18 - x$
	$y = x - 18$

   d)

The point of intersection is $(93, 75)$.

   e) Yes, this confirms the inferences drawn from the values in the table in part a) because 93 is between 90 and 100, and 75 is between 68 and 78.

3. a) $x + y = 15\,000$
        $0.065x + 0.05y = 885$

   b) $y = -x + 15\,000$
        $y = -1.3x + 17\,700$

   c) The point of intersection is $(9000, 6000)$. Josee invested $9000 at 6.5% interest per year and invested $6000 at 5% interest per year.

4. a) $x + y = 5$
   b) $0.4x + 0.25y = 0.32(5)$
   c) $y = -x + 5$ and $y = -1.6x + 6.4$
   d) The point of intersection is $\left(\frac{7}{3}, \frac{8}{3}\right)$ or approximately (2.3, 2.7). The chemist needs about 2.3 L of 40% bromine solution and about 2.7 L of 25% bromine solution.

5. a) Answers may vary. Example:
   $l = 3w$

w	2	5	10	15	20
l	6	15	30	45	60

   $2l + 2w = 72$

w	2	5	10	20	30
l	34	31	26	16	6

   b)

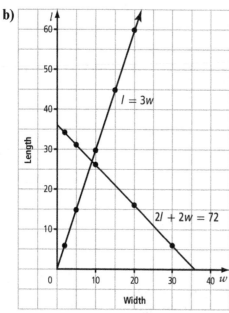

   From reading the graph, the point of intersection can be estimated to be about (8, 27).
   c) The actual point of intersection is (9, 27).
   d) The width of the rectangle is 9 m and its length is 27 m.

6. a) $c + p = 0.5$
   $12c + 3p = 0.5(5)$
   b) $p = -c + 0.5$
   $p = -4c + 0.8\overline{3}$
   c) The point of intersection is approximately (0.11, 0.39). The company should use 0.11 kg of cashews and 0.39 kg of peanuts per bag.

7. a) $A = 1200 - 20s$
   $A = 200 + 30s$
   b) 20 s after the time interval begins; 800 m

8. a) The first equation means that the difference in elevation between Mount Columbia and Cypress Hills is 2279 m. The second equation means that the sum of the elevations is 5215 m.
   b) $s = a - 2279$ and $s = -a + 5215$
   c) The point of intersection is (3747, 1468). Mount Columbia has an elevation of 3747 m and Cypress Hills has an elevation of 1468 m.

9. a) The first restaurant charges $175 for room rental and $20 per person. The second restaurant charges $100 for room rental and $22.50 per person.
   b) The point of intersection is (30, 775).
   c) The first restaurant is cheaper if there are more than 30 guests to a maximum of 100 guests: $30 < n \le 100$. The second restaurant is cheaper if there are fewer than 30 guests: $0 < n < 30$.

10. a) Driver B left one hour later than Driver A.
   b) Driver B
   c) Driver B has caught up to and passed Driver A.
   d)

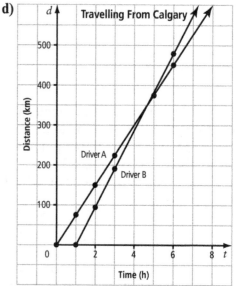

   From the graph, you can estimate that it takes approximately 5 h for the drivers to travel the same distance.

11. a) $2.5(s + c) = 50$; $4(s - c) = 50$

b) $s = -c + 20$; $s = c + 12.5$; the point of intersection is (3.75, 16.25).

c) The boat's speed is 16.25 km/h and the current's speed is 3.75 km/h.

12. a) One tank has 120 L. The other tank has 10 L.

b) The 120-L tank is draining and the 10-L tank is filling.

c) At 10 min, both tanks contain 90 L of water.

d) The slopes of the lines represent the rates at which the tanks are draining or filling. Use two points on each line and the slope formula to calculate slope. First line: Use points (0, 120) and (10, 90).

$$m = \frac{y_2 - y_1}{x_2 - x_1}$$

$$m = \frac{90 - 120}{10 - 0}$$

$$m = \frac{30}{10}$$

$$m = -3$$

The first tank is draining at a rate of 3 L/min.

Second line: Use points (0, 10) and (10, 90).

$$m = \frac{y_2 - y_1}{x_2 - x_1}$$

$$m = \frac{90 - 10}{10 - 0}$$

$$m = \frac{80}{10}$$

$$m = 8$$

The second tank is filling at a rate of 8 L/min.

e) $V = 120 - 3t$ and $V = 10 + 8t$

13. a) The point of intersection is (1, 70).

b) Company A will charge less.

c) A: $C = 45 + 25t$
B: $C = 30 + 40t$

14. Answers may vary. Example:

a) Charges for Company A are $100 for a sign-up fee and $18.50 per month. Charges for Company B are $75 to sign up, plus $20 per month. Which company should you choose?

b) A $900 deposit is put into two different investments. One part earns interest at a rate of 5% per year; the other earns interest at 4.5% per year. If total interest earned in one year is $74, how much money was invested at each rate?

c) One person is 8 years older than another. Five times the first person's age added to 9 times the other person's age totals 100 years. Find the age of each person.

15. Answers may vary. Examples are:
$x + y = 27$ and $x - y = -21$ or $y - 6x = 6$ and $3x + y = 33$

8.3 Number of Solutions for Systems of Linear Equations

1. a) no solution; lines have same slope and different y-intercepts

b) one solution; lines have different slopes

c) infinite number of solutions; lines are multiples of each other (same slope and same y-intercept)

d) no solution; lines have same slope and different y-intercepts

e) one solution; lines have different slopes

2. a) $2x - 3y = C$, $C \neq 8$

b) $x - 3y = 8$ or any other change to the coefficient of x or y

c) $4x - 6y = 16$ or any other multiple of the first equation

3. a) no solution

b) no solution

c) one solution

d) one solution

e) one solution

4. a) no solution

b) one solution

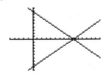

c) an infinite number of solutions

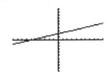

5. For a system of linear equations in the form $Ax + By = C$ and $Dx + Ey = F$:

  a) If the coefficients D, E, and F are the same multiple of coefficients A, B, and C, respectively, then there will be an infinite number of solutions.

  b) If coefficients D and E are the same multiple of coefficients A and B, respectively, but F is not this same multiple of C, then there will be no solution.

  c) In all other cases, there will be one solution.

6. **a)** $7x - 3y = C$, $C \neq 12$

  b) $14x - 6y = 24$ or any other multiple of the given equation

  c) Example: $7x - 3y = 12$. Only coefficient A in the equation of the second line has to be different as that is the number that dictates the slope.

7. Jocelyn: $E = 1200 + 0.03s$;
Mario: $E = 1000 + 0.045s$;
Kendra: $E = 2000 + 0.03s$;
Pavel: $E = 2000 + 0.03s$

  a) Jocelyn and Kendra or Jocelyn and Pavel

  b) Kendra and Pavel

  c) Jocelyn and Mario, or Mario and Kendra, or Mario and Pavel

8. **a)** $C = 20 + 0.35t$
$C = 15 + 0.4t$

  b) $C = 20 + 0.35t$
$C = 15 + 0.35t$

  c) $C = 20 + 0.35t$
$C = 20 + 0.35t$

9. **a)** Ling is correct. The slopes are similar, but the lines are not parallel and will intersect at (37.5, 25). Since the slopes of the lines are different, the system must have one solution.

  b) The system can be solved by comparing coefficients. Because the left sides of the equations are identical, any value of y that is substituted will result in the same value on the left side of each equation. However, only one value of x (37.5) will yield equivalent values on the right side of the equations. Therefore, the system has only one solution.

10. **a)** Gold Coast: $E = 1.25k - 40$; The Salmon House: $E = 1.00k - 25$

  b) one solution

  c) The point of intersection is (60, 35). A fisher should bring a catch to The Salmon House when $k < 60$ kg because of the lower processing fee and to Gold Coast Fishery when $k > 60$ kg because of the higher rate of pay per kilogram.

  d) There would be no point of intersection and The Salmon House would be the better choice regardless of the size of the catch.

11. **a)** $C \neq 60$

  b) $C = 60$

12. **a)** $A = 1$

  b) $A \neq 1$

13. **a)** $h = 5w$ and $h = 6w - 24$

  b) one solution

  c) (24, 120); The solution represents the time when both towers are the same height. Each tower will be 120 ft in height 24 weeks after construction starts on the first tower.

14. **a)** The equations would be $x + y = 20$ and $x - y = 10$. This would lead to one solution since natural numbers that satisfy both equations can be found easily.

  b) The equations would be $x + y = 10$ and $x - y = 20$. This would lead to no solution since a negative number is needed to satisfy this system of linear equations, but a negative number is not a natural number.

  c)

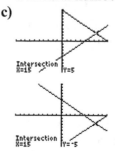

  d) The difference is due to the domain being N, which does not include negative numbers.

15. Let d represent distance, in metres Let t represent time, in seconds.

  a) $d = 220 + 3.1t$ and $d = 198 + 3.6t$; There is one solution. Boat C catches up to Boat A in 44 s at 356.4 m into the race.

  b) $d = 220 + 3.1t$ and $d = 230 + 3.2t$; There is one solution; however, at the point of intersection the value of t is less than zero, which is outside the range for time ($t \geq 0$). Boat D has already overtaken Boat A, which will not catch up.

  c) $d = 206 + 3.4t$ and $d = 230 + 3.2t$; There is one solution; however, at the point of intersection the value of d is greater than 500, which is outside the domain for distance ($d \leq 500$). Boat B is gaining on Boat D, but will not catch up before Boat D crosses the finish line.

16. Eva is correct. Vince is correct in saying that the lines will intersect, but the intersection is at a negative time and a negative volume, which is not allowed in the context of the problem. In this problem, the domain of time is $t \geq 0$ and the range of volume is $V \geq 150$.

17. a) $\dfrac{a}{d} = \dfrac{b}{e} \neq \dfrac{c}{f}$ **b)** $\dfrac{a}{d} = \dfrac{b}{e} = \dfrac{c}{f}$

Chapter 8 Review
8.1 Systems of Linear Equations and Graphs

1. a) yes
   b) no

2. a) approximately (3.48, −0.39)
   b) approximately (−15.45, 7.05)

3. a) (2, 4)
   b) $y = -2x + 8$ and $y = \frac{1}{2}x + 3$

4. a) The solution is (2, 55).
   b) After 2 h, the second cyclist has caught up to the first cyclist at a distance of 55 km.

8.2 Modelling and Solving Linear Systems

5. a) $C = 0.50t$
        $C = 25 + 0.25t$

b) $x + y = 23$
       $0.10x + 0.25y = 3.35$
   c) $d = 85t$
        $d = 100(t - 1)$

6. a) Basic cost is the y-intercept of the graph. For DirectCar, this is $60. For Wheels To Go, the basic cost is $40. The slope of the graph represents the charge per kilometre of distance travelled. For DirectCar, the charge is $0.50/km. For Wheels To Go, the charge is $0.75/km.
   b) Wheels To Go
   c) Choose DirectCar when $d > 80$ km.
   d) Charges are equal (a total of $100) at 80 km. Choose Wheels To Go when $d < 80$ km and choose DirectCar when $d > 80$ km.

7. a) $V = 12.5 - 1.4t$
        $V = 1.4t$

  b)

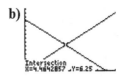

Intersection
X=4.4642857 Y=6.25

  c) The point of intersection is approximately (4.46, 6.25). After about 4.46 min, the truck and the bin both have 6.25 m³ of grain in them.

8. a) $A = 885 - 35t$
        $A = 1450 - 60t$
   b) The solution is (22.6, 94).
   c) After 22.6 s, both files have 94 MB left to download.

8.3 Number of Solutions for Systems of Linear Equations

9. a) $x + y = 45$
        $x = 3y - 15$
   b) Bill is 30. Nancy is 15.

10. a) no solution; lines have same slope but different y-intercepts so they are parallel
   b) an infinite number of solutions; second equation is a multiple of the first
   c) one solution; lines have different slopes and therefore must intersect at one point

11. no solution

12. a) P and R, P and S, P and Q, Q and R, and Q and S
b) R and S

13. a) $p + d = 24$ and $2p + 4d = 82$
b) solution is (7, 17), i.e., 7 parrots and 17 dogs
c) With 83 legs, the solution would not be a whole number of normal parrots or dogs.
d) Even though the slopes of the lines are different and the lines intersect, the domain and range are N, not R.

Chapters 1–8 Cumulative Review

1. 2.5 cm or about 10 in.

2. 1077.2 yd²

3. a)

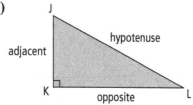

b) $\tan J = \dfrac{KL}{JK}$, $\sin J = \dfrac{KL}{JL}$, $\cos J = \dfrac{JK}{JL}$

4. a) perfect square **b)** perfect cube
c) perfect cube **d)** both
e) both **f)** perfect square

5. a) $-29n^2 + 34n + 9$
b) $-6s^4 + 17s^3 + 41s^2 - 12$

6. Graphs may vary. Example:

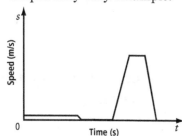

7. a) $y = -\dfrac{2}{5}x - 3$
b) $y = 12$

8. To verify if the given point is a solution, substitute the coordinates of the point for x and y in each equation. If the values work in both equations, then the point is a solution.
a) yes **b)** no

9. a) 1 652 959 **b)** 460 166

10. a) 36.0°
b) 57.8°
c) 15.6°

11. a) Answers may vary. Example: The independent variable is time, t. The dependent variable is population, p.
b) The graph is linear because the number of students grows at a constant rate (89 students) each year.
c) $P = 89t + 3420$
d) 4399
e) 1979

12. a) (1, 1) **b)** (6, −3)

13. a) $s = 3.28$ cm
b) $s = 43.09$ cm
c) $r = 4.42$ cm

14. a) $6ab$
b) $18xy^2$
c) p^2q^2

15. a) (0, 3), (−1, 0), $3x - y + 3 = 0$
b) (−2, 0), $x + 2 = 0$

16. 1.5 cm; length of a thumbtack

17. 89 in²

18. The castle is 5.87 m taller than the boy's height.

19. a) $\dfrac{1}{x^{\frac{5}{4}}}$ **b)** $\dfrac{1}{512h^{\frac{27}{2}}}$
c) $12^{\frac{31}{35}}$ **d)** $\dfrac{4096}{x^{\frac{20}{3}}}$

20. a) $(c - 12)(c + 12)$
b) $(1 + 16y^2)(1 - 4y)(1 + 4y)$
c) $54(h - 3f)(h + 3f)$
d) $(x - 3)(x + 3)(x - 2)(x + 2)$

21. [−32.6, 162.7]

22. a) $y = -2x - 7$, $2x + y + 7 = 0$
b) $y = \dfrac{1}{3}x + \dfrac{22}{3}$, $\dfrac{1}{3}x - y + \dfrac{22}{3} = 0$

23. a) $(x + 9)(x - 6)$
 b) $(3x - 1)(x + 3)$
 c) $2(5m - n)(2m - n)$
 d) $(2x + 3y)(6x - y)$
 e) $3t(s + 4)(s - 3)$

24. a) The variable w represents the number of minutes that each tank has been draining.
 b) $T(4) = 80$ and $H(4) = 96$. 80 L of water remain in the first tank after 4 min. 96 L of water remain in the second tank after 4 min.
 c) $w = 15$; After 15 min, 25 L will remain in the first tank.
 d) Tank 1: $0 \le w \le 20$, $0 \le T(w) \le 100$;
 Tank 2: $0 \le w \le 20$, $0 \le H(w) \le 120$

25. a) 98 174.77 ft³   **b)** 1321.04 cm³
 c) 4928 ft³   **d)** 11 742.10 cm³

26. 11°

27. 49 mph

28. $y = \left(-\frac{1}{3}\right)x + 3$

29. a)

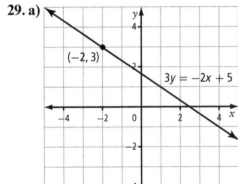

 b)

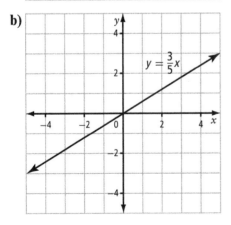

c)

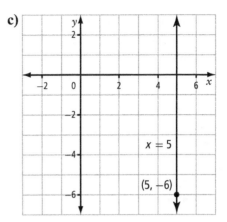

d)

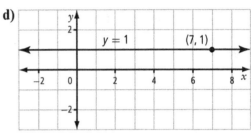

30. $y = \frac{7}{6}x - \frac{1}{2}$

31. a) no solution; both lines have the same slope but different y-intercepts
 b) one solution; the lines have different slopes
 c) infinite number of solutions; both lines have the same slope and the same y-intercept

32. a) $x + y = 14$ and $0.25x + 0.10y = 2.90$, where x represents the number of quarters and y represents the number of dimes
 b) 10 quarters and 4 dimes

33. a) 478 km   **b)** 407 ft

34. 2714.68 cm³

35. 35.75 m

36. a) $(18x)^{\frac{5}{2}}$ **b)** $7^{\frac{2}{3}}$
 c) $z^{\frac{2}{5}}$ **d)** $\frac{a}{b}$

37. a) $(4s - 3)^2$
 b) $27s(2s + 1)^2$
 c) $(15 - 4y)^2$

Chapter 8 Extend It Further

1. Achilles will catch up to the tortoise at a distance of 11.1 units from the starting point regardless of their speeds. Algebraically:

$$d_{\text{tortoise}} = d_{\text{Achilles}}$$
$$100 + rt = 10rt$$
$$100 = 9rt$$
$$11.1 = rt$$

2. **a)** $m = 5.5, n \neq 2$
   b) $m = 5.5, n = 2$

3. **a)** Let x represent the first digit and let y represent the second digit: $x + y = 10$ and $x - y = 2$
   b)

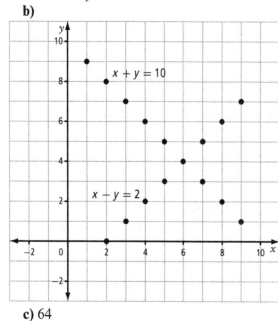

   c) 64

4. **a)** $y = x + 2, x - 2y + 7 = 0$
   b)

```
      y
    8
              y = 2 + x
    6
                  x - 2y + 7 = 0
    4

    2

    0       2       4       6  x
```

   c) 77 units^2

5. **a)** $(4, 1.5)$
   b) $x = 4$ and $y - 6 = -\dfrac{9}{8}x$

6. **a)** $A + 3B = -1, 2A + B = 8$
   b) $A = 5, B = -2$

7. 6 units

8. 27

9. 256

10. 16

11. -1

Chapter 9 Solving Systems of Linear Equations Algebraically

9.1 Solving Systems of Linear Equations by Substitution

1. **a)** $x = 13.5$ and $y = 11.5$
   b) $x = -11$ and $y = -44$
   c) $x = -1$ and $y = 20$
   d) $x = 2$ and $y = -3$
   e) $x = 5$ and $y = -1$
   f) $x = 2$ and $y = 3$

2. Method 1: Isolate the variable x in the equation $2x - y = -5$.
$$2x - y = -5$$
$$2x - y + y = -5 + y$$
$$2x = -5 + y$$
$$\frac{2x}{2} = \frac{-5 + y}{2}$$
$$x = \frac{-5 + y}{2}$$
Substitute for x in the equation $5x + y = -2$. Then, solve for y.
$$5x + y = -2$$
$$5\left(\frac{-5 + y}{2}\right) + y = -2$$
$$\frac{-25 + 5y}{2} + y = -2$$
$$2\left(\frac{-25 + 5y}{2} + y\right) = 2(-2)$$
$$-25 + 5y + 2y = -4$$
$$-25 + 7y = -4$$
$$-25 + 25 + 7y = -4 + 25$$
$$7y = 21$$
$$\frac{7y}{7} = \frac{21}{7}$$
$$y = 3$$

Substitute $y = 3$ in the equation $2x - y = -5$ and solve for x.
$$2x - y = -5$$
$$2x - 3 = -5$$
$$2x - 3 + 3 = -5 + 3$$
$$2x = -2$$
$$\frac{2x}{2} = \frac{-2}{2}$$
$$x = -1$$
The solution is $x = -1$ and $y = 3$.

Method 2: Isolate the variable y in the equation $5x + y = -2$.
$$5x + y = -2$$
$$5x - 5x + y = -2 - 5x$$
$$y = -2 - 5x$$
Substitute for y in the equation $2x - y = -5$. Then, solve for x.
$$2x - y = -5$$
$$2x - (-2 - 5x) = -5$$
$$2x + 2 + 5x = -5$$
$$7x + 2 = -5$$
$$7x + 2 - 2 = -5 - 2$$
$$7x = -7$$
$$\frac{7x}{7} = \frac{-7}{7}$$
$$x = -1$$
Substitute $x = -1$ in the equation $5x + y = -2$ and solve for y.
$$5x + y = -2$$
$$5(-1) + y = -2$$
$$-5 + y = -2$$
$$-5 + 5 + y = -2 + 5$$
$$y = 3$$
The solution is $x = -1$ and $y = 3$.
Example: I prefer the second method where I solved for y. The coefficient on y was 1, so there were no fractions involved. In the first method, where I solved for x, there were fractions. Fractions involve more complicated computations than integers do.

3. The point $(2, 4)$ is not the solution to the system $3x - y = 2$ and $x + y = 5$. The point $(2, 4)$ lies on the line of the first equation because substituting 2 for x and 4 for y results in a true statement.
$$3x - y = 2$$
$$3(2) - 4 = 2$$
$$6 - 4 = 2$$
$$2 = 2$$
However, the point $(2, 4)$ does not lie on the line $x + y = 5$ because replacing x with 2 and y with 4 does not result in a true statement.
$$x + y = 5$$
$$2 + 4 \neq 5$$

4. 6000

5. 400 shares of the $4.50 stock and 880 shares of the $2.50 stock

6. Let C represent the number of cans. Let B represent the number of bottles.
Write an equation to represent the total number of cans and bottles collected.
$C + B = 900$
Write an equation to represent the total amount of money, in dollars, received.
$0.1C + 0.25B = 145.20$
Solve the system of linear equations by substitution. Solve for C in the first equation.
$$C + B = 900$$
$$C + B - B = 900 - B$$
$$C = 900 - B$$
Substitute for C in the second equation and solve for B.
$$0.1C + 0.25B = 145.20$$
$$0.1(900 - B) + 0.25B = 145.20$$
$$90 - 0.1B + 0.25B = 145.20$$
$$90 + 0.15B = 145.20$$
$$90 - 90 + 0.15B = 145.20 - 90$$
$$0.15B = 55.20$$
$$\frac{(0.15B)}{0.15} = \frac{(55.20)}{0.15}$$
$$B = 368$$
Substitute $B = 368$ in the first equation and solve for C.
$$C + B = 900$$
$$C + 368 = 900$$
$$C + 368 - 368 = 900 - 368$$
$$C = 532$$
The team brought in 532 cans for recycling.

7. 14

8. 15 new wave songs and 3 hip-hop songs; It is assumed that the station plays the same number of each song in each hour.

9. Jane is 26. Tim is 14.

10. 42

11. music video: $12.50; CD: $4.75

12. Team A: 16 wins, 4 losses;
Team B: 4 wins, 16 losses

13. No. The correct system of linear equations is $T + Q + 45 = 125$ and $2T + 0.25Q + 45 = 184$. $T = 68$ and $Q = 12$. The coins in the machine consisted of 12 quarters, 45 $1 coins, and 68 $2 coins.

14. Step 2; The correct line is $2x - 15x + 10 = 23$. The solution is $x = -1$ and $y = 5$.

15. Let x represent the distance over which Mandy drove at a speed of 80 km/h. Let y represent the distance over which Mandy drove at a speed of 100 km/h.
Write an equation to represent the total distance driven.
$x + y = 400$
Write a second equation to express the time of the trip in terms of speed and distance travelled. (Recall that time equals distance divided by speed.)
$\frac{x}{80} + \frac{y}{100} = 4.5$
Isolate the variable y in the equation $x + y = 400$.
$$x + y = 400$$
$$x - x + y = 400 - x$$
$$y = 400 - x$$
Substitute for y in the equation $\frac{x}{80} + \frac{y}{100} = 4.5$.
$$\frac{x}{80} + \frac{y}{100} = 4.5$$
$$\frac{x}{80} + \frac{400 - x}{100} = 4.5$$
Multiply each term of the equation by the lowest common multiple of the denominators to clear out the fractions. The lowest common multiple of 80 and 100 is 400.
$$400\left(\frac{x}{80} + \frac{400 - x}{100}\right) = 400(4.5)$$
$$\frac{400x}{80} + \frac{400(400 - x)}{100} = 1800$$
$$5x + 4(400 - x) = 1800$$
solve for x.
$$5x + 4(400 - x) = 1800$$
$$5x + 1600 - 4x = 1800$$
$$x + 1600 = 1800$$
$$x + 1600 - 1600 = 1800 - 1600$$
$$x = 200$$
Substitute $x = 200$ in the equation $x + y = 400$ and solve for y.
$$x + y = 400$$
$$200 + y = 400$$
$$200 - 200 + y = 400 - 200$$
$$y = 200$$
Mandy drove a distance of 200 km at a speed of 100 km/h.

16. $y = 4$

17. a) There is one solution. The slopes of the lines are different, which means that the lines intersect.

b) The point of intersection is located in the first quadrant. Rewrite each equation to isolate the variable y and enter the new form of the equations into a graphing calculator.

$$5x - 4y = 0 \qquad\qquad x + 3y = 15$$
$$5x - 5x - 4y = 0 - 5x \quad x - x + 3y = 15 - x$$
$$-4y = -5x \qquad\qquad 3y = 15 - x$$
$$\frac{-4y}{4} = \frac{-5x}{4} \qquad\qquad \frac{3y}{3} = \frac{15}{3} - \frac{x}{3}$$
$$y = \frac{5}{4}x \qquad\qquad y = 5 - \frac{x}{3}$$

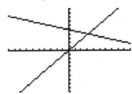

The point of intersection is in the first quadrant.

18. $x = 14$, $y = 19$, and $z = -8$

19. a)

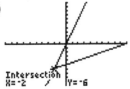

b) $x = -2$ and $y = -6$

c) Example: The methods are similar in that they produce the same solution. The difference is that the graphing method allows you to see how the two variables relate.

d) Example: I prefer the substitution method because there is a coefficient of 1 in one of the equations. This makes it simple to solve for the variable so that it can be substituted into the second equation.

9.2 Solving Systems of Linear Equations by Elimination

1. a) $x = -1$ and $y = 3$ **b)** $x = 1$ and $y = 1$
c) $x = 1$ and $y = 2$ **d)** $x = 8$ and $y = -2$
e) $x = -3$ and $y = 12$

2. a) $x + 3y = -1$ **b)** $2x + 3y = 1$
$\qquad 2x + 4y = 12$ $\qquad 4x - 2y = 10$

c) $3x - 2y = 5$ **d)** $x - 3y = -4$
$\qquad -5x + 4y = 1$ $\qquad 4x + 2y = 12$

e) $3x + 2y = -9$
$\qquad 2x + 3y = 9$

3. a) $x = 20$ and $y = -7$ **b)** $x = 2$ and $y = -1$
c) $x = 11$ and $y = 14$ **d)** $x = 2$ and $y = 2$
e) $x = -9$ and $y = 9$

4. a) $x = 2$ and $y = 3$

b) Multiply each term of the equation $\frac{1}{2}x - \frac{1}{3}y = 1$ by the lowest common multiple of the denominators to clear out the fractions. The lowest common multiple of 2 and 3 is 6.

$$6\left(\frac{1}{2}x - \frac{1}{3}y\right) = 6(1)$$
$$\frac{6}{2}x - \frac{6}{3}y = 6$$
$$3x - 2y = 6$$

Multiply each term of the equation $x + \frac{1}{4}y = 2$ by the lowest common multiple of the denominators to clear out the fractions. The lowest common multiple of 1 and 4 is 4.

$$4\left(x + \frac{1}{4}y\right) = 4(2)$$
$$4x + \frac{4}{4}y = 8$$
$$4x + y = 8$$

Eliminate variable y. The lowest common multiple of 1 and 2 is 2. Multiply the equation $3x - 2y = 6$ by 1 and multiply the equation $4x + y = 8$ by 2.

$$3x - 2y = 6 \qquad\qquad 4x + y = 8$$
$$1(3x - 2y) = 1(6) \qquad 2(4x + y) = 2(8)$$
$$3x - 2y = 6 \qquad\qquad 8x + 2y = 16$$

Add the two equations to eliminate y.

$$\begin{array}{r} 3x - 2y = 6 \\ + (8x + 2y = 16) \\ \hline 11x = 22 \end{array}$$

Solve for x.
$$\frac{11x}{11} = \frac{22}{11}$$
$$x = 2$$

Substitute $x = 2$ into the second equation and solve for y.

$$x + \frac{1}{4}y = 2$$
$$2 + \frac{1}{4}y = 2$$
$$2 - 2 + \frac{1}{4}y = 2 - 2$$
$$\frac{1}{4}y = 0$$
$$y = 0$$

The solution to the system is $x = 2$ and $y = 0$.

c) $x = -6$ and $y = 10$

5. a) The two equations are the same. Therefore, the solution is an infinite number of points. Another method of finding the solution is to write each equation in "$y =$" form and enter it into a graphing calculator.

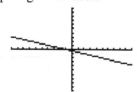

b) The two equations represent lines with the same slope. The lines are parallel and do not intersect. Therefore, there is no solution. Another method of finding the solution is to write each equation in "$y =$" form and enter it into a graphing calculator.

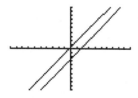

6. 24 $2 coins and 112 $1 coins

7. The initiation fee is $45 and the monthly fee is $25.

8. The daily rental charge was $28 and the charge per kilometre was $0.25.

9. $300 at 12% and $360 at 10%

10. 175 motorcycles and 325 cars

11. adult: $19; child: $11

12. 0.9 miles

13. 2050 vehicles

14. Let C represent the number of oranges purchased.
Let G represent the number of granola bars purchased.
Write an equation to represent the total number of snacks purchased.
$C + G = 50$
Express the cost of the snacks in terms of the price of each item. Since oranges cost $2.40 per dozen, the price of one orange is $\frac{\$2.40}{12} = \$0.20$. Since the price of a 5-bar box of granola is $3.25, the price of one bar is $\frac{\$3.25}{5} = \$0.65$.
Write an equation to represent the total amount of money that Shanice spent.

$0.2C + 0.65G = 19$

Eliminate the variable C. Multiply the second equation by 5 to make the coefficient of C equal to 1.

$$5(0.2C + 0.65G) = 5(19)$$
$$C + 3.25G = 95$$

Subtract this new form of the second equation from the first equation.

$$\begin{array}{r} C + G = 50 \\ -(C + 3.25G = 95) \\ \hline -2.25G = -45 \end{array}$$

Solve for G.

$$-2.25G = -45$$
$$\frac{-2.25G}{-2.25} = \frac{-45}{-2.25}$$
$$G = 20$$

Therefore, Shanice bought 20 granola bars, or 4 boxes of bars.

15. Cashews cost $2.60 per pound. Peanuts cost $1.50 per pound.

16. a) Let T represent the 10s digit. Let D represent the 1s digit.
The original number may be expressed as $10T + D$.
The number with the digits of the first number reversed is represented as $10D + T$.
Write an equation to represent the sum of the digits.
$T + D = 14$

Write an equation to represent the number formed by reversing the digits that is 36 more than the original number.

$10D + T = 36 + 10T + D$

Rewrite the equation to be in the same form as the first equation.

$$10D + T = 36 + 10T + D$$
$$10D + T - 10T - D = 36 + 10T - 10T + D - D$$
$$-9T + 9D = 36$$

Solve the system using elimination. Eliminate the variable T. The lowest common multiple of 1 and 9 is 9. Multiply the first equation by 9 and multiply the second equation by 1.

$T + D = 14$	$-9T + 9D = 36$
$9(T + D) = 9(14)$	$1(-9T + 9D) = 1(36)$
$9T + 9D = 126$	$-9T + 9D = 36$

Add the two equations.

$$9T + 9D = 126$$
$$+(-9T + 9D = 36)$$
$$18D = 162$$

Solve for D.

$$18D = 162$$
$$\frac{18D}{18} = \frac{162}{18}$$
$$D = 9$$

Substitute $D = 9$ in the first equation and solve for T.

$$T + D = 14$$
$$T + 9 = 14$$
$$T + 9 - 9 = 14 - 9$$
$$T = 5$$

The solution is $T = 5$ and $D = 9$.
Therefore, the original number is 59.

b) 56

17. $m = 7$ and $n = 2$

18. Example: **a)** $4x + 2y = 6$
b) $2x + y = 5$ **c)** $y = -10$

19. $A = 3$

20. a) $x = -1$ and $y = 1$ **b)** $x = -1$ and $y = 1$
c) Example: I prefer the elimination method because using substitution involved using fractions.

d) Example: When using the substitution method, I look for a coefficient of 1 in one of the equations. If there is no coefficient of 1, then I use the elimination method.

9.3 Solving Problems Using Systems of Linear Equations

1. a) $x = -2$ and $y = -6$ **b)** $x = 0$ and $y = 3$
c) $x = 2$ and $y = -2$ **d)** $x = 0$ and $y = -5$
e) $x = -20$ and $y = 7$

2. a) Solve by elimination.
Eliminate the variable x. The lowest common multiple of 2 and 8 is 8. Multiply the first equation by 4 and multiply the second equation by 1.

$2x - 5y = -18$	$8x - 13y = -58$
$4(2x - 5y) = 4(-18)$	$1(8x - 13y) = 1(-58)$
$8x - 20y = -72$	$8x - 13y = -58$

Subtract the second equation from the new form of the first equation.

$$8x - 20y = -72$$
$$-(8x - 13y = -58)$$
$$-7y = -14$$

Solve for y.

$$-7y = -14$$
$$\frac{-7y}{-7} = \frac{-14}{-7}$$
$$y = 2$$

Substitute $y = 2$ in the first equation and solve for x.

$$2x - 5y = -18$$
$$2x - 5(2) = -18$$
$$2x - 10 = -18$$
$$2x - 10 + 10 = -18 + 10$$
$$2x = -8$$
$$\frac{2x}{2} = \frac{-8}{2}$$
$$x = -4$$

The solution is $x = -4$ and $y = 2$.

b) $x = \frac{3}{14}$ and $y = \frac{15}{14}$

c) $x = 3$ and $y = -3$

3. The width is 1080 m and the length is 2120 m.

4. He should invest $6000 at 9% and $6000 at 11%.

5. 15 mph

6. $1.50

7. Let H represent the amount of hay. Let G represent the amount of grain.
Write an equation to represent the daily amounts of hay and grain that are fed to the horse.
$H + G = 20$
The total cost to feed the horse for 60 days is \$702. Therefore, the daily cost is $\frac{\$702}{60} = \$11.70$.
Write an equation to represent the cost of feeding the horse each day.
$0.08H + 2.10G = 11.70$
Solve by substitution. Solve for H in the first equation.
$H + G = 20$
$H + G - G = 20 - G$
$H = 20 - G$
Substitute $H = 20 - G$ into the second equation and solve for G.

$$0.08H + 2.10G = 11.70$$
$$0.08(20 - G) + 2.10G = 11.70$$
$$1.6 - 0.08G + 2.10G = 11.70$$
$$2.02G = 10.10$$
$$\frac{2.02G}{2.02} = \frac{10.10}{2.02}$$
$$G = 5$$

Substitute $G = 5$ into the first equation and solve for H.

$$H + G = 20$$
$$H + 5 = 20$$
$$H + 5 - 5 = 20 - 5$$
$$H = 15$$

The solution is $H = 15$ and $G = 5$. Therefore, the horse is fed 15 lbs of hay and 5 lbs of grain per day.

8. The team made 32 field goals and 6 three-point shots.

9. 250

10. Tom spent 25 h swimming and 45 h biking.

11. The hourly wage for outdoor work is \$18 and the hourly wage for indoor work is \$15.

12. a) $y = 0.15x + 25$, $y = 0.10x + 30$
b) 100 km

13. a) $2W + T = 26$, $3T = W + 1$
b) 11

14. a) 458 km **b)** 38.93 L

15. The slower snowmobile rider rides at 40 km/h. The faster snowmobile rider rides at 55 km/h. The assumption is that both riders are riding at a constant rate of speed.

16. 771.4 mL

17. Let C represent the number of correct answers. Let I represent the number of incorrect answers.
Write an equation to represent the total number of answers on the test. The assumption is that all questions were answered.
$C + I = 76$
Write an equation to represent the total score achieved.
$C + (-0.2)I = 58$
Solve for C in the first equation.
$$C + I = 76$$
$$C + I - I = 76 - I$$
$$C = 76 - I$$
Substitute $C = 76 - I$ into the second equation and solve for I.
$$C + (-0.2)I = 58$$
$$76 - I + (-0.2)I = 58$$
$$76 - 1.2I = 58$$
$$76 - 76 - 1.2I = 58 - 76$$
$$-1.2I = -18$$
$$\frac{-1.2I}{1.2} = \frac{-18}{1.2}$$
$$I = 15$$
Substitute $I = 15$ into the first equation and solve for C.
$$C + I = 76$$
$$C + 15 = 76$$
$$C + 15 - 15 = 76 - 15$$
$$C = 61$$
Therefore, the student answered 61 questions correctly.

18. 62.5 square units

19. a)–c) Answers may vary.

Chapter 9 Review
9.1 Solving Systems of Linear Equations by Substitution

1. a) $x = -2$ and $y = 5$ **b)** $m = 2$ and $n = 1$
c) $a = 1$ and $b = 4$ **d)** $w = -2$ and $z = 7$

2. a) no solution
b) an infinite number of solutions

c) one solution, $x = -\frac{14}{3}$ and $y = \frac{16}{3}$

d) one solution, $x = -3$ and $y = 3$

3. The length of the bridge in Kobe, Japan, is 1992 m and the length of the Capilano Bridge is 137 m.

4. 60 goals

5. Let x represent the length of the shorter piece of board. Let y represent the length of the longer piece.
Write an equation to represent the total length of the board.
$x + y = 180$
Write an equation to represent the relationship between the lengths of the two pieces of board.
$3y = 85 + 4x$
Isolate x in the first equation.
$$x + y = 180$$
$$x + y - y = 180 - y$$
$$x = 180 - y$$
Substitute $180 - y$ for x in the second equation.
$$3y = 85 + 4x$$
$$3y = 85 + 4(180 - y)$$
$$3y = 85 + 720 - 4y$$
$$3y = 805 - 4y$$
Solve for y.
$$3y = 805 - 4y$$
$$3y + 4y = 805 - 4y + 4y$$
$$7y = 805$$
$$\frac{7y}{7} = \frac{805}{7}$$
$$y = 115$$
Substitute $y = 115$ into the first equation and solve for x.
$$x + y = 180$$
$$x + 115 = 180$$
$$x - 115 - 115 = 180 - 115$$
$$x = 65$$
Therefore, the lengths of the two pieces of board are 115 cm and 65 cm.

6. 864 burgers

9.2 Solving Systems of Linear Equations by Elimination

7. **a)** $x = 2$ and $y = -3$
   b) $x = -1$ and $y = 5$
   c) $x = -\frac{6}{5}$ and $y = \frac{17}{15}$

d) $x = -2$ and $y = 3$
e) $x = 4$ and $y = 2$

8. Let M represent the monthly charge. Let T represent the text message charge.
Write an equation to represent Wade's January bill.
$M + 300T = 63$
Write an equation to represent the total of Wade's bills in February and March.
$2M + 675T + 12 = 142.50$
Rewrite the equation in the form $ax + by = c$.
$$2M + 675T + 12 = 142.50$$
$$2M + 675T + 12 - 12 = 142.50 - 12$$
$$2M + 675T = 130.50$$
Eliminate the variable M. The lowest common multiple of 1 and 2 is 2.
Multiply the first equation by 2.
$M + 300T = 63$
$2(M + 300T) = 2(63)$
$2M + 600T = 126$
Subtract the second equation from the first equation.
$$\begin{array}{r} 2M + 600T = 126 \\ -(2M + 675T = 130.50) \\ \hline -75T = -4.50 \end{array}$$
Solve for T.
$$-75T = -4.50$$
$$\frac{-75T}{-75} = \frac{-4.50}{-75}$$
Substitute $T = 0.06$ into the first equation and solve for M.
$$M + 300(0.06) = 63$$
$$M + 18 = 63$$
$$M + 18 - 18 = 63 - 18$$
$$M = 45$$
Therefore, the monthly charge is $45.00 and the text charge is $0.06 per message.

9. $m = -1$ and $n = 2$

10. **a)** yes   **b)** yes
    c) no   **d)** no

11. $650 at 10% and $1450 at 7%

12. 10.75 m by 23.75 m

13. Marmot Basin has 86 runs and Sunshine Village has 107 runs.

9.3 Solving Problems Using Systems of Linear Equations

14. a) There is no solution.

b) The two lines are parallel and do not intersect. Therefore, there is no solution.

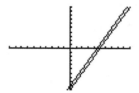

15. Michele ran 15 km.

16. Let F represent the fixed weekly wage. Let C represent the commission rate.

Write an equation to represent wages paid for the first week.

$F + 15\,500C = 1015$

Write an equation to represent wages paid for the second week.

$F + 9800C = 844$

Isolate F in the first equation.

$F + 15\,500C = 1015$

$F + 15\,500C - 15\,500C = 1015 - 15\,500C$

$F = 1015 - 15\,500C$

Substitute $F = 1015 - 15\,500C$ into the second equation.

$F + 9800C = 844$

$1015 - 15\,500C + 9800C = 844$

$1015 - 5700C = 844$

$1015 - 1015 - 5700C = 844 - 1015$

$-5700C = -171$

Solve for C.

$-5700C = -171$

$\dfrac{-5700C}{-5700} = \dfrac{-171}{-5700}$

$C = 0.03$

Substitute $C = 0.03$ into the second equation and solve for F.

$F + 9800C = 844$

$F + (9800)(0.03) = 844$

$F + 294 = 844$

$F + 294 - 294 = 844 - 294$

$F = 550$

Avatar's fixed wage is $550 and his rate of commission is 3%.

17. 2.5 km

18. 2.25 mph

19. $63.75

20. 900 kW

21. 13.5 t

Chapters 1–9 Cumulative Review

1. To verify if the given point is a solution, use the values of x and y in both equations. If the values work in both equations, then the point is a solution.

a) Yes   **b)** No

2. $238.36

3. a) $\dfrac{4}{5}$ **b)** $\dfrac{3}{5}$

c) $\dfrac{3}{5}$ **d)** $\dfrac{4}{5}$

e) $\dfrac{4}{3}$ **f)** $\dfrac{3}{4}$

4. a) 64   **b)** -625

c) 49   **d)** $-\dfrac{27}{5}$

e) $\dfrac{3}{64}$ **f)** $-\dfrac{1}{125}$

5. a) $-56n^2 + 102n - 27$

b) $-4s^4 - 6s^3 + 21s^2 + 13s - 15$

6. Example: It takes Jon 5 s to reach the bottom of the first hill on his bike. For a few seconds, Jon pedals to maintain his speed on a flat section of road. He then begins to go down a second hill and continues to accelerate. At the bottom of the hill, the road rises up. Jon coasts up the third hill as his speed slows. At the top, Jon maintains his speed by pedalling until he reaches a slight decline, at which point he begins to accelerate again. He then maintains this speed by pedalling.

7. a) $(6, -10)$

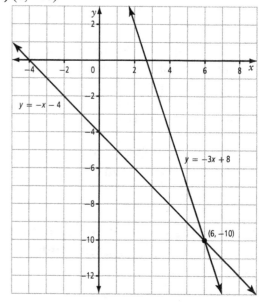

b) $(-3, 0)$

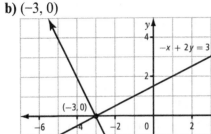
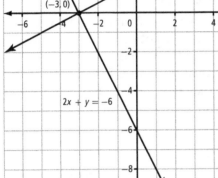

c) $(1, -7)$

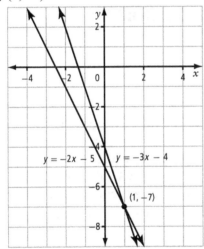

8. a) $26.2°$ **b)** $67.4°$
  c) $14.3°$

9. a) slope is -5, y-intercept is $(0, 8)$
  b) slope is $\frac{3}{7}$, y-intercept is $\left(0, -\frac{10}{7}\right)$

10. a) $2674.75\ \text{cm}^2$ **b)** $133.88\ \text{in.}^2$
   c) $10\ 908\ \text{cm}^2$ **d)** $3019.07\ \text{cm}^2$

11. a) domain: $\{x \mid x \in \mathbb{R}\}$; range: $\{y \mid y \in \mathbb{R}\}$;
    intercepts are $(-1, 0), (0, -2.5)$; slope is
    $-\frac{5}{2}$; equation of the line in general form
    is $5x + 2y + 5 = 0$
  b) domain: $\{x \mid x \in \mathbb{R}\}$; range: $\{-4\}$;
    y-intercept is $(0, -4)$; slope is 0; equation
    of the line in general form is $y + 4 = 0$

12. a) $2ab^2$ **b)** $9xy^2$
  c) pq

13. a) linear
  b) Example: Let n represent the quantity,
    in kilograms, of honey sold. Let R
    represent the sales revenue, in dollars.
    In this situation, n is the independent
    variable and R is the dependent variable.
    In order to calculate the money earned
    from sales, first you need to know
    how much honey was sold. Therefore,
    revenue is dependent on the amount of
    honey that is sold.

  c)

n	$R\ (\$)$	n	$R\ (\$)$
0	0	50	549.00
10	109.80	60	658.80
20	219.60	70	768.60
30	329.40	80	878.40
40	439.20	90	988.20

  d) The data would be discrete if the
    beekeeper sells honey only in quantities
    that are in whole units. The data would
    be continuous if the beekeeper sells
    honey in quantities of any weight.

  e)

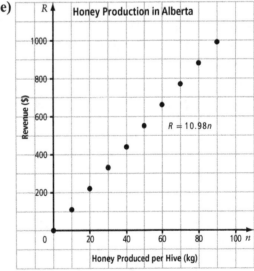

14. a) one solution
  b) no solution
  c) infinite number of solutions

15. 3.65cm; Example: length of a nail

16 a) $(2, 4)$ **b)** $(0, -5)$

17. a) 14.6 **b)** 8.1
   c) 106.7

18. a) $x^{\frac{23}{5}}$ **b)** $\frac{1}{64}$

c) z^4 **d)** $\frac{1}{5p^{\frac{5}{2}}}$

e) $x^{200}y^{125}$ **f)** $\frac{x^{\frac{9}{4}}(0.16)^{\frac{3}{4}}}{y^{\frac{9}{2}}}$

19. a) $(4x-1)(x+2)$
  b) $(x-3)(x-6)$
  c) $-3(2m-3n)(4m-n)$
  d) $(7x+2y)(5x-3y)$
  e) $12t(s+6)(s-4)$

20. a) $(4, -2)$ **b)** $(-1, 8)$

21. 176 miles; 50 km; 66 ft; 213 m

22. a) 0.67 ft **b)** 5.85 cm
  c) 4.33 m **d)** 9.40 cm

23. a) $\frac{4}{9}$, $0.777...$, $\sqrt[3]{634}$, $\sqrt{82}$; The last two numbers are irrational.
  b) $\sqrt[5]{67}$, $\sqrt[4]{1296}$, $14\frac{1}{3}$, $\sqrt{289}$; $\sqrt[5]{67}$ is irrational.

24. $[-18.4, 69.8]$

25. a) slope-intercept form: $y = 3x + 5$; general form: $3x - y + 5 = 0$
  b) slope-intercept form: $y = \frac{3}{4}x - \frac{45}{4}$; general form: $3x - 4y - 45 = 0$

26. a) $(c-13)(c+13)$
  b) $(9+4y^2)(3-2y)(3+2y)$
  c) $7(5h-12f)(5h+5f)$
  d) $(x-4)(x+4)(x-5)(x+5)$

27. a) Example: domain: $\{x|0 \le x \le 30\ x \in \mathbb{N}\}$; range: $\{y|y \ge 40, y \in \mathbb{N}\}$

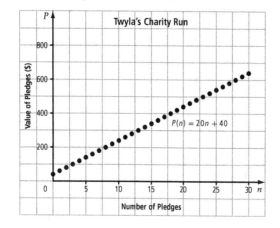

Twyla's Charity Run
$P(n) = 20n + 40$
Number of Pledges
Value of Pledges ($)

  b) If there were 9 pledges, there would be a total of $220 in funds.
  c) 24 pledges

d) This situation depicts a function because for every value in the domain there is a unique value in the range.

28. $y = \frac{5}{4}x + \frac{5}{2}$

29. a) $(3s-9)^2$ **b)** $s(4s+12)^2$
  c) $(16-5y)^2$

30. a) 15.2 cm; 152 mm **b)** 5.98 in.
  c) No, it is not necessary to measure the figure three times. It only needs to be measured once. That measurement can then be converted to the other required units.

31. 6.3 ft

32. a) $2\sqrt{10}$ **b)** $3\sqrt{2}$
  c) $3\sqrt[3]{4}$ **d)** $3\sqrt[4]{2}$

33. A: undefined; B: $-\frac{3}{5}$; C: $\frac{1}{5}$; D: 5; E: 0

Chapter 9 Extend It Further

1. C

2. D

3. B

4. A

5. Adding the two equations yields $444x + 444y = 888$, or $x + y = 2$. Subtracting the two equations yields $198x - 198y = 198$, or $x - y = 1$. The solution to the system of linear equations $x + y = 2$ and $x - y = 1$ is $\left(\frac{3}{2}, \frac{1}{2}\right)$.

6. $(40.5, 39.5)$

7. Let x be the volume of the tank, in litres. Let m be the fill rate of hose M, in litres per hour. Let n be the fill rate of hose N, in litres per hour.

$$\frac{x}{m+n} = 4.8$$
$$\frac{x-2m}{m+n} = 3.6$$

The solution is $m = 12$, $n = 8$, and $x = 96$ L. Hose N will fill the tank in $\frac{96}{8} = 12$ h.

8. $x = \frac{21}{16}$, $y = \frac{28}{67}$

9. a) $a = 4$, $b = 2.7$ **b)** $15.34

10. 9.6 m/s

11. 121 407 or 220 407

12. -1

Unit 4 Review

1. A
2. B
3. A
4. A
5. B
6. A
7. C
8. C
9. C
10. B
11. D
12. C
13. C
14. A
15. D
16. D
17. 16
18. 17
19. 7
20. 9
21. 5

22. **a)** $2x + y = 10$
    $3x + 2y = 17$
    b) mass of each cylinder = 3 kg, mass of each rectangular block = 4 kg

23. **a)** $x = -\dfrac{6}{25}, y = -\dfrac{14}{25}$
    b) $x = -\dfrac{24}{5}, y = -\dfrac{19}{2}$

24. **a)** Answers may vary.
    b) 7 h on the highway, 3 h in the city
    c)

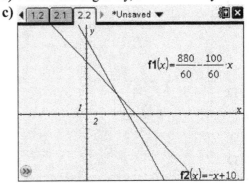

25. **a)** $x + y = 180$
    $x - 3y = -12$
    b) Answers may vary.
    c) 132° and 48°

26. $A = 3, B = 1$

Practice Final Exam

1. B
2. A
3. C
4. A
5. A
6. B
7. A
8. 44 in.
9. D
10. B
11. 4
12. B
13. D
14. 0.1 m^3
15. C
16. D
17. A
18. C
19. 216
20. D
21. C
22. 1
23. A
24. A
25. D
26. C
27. B
28. B
29. B
30. D
31. B
32. D
33. C
34. A
35. 4.5
36. 3

37. C
38. D
39. 72 km
40. C
41. A
42. C
43. C
44. D
45. 32°
46. a) Rate of change $= \frac{600 \text{ m}}{8 \text{ min}} = \frac{75 \text{ m}}{\text{min}}$. The rate of change is 75 m per minute.

b)
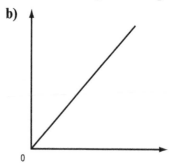

c) 24(tan 14°) + 24(tan 38°) = 5.983 872... + 18.750 854 = 24.734 726... The chairs are approximately 25 ft apart.

47. Example:
- Stage A: The car starts from rest and accelerates at a constant rate to reach a speed of 90 km/h, which it maintains for almost 2 h.
- Stage B: The car decelerates quickly over a short period of time to 50 km/h (perhaps while entering the outskirts of a town.
- Stage C: The car accelerates back up to 90 km/h.
- Stage D: The cruise control is set and the car travels at a constant speed of 90 km/h for more than 2 h.
- Stage E: The car decelerates and stops. The approximate trip time is 5 h.

48. a) The solution is $(1, 2)$.

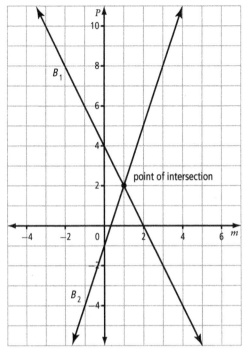

b) $3(1) + \frac{3}{2}(2) = 6$

c) After 2 months (since at 2 months the profit is \$0)

d) Answers may vary. Example: In order to launch the new product, the company has start-up production costs, which in this case amount to \$1000.

e) Trial 1:

B_1: $P = \frac{1}{2}m + \frac{3}{2}$

B_2: $P = \frac{1}{2}m + \frac{3}{2}$

Both equations are identical. Therefore, there is an infinite number of solutions. The company would be unable to use these equations to compare sales of the two products.

Trial 2:

B_1: $\frac{6}{5}P = 3m - 2$

$\qquad P = \frac{5}{2}m - \frac{5}{3}$

B_2: $\frac{1}{5}P = \frac{1}{2}m - \frac{2}{3}$

$\qquad P = \frac{5}{2}m - \frac{10}{3}$

The lines representing these equations are parallel. Therefore, they have no points in common. The company would be unable to find a common time period for sales of the two products.